A-Level
Sociology

Exam Board: AQA

Revising for Sociology exams is stressful, that's for sure — even just getting your notes sorted out can leave you needing a lie down. But help is at hand...

This brilliant CGP book covers **everything you'll need to learn** for **both years** of the course, including **every optional topic** and all the crucial **sociological studies**. And of course, everything's explained in CGP's straightforward style.

We've also included **exam-style questions** throughout the book, along with a section of advice on how to pick up as many marks as possible in the final tests!

A-Level revision? It has to be CGP!

Contents

We deliberately haven't included answers to the questions — that's because there are lots of valid ways to give your answers. Instead, we've put in a section on how to write answers and do well.

Published by CGP

Editors:
Emma Bonney, Emma Cleasby, Sharon Keeley-Holden, Caley Simpson and Rebecca Tate.

Contributors:
Anna Hazeldine, Sean Purcell, Neil Renton, Frances Rippin, and Andrew Walker.

Acknowledgements:

Government Statistics or National Statistics. Source: Office for National Statistics licensed under the Open Government Licence v. 3.0
https://www.nationalarchives.gov.uk/doc/open-government-licence/version/3/

Page 24: The classification of one in ten children as poor. From *Poverty in Britain: what can we learn from household spending?* by Mike Brewer, Alissa Goodman and Andrew Leicester, published in 2006 by the Joseph Rowntree Foundation. Reproduced by permission of the Joseph Rowntree Foundation.

Page 27: Research on ethnic minority workers and promotion. From *In-work poverty, ethnicity and workplace cultures* by Maria Hudson and Gina Netto et al, published in 2013 by the Joseph Rowntree Foundation. Reproduced by permission of the Joseph Rowntree Foundation.

Page 27: Table of ethnicity and free school meal entitlement. Contains Parliamentary information licensed under the Open Parliament Licence v. 3.0
http://www.parliament.uk/site-information/copyright/open-parliament-licence/

Page 33: International reading and science rankings. From OECD (2014), *PISA 2012 Results in Focus, What 15-year-olds know and what they can do with what they know.*

Pages 48, 72, and 75: Employment, childbearing and death rate statistics. Crown copyright - from Social Trends 38 (2008)

Pages 54, 82, 96 and 194: Life expectancy, wealth, working-class health and infant mortality statistics. Crown copyright - from Social Trends 33 (2003)

Pages 63 and 66: © NatCen. Source: Kathleen Kiernan 'Men and women at work and at home' in Roger Jowell, Lindsay Brook, Gillian Prior and Bridget Taylor, editors (1992) 'British Social Attitudes: the 9th Report' Aldershot: Dartmouth Publishing Company

Page 64: Margaret Thatcher quote. Source: Margaret Thatcher Foundation

Pages 68 and 204: Information on referrals to social services, and ethnicity and housing. Contains public sector information licensed under the Open Government Licence v. 2.0 http://www.nationalarchives.gov.uk/doc/open-government-licence/version/2/

Page 68: Statistics Copyright © United Nations 2000-2008

Pages 74, 83, 124, 126, 128, 135, 148, 150, 175, 181, 194, 198, 207, 208: Information on visa applications, relative poverty, crime detection rates, crime and ethnic minorities, percentage of crimes solved, women and the justice system, domestic violence, burglary, violent crime, religion and age, prevalence of Christianity, age and new media, disability statistics, life expectancy and occupation, women in work, ethnicity and occupation, ageing population, and disability and education. Contains public sector information licensed under the Open Government Licence v. 3.0
http://www.nationalarchives.gov.uk/doc/open-government-licence/version/3/

Page 78: Statistics from the National Society for the Prevention of Cruelty to Children (NSPCC) © 2008 NSPCC

Pages 80 and 81: Poverty statistics published under a Creative Commons Attribution-ShareAlike 2.0 UK: England & Wales License -
http://creativecommons.org/licenses/by-sa/2.0/uk/

Page 81: Poverty statistics. From *Poverty and social exclusion in Britain* by David Gordon et al, published in 2000 by the Joseph Rowntree Foundation. Reproduced by permission of the Joseph Rowntree Foundation.

Page 83: Paid work and ethnicity statistics. From *Poverty among ethnic groups how and why does it differ?* by Peter Kenway and Guy Palmer, published in 2007 by the Joseph Rowntree Foundation. Reproduced by permission of the Joseph Rowntree Foundation.

Page 99 and 208: Discrimination by health care professionals. Source: Mencap

Page 131: Information on illegal logging. *Goncalves, Marilyne Pereira; Panjer, Melissa; Greenberg, Theodore S.; Magrath, William B.. 2012. Justice for Forests : Improving Criminal Justice Efforts to Combat Illegal Logging. Washington, DC: World Bank. © World Bank. https://openknowledge.worldbank.org/handle/10986/6011 License: CC BY 3.0 IGO.*

Page 149: Religious participation and class. From "Men practising Christian worship" report found at
http://cvm.org.uk/downloads/YouGov-CVMreport.pdf

Page 166: Data used in graph. COPYRIGHT © UNITED NATIONS 2015 (Accessed 06/01/2016.)

Page 171: Garment industry, women in EPZs and women in the garment industry. Source: International Labour Organization (2014)

Page 202: Information on female professors. Source: Higher Education Statistics Agency

Page 202: Gender pay gap. Source: © European Union, 1995-2016

Page 211: Information on reading level: From The Reading Gap: The socio-economic gap in children's reading skills: A cross-national comparison using PISA 2009 by John Jerrim, published in 2013 by the Sutton Trust. Reproduced by permission of the Sutton Trust.

The questions in this book are NOT AQA questions and have been neither provided nor approved by AQA.

ISBN: 978 1 78294 356 3

With thanks to Duncan Hall, Glenn Rogers and Caley Simpson for the proofreading.
With thanks to Ana Pungartnik for the copyright research.
Cover photo © iStockphoto.com/Kativ

Clipart from Corel®
Printed by Elanders Ltd, Newcastle upon Tyne.

Based on the classic CGP style created by Richard Parsons.

Text, design, layout and original illustrations © Coordination Group Publications Ltd. (CGP) 2016
All rights reserved.

Themes in Sociology

OK, so before you get going with all the ins and outs of sociology, I'm going to try to answer some key questions. Starting with "what actually is sociology anyway?" Well, that's an excellent question...

Sociology is the **Study of Society**

1) Sociology is the study of **human society**, including its **development**, **functions** and **organisation**.

2) There are generally considered to be **three** 'founding fathers' of sociology — **Karl Marx**, **Emile Durkheim** and **Max Weber**. There's more information on their beliefs over the next couple of pages, but here are the **basics**:

Karl Marx (1818-1883)	**Emile Durkheim (1858-1917)**	**Max Weber (1864-1920)**
Marx believed that **capitalism** oppresses the **working class**, and that there needs to be a **revolution** to make all people **equal**.	**Durkheim** was a **functionalist**. He believed that society is made up of different **institutions**, each with its own **function** — these institutions work in **harmony** to create a **stable society**.	**Weber** believed that sociologists should study both **structures** and **actions** to understand society. He thought that an individual's behaviour is shaped by **structural factors** (such as the **law**) and **subjective factors** (such as **emotion**).

Culture, Socialisation and **Identity** are **Core Themes** in Sociology

There are some **key ideas** that you need to be able to **apply** to **many different topics** of your sociology course. They're covered **briefly** here, but they'll pop up **throughout** this book — you have been warned...

Culture is a Society's **Way of Life**

1) The **culture** of a group of people refers to the way they **live** — their **language**, **beliefs**, **norms**, **values**, **knowledge** and **skills**. It **reinforces** the sense of **community** in a society.

2) Cultures **vary** from **place to place** — e.g. **British** culture is different to **Indian** culture. It also varies with **time** — **today's** culture is very different to the culture of **100 years ago**.

> Norms are behaviours and views that society sees as normal. Values are beliefs and ideas about what is right and wrong.

> There's more detail about culture on pages 36-37, socialisation on pages 40-41 and identity on pages 44-45, but these pages contain more detail than you need to learn (unless you're studying that optional topic).

Socialisation is how **Culture** is **Passed On**

1) **Socialisation** is the way in which **culture** is passed on from **generation to generation**.

2) It begins in **childhood**, where you **learn** how to **behave** and what to **believe**, and continues into adult life. Socialisation comes from **families**, **schools**, **friends**, **religion**, the **media** and **work**.

3) A society's **values** are **internalised** by socialisation, so that they become part of your **way of thinking**.

Identity is quite a **Complex Idea** in Sociology

1) **Identity** is hard to define — there are different **levels** to it. The most **basic** level of your identity is made up of **simple facts** — your **name**, **age**, **appearance** etc.

2) On a **deeper** level (the one sociologists are more interested in), your identity is the way **you see yourself**, and the way you are viewed by **others**. This is called your **social identity**. It's influenced by things like **class**, **ethnicity**, **gender**, **age** and **sexuality**, and also by your **roles** in society — e.g. **teacher**, **friend**, **cousin**.

Chuck saw himself as a sensitive poet. Unfortunately, society just saw him as a firefighter.

Globalisation is a **Very Important Idea**

Globalisation is the idea that the **world** is becoming **more connected**. Improved **technology** and **communication**, an increase in **transnational corporations (TNCs)** and more **migration** have all meant that **national boundaries are breaking down**. Globalisation affects many different areas of sociology — e.g. some sociologists say that **culture** is now globalised.

Themes in Sociology

Social Differentiation, Stratification and Power are also Core Themes

There are a few more **key ideas** that you need to get to grips with. As on the previous page, they **apply** to many **different aspects** of sociology, so they appear throughout the book.

Social Differentiation is the way society is Divided Up

Any society can be **divided up** into **different groups** — this is known as **social differentiation**. The groups can be based on **biological** features (e.g. age, sex), **cultural** features (e.g. class, religion) or more personal characteristics, like abilities. You'll see **many different examples** of social differentiation throughout sociology.

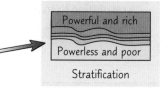
There's another form of differentiation in sociology called structural differentiation. This is when different institutions in society become more and more specialised.

Stratification is the way society is Divided Into Layers

Stratification also splits society into **different groups**, but the groups are **ordered in layers**, with a definite **hierarchy**. The groups can be based on things like **status**, **income**, **religion**, **ethnicity**, **gender** and **age**, but are usually based on **social class** (especially in **Western** societies). The **top layer** is made up of the **richest** and **most powerful** people, and the **bottom layer** is the **poorest people** who have the **least power**. In between, there are many different layers, known as **strata**.

Powerful and rich
Powerless and poor

Stratification

Power is usually based on Wealth

1) **Power** can be seen as the **ability** to get someone to **do something** that they **wouldn't normally do**. A lot of sociology focuses on the **balance** (or **imbalance**) of **power** in society.

2) A person usually has power because of their **wealth**, **job** or **social class**, but could also have it because of their **gender** or **religion**, for example.

3) Some sociologists argue that people who have power use it to **control society** so that they can **remain** in power (e.g. by **oppressing** those with less power).

There are Different Sociological Methods and Theories

1) Sociologists do **research** to try to find **explanations** for how society works and why it changes. They can use different **research methods** for this, including:

- interviews
- questionnaires
- observations
- documents
- government statistics
- experiments

See Section One for more on research methods.

Louisa (third from right) was covertly observing the 2nd Highland Regiment.

2) Once the data has been **collected**, it needs to be **analysed** and **interpreted**. Sociologists look for **patterns** and **correlations**, and use these to draw **conclusions**.

3) Sometimes, sociologists carry out research that relates to the **main theories** of sociology. The main theories are **Marxism**, **functionalism** and **interactionism** (also called **interpretivism**), as well as **feminism** and **postmodernism**. There are also subcategories, such as **neo-Marxism** and **radical feminism**. There's a bit more **detail** about these theories over the next few pages, and they'll come up **throughout this book** as well.

Sadly, the examiners have all the power...

Remember, you need to be able to relate all these core themes to the sociology topics you're studying. You won't get an exam question just about 'power' — it'll be about power in relation to education, or health, or whatever topics you've learnt about. Unfortunately, you don't need to know about power in relation to superheroes or villains, or the power to travel through time.

Sociological Theories

There are lots of different theories about how society shapes individuals — or how individuals shape society. You need to have a decent idea of what functionalism, Marxism and interactionism are, as well as a couple of other theories.

Functionalism Says the Individual is the Product of Society

1) **Emile Durkheim** believed that society is made up of various **institutions**, each of which has a useful **function**. So Durkheim and his followers are known as **functionalists**.

2) They look at **how society is structured** — you can call functionalism a **structural theory**. Functionalists look at how institutions in society work, and how they **affect individuals**. Here are some examples:

   • The Family — has the function of socialising children.
   • Education — has the function of preparing young people for adult society.
   • Religion — has the function of uniting society through shared beliefs.

3) Functionalists believe that the **institutions** of society are structured to allow society to **run as smoothly as possible**.

Functionalism is a type of consensus structuralism because it states that society is structured to function harmoniously.

Not Everyone Agrees with Functionalist Thinking

1) **Interactionists** (also called **interpretivists**) think that functionalists don't focus enough on the **individual** (see p.4).

2) **Marxists** say functionalism ignores the **unequal power** of some groups. They think that society is structured to **serve the interests of the rich**, not to keep society ticking along as smoothly as possible.

Marxism Says the Individual is the Product of Economic Forces

Karl Marx focused on the **effects of capitalism**. He thought that a society's **economic system** (the **infrastructure**) influenced its non-economic institutions (the **superstructure**), and that the superstructure, in turn, determined the society's **beliefs** and **values**.

Karl Marx

Marxists believe that the most important force in society is class conflict

1) In **capitalist societies**, workers are employed to produce goods which are sold by their employers at a **profit**.

2) Only a bit of this money ends up in the workers' wages — most of it's **kept by the employer**.

3) Marx said that if workers were allowed to **notice the unfairness** of this, they'd revolt. So, to **avoid revolution**, the **capitalist system shapes the superstructure** to make sure that the workers accept their lot in life.

4) **Institutions** like the family, education and religion are part of the **superstructure**. They **lead individuals** into **accepting** the **inequalities of capitalism**.

Marxism is a type of conflict structuralism because it states that there is conflict between the two main classes of society.

Marx believed that society was divided into **two classes**:

• The **bourgeoisie** were the **ruling class** — they were the minority but had all the money and power.
• The **proletariat** were the **working class** — they formed the majority of society but had little or no power.

> **Neo-Marxism** is a **20th century** version of Marxism, developed to be more **relevant** to the modern world. Neo-Marxists focus on **ideology** (a set of **ideas** and **beliefs** about how things should be). They study how this ideology is **communicated** and **enforced** by the **ruling class** to maintain its **power**.

Not Everyone Agrees with Marx either...

1) **Functionalists** say Marx put too much emphasis on the role of **economic structures** in shaping ideas and beliefs.

2) **Interactionists** say he placed too much emphasis on **class** and not enough on individuals.

3) **Postmodernists** say social class doesn't have such an important influence on **individual identity** any more. They say people are defined by the **choices** they make, not by whether they're a worker or a boss.

THE BASICS OF SOCIOLOGY

Sociological Theories

Feminists Say *Women* are *Oppressed* by *Men*

Feminists believe that society is **patriarchal** — that it's **run by men**, and that things are done in men's **best interests**. They believe that there are many **inequalities** in society based on gender, and want to make society more **balanced**. There are many different **strands** of feminism — the main ones are:

Feminism is also a structuralist theory.

Liberal Feminism

Liberal feminists want **equal rights** and **opportunities** for women. They believe that introducing more **opportunities** for women into the **existing structures** of society (e.g. the legal system) is the **best way** to try to bring about **equality**.

Radical Feminism

Radical feminists believe that society is **structured to oppress women**, and that **society itself** needs to change. They believe there's an **imbalance of power** in all relationships, and that all women are always expected to be **subservient** to all men.

Marxist Feminism

Marxist feminists combine the beliefs of **Marxism** and **feminism** — they believe that **women are exploited** by **capitalist societies** (which are run by **men**).

Feminists don't even agree with *Each Other*...

Radical feminists criticise **liberal** feminists for not acknowledging that it's more than just **institutions** that are patriarchal — it's **all relationships**. For example, **families** have a male-dominated structure too.

Interactionists Say *Individual Actions* are Most Important

1) Many sociologists say that society is actually determined by the **behaviour and interaction of individuals**. Theories like this are called **action theories** because they emphasise the **action** of individuals, as opposed to **structural theories** like functionalism and Marxism, which are all about the big structures of society.

2) **Interactionist** (or **interpretivist**) theories start with the idea that all individuals **interpret** society around them — people **try to make sense** of society. Interactionists say that culture comes from **people's own ideas** of how people **interact** with each other.

3) Interactionists don't say structures aren't important, but they do suggest that each of us **responds** to social structures in our **own way**. We aren't just products of socialisation — we all have **free will** and make **choices**. An important point here is that the **results of individual choice** can be **large-scale social change**. For example, **Jonathan Gershuny (1992)** made an interactionist analysis of gender roles in the home.

> 1) Some **women decided** they wanted to **work outside the home**. That's the **individual choice** bit.
>
> 2) Male partners then took on **more childcare** and housework. It became **acceptable** for men to adopt roles in the family that had been considered **feminine**. That's the **large-scale social change** bit.

What do you know... *Not Everyone Agrees* with the *Interactionists*

Marxists say interactionists don't pay enough attention to **conflict** or to the fact that some social groups are more **powerful** than others. **Functionalists** say they don't acknowledge the importance of the **socialisation process**.

Learn the *Main Points* of Each Theory

To **sum up** — here's a nice table showing the **main ideas** of functionalism, Marxism, interactionism and feminism.

Functionalism	Marxism	Feminism	Interactionism
Society is made up of different institutions that function together as a whole.	Society is split into two classes. The ruling class oppress and exploit the working class.	Society is patriarchal and women have fewer rights and opportunities than men.	The behaviour of and interaction between individuals determine how society works.

Sociological Theories

New Right Sociologists Say *Traditional Values* are Important

1) Like **functionalism**, the New Right is a form of **consensus structuralism**. New Right theorists are **similar** to functional theorists in that they believe society needs **values** and **institutions** to maintain **social order**. New Right theories focus on subjects such as **family**, **education** and **welfare**.

2) They argue that a **nuclear family** is one of the most important social institutions. They argue that **traditional roles** within the nuclear family (the **man** goes out to **work** and the **woman** stays at **home**) are **crucial** to maintain **social order**.

A nuclear family is made up of parents and their dependent children, all living together.

3) New Right sociologists such as **Charles Murray** say that the traditional family is **under threat**, which has led to a **decline** in **moral standards** and the **breakdown of society**.

Feminists disagree with the *New Right*

As you've probably guessed by now, not everyone **agrees** with New Right theories. In fact, not many people agree with them — in particular, **feminists** criticise the New Right's ideas of **traditional roles** within the family, which they see as being **oppressive to women** and reinforcing a **patriarchal** society.

Postmodernists Say *Society* is *Changing*

Postmodernism came about as a **reaction** to **modernism** — so let's start with a **brief explanation** of modernism:

> **Modernism** is the period of **industrialisation** and **urbanisation** that began with the **Industrial Revolution**, when **rational**, **scientific** thinking was valued. Modernist theories include **Marxism** and **functionalism**. Modernist theories are also known as 'metanarratives' (**big, all-encompassing stories** that explain why things are as they are).

Postmodernists say that society has **moved on** from modernism — it's no longer **ordered** and **structured** in the same way. Society is a lot more **flexible**, and there's more **choice** of **cultures** and **lifestyles** due to increased **globalisation**. They claim that **metanarratives** are no longer appropriate — there are **many different ways of understanding** society, rather than one universal truth or theory.

Other Sociologists disagree with *Postmodernists* (of course they do)

1) **Functionalists** disagree with postmodernists because postmodernism ignores the role of **institutions**.

2) **Interactionists** disagree with postmodernists because postmodernism ignores how individuals **interact**.

3) **Marxists** disagree with postmodernists because postmodernism ignores **inequalities**. No one's ever satisfied.

You've probably realised by now that pretty much **all** the theories **criticise each other**. If you know what **each group** of sociologists believe, then you can probably work out what they think of a **particular theory** or idea (and why).

Practice Questions

Q1 What is 'socialisation'?
Q2 Name three different research methods.
Q3 What's the main difference between structural and interactionist approaches?
Q4 Give two examples of consensus structuralism.
Q5 Name three strands of feminism.

Exam Question

Q1 Outline two key ideas of Marxism. Explain each one. [10 marks]

I'm a post-Marxist neo-functionalist feminist...

*These theories come up again and again throughout sociology, so **learn these pages**. Make sure you can jot down a few sentences about what functionalists, Marxists and interactionists think about the relationship between individuals and society, and the main arguments of feminism, the New Right and postmodernism too. Then take a deep breath before carrying on.*

Research and Methods

Sociologists do research to get evidence which helps them understand society.
Unfortunately, it's not all that straightforward to study human behaviour. If only we were ants in an ant farm.

Sociologists Have Three Aims When Collecting and Using Data

1) Sociologists try to make their research **reliable** and **valid**.

- **Reliable** research can be repeated to get the same results. Reliable data is data that another researcher would be able to get by using the exact same methods.
- Sociological research isn't generally as reliable as research in the natural sciences (physics, biology, chemistry, etc.).

- Valid data is a true picture of what the researcher is trying to measure.
- Even reliable data isn't always valid. For example, you could use unemployment statistics to measure how many people don't work. This wouldn't give a true picture, because these statistics don't include students who don't work, or people who are unable to work.

There are several reasons why research may **not** give a true picture:

- Respondents in an interview may **forget** things, **exaggerate** or just plain **lie**, e.g. they may say they recycle all their rubbish when really they don't.
- Asking people about their attitudes to an event a **long time afterwards** often isn't valid. People **change their views** over time, and may **alter their description** of the past in the light of their **current beliefs**.

2) You can't research the whole population, so you have to take a **sample** (see p.13). Sociologists try to make their samples **representative** — reflective of the population as a whole. To do this, it needs similar proportions of different ages, genders, classes and ethnic groups. If a sample is **representative** then sociologists can **generalise** — i.e. conclude that the results are likely to apply to the entire population.

3) Sociologists aim to be **objective** and **avoid bias**.

Primary Data is Collected First-Hand

The researcher collects primary information **first-hand** — they find it themselves. You could use methods like **interviews**, **questionnaires**, **observations** or **experiments**. You generate quantitative or qualitative data (see p.7).

1) Primary data is obtained from **first-hand research**. It doesn't rely on **another sociologist's research** and you can carefully **choose your method** to make your data as valid and reliable as possible.
2) Primary data is always **brand new** and **bang up to date**.
3) **Some methods** of getting primary data can be **expensive** and **time-consuming**.
4) **Some methods** may put the researcher in a **dangerous situation**.
5) **Some methods** may be **unethical** if you don't give **informed consent** (p.9).
6) The **researcher's own values** may mess with the research process. This creates **bias**.
7) You **can't always get access** to the group you want to study.

Secondary Data is Existing Information

Secondary data sources include **official statistics**, **diaries**, **letters**, **memoirs**, **emails**, **TV documentaries** and **newspapers**. You gather the data together and analyse it, but you don't generate the data.

1) You can **quickly** and easily collect secondary data.
2) You can **easily** use **secondary data** to **compare different societies**.
3) With secondary data you can study **past events and societies**. You can **compare past and present**.
4) You don't have to worry about **informed consent**.
5) The **existing data** may not be **valid** or **reliable** — you're **stuck** with the way the research was **originally done**.
6) Documents may not be **authentic**, **representative** or **credible**. Official statistics can be **biased**.
7) You **might not be able to find** the information that you need from existing data.
8) **Your values** don't influence the **collection** of the data (though they might influence your **choice of sources**), but the **researcher's values** might have ruined the validity of the **original research**. **Your values** can get in the way of **how you analyse** the data.

Research and Methods

Quantitative Data can be Reliable but Not Very Valid

Quantitative data is numbers and statistics. You can easily put quantitative data into a graph or a chart.

There are several advantages of using quantitative data in sociological research...
1) With quantitative data, you can **test your hypothesis** and look for **cause and effect** relationships.
2) You can **compare** your statistics against existing statistics, and look for **trends over time** and between societies.
3) It's **easy to analyse tables**, **charts** and **graphs** — especially line charts, bar graphs and pie charts.
4) You can **repeat** questionnaires and structured interviews to **test reliability**.
5) Quantitative methods allow **large samples**, so the findings can **represent** the **general population**.

However, quantitative data also has its problems...
1) **Statistics** can **hide reality**. **Categories** in **interviews** or **questionnaires** can **distort** the truth.
2) Statistics don't tell you anything about the **meanings**, **motives** and **reasons** behind behaviour — there's not much **depth** and **insight** into **social interaction**.
3) Statistics can be **politically biased**. The method may have been chosen in order to get the 'right' data.

Qualitative Data can be Valid but Not Very Reliable

Qualitative data gives a detailed picture of what people do, think and feel. It's **subjective** — it involves **opinions**, **meanings** and **interpretations**. You can't easily turn qualitative data into a list of numbers or a graph.

The motives behind some behaviour can present a difficult challenge for the sociologist.

There are plenty of reasons why using qualitative data is a good idea...
1) **Qualitative sociological data** gives **insight** into **social interaction**. It's a **detailed description** of social behaviour.
2) Qualitative data lets you find out the **meanings** and **motives** behind behaviour.
3) You don't have to **force** people into **artificial categories** like in questionnaires.
4) Qualitative methods let you build up **trust** and research **sensitive topics**.

There are also some drawbacks of using qualitative data in research...
1) Qualitative investigations are **difficult to repeat** — they **aren't very reliable**.
2) The research is often on a **small scale** — so the findings might not **represent** the whole population.
3) **Positivists** say qualitative results **lack credibility** because they're **subjective** and open to interpretation.
4) The **researcher** can get the **wrong end of the stick** and **misinterpret** the group or individual they're studying.

Practice Questions

Q1 Give one reason why research may not be valid.
Q2 What is meant by the term 'representativeness'?
Q3 Give two strengths of primary data.
Q4 What is the difference between quantitative and qualitative data?
Q5 Give two criticisms of qualitative data.

Exam Questions

Q1 Outline two drawbacks of using secondary data in sociological research. Explain each one. [10 marks]

Q2 Outline two disadvantages of using quantitative data in sociological research. Explain each one. [10 marks]

Ready, aim, research...

Data is to the sociologist what clay is to the sculptor, or what pigeon liver and celeriac are to the chef — you can't do great work without the best raw materials. Studying methodology may not have the Hollywood glamour of criminology or the rustic charm of politics, but without data sociologists have nothing to do. So you'd best learn where and how to find it.

Key Issues in Research and Methods

Sociologists use different methods to carry out their research, and lots of issues determine which method they choose.
You can separate them into three groups — theoretical issues, practical issues and ethical issues.

Theoretical Issues Affect Your Choice of Method

Two important **theoretical approaches** to sociology are **positivism** and **interpretivism**.
You need to know how they affect someone's choice of research method.

> **Positivism** looks at the **institutions** in society. It's called **macrosociology**.
> **Interpretivist sociology** looks at the **individual**. It's called **microsociology**.

Jake's parents had developed
a perfect method for
keeping him out of trouble.

Positivists Use Reliable Methods That Give Quantitative Data

1) **Positivists** say behaviour is influenced by **external social factors**.

2) They think sociology should be **scientific** and **analyse 'social facts'**. Social facts are things that **affect behaviour** and can be **easily measured**. They're **external** things like laws, **not internal** things like people's opinions.

3) So positivists measure human behaviour using **quantitative data**.

4) They use **statistics** to measure the **relationships** between different factors. They're interested in **cause and effect** relationships, e.g. the factors that cause underachievement in schools.

5) They use sources like **questionnaires** and **official statistics**. These are **objective** and **reliable**.

Interpretivists Use Valid Methods That Give Qualitative Data

1) **Interpretivists** (also called **interactionists**) believe that you can only really **understand** human behaviour using **empathy** — by putting yourself in **other people's shoes**. They think that it is important to uncover and understand the **meaning** individuals give to **their actions** and to **the actions of others**.

2) **Interpretivist sociologists** use methods that let them discover the **meanings**, **motives** and **reasons** behind **human behaviour** and **social interaction**.

3) Interpretivists reckon that the **scientific** methods used in **positivist** research **don't tell you much** about how **individual people** act in society. They don't believe in the existence of 'social facts' — they think that the findings of research are always **subjective** (they depend on your opinion).

4) Interpretivists say you can't count meanings and opinions and turn them into statistical charts. They reckon **sociology isn't scientific** because **humans can't be measured** like ants in an ant farm. People don't always understand questions in questionnaires and they don't always tell the truth to researchers.

5) Interpretivists like to use methods that produce **qualitative** data — they try to understand human behaviour from the point of view of the **individual person**. They use methods like **participant observation** and **unstructured interviews** to build up a **rapport** (a feeling of mutual trust and understanding) with individuals, so they can produce a valid and detailed picture of what they think.

> Participant observation means being actively involved in the research as both participant and observer.

Practical Issues also have an Impact on Method

1) **Time** — Some methods need more time. **Covert participant observation** (see p.17) takes a **long time**. The researcher has to get into the group they're studying and win their trust before starting the actual research. A **social survey** (p.13) doesn't need the researcher to participate all the time and the **workload can be shared** in a team.

2) **Money** — This affects the **length** and **method** of the research. Money is needed to **pay the researcher**, for **transportation** to interviews, and to pay for **resources** like computers. **Large-scale social surveys** are **expensive**. The 2011 census cost £480 million. A small focus group will cost a lot less.

3) **Characteristics and skills of the researcher** — It'd be difficult for a **female** researcher to be involved in a participant observation of **monks** in a monastery. Some researchers may be OK with **dangerous situations** and others may prefer to **stay at their desk** and do **detailed analysis** of statistics.

4) **Access and opportunity** — If researchers **don't have access** to certain groups to carry out interviews or observations then they have to turn to **secondary sources**.

Key Issues in Research and Methods

Ethical Issues can be grouped into Four Main Areas

Studies should **try** to meet these **four ethical ideals**. Some studies **fall short**, and some **methods** deliberately avoid them.

1) **Consent** — All participants must have openly agreed to take part.
2) **Avoidance of deception** — Researchers should be open and honest about the study and its implications.
3) **Confidentiality** — The details of all participants and their actions must remain confidential and private.
4) **Avoidance of harm** — Participants should not be physically or psychologically harmed by the research process.

Covert Studies are Criticised for not getting Free, Informed Consent

1) The researcher should get participants' **consent** before they conduct their study. Sociologists should be **open** and **honest** about the work they wish to carry out. It's important that the respondent knows what they're signing up for.
2) People with **learning difficulties** may **not fully understand** what participation would entail. This is problematic. It can be argued that **uninformed consent** isn't really consent at all.
3) Consent can be **difficult to obtain**, especially from **secretive** groups (e.g. Scientologists, the Freemasons, gangs) or when the research is about a **sensitive** topic (e.g. crime, sexuality).

1) Covert methods (e.g. **covert participant observation**, see p.17) involve **not telling** the group being studied that they actually are being studied. They're often criticised for their **lack of honesty** and the absence of **true informed consent**.
2) Covert participant observers argue that to **negotiate access** into **sensitive** or **dangerous** groups such as criminals, the researcher often has to either **pretend to be part of the group**, or not inform the group of the **true purpose** of the study.

	Laud Humphreys' "Tearoom Trade" (1970) was a covert observation of secretive homosexual activity
The group:	The group Humphreys wished to study were men who engaged in homosexual activities in **public places** (especially public toilets). They were **secretive** about their activities for three main reasons — homosexuality was **taboo** in mainstream society, sexual activity in public is **against the law**, and some of the men may have been married men leading a "secret life".
Covert study:	Humphreys probably wouldn't have gained access to this group if he'd openly and honestly informed them about the nature of the research and then sought their permission. Even if he did gain their permission, it's likely that they'd have **acted very differently** if they were aware that they were being observed. Humphreys therefore posed as someone who watches homosexual acts for a sexual thrill. This enabled him to gain the **trust** of the group and observe **genuine actions**.

Other sociologists argue that work like Humphreys' shouldn't be conducted, even if it gives valuable insights to sociology.

Milgram was Criticised for Deceiving his Participants

	Milgram (1974) was not honest with participants in his experiments on obedience
Background:	Milgram conducted a series of experiments in which volunteers were told to administer electric shocks to another person (who was actually an actor) on the other side of a glass screen, when that person failed to give the correct answers in a memory test. Many volunteers kept on giving punishment shocks until the actor pretended to pass out.
Deception:	• Milgram lied about the purpose of the experiment. He told the volunteers that they were doing an experiment about **memory**. • The electric shocks **weren't real**. The person who the volunteers were "shocking" was an actor, pretending.
Results:	The results of the experiment were **very useful**. The experiment showed how people are ready to **obey** authority without **question**. This helped people understand how **ordinary people** take part in war crimes and genocide.

The experiment **wouldn't have worked** if the volunteers **knew** the real purpose of the experiment. If they knew that their **obedience** was being tested, they might have deliberately been less obedient. If they knew the shocks weren't real, they wouldn't have behaved in the same way. Milgram **had to be dishonest** for the experiment to work at all.

This experiment has been **repeated** more recently, but with adjustments to try to reduce the risk of **psychological harm**. Many of Milgram's original participants showed signs of **distress** during the experiment, and some of them were disturbed by how **easily** Milgram had **manipulated** them. However, Milgram did **debrief** all of his participants afterwards so they all **understood** the study, and did **follow-up work** to check on their psychological state. He found that some participants saw the experiment as a **valuable learning experience**.

Key Issues in Research and Methods

Respondents have a Right to Confidentiality

1) All respondents taking part in a piece of research must have their **basic right to privacy** valued and **upheld**. The **data** gathered from them and their **personal details** must not be distributed to anyone **outside** the **research process**.

2) When the report is finally produced, respondents must be made **anonymous**. Any descriptions of people, geographical locations and institutions have to be written in a way that prevents readers from easily recognising the participants. **False names** may be used — in which case the researcher should **clearly state** that false names have been used, in case someone who **shares** the name is **mistakenly identified** as having taken part in the research.

3) Of course, if a researcher **breaches** trust and confidentiality, potential participants will be **put off** taking part in future studies. Research participants must feel they can **trust** the researcher, especially if the research is of a sensitive nature — e.g. a self-reported crime study, or a sexual health survey.

Researchers must make sure that Nobody is Harmed by Taking Part in a study

1) Emotional and physical harm is **never acceptable** in sociological research, and work is actively criticised and rejected if it has allowed harm to come to those involved.

2) Researchers studying topics such as **mental health** or **geriatric care** may have contact with **vulnerable groups** of people, or witness **situations** and **experiences** that cause individuals **harm** — e.g. inappropriate living conditions, or abuse by carers. There is an ethical question as to whether they should **stop** or **suspend** the research in order to **remove** the individual from the dangerous situation.

3) Some topics that are discussed may be **traumatic** for the respondents — they would need to be **informed** of the possible temporary mental and emotional harm before starting the study. Remember, it's important to make sure that all consent is **informed consent** (i.e. that the person fully understands all the implications and aspects of the research before they agree to take part).

Some Sociologists can justify Bending or Breaking ethical rules

There's a lot of **good** that can come from sociological research. Many sociologists can **justify** breaking or slightly bending some of the **ethical rules** — if the data that they'll gather is likely to make a beneficial contribution to society. This justification becomes even stronger if potential ethical problems are minimised — e.g. if there's **minimal harm** and **full confidentiality**, but just a **wee bit of deception** (the basis of covert participant observation).

1) For example, **Nigel Fielding (1981)**, in a study of the **National Front** (an extreme right-wing political party with a secretive hierarchy) argues that he needed to conduct covert research otherwise he wouldn't have been able to gain access to the group and gather information.

2) **"James Patrick" (1973)** was a false name given to a researcher conducting a study on **violent gangs** in Glasgow — to ensure his **own safety** and protection.

3) **Roy Wallis (1977)** wasn't entirely **honest** when researching Scientology. He didn't say he was a sociologist when he signed up to a Scientology course. If he had been honest, the Scientologists may have told him to go away. Wallis was also forced to **name** some of his sources, during a **legal battle** between the Church of Scientology and another researcher. This broke the rule on **privacy** and **anonymity**, but in this case Wallis had **no choice**.

Practice Questions

Q1 What are the four main ethical considerations a sociologist needs to be aware of in their study?

Q2 Why are covert methods seen as unethical?

Q3 Give two reasons that sociologists might use to justify breaking ethical rules.

Exam Question

Q1 Outline two reasons why ethics are important in sociological research. Explain each one. [10 marks]

Danger, sociologists at work...

Well, obviously you wouldn't decide to do a covert observation of how people react to being hit on the head. Because that would be wrong. The key point is that sometimes there are justifications for breaking ethical guidelines, but only when the research is likely to provide such useful information that it's worth it. Most of the time, the best option is to stick to the rules.

Research Design

The first step in sociological research is figuring out what you're going to research.
The second step is condensing your topic down into a single question, or a single hypothesis.

Sociologists pick a **Topic** based on their own **Preference** and **Knowledge**

1) Sociologists often **specialise** in different fields of the subject and therefore will often choose a topic that they have experience or knowledge of — for example, **Steve Bruce** specialises in **religion**.

2) Sociologists try to pick a topic that they think they'll find **enjoyable** and **interesting** to research. It's best not to try a piece of research that you won't enjoy — it only leads to a poorly constructed report that may be either flawed or just plain boring.

3) Also, certain topics become popular in sociology at different times. For example, research in the **mid-twentieth century** often focused on **stratification** and the **class system**. **Nowadays**, the focus of sociologists has moved on to other topics such as **World Sociology**. To gain **prestige**, **funding** and public or academic **interest**, sociologists are more likely to focus their research on topics that are currently **in vogue**.

4) Sociologists and other academics who want to make a **change** in society prefer research that could help develop **solutions** to **social problems**.

5) Sociologists may feel that a particular issue is **neglected** by other researchers, so they'll research the issue to try and '**plug the gap**' — and encourage others to embrace the issue as well.

Funding and Cooperation for Research have an impact on the choice of Topic

1) There are a wide range of potential **sources of funding**. Some research is funded by **charities**, e.g. the Joseph Rowntree Foundation. Some is funded by **industry**. Some is funded by the **government**. A lot of quantitative studies are done **directly** by **government agencies**.

2) The organisation which funds the research is sometimes called a **gatekeeper**, because it often has the final say in the **choice of topic**, the **way** that the topic is **researched** or whether a topic gets researched at all. Government agencies often do research into areas covered by current or proposed **government policy**. **Industrial** grant providers tend to fund research that gives their industry some **practical benefit**.

3) Additionally, a researcher needs to decide whether or not they will be able to get the **cooperation** of the groups they'll be studying if they choose a particular topic. If potential subjects refuse to give their help for the research, then the topic may not be viable.

The researcher's **Career** in **Sociology** is another factor in selecting a topic

1) Sociologists have their eye on their **careers**, just like everyone else. Researchers would jump at the chance to conduct a study that improves their **employability**. Interesting, original or popular topics that are well researched, with good clear results, improve an academic's chance of having their work **published**. Getting work published, particularly in one of the **big sociological journals**, really **improves a researcher's standing** in academia.

2) A quick way for a sociologist to progress in their career is to respond to another sociologist's work. The aim can be either to **prove** the other sociologist **wrong**, or to **add something** to their research. Practically speaking, this could mean investigating the same topic, but using slightly different methods, or investigating a different group of people.

3) This can mean that particular social groups are researched a lot. For example, **routine office workers** are frequently researched in order to test out **theories of stratification** — some systems classify them as working class and some as middle class. Each sociologist who wants to **disprove** or **add to** earlier research on classification has to research **yet another** bunch of routine office workers. Beekeepers **never** get this level of interest from sociologists.

Reviewing the Field is crucial to a good research topic

1) **Reviewing** and **critiquing** existing **data** and **literature** is an important feature in any sociological report. It requires the researcher to spend time reading **articles**, **publications** and other sources of information already produced on the subject.

2) The researcher then **analyses** this material to help clarify the issues around the subject.

"Lush, undulating, 4/5"

3) Reviewing the field gives the researcher useful information on the types of **methodology** used in **previous studies**. They can see whether specific methods, e.g. structured interviews, worked in the past. They can see if research samples were big enough, and form ideas about how big their own sample should be.

Research Design

Research Questions give Focus to sociological research

1) Once the researcher has chosen a broad topic area, they need to **narrow down** the focus of their research so they don't spread their work out too thinly and end up with not enough detail. They do this by coming up with a **single research question** that their research aims to **answer**.

2) A good research question should focus on **one part** of the topic, and it should be **clear** and **easy to research**.

3) Questions should be as **value-free** as possible. In other words they shouldn't be **biased**, or **suggest potential social changes**. So, "Should governments provide vocational education to 14-year-olds?" isn't a good research question because it asks for a **value judgement** on social policy. "What are the attitudes of employers, parents and teachers towards vocational education for 14-year-olds?" is **better**.

Hypotheses are Statements that make Predictions that can be Tested

1) A hypothesis is a **statement** that makes a **prediction**. A hypothesis acts as a **starting point** for research. The research will aim to either **show that the hypothesis is true**, or **show that it's false**.

2) A hypothesis states a **relationship** between **two factors** — e.g. "Sociology teachers wear corduroy trousers" or "Material deprivation causes educational underachievement".

Terms like "democracy" need to be Operationalised — i.e. Made Measurable

1) Sociology prides itself on giving names to **concepts** and **ideas** that aren't **easily explained** or measured. For example, it's **tricky** to measure things like 'democracy', 'development' and 'culture'.

2) You end up measuring these concepts by measuring **something else** that's **linked** to the tricky concept — sociologists call this an **indicator**. This is called '**operationalising**' a concept. It means making it operational, or workable, by finding a way to measure it.

3) Researchers do this **every time** they conduct a piece of research, because you **can't research** something if you **can't measure** it. Each difficult concept needs an **indicator**, e.g. electoral participation or diversity of electoral results for democracy.

4) Researchers need to be able to **justify** how they **operationalised** their concepts in their final report. This is often a **subjective** process and the way a researcher operationalises may be **criticised** by other sociologists.

Triangulation is where you Combine Methods or Data

Triangulation is when sociologists try to combine different methods or data to **get the best out of all of them**.

1) Triangulation gives a more **detailed picture** than when you only use one method, so it's more **valid** (see p.6).

2) When you triangulate, you can **check** different sets of data against each other.

3) Triangulation combines **strengths** and **weaknesses** of different types of data.

4) It can be **expensive** and **time-consuming** to do the same research by lots of methods. Sometimes it's **not possible** to use triangulation — e.g. when there's only one viable method to get the data.

A Pilot Study is a Small-Scale Practice Run

1) A **pilot study** lets you test the **accuracy** of your questions, and check if there are any **technical problems** in your **research design**. You can use them to make studies **more valid** and **reliable**, test how **long** the research will take, and **train** your interviewers.

2) Though they can be **time-consuming**, **expensive** and create lots of **work**, they show that the project is **feasible**, and can help you secure **research funding**.

Not that sort of pilot.

Research Design

Social Surveys Give Quantitative Data

1) **Social surveys** collect information about large target populations, using **questionnaires** or **interviews**.
2) Social surveys tend to be used by **positivists** as a **primary source** of **quantitative data**. This data can be analysed to discover overall **patterns** and **trends**.
3) They're **reliable**, so they're used by **government agencies** and **research companies**.

The target population is the group that is being studied, e.g. 'women over 50'.

Before You Can Start a Social Survey You Need a Sample

1) It's **too expensive** and **time-consuming** for sociologists to survey the **whole target population**. They select a **sample**.
2) If the **characteristics** of the **sample** reflect the **characteristics** of the **target population** — with similar proportions of people in terms of age, class, ethnicity and gender — then the sample can be said to be **representative** of that target population. The extent to which a sample represents the target population is known as its **representativeness** (p.6).
3) If the sample is sufficiently **large** and **representative**, then it should be possible to make **generalisations** from it about the **wider target population**. The extent to which you can accurately do this is the sample's **generalisability**.

Representative Sampling

Representative sampling involves picking names out of a 'sampling frame'. A sampling frame is a **complete list** of the population being sampled, which needs to be **accurate**, **complete** and without any **duplicate** entries.

1) In simple random sampling, names are taken completely at random, e.g. randomly selected from a list by a person or a computer, so each member of the population has an equal chance of being selected.
2) Systematic sampling involves choosing a random starting point in the sampling frame and selecting every nth value, e.g. every fifth name. There may be bias if there's an underlying pattern in the sampling frame.
3) Multi-stage sampling means selecting a sample from within another sample. It's often used to select samples for opinion polls to measure voting intention. First, a selection of constituencies is chosen to represent the whole country, then postcodes within that constituency are selected, then houses from those postcodes.
4) In stratified random sampling the population is put into segments called 'strata' based on things like age, gender or income — e.g. age 18-24, 25-34, 35-44, 45-54, 55-64, 65+. Names are selected at random from within each segment.
5) Quota sampling is a bit like stratified random sampling, but it's not random. The selection is made by the interviewer, who'll have a quota to meet — e.g. "interview 20 women between 25 and 34". Interviewers tend to pick people who look 'nice', which introduces bias. It's quick and useful, though.

Non-Representative Sampling

Some target populations may be **difficult** to **access** — e.g. criminals, the very young or very old — or the characteristics of the population may be **unknown**. In these cases you can use **non-representative sampling** methods.

1) **Snowball sampling** means finding **initial contacts** and getting them to **give you more names** for your research.
2) **Purposive sampling** is when researchers select non-representative samples, often in order to **falsify** a hypothesis. E.g. **feminist** sociologists trying to disprove the idea that gender roles are determined by biological difference deliberately looked for samples where women's roles **weren't different from men's roles**, or weren't traditionally 'feminine'.
3) **Opportunity sampling** is used when researchers need to select a non-representative sample **quickly** and **easily**. Researchers can use **captive audiences** — these are **groups** of people who are gathered together for another reason, like a group of **school-children** or **office workers**. Researchers also go to **public areas** and select people who are nearby.

Practice Questions

Q1 Why is reviewing the field useful?
Q2 Name and explain one representative and one non-representative sampling method.

Exam Question

Q1 Outline two advantages of conducting a pilot study. Explain each one. [10 marks]

The scarecrow award — for being outstanding in your field...

Now you know how sociologists plan research — pick a topic, check out previous studies, formulate a question, make some hypotheses, operationalise the concepts, do a pilot and choose samples. Oh, and find funding. I definitely would've been a researcher if I'd known it was that easy. Revise these pages and maybe you can become the sociologist I can only dream of being.

SECTION ONE — SOCIOLOGICAL METHODS

Questionnaires

Are questionnaires A) the main way to conduct a social survey, or B) flashy people who enjoy asking questions? (Hint: It's A.)

Questionnaires Mainly Give Quantitative Data

1) **Questionnaires** mainly use **closed questions** and **multiple-choice answers**.
e.g. *"What's your favourite fish? a. Haddock b. Cod c. Salmon d. Hake e. Other"*

2) Some questionnaires use **open-ended** questions. e.g. *"What's your favourite fish?"*

3) The **reliability** and **validity** of a questionnaire depends on **how it's designed**.

   • **Closed** questions give you **quantitative** data, which **positivists** like.

   • **Open-ended questions** can give you some insight into **meanings** and **motives**. They give you **qualitative** data, which **interpretivists** prefer.

Reginald was lamenting the lack of an 'all of the above' option.

Questionnaires should...

1) Use **clear, simple questions** which are **easy to understand**.
2) Give **clear instructions** and make it **easy** for the respondent.
3) Have a nice **clear layout** that doesn't **intimidate** people.
4) Give a **range of options** on **multiple-choice** questions.
5) **Measure** what **you want to measure**.

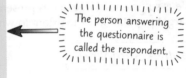
The person answering the questionnaire is called the respondent.

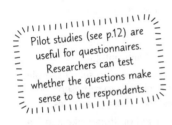
Pilot studies (see p.12) are useful for questionnaires. Researchers can test whether the questions make sense to the respondents.

Questionnaires shouldn't...

1) Ask **embarrassing, threatening** or **complex** questions.
2) Ask **two questions instead of one**.
3) Be **too long**.
4) Use **sociological** terms that **few people understand**.
5) **Lead** the respondent to **answer a question** in a **particular way**.

1) Questionnaires can be used to investigate topics such as **TV viewing habits**, **purchasing habits**, **voting behaviour** and **experiences of crime**.

2) The **Crime Survey for England and Wales (CSEW)** is a questionnaire that is carried out **continually** by the British government. They survey about **38 000** people a year and publish new results **annually**.

3) The **British Social Attitudes Survey** is carried out annually by the **National Centre for Social Research**. Each year they select around **3000** British adults at random and send them a questionnaire.

Questionnaires have several Advantages

1) Questionnaires are **easy to administer**, and they can collect a **lot of data** in a **short time**. Closed questions provide quantitative data which can be **quickly** analysed too.

2) Questionnaires are **reliable**.

3) Questionnaires are **anonymous** and don't require the respondent to sit **face-to-face with an interviewer**. This makes them suitable for **sensitive topics**. For example, the National Survey of Sexual Attitudes and Lifestyles was a **postal questionnaire** rather than a face-to-face structured interview.

4) A **large sample** can be given a questionnaire, so if the sample is representative (see p.6), the questionnaires should produce **representative data** that can be used to make generalisations.

Questionnaires have Limitations — they aren't very Valid

1) Respondents **may not tell the truth**. They may lie, or they may be mistaken.

2) Questions may be **misleading** or **mean different things** to **different people**. This means they may not accurately measure what you **want to measure**.

3) Respondents can't give any **extra information**, even if it would be really helpful to the researcher.

4) Because the respondent fills in the questionnaire on their own, there's no one there to **explain** the questions if the respondent doesn't understand them.

5) Postal questionnaires have a **low response rate**. If it's **too low** it won't be a **representative** sample.

Interviews

There are two kinds of interview — structured and unstructured. Sociologists use interviews when they want to be able to have a chat with their respondents. Well... okay, it's a little bit more complicated than that.

An **Interview** is a **Conversation** Between a **Researcher** and a **Respondent**

1) An **interview** is a **conversation** between a **researcher** and an **interviewee** where the researcher asks a set of questions.
2) You have to pick the **sample**, organise the **interview**, select / train your **interviewers**, **ask the questions** and **record the answers**. **Bias** can get in the way at each stage. An interviewer should create a **friendly relaxed atmosphere**.

Structured Interviews are Questionnaires given Face to Face

1) **Structured interviews** are like **questionnaires** given to **individuals** or **groups**, except an interviewer is present to ask the questions.
2) **Structured interviews** ask the **same questions** each time. The questions are closed questions, with set **multiple-choice answers**.
3) They give **quantitative data** and they're very **reliable**.
4) They're used in **large-scale social surveys**.
5) The main plus point over a postal questionnaire is that the interviewer can **explain** and **clarify** the questions.
6) Also, most structured interviews get a much **higher response rate** than questionnaires. People tend to agree to be interviewed (unless the research topic is sensitive or taboo).
7) However, they're **more expensive** than questionnaires — you need to **pay for the interviewer**.
8) The interviewer has to **follow the list of questions** so they **can't ask for more detail** if the respondent says something **particularly interesting**.

Unstructured Interviews give Qualitative Data

1) **Unstructured interviews** are **informal**, with **no rigid structure**.
2) They are also **flexible** — they can be used to find out facts or attitudes.
3) They're good for researching **sensitive issues** where the interviewer has to gain the respondent's **trust** — for example, sexuality, domestic violence or crime.
4) They use **open-ended questions** and give **qualitative** data. They're quite **valid**.
5) The interviewer needs to have **skill** so they can **probe** to **find out more detail** about the interviewee's **opinions**.
6) They're used with **smaller samples**, which means they're **not very representative**.
7) It takes a **long time** to write up an **unstructured interview** — you have to write down a **whole conversation**, not just the **answers** to particular **multiple-choice questions**.

Pilot studies allow the researcher to find out what kind of question gets a substantial response. They also tell the researcher whether they need to warm up with a gentle chat to gain rapport with the respondent before asking more meaty questions.

In constrast, Becker (1970) suggested that an aggressive interview style could actually uncover more honest responses that a participant might otherwise have kept to themselves.

Interviewers can have an effect on people's answers

1) Respondents in interviews may give the sort of answer they think the interviewer wants to hear — or the exact opposite, if they're feeling uncooperative.
2) Interviewers can give subtle direction towards certain responses — often without realising they're doing it.
3) These are known as 'interviewer effects' (or 'researcher effects'). They make the data less valid.

Practice Questions

Q1 Give two advantages and two disadvantages of questionnaires.
Q2 Give two differences between structured and unstructured interviews.
Q3 What are 'interviewer effects'?

Exam Question

Q1 Outline two disadvantages of using interviews as a method of data collection. Explain each one. [10 marks]

Sociologists could be everywhere, watching us... shhhh...

Don't just learn what questionnaires and interviews are — you have to be aware of their pros and cons. You might also be asked whether one of these methods would be appropriate for educational research (there's more about that on p.34-35).

Experiments

You can use experiments to give you quantitative primary data.
Observation will give mostly qualitative primary data, and there are lots of different types.

Experiments Let You Find Cause and Effect

1) Experiments are used by **natural scientists** — biologists, chemists etc.
2) The researcher starts with a **hypothesis** and they use the experiment to **test** it out.
3) All the variables are kept constant, apart from the one you're interested in — the **independent variable**. Scientists **change the independent variable** and observe the effects on the **dependent variable**. If you were testing the effects of temperature on electrical resistance, **temperature** would be the **independent variable** which **you control** and **electrical resistance** would be the **dependent variable** which you **measure**.
4) The results are **turned into numbers** — the scientist looks for **patterns** and **cause-and-effect** relationships.
5) This method has been developed and used by **social scientists** to look for **social** causes and effects.

There are Two Kinds of Experiment

1) **Lab experiments** are done in a **controlled environment**. The researcher **changes** the **independent variable**, and observes the effect on the **dependent variable**. The researcher usually uses a **control group**, which is **left alone** to see what happens if you **don't do anything** to the **independent variable**. This method is often used by psychologists.
2) **Field experiments** are a response to the criticisms of lab experiments. They take place outside of the lab in **real social settings**, and those involved are often **unaware**. This method is used by **interpretivist** sociologists.

Strengths of lab experiments
1) The **researcher** has **control** over the experiment.
2) You get **quantitative** data.
3) You can **replicate** the research.

Limitations of lab experiments
1) It's **hard** to **reproduce real social situations** in a lab — lab experiments are **artificial**.
2) It is **difficult** to **isolate single variables**. **Social behaviour** is influenced by **many factors**.
3) There are often **moral** and **ethical** issues in lab experiments.
4) People may feel **intimidated** or **act differently** in the lab.

Strengths of field experiments
1) They're done in **natural social settings** and are more like **real life**.
2) They can show the **hidden meanings** of everyday social interaction.

Limitations of field experiments
1) You **can't control the variables** like you can in lab experiments.
2) If people **know they're being studied** they may **change** their **behaviour**.
3) There's an **ethical problem** in carrying out experiments when the subjects **aren't aware** that they are taking part in an experiment.

In any kind of experiment, researchers can measure things in a biased way if they have expectations about the results.

When People Know They're Being Studied, They Sometimes Act Differently

1) When people are more **interested** in something, they **try harder**. They may try harder at what they're doing because they know they're being observed and want to appear in a good light. This is called the **Hawthorne effect**.
2) People usually have an idea of what kind of **response** the **researchers want**. People often either give the researchers the **response they think they want** or the **exact opposite** — depending on whether they want to please the researchers or whether they want to be stubborn.
3) These effects mean data from experiments may not be **valid**.

SECTION ONE — SOCIOLOGICAL METHODS

Observations

Observation is Watching Behaviour in Real-Life Settings

1) In **covert observation**, the researcher **doesn't tell the group** they're being observed. The British Sociological Association (BSA) advise that you should only use covert participant observation when there's **no other way** of obtaining the data. For example, **Nigel Fielding (1981)** used covert observation when researching the National Front (a far right-wing political party) because he believed he would encounter hostility if they knew he was a sociologist.

2) **Overt observation** (direct observation) is when the group is aware of the research and they know who the researcher is. For example, **Beverley Skeggs (1991)** used overt observation when studying female sexuality among students at a college.

3) **Participant observation** is when the researcher **actively involves themselves in the group**.

4) **Non-participant observation** is when the researcher **observes** the group but isn't actively part of the group.

> Interpretivists prefer observation because the researcher can get to the action. It tends to produce qualitative data that's more valid than data from questionnaires.

Participant and Non-Participant Observation Have Pros and Cons

1) Participant observation gets the researcher **right to where the action** is — so they can **check out the dynamics of a group** from **close up**.

2) **Participant observation** allows you to research the workings of deviant groups.

3) The researcher gets **first-hand insight** of people in **natural real-life settings**.

4) If it's **covert**, people **can't mislead** the researcher.

But...

1) The researcher may get too involved and find it **hard to stand back** and **objectively observe** the group.

2) **Overt research** may **influence** the behaviour of the group.

3) The researcher in a **covert observation** may join in with illegal acts if they're in a deviant group.

4) You **can't repeat the research**. It **lacks reliability**. A covert observer may find it difficult to remember all the events and accurately record them.

5) There are **ethical** and **practical** problems in **getting in, staying in** and **getting out** of the group.

6) The research usually includes a **small group** so it's not **representative** of the population.

7) It is **hard work, time-consuming** and **expensive**.

1) In **non-participant** observation, the researcher **isn't drawn into the group** so they can be more **objective** about the group's behaviour.

2) If you want to observe **deviant** groups, you have to be very **inconspicuous**.

But...

1) **Observing from the outside** stops you from getting to where the **action** is.

2) **Overt research** may **influence** the **behaviour** of the group.

By day three of her covert participant observation of landscape painters, Jules was blending in seamlessly.

Practice Questions

Q1 Name two advantages of field experiments over laboratory experiments.

Q2 What is the 'Hawthorne effect'?

Q3 What is the difference between overt and covert observation?

Exam Question

Q1 Outline two disadvantages of using participant observation to conduct sociological research. Explain each one. [10 marks]

Anyone up for an experiment on how people cope with being millionaires...

If you're not really into science, this business about dependent and independent variables might seem a tad confusing. Don't be too confused — just remember that the dependent variable is the one you measure to see how it's changed. When it comes to the stuff on observations, remember to think about the reliability and validity of the different types.

In-depth Research Methods

This page covers some specific types of research methods that study particular groups in a very detailed way.

Case Studies *focus on just* One Thing

1) Case studies are **detailed investigations** of **a specific thing** — e.g. one person, one group, one institution or one event.

2) One particular kind of case study is the **life history**, which studies one person's whole life.

3) Examples of case studies include **Willis's (1977)** study of one group of boys in a school (p.23) and **Venkatesh's (2008)** study on the organisation and impact of one criminal gang.

4) **Interpretivists** like case studies because they can provide very **detailed data**, and they can give the researcher great **insight** into the subject under investigation.

5) **Positivists** dislike case studies as they **aren't representative** of wider populations, and so they can't be used to make accurate generalisations because of the **small sample size**.

Focus Groups *are a Type of* Semi-Structured Observation

1) A **focus group** is a **small sample**, perhaps fewer than ten people. The sample are **put in a room together**, and asked to talk about a particular issue or to try to answer a specific set of questions. The discussion is **observed by a researcher**.

2) Because this is more like a **natural conversation**, the subjects may feel **more able to express themselves** than if they were speaking **directly to an interviewer**. Sometimes the focus group is **left alone** and a **video camera** or **audio recorder** is used to **record the discussion for later analysis**. Sometimes researchers **stay with the group** and **take part in the discussion** — they use the focus group to conduct a **group interview**.

Longitudinal Studies *are* Social Surveys *over a Period of* Time

Longitudinal studies are done at **regular intervals** over a **long period of time**. They're often **large-scale quantitative** surveys, and they tend to be used by **positivists**. However, some studies like the TV programme *Seven Up* are more **qualitative**.

Strengths of longitudinal studies

1) You can **analyse changes** and **make comparisons** over time.

2) You can study how the **attitudes** of the sample **change** with time.

Limitations of longitudinal studies

1) It's **hard** to recruit a **committed sample** who'll want to **stay** with the study.

2) It's **hard to keep contact** with the sample, which may make the study less valid.

3) You need **long-term funding** and you need to **keep the research team together**.

4) Longitudinal studies rely on **interviews** and **questionnaires** which might not be **valid** or **reliable**.

Seven Up was a TV documentary that asked 14 kids aged 7 what they thought about life, and what they wanted to be when they grew up. The programme makers came back to interview the children every seven years. The latest instalment was *Fifty-Six Up*.

Ethnography *Studies the* Way of Life *of a Group*

1) **Ethnography** is the scientific description of a specific culture by someone with first-hand experience of observing that culture. It was first used by **anthropologists** to study **traditional societies**. They joined the community, learnt the language, and noted their observations.

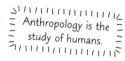

Anthropology is the study of humans.

2) It is based on small-scale fieldwork that tends to produce **qualitative** data. It's **valid** because you can study behaviour in **natural settings**.

3) You can use ethnography to see what a whole **community** get up to, or to find out just one **individual's life history**.

4) You can use all sorts of methods to get **primary data**, including **case studies**, **focus groups** and **longitudinal surveys** and **observations** (p.17).

5) Researchers may also analyse **documents** such as **diaries** and **letters**, which are **secondary data** (p.19).

- Ethnography is **in-depth research** which gives **inside knowledge** about a community.

- You get a **valid** picture from ethnography, but it relies on the **researcher's interpretations** of what people do and say.

- It's **difficult** to **make generalisations** from small-scale research, and it may not be **reliable** (it's difficult to reproduce).

Secondary Data

You can get quantitative secondary data from statistics, and qualitative secondary data from documents.

Statistics are a Source of Secondary Data

Official statistics are a source of secondary data. They're produced by local governments, central government and government agencies.

1) **Hard statistics** are **objective**. Politicians can't fiddle with them. Statistics on births and marriages are hard statistics.
2) **Soft statistics** are more **subjective**. Politicians can fiddle with them. Statistics on **crime**, **poverty** and **unemployment** are soft statistics. In the 1980s and 1990s, the government **changed the method** used to **measure unemployment** over 20 times.
3) **Social Trends** was a collection of **government surveys** published annually until 2012 — a **great source** of **secondary data**.
4) The **UK census** is a survey of every household every 10 years. Every household has to fill in the form **by law**.
5) The **Crime Survey for England and Wales (CSEW)** looks at victims of crime. The data is collected by a questionnaire.

Non-official statistics are statistics collected by organisations other than the government. For example:

1) **TV ratings** collected by the **British Audience Research Bureau**.
2) **Surveys** carried out by **special interest groups**, such as charities, or by other **sociologists**.

Documents and Mass Media are a Source of Secondary Data

1) A document is **written text**. It can be either on paper or in a digital format, e.g. an online text.
2) Documents can be **personal** — like **letters**, **diaries**, **autobiographies** and **memoirs**. Documents can also be **official**, like **school** records, **health** records, **church** records and **social work** records. **Public** documents are produced by charities, businesses and local government.
3) Documents can be **expressive** — more to do with **meanings**, like a **diary**. Documents can be **formal** — like **official documents**. **Interpretivists** prefer **expressive** documents because they're a big source of **qualitative data**.
4) **Content analysis** is a method of **systematically** analysing a communication (e.g. a speech, film or letter) to understand its **meanings**. It is often used to study the mass media, e.g. research by the Glasgow University Media Group.
5) There are **problems** with documents. They can be **difficult to understand** if they're old. They might be **fakes**. They might contain **lies** — especially personal documents.

Sociologists Compare Different Secondary Documents

1) Sociologists look for **similarities** and **differences** between secondary documents. They can compare different **times**, different **cultures** and different **groups** within society by looking at secondary data.
2) Researchers can analyse real social behaviour and make comparisons without having to set up artificial experiments.
3) Durkheim used this **comparative method** in his famous 1897 study of suicide. He looked at the rates of suicide in different European societies. He found that the suicide rate was **consistent over time**, **but varied between societies** and varied for **different groups** within society.

Practice Questions

Q1 What is ethnography?
Q2 Give three examples of official statistics.
Q3 What is the difference between hard and soft statistics?

Exam Questions

Q1 Outline two problems of using longitudinal studies as a sociologist. Explain each one. [10 marks]

Q2 Outline two advantages of using documents as a source of data. Explain each one. [10 marks]

Studying research methods? Infiltrate a gang of sociologists...

I once infiltrated a chocolate factory in the name of ethnography. I got caught sampling a box of triple-layered chocolate bars and had to leave pretty quickly. Make sure you know the kinds of secondary data and in-depth research methods sociologists use.

The Role of the Education System

Different theories try to explain the role or function of education in society. Some of them look at the positive functions, some look at how education maintains inequality, some look at education as a business. Time to learn about learning.

*Functionalism Says Education Has **Three Functions** that Help Society*

1) Education plays a part in **secondary socialisation**, passing on **core values**.
2) Education **sifts and sorts people** for the **appropriate jobs**. This is called the **allocation** function.
3) Education teaches the **skills** needed in **work** and by the **economy**.

1) **Durkheim** said that education passes on **norms** and **values** in order to **integrate** individuals into society. Education helps to **create social order** based on cohesion and value **consensus**, and to strengthen **social solidarity**.

2) **Parsons** describes school as a bridge between the family and adult roles of society. Schools pass on a **universal value** of **achievement**. Parsons says that education **selects** children into **appropriate roles** because it's **meritocratic** (meaning that the best students rise to the top). He agrees with Durkheim that education helps to make people agree about norms and values.

3) **Davis and Moore (1945)** say that every society sorts its members into different positions. They think that there are **rules** for how education does this — called "**principles of stratification**". They believe that there has to be a system of **unequal rewards** (more money or status) to **motivate** people to train for the top positions.

The **functionalist** perspective says that education is **meritocratic**. A **meritocracy** is when social **rewards** are allocated by **talent** and **effort** rather than because of a position someone was **born** into.

Talent + motivation + equal opportunity = qualifications and a high position in society

*Marxism Says **Education Legitimises Inequality** through **Ideology***

1) Education **prepares children** for the **world of work** by giving them **skills** and **values** employers need.
2) Education passes on **ruling class ideology** that **supports capitalism**.
3) Education **legitimises inequality**.

1) **Bowles and Gintis (1976)** say that there's a **correspondence** between **pupil experiences of school** and **adult work**. Pupils are **prepared** for the world of work by the school system:
   - Pupils are taught to accept the **hierarchy** at school. Work also has a hierarchy.
   - Pupils are **motivated by grades** to do **boring work**. Workers are **rewarded with pay** to do **boring work**.
   - The **school day** is broken into **small units**. So is the **work day**.
   - At school and work **subservience** (following the rules) is **rewarded**.

2) Bowles and Gintis say that the '**hidden curriculum**' (see p.22) also **prepares people for work**.

3) Marxists claim that, as well as these skills and values, education also passes on **capitalist ideology**. **Althusser**, a neo-Marxist, sees education as part of the "ideological state apparatus". In other words, it's a **tool** of capitalism which is used to pass on the belief that society is fair, even though it isn't — it **legitimises inequality**. Althusser thinks education produces a **docile and obedient workforce** who will not challenge authority.

4) **Willis (1977)** says that education **doesn't turn out** an **obedient workforce**. Some kids form an **anti-school subculture** and cope with school and then adult work by mucking about (see p.23).

5) **Bourdieu** used the concept of **cultural capital** (language, skills, knowledge and attitudes) to explain how middle-class children generally go on to fill the top jobs in society (there's **plenty** on this on p.25).

6) Marxists say that education **legitimises** this inequality through **meritocracy**. They claim that meritocracy is a **myth**, so **working-class pupils** are blamed for their poor results, when in fact they're a result of their **social class**.

*There are **Similarities** and **Differences** Between Functionalist and Marxist Views*

1) Both functionalism and Marxism look at the **big picture** — institutions and the whole structure of society. They tend to **ignore social interaction** — with the exception of Willis. Both say education has a **huge impact** on the individual and that it's **closely linked** to the **economy** and **work**.

2) The biggest **difference** is how they see **inequality**. Marxists say education helps to **reproduce and legitimise inequality**. Functionalists say education passes on the value of **meritocracy** and lets people **better themselves**.

The Role of the Education System

There are **Problems** with **Functionalist** and **Marxist Views**

Criticisms of Functionalism

1) Evidence of **differential achievement** in terms of class, gender and ethnicity suggests that education is **not meritocratic**.
2) **'Who you know'** is still more important than 'what you know' in some parts of society. So the allocation function isn't working properly.
3) It can be argued that the education system **doesn't prepare people** adequately for **work**. For example, the lack of engineering graduates indicates education is failing to produce what **employers** and the **economy** needs.
4) Functionalism doesn't look at how education may serve the interests of particular groups in terms of **ideology** and **values**. It **doesn't explain conflict**.

Criticisms of Marxism

1) Marxism assumes people are **passive victims**. It **exaggerates** how much working-class students are **socialised** into **obedience**. Willis showed how students actually resist authority.
2) Most people are **aware of the inequality** in education, and **don't think** that this inequality is **legitimate**.

The problem with both approaches is that they don't look at interaction and social processes within the school (see p.24-25).

Feminists say that the Education System is **Patriarchal**

1) Some feminists argue that the hidden curriculum (p.22) unofficially **reinforces gender differences**.
2) There are still **gender differences** in **subject choice** in schools. Gender stereotyping may still exist.
3) Girls are now outperforming boys at school — but **boys** still **demand more attention** from the teacher.
4) **Men** seem to dominate the top positions in schools (**head teacher**, **deputy head**) and even more so in universities.

Liberal feminists want **equal access to education for both sexes**.
Radical feminists believe men are a bad influence, and want **female-centred education** for girls.
Marxist feminists want to consider gender inequalities **combined with inequalities** of **class** and **ethnicity**.

The **New Right** believes that **Education** should provide **Individual Choice**

1) **New Right** theorists believe in the power of **individual choice**, and prefer this to the **state intervening** in people's lives.
2) They claim that the role of a school should be more like the role of a **business**. Businesses have to **compete** with one another to **attract consumers** and provide those consumers with the products they **want** and **need**. New Right theorists claim that this forces all businesses to **continually improve their standards**.
3) State schools are run by the **state**, so they **don't** have to **compete** for their consumers (pupils, parents and employers). New Right theorists say that this has caused **poor standards**. They want to **accelerate** the creation of an **'education market'** (see p.31), where a school's role is to provide what its community **wants** and **needs**.

Practice Questions

Q1 Name three functions that the education system performs, according to functionalists.
Q2 What is meant by meritocracy?
Q3 Give two problems with the Marxist theory of education.
Q4 What are the differences between Marxist and functionalist approaches to education?
Q5 Why do New Right theorists believe that schools should be run more like businesses?

Exam Questions

Q1 How does schooling in capitalist societies mirror the working world? Outline two ways. [4 marks]

Q2 Evaluate the Marxist idea that the function of the education system is to pass on ideology and reproduce the existing class structure. [30 marks]

I like this idea of consumer power — all breaks and no lessons, please...

Mmm, there are lots of theories here. But if you know what functionalism, Marxism, feminism and the New Right are, then their views of school **aren't that surprising**. What's that, Marxists think education reproduces class inequality? Shocker.

Relationships and Processes within Schools

These pages are all about what actually happens inside schools, day in, day out. Most people experience a school at some point in their lives, so you should be able to relate to quite a bit of this stuff. Which should make it easier to learn. Dandy.

School also Teaches you a **Hidden Curriculum**

1) As well as the **formal curriculum** of subject content (English, science, geography and so on), schools pass on a set of **social norms** and **values** to their students. This is called the **hidden curriculum**.

2) Turning up to lessons **on time**, dressing **smartly** in the correct uniform and **working hard** to **achieve rewards** are all part of the hidden curriculum. They all teach students things they will need in **adult life**.

3) The hidden curriculum is part of many areas of school life. For example, a **hierarchy** of management staff, teaching staff and students teaches **respect for authority**. Punishments for failing to do homework teach students about the importance of **following instructions**.

The chaps had searched all night for the hidden curriculum, but without success.

Labelling Theory says that Teachers can create Self-Fulfilling Prophecies

1) **Labelling theory** was a very popular idea in sociology in the 1970s and 1980s. It states that people **decide** on the **characters** of others and **treat** them accordingly, whether the label is 'fair' or not.

2) According to this theory, **labels** are an important part of **teacher-pupil relationships**. If a student is labelled by their **teacher** as a 'troublemaker', they're **disciplined more harshly** than their classmates. Meanwhile, a student labelled as a 'bright spark' is given encouragement to help them to **succeed even further**.

3) Labelling can create a **self-fulfilling prophecy**. This is where the student **internalises** the label they've been given as part of their **identity** (see p.23), and 'acts up' to the label. For example, 'troublemakers' might behave poorly because that is how they think their teacher **expects** them to behave anyway.

> Some studies have shown that teachers label students based on **ethnic**, **gender** and **class stereotypes**. E.g. **Gillborn and Youdell (2000)** found that **black pupils** were more likely to be **disciplined** than their white classmates for the **same behaviour**, and black students felt that their teachers had **low expectations** of them.

There are **Different Ways** to **Organise Teaching** in a School

The ways in which schools decide to **sort** their pupils into **classes** can have a **big impact** on pupil achievement.

Streaming	Setting	Mixed Ability
Students are sorted into classes according to ability, and they stay in these groups for all or most of their subjects.	Students are sorted into classes according to ability, but on a subject-by-subject basis. E.g. a student could be in the top class for maths and the lowest class for music.	Students are sorted into classes that aren't based on ability, so that the highest and lowest achieving students are taught together.

1) There are possible **advantages** and **disadvantages** to each of these systems.

2) The main argument in favour of **setting** and **streaming** is that students can work at their own **level** and **pace**.

3) One problem with **streaming** is that students are likely to be **better** at **some subjects** than **others**, so some 'bottom stream' students **aren't challenged enough** in certain subjects, whilst some 'top stream' students **struggle** in some subjects.

4) Both **setting** and **streaming** can lead to **low self-esteem** for those in the lowest ability classes. **Ball (1981)** also found that teachers had **high expectations** for the highest ability classes. These students received even more attention and encouragement, while those in the lower classes suffered from **negative labelling** and performed poorly — setting and streaming can actually **increase** the differences in student achievement.

5) **Mixed-ability** classes can avoid worsening **gaps** in pupil achievement, but studies have shown that teachers still hold **low expectations** for lower ability students, and often **lower the level** of their teaching to suit them. This can mean that there isn't enough challenging work for the higher ability students.

Relationships and Processes within Schools

Pupils can Form Subcultures within Schools

A subculture is a group who share ideas and behaviour patterns which are different from the mainstream culture.

1) Two of the most commonly discussed subcultures are **pro-school** and **anti-school**, but there are **many** different subcultures within a school, e.g. sporty students, academic achievers or "lads".

2) Subcultures can have a **positive** or a **negative** effect on student **achievement**.

3) There is much debate about **how** and **why** students form subcultures within schools:

Streaming

Lacey (1970) claimed that it was a result of streaming. He conducted his study in a grammar school (p.30). Even though all pupils had been selected as "bright" at age 11, bottom stream pupils still formed an anti-school subculture, because they were labelled as failures.

Ethnicity

Fuller (1984) looked at a group of black girls in Year 11 at a comprehensive school. They were high ability, but felt that their teachers were racist, so they didn't work for their teachers' approval. Instead, they formed a subculture, worked alone and succeeded.

Social class

Willis (1997) studied a group of boys who had formed an anti-school subculture. He found that the 'lads' deliberately disrupted lessons as a way of gaining respect from others within the subculture. He also observed that these boys were working-class and likely to get manual jobs after school — they seemed to believe that school was of no use to them in the future.

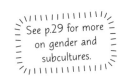
See p.29 for more on gender and subcultures.

Identity is a More General Way of Studying School Pupils

1) Factors such as labelling, self-fulfilling prophecies, the organisation of teaching, and subcultures all have an **impact** on the achievement of school pupils, and it can be hard to work out the **specific** effects of each factor.

2) Instead, considering a pupil's **identity** (the way they view themselves, and the way others view them — see p.1) can be a way of **bringing together** all of these factors, and thinking about them alongside factors outside of school, such as parental attitude and whether they're suffering from poverty.

> For example, if a **male pupil** identifies himself as '**non-academic**', this may have **begun** with a **teacher label**, but the biggest factor may **now** be a **subculture** of other, like-minded pupils, who are also 'non-academic'. He may choose to take a physical education GCSE, because he thinks of it as a **traditionally male** subject and he's already in a **top-ability set**, while adopting an **anti-school attitude** in English and history lessons. At home, he may not have access to **books** that would help his English or history performance. Overall, the difference in his **achievement** in various subjects gets **larger**.

3) One **disadvantage** of studying pupils' identities is that they're very **complex**. If a sociologist wants to study the effect of a **specific process** within school (such as setting) on achievement, then identity can make this difficult. Using the example above, if this student's achievement fell in history, it would be tricky to work out whether this was due to the set he was in, or one of the various factors that form his 'non-academic' identity.

Practice Questions

Q1 What is the hidden curriculum?

Q2 How can teacher labels lead to the formation of self-fulfilling prophecies?

Q3 Define the term 'subculture' and give two examples of subcultures which could appear in a school.

Exam Question

Q1 Why might subcultures form in schools? Outline two reasons. [4 marks]

"Yes, I did stick loo roll to the ceiling, but I was fulfilling a negative label, sir..."

Even if sociology can't get you out of detention, it can tell you a lot about how schools work. All of these processes and relationships affect pupil achievement, so make sure you're clear on key terms like streaming, labelling and pupil subcultures.

Class and Differential Achievement in Education

Sociologists have investigated how social class affects how well people do at school.
Financial and cultural factors are studied, as well as in-school factors like streaming.

Social Class tends to Affect Educational Achievement

1) Pupils from **professional** backgrounds are significantly **more likely** to enter **higher education** than those from unskilled backgrounds.

2) Pupils from **middle-class** backgrounds are more likely to study for **A-levels**, whereas **working-class** pupils are more likely to take **vocational** qualifications.

3) Pupils from disadvantaged backgrounds are **less likely** to start school being able to **read**.

I wonder if class affects how well you do in a school of fish.

4) Pupils from **unskilled backgrounds** on average achieve **lower scores** on SATs and in GCSEs and are more likely to be placed in **lower streams** or sets.

Some sociologists have suggested that different socio-economic groups have **different relative IQs**, and this accounts for discrepancies in educational attainment (**Eysenck (1971)** and others), but this is **very controversial**. It's also difficult to work out whether or not any **potential** IQ differences would be more **important** to achievement than social factors.

Processes Inside School — Labelling, Streaming and Subcultures are Factors

1) **Negative labelling** of students can lead to a **self-fulfilling prophecy of failure** (p.22). **Becker (1971)** and **Keddie (1971)** say that teachers tend to evaluate pupils in comparison to an imaginary **ideal student**, by looking at their **social class** (as well as appearance, personality and speech).

2) **Ball (1981)** found that the pupils in top **streams** (p.22) tended to be from **higher social classes**.

3) As a response to negative labelling and frustration with low status, pupils may form **anti-school subcultures** (p.23). **Woods (1983)** argued that there are lots of different reactions to school, but **non-conformist** reactions were more likely to come from **working-class** students.

These explanations are useful when looking at **day-to-day experiences** in schools. The problem is that they don't explain how **factors outside of school** (e.g. poverty, cultural deprivation) can influence achievement.

Material Deprivation Outside School Can Affect Achievement

The theory of **material deprivation** says that **economic poverty** is a big factor in low achievement at school.

1) In 1997, the **Joseph Rowntree Foundation** classified **one in ten** children as **poor** — which was defined as being in a family that couldn't afford at least three things other families took for granted.

2) **Halsey (1980)** found that the **most important factor** preventing working-class students staying on at school was a **lack of financial support**.

3) **Douglas (1964)** found that children in **unsatisfactory living conditions** (poor housing, lack of nutritious food, overcrowding) didn't do very well in ability tests compared to kids from comfortable backgrounds.

4) **Unemployment** or **low income** means less money for books, internet access and school trips. Low income families can't afford **nurseries** and **private schools** and they can't afford to support their kids through **uni**.

5) Poverty and unsatisfactory living standards may cause **health problems** and **absence from school**.

Cultural Deprivation Outside School Can Affect Achievement

The theory of **cultural deprivation** says that **working-class culture** and **parenting** aren't aimed at educational success.

1) **Douglas (1964)** thought the **level of parental interest** was the most important factor in affecting achievement. For example, middle-class parents are more likely to attend open evenings. Bear in mind though that **working-class parents** may not go to open evenings because they work **inconvenient shifts** — not because they aren't interested.

2) Some sociologists say that working-class kids don't have the **knowledge** and **values** that help achievement. **Books, museum visits, home internet access** and **parental knowledge of education** may help middle-class pupils to succeed.

3) Some **styles of parenting** emphasise the importance of education more than others.

Class and Differential Achievement in Education

Some Sociologists say **Class Affects Attitudes** to **Education**

1) **Sugarman (1970)** said that pupils from non-manual backgrounds and manual backgrounds have **different outlooks**. The pupils from **manual** backgrounds lived for **immediate gratification**. The pupils from **non-manual backgrounds** were **ambitious** and **deferred their gratification** — they invested time in studying and planned for the future.

2) **Leon Feinstein (2003)** found that social class continued to have a **significant impact** on educational achievement. He argued that **redistributive policies** (like Sure Start — see p.32) should carry on throughout a **student's entire education**, rather than being restricted to their pre-school years.

3) **Hyman (1967)** said that the **values** of the working class are a **self-imposed barrier** to improving their position. He said that the working class tend to place a **low value** on education.

> ethnocentric = prioritising the values and culture of a particular group.

> But...
>
> Material and cultural deprivation theories **don't** explain how **factors inside school** affect achievement.
>
> **Cultural** deprivation theory **generalises a lot** about differences between middle-class and working-class life. It **ignores** working-class families who **do** place a high value on education, and tends to **assume** that working-class families have **no culture** at all, or that working-class culture can't be **relevant** to school. This is **ethnocentric**.
>
> The **method** may be **unsound**, e.g. attending parents' evenings might not be a good measure of parental interest.

The two Bs (**Bernstein** and **Bourdieu**) Investigated **Differences** in **Achievement**

1) Bernstein (1970) found that working-class pupils in the East End of London weren't comfortable with the style of language required by school. They used a restricted code — short forms of speech.

2) Middle-class students knew how to use the same elaborated code as the teachers — a much more wordy style of speech with everything made very explicit.

3) In terms of language, the working-class kids were at a disadvantage.

1) Bourdieu (1971, 1974) reckons middle-class students are at an advantage because they have the right kind of "cultural capital" — the right language, skills, knowledge and attitudes.

2) He thought that the more cultural capital you have, the more successful you'll be in education — and he believed that working-class pupils don't have access to cultural capital.

3) Middle-class families pass on cultural capital and expectations from parents to children. This is called cultural reproduction.

Problems with Bernstein's theory	Problems with Bourdieu's theory
There are **variations within** the middle class and working class. Different sections of these groups **vary** in how they use the **elaborate code** — the 'posh language' of teachers.	**Halsey et al (1980)** found that **material factors** are important. **Lack of money** may **stop kids staying on at school** or **getting to university**.
Some sociologists have developed his ideas to say working-class speech patterns are inferior or somehow 'wrong' — controversial... **Labov (1973)** thinks the elaborated speech code is just **different**.	**Not all working-class students fail**, even if they don't have cultural capital.

Practice Questions

Q1 Explain how processes outside school can cause underachievement by children from working-class backgrounds.

Q2 In what way might cultural deprivation theory be considered ethnocentric?

Q3 What is cultural capital and who does it help in education?

Exam Question

Q1 Analyse two explanations for why children from lower social classes may underachieve in school. [10 marks]

Immediate gratification sounds good to me...

A warning — the exam might ask you something like "Assess how factors inside and outside school affect achievement".
To answer that, you'd need to look at home and school factors for ethnicity, gender AND class. So revise p.26-29 as well.

Ethnicity and Differential Achievement in Education

Ethnicity is another factor that can influence how well people do at school.
Quick reminder — ethnicity means the shared cultural traditions and history which are distinct from other groups in society. Modern Britain is said to be a multicultural society made up of many different ethnic groups.

Some **Ethnic Groups** Do **Better** Than **Others**

There are big **variations** between the **average achievement level** of different ethnic minority groups.

Higher levels of achievement

1) **Chinese** pupils are the highest achievers at GCSE. **Indian** pupils also perform above the national average.

2) Students who are from **mixed ethnicity** backgrounds tend to perform above the national average at GCSE.

3) **Female black** and **male Asian** groups have some of the highest rates of students entering **higher education**.

All these statistics are averages. If you look at someone and say "she does well 'cos she's Chinese" you might be wrong.

Lower levels of achievement

1) **Fewer black pupils** get 5 A*-C passes at GCSE than any other major ethnic group.

2) **Roma, white** and **Bangladeshi** students are the least likely to continue into **higher education**. (However, it's worth noting that Bangladeshi pupils achieve **above** the national average at **GCSE**.)

There must be reasons behind these statistics — probably more than one factor, and probably some **social** and **economic** factors.

Some people say that **intelligence is inherited** — i.e. people underachieve because they've inherited low IQ.

However, **IQ tests** can be **biased**. Sometimes they ask things that aren't really a test of brains, but really a test of **cultural knowledge**. The **Swann Report (1985)** found that if you took into account social and economic factors there were **no significant differences in IQ** whatsoever between different **ethnic groups**.

Processes Inside School — **Labelling**, **Curriculum** and **Prejudice** are Factors

Labelling theory

Labelling theory says that teachers have **different expectations** of **different ethnic minority groups**. **Gillborn (1990)** found that teachers sometimes **negatively label black students**. African-Caribbean students were seen as a **challenge** to school **authority** — and were more likely to be excluded from school. Gillborn calls this the 'myth of the black challenge'. Teachers had high expectations of Asian students, which could lead to a self-fulfilling prophecy of **success**. In contrast, negative labelling could result in a **self-fulfilling prophecy of failure**.

School Curriculum

The school curriculum could also be seen as **ethnocentric** — i.e. that it might fit the mainstream, white, middle-class culture better than other ethnicities. It could be **Europe-centred** too. Languages in the National Curriculum are mainly **European** — even though Mandarin Chinese is being taught more, kids usually learn French and German. **Assemblies, school holidays** and even **history lessons** may not fit with the culture and history of particular groups.

Institutional Racism

Some sociologists see British education as 'institutionally racist'. This is where **policies** and **attitudes** unintentionally discriminate against ethnic minority groups. **Wright (1992)** found that even though members of staff said they were **committed to equal opportunities**, Asian girls got **less attention** from teachers and felt their cultural traditions were disapproved of (e.g. they might get told off for wearing a headscarf if it isn't part of the school uniform). **African-Caribbean boys** were more likely to be punished and **sent out of class**.

1) Some sociologists say that these factors may lead to **low self-esteem** for ethnic minorities. **Coard (1971)** said that black students are made to feel inferior in British schools.

2) On the other hand, **Mirza (1992)** found that black girls had **positive self-esteem** and **high aspirations**. The girls experienced discrimination but had **strategies** to minimise the effects of racism. It **wasn't low self-esteem** that affected their achievement — it was being **unwilling to ask for help**, or unwilling to **choose certain subjects**.

Ethnicity and Differential Achievement in Education

Factors Outside School — *Cultural Deprivation* Can Affect Achievement

1) **Language** can be a barrier for children from **immigrant families** when they **first arrive** in the UK.
2) However, the **Swann Report** found that **language didn't affect progress** for **later generations**.
3) **Driver and Ballard (1981)** also found that Asian children whose **first language** was **not English** were **as good at English** as their **classmates** by the age of 16.
4) **Labelling theorists** would say that language might not be a barrier, but **dialects** or having an **accent** might **influence teacher expectations** and lead to **negative labelling**. For example, a teacher might **assume** that a child isn't good at English because they have a foreign accent and put them in a lower set.

1) Some studies say that **family life varies** for different groups and this can influence achievement.
2) **Driver and Ballard (1981)** say that the **close-knit extended families** and **high parental expectations** increase levels of achievement in **Asian communities**.
3) **Archer and Francis (2006)** found that **Chinese parents** saw education as hugely important and this seemed to create a **desire for achievement** in Chinese families.
4) Some sociologists say the relatively high levels of **divorce** and **single-parenthood** in African-Caribbean households could result in **material deprivation**. On the other hand, the **independence of African-Caribbean women** can mean that girls get **positive role models**.

Ethnicity Combines with Material Deprivation to Affect Achievement

On their own, cultural factors and factors inside school may not seem all that convincing.
If you bring **material factors** and **social class** into the equation you get a more complex picture.

1) The Swann Report found that socio-economic status was a factor in the lower levels of achievement of African Caribbean pupils.
2) Pakistani, Bangladeshi and African Caribbean groups are more likely to be in lower class positions such as routine occupations (assembly line workers, factory workers) and elementary occupations (cleaners, labourers). This may result in poor housing, periods of unemployment, poverty and material deprivation.
3) Chinese, African Asian and Indian groups are more likely to be in higher class positions and less likely to experience material deprivation.

Some recent studies have claimed that **prejudice** in society may contribute to these lower class positions. Research by the **Joseph Rowntree Foundation** found that **ethnic minority** workers in **low-paid jobs** often face **barriers** to **promotion**.

Free school meals are given to children from families on certain financial **benefits**, so they can be a good **indicator** of material deprivation:

African Asians means people of Indian origin who lived in Kenya and Uganda and then moved to Britain in the 1970s.

Ethnic group	% of pupils at end of KS4 entitled to free school meals
Bangladeshi	38.5%
Pakistani	28.0%
Indian	9.7%
Chinese	7.4%

Data from the year 2012-2013.

Practice Questions

Q1 Why do sociologists dislike genetic explanations of intelligence and educational success?
Q2 Name one factor inside school that explains the underachievement of some ethnic minority groups.
Q3 Give an example of how social class combines with ethnicity to affect achievement.

Exam Question

Q1 Evaluate the idea that factors inside the school are the most significant in explaining the educational achievement of different ethnic minority groups. [30 marks]

It's more complicated than you might have thought...

Remember that not all ethnic minorities underachieve — so don't go storming into your exam answer with a pre-prepared rant that it's all about white / black racism. There are always several different factors that affect each ethnic group.

SECTION TWO — EDUCATION

Gender and Differential Achievement in Education

Gender is another factor that can influence how well people do at school.
Since the 1980s, things have changed. Sociologists used to talk about female underachievement.
Now there are worries that boys are falling behind. Geez Louise, make your minds up...

Four Facts *about* Gender *and* Differential Educational Achievement

Boys used to outperform girls at school in the UK — this had a lot to do with the fact that female education was seen as **less important** for much of history. However, there's been a shift, and it's now **boys** who are **falling behind**:

1) Girls get better results in primary school National Curriculum tests.
2) Girls get better results in nearly every subject at GCSE.
3) Girls are more likely to pass their A-levels.
4) More women than men go on to university in the UK.

Factors Inside School *Explain Why* Females Now Do Better

1) **Mitsos and Browne (1998)** say teaching has been **feminised**. Women are **more likely to be classroom teachers**, especially in primary schools. This gives girls **positive role models**.

2) **Textbooks** and **teaching resources** have changed and are less likely to **stereotype girls** into passive roles.

3) The National Curriculum **forced** girls to do **traditionally 'male'** subjects. For example, more girls started to do **science**. Other Local Education Authority and government initiatives tried to encourage girls to do these subjects, e.g. WISE (Women In Science and Engineering) and GIST (Girls Into Science and Technology).

4) **Swann and Graddol (1993)** think that high female achievement is a result of the **quality of interaction** they have with their **teachers**. Most of the time teachers spend with girls is used to **help with their work** but most teacher time spent with boys is focused on **behaviour management**.

5) **Jackson (1998)** says that schools label boys **negatively**. Boys are associated with poor behaviour, which gives the school a bad name, and with **low achievement**, which lowers the school's **league table position**. This negative label becomes a **self-fulfilling prophecy**.

Archer (2006) *says that Females Still Face* Problems at School

1) **Archer (2006)** argues that the current **underachievement** by boys in education masks the **continuing problems** that girls still face.

2) She claims that **high-achieving Asian** and **Chinese** girls get negatively labelled by teachers as **robots** who are **incapable of independent thought**.

3) She also argues that **black working-class girls** are negatively labelled as **loud and aggressive**.

4) She concludes that the ongoing achievement of girls is '**fragile and problematic**'.

Factors Outside School *Explain Why* Females Now Do Better

1) Some sociologists argue that girls are **socialised** into ways of behaving that are **well-suited** to classroom environments — to be quieter, to listen to authority figures and to read a lot.

2) Policies such as the **Equal Pay Act** and **Sex Discrimination Act** have helped to create **more equal opportunities** in the wider society. This has **changed the values** of society and attitudes in school.

> The Equal Pay Act (1971) makes it illegal to pay men and women different wages for the same work. The Sex Discrimination Act (1975) means employers can't discriminate on the basis of gender.

3) **Sue Sharpe (1994)** found that girls' priorities have changed. They now want **careers** and qualifications. More women go out to work, so girls see **positive role models** in work. Girls nowadays often want to be **financially independent**.

4) The **feminist** movement caused a **change in female expectations**, and made more people **aware of inequality**. People are now more careful about negative stereotyping, sex discrimination and patriarchy.

5) Changes in the **labour market** have created opportunities for women. Since the 1970s, there has been a **continual increase** in the size of the **service sector** (jobs like healthcare and retail), which is traditionally female-dominated, and a **shrinking** of the **primary sector** (e.g. farming and mining), which is traditionally male-dominated.

6) Changes in **family structure** have changed female aspirations. On average, women now marry and have children **later in life**, so they can pursue a career first. There's also been a move towards **more equal roles within households** (p.49), partly as a result of the feminist movement, so that women are more able to seek work **outside** of the home.

Gender and Differential Achievement in Education

There are Several **Reasons** Why **Some Boys Underachieve**

1) Boys may be having an **identity crisis**. The rise of **female independence**, the decline of the **breadwinner** role for men and the rise in **male unemployment** might mean that boys don't see the point of education. This may lead to anti-school subcultures.

2) **Interpretivists** say that teachers have **lower expectations of boys**. Teacher expectations may lead to a **self-fulfilling prophecy** of poor behaviour. **Negative labelling** may explain why they're more disruptive. Boys are more likely to be **excluded** from school.

3) The **feminisation** of **teaching** means that boys don't have as many **role models** in the classroom.

4) **Reading** can be seen as 'girly'. Boys who **avoid books** may not develop vital **communication skills**.

Burly men in Santa hats can read books, too.

Subcultures help to Explain **Gender** and **Achievement**

Negative labelling and putting students into different **streams** or **sets** can cause some pupils to rebel against the school's values. They form **subcultures**. These can be either **pro-school** or **anti-school** subcultures.

1) In the 1970s **Willis** looked at why working-class kids get working-class jobs. He studied a group of boys later called "Willis's lads". The lads **rejected school** and formed an **anti-school subculture**. They **coped** with their own underachievement by having a **subculture where education didn't matter**, and where having a laugh was more important.

2) **Mac an Ghaill (1994)** says that **subcultures are complicated**. There are **lots of different types**. Boys may join a **macho lad subculture** because of a crisis of masculinity. But boys could also join **pro-school subcultures** and be proud of academic achievement.

3) **Fuller (1980)** studied a group of **African-Caribbean girls** in **London** who formed a **subculture** that worked hard to prove negative labelling wrong.

There are **Different Ways to Explain Gender** and **Subject Choice**

Girls tend to choose **essay-based** A-levels like English and religious studies.
Boys tend to go for **technical** ones like maths and physics.

1) **Subject choice** may still be influenced by **gender socialisation**. The ideas of **femininity** and **masculinity** can create different **expectations** and **stereotypes** of what pupils should study.

2) **Kelly (1987)** found that **science** is seen as a **masculine subject**. Boys dominate the science classroom.

3) **Parental expectations** may encourage students to follow what they see as the traditional 'normal' choice for their gender. There's a pressure to **conform** to a social norm.

4) **Teachers** may also have an effect on subject choice. Most physics teachers are male, for example, meaning that there are more male than female **role models** within this subject.

In 2015, 28 500 boys and 7787 girls entered the A-level physics exams.

Practice Questions

Q1 Give two stages of education where girls tend to outperform boys.
Q2 Give two reasons why subcultures are formed by some pupils.
Q3 Give one reason why boys and girls might choose different subjects.

Exam Question

Q1 By applying material from Item A, analyse two explanations for why girls now do better than boys in school. [10 marks]

> **Item A**
> Girls now get better results than boys in primary National Curriculum tests, and this performance continues to GCSE level, where girls achieve higher grades in nearly every subject. This is in stark contrast to historical gender trends in education.

Girls are DOOMED... no wait, boys are DOOMED... no wait... ah, forget it...

*Remember that there's a **lot of generalisation** with all of the sociological theories in this book. You can't just assume that Josephine beat Joseph in the sociology exam because she's a girl. She might have done more revision. (No hints here.)*

State Policy and Education

All governments are interested in education. The 1870 Forster Education Act introduced elementary schooling for 5–10 year olds in England and Wales. Since then there have been some major changes. Place your votes, please.

The **1944 Education Act** Introduced the **Tripartite System** and the **11+**

Before the **Second World War**, many poor people couldn't afford **secondary education** because it wasn't **free**. The **1944** Act (often called the **Butler Act**) made secondary schools free for all and raised the **leaving age** to 15. You took the **11+ exam** (like an IQ test) at the end of primary school and then went to one of **three types** of school:

1) Grammar schools were for the able kids who passed the 11+. Pupils were taught traditional subjects ready for university. About 20% of kids got in to grammar school.

2) Secondary modern schools were for the 75-80% of pupils who failed the 11+. Secondary moderns offered basic education.

3) Technical schools were meant to provide a more vocational education for those pupils with aptitude for practical subjects.

This system took a largely functionalist approach (since it was based on the idea of role allocation — see p.20).

This **tripartite system** aimed to improve the education of all children, but several problems remained:

1) The **11+ didn't necessarily measure your intelligence**. It was **culturally biased**, and suited the middle class more than the working class. It actually **legitimised** social class inequality, by incorporating it into a **system**.

2) **Few technical schools were built**, so the vocational part of the plan didn't work that well. Most children ended up either at grammar or secondary modern schools. These schools were supposed to have '**parity of esteem**' — they were supposed to be considered as having **equal value** — but grammar schools were seen as the best.

3) Kids who failed the 11+ were **labelled as failures**, which sometimes turned them off education.

4) If well-off middle-class pupils failed, their parents could still afford to send them to **private schools**.

In **1965** the Labour Government made Schools **Comprehensive**

The Labour government insisted that Local Education Authorities (LEAs) **reorganised most schools** so that everyone had **equality of opportunity**. 'Comprehensive school' means it's universal — everyone's meant to get the same deal.

Positive aspects of the comprehensive system	Criticisms of the comprehensive system
There's no 11+, so 80% of the school population don't get labelled as failures.	Most comprehensive schools still sort pupils into streams or sets (p.22) depending on test scores, so it's still possible to feel like a failure without the 11+.
High-ability pupils generally still do well with this system. Lower-ability pupils do better in comprehensive schools than in the old secondary moderns.	Comprehensives in working-class areas have worse GCSE results than those in middle-class areas.

Comprehensive schooling **hasn't achieved equality of opportunity**. Schools tend to be 'single-class', depending on the **local area**. Where people can afford to live (and how good the local schools are) is important in educational attainment.

In **1976** the Push for **Vocational Education** Started

In 1976, Labour Prime Minister James Callaghan made a speech saying that British education and industry was in decline because schools didn't teach people the **skills they needed in work**. All governments since then have had policies designed to create a closer link between school and work. This is called **vocationalism**. These vocational reforms include:

1) **Youth Training Schemes** (**YTS**) started in 1983. These were job training schemes for school leavers aged 16-17.

2) **NVQs** (1986) and **GNVQs** (1992) were introduced — these were **practical qualifications**.

3) The **New Deal**, introduced in 1998, meant people on benefits had to attend courses if they didn't accept work.

There are some **problems** with vocational education:

1) Some sociologists argue that vocational education aims to teach **good work discipline**, not skills.

2) Some Marxist sociologists say that vocational training provides **cheap labour** and that governments encourage people into training schemes to **lower unemployment statistics**.

3) Vocational qualifications often aren't regarded as **highly** as **academic qualifications** by universities and employers.

4) Some feminist sociologists argue that vocational qualifications **force** girls into traditionally 'female' jobs, such as beautician and childminder.

State Policy and Education

The *1988 Education Reform Act* — *Choice, Inspections and More Tests*

In the late 1980s, the **Conservative** government introduced some **major reforms** in education.
These reforms were based on **New Right** ideas (see p.21), so they were focused on:

- widening **choice** within the education system.
- encouraging **more competition** to create a '**market**' in schools (this is called **marketisation**).

Education should link to the economy

The government introduced **more vocational courses** and more **work placement schemes**.

There should be better standards in education

1) The government introduced a **National Curriculum** of **compulsory subjects** for all **5- to 16-year-olds**.
   English, maths and science ('**core subjects**') had to be given more space in the timetable.

2) **OFSTED** (Office for Standards in Education) was set up to **inspect** schools and make sure they were
   doing a **decent job**. You might have seen **teachers** getting somewhat **frantic** before an inspection.

3) Schools could **opt out** of their local education authority and become **grant-maintained schools**.
   This means that they got money **straight from the government** and could **spend it how they liked**.
   The government believed this would **improve standards**.

There should be a system of choice and competition

1) Parents could **choose** which school to send their child to — if the school had **space**.

2) Parents could use **league tables** to help them choose. **League tables** show **how
   many** kids at each school **pass their exams**, and how many get **good grades**. ⬅

3) Schools worked like **businesses** and **advertised** for students.

> David (1993) describes this situation as a 'parentocracy', because the power in education is held by parents, rather than by teachers and schools.

There should be more testing and more exams

1) Pupils had to sit **SATs** at **7, 11 and 14**, and **GCSEs** at **16**.

2) The results could be used to form **league tables**, and to monitor school **standards**.

There are several criticisms of these policies:

1) Sociologists like **Whitty (1998)** argue that middle-class parents have an **advantage** in an educational **market**. Since
   they are more likely to have succeeded in education themselves, they have the **knowledge** and **attitudes** (what Bourdieu
   called **cultural capital** — see p.25) to choose a good school for their child. They may also have the **financial** capital
   to **move** to an area with better schools. Increasing parental choice can actually **reinforce social class inequality**.

2) Constant **testing** can be **stressful** for students, and can encourage **labelling** and **self-fulfilling prophecies** (p.22).

3) **Ball (1995)** claimed that the new **National Curriculum** was the 'curriculum of the dead',
   because its emphasis on the core subjects was **outdated**.

Practice Questions

Q1 What was the aim of the 1944 Education Act?

Q2 Name the three types of school in the tripartite system.

Q3 Briefly explain two problems with comprehensive schools.

Q4 Briefly describe two changes brought about by the 1988 Education Reform Act.

Q5 Explain one way in which middle-class parents may benefit from an education 'market'.

Exam Question

Q1 Evaluate the idea that social policies in education reproduce and legitimise social class inequalities.   [30 marks]

They'll never make their minds up...

*Governments have been trying to "Sort Out Education Once And For All" and "Shake Up Britain's Failing Schools" for ages.
But whatever happens, kids go to school, teachers teach them things, and there are exams at the end of it all...*

State Policy and Education

These pages examine and evaluate the motivation behind recent state policies in education.

New Labour *(1997-2010)* Followed *Third Way* ideas

When Labour took power, they wanted to intervene to do something about **educational inequality**, but they also wanted **choice** and **diversity**. This approach is called '**third way politics**' — it's a bit like the old Labour policies of **state intervention** and the New Right policies of marketisation **combined**. Party leaders called themselves 'New Labour'.

1) New Labour continued the process of **marketisation** begun by the previous Conservative government. For example, they allowed schools to **specialise** in certain subjects — e.g. by becoming Music Colleges or Mathematics Colleges — to try to **create diversity** and **increase choice for parents**. They also allowed **faith schools** to be set up.

2) New Right thinking made education more **privatised**. Agencies were given **contracts** for things like improving reading and writing in primary schools. New Labour claimed that this would improve efficiency and standards, because the contracts were **competitive**, but some people argue that the **privatisation** of education takes too much control away from schools.

3) The government also pursued some **interventionist** policies, such as:

- reducing infant class sizes to a maximum of 30.
- introducing numeracy hour and literacy hour in primary schools.
- trying to increase the number of people going to university.

4) A big change in education for 16- to 18-year-olds came with **Curriculum 2000**. Policy changed to make A-level education broader. A **vocational A-level** was introduced (intended to be of equal worth to an academic A-level). **Key skills** qualifications were also launched, and were supposed to be useful for all jobs.

Some Policies Aimed to *Promote Gender Equality*

Girls

The **1988 National Curriculum** gave all pupils equal entitlement to all subjects for the first time. This has been credited with the increased achievement of girls in the last 20 years.

Initiatives such as the **Computer Club for Girls** (CC4G), **Women Into Science and Engineering** (WISE) and **Girls In Science and Technology** (GIST) encourage girls to get involved with subjects they have **traditionally avoided**.

Boys

In 1999 the government gave **grants** to primary schools to hold **extra writing classes** for boys to help push up their **SATs scores**. In 2005 the **Breakthrough Programme** introduced **mentoring, after-school classes** and **e-tutorials** for teenage boys in an attempt to improve their exam performance.

Some New Labour Policies Aimed to *Reduce Class Inequality*

Compensatory education tries to make up for **material** and **cultural deprivation**, by giving **extra help** to those who need it. This is an **interventionist** approach. New Labour introduced several compensatory policies during their time in power:

1) **Sure Start** began in 1999. It was a government programme to improve early education and childcare in England, and offered up to two years of **free childcare** and **early education** to all three- and four-year-olds.

2) The **Education Maintenance Allowance (EMA)** gave up to £30 per week to students who stayed on in education post-16. A series of **bonuses** were available for good attendance and progress. EMA was **means-tested** so only children from poorer families could benefit from it.

The EMA was ended in England by the new government in 2010.

3) **Education Action Zones** were introduced in 1998 as a way of tackling educational inequality by **area**. Local public, private and voluntary organisations worked together and combined their **resources** to try to raise standards.

4) **Free school meals** (which were means-tested) and **breakfast clubs** also aimed to reduce class inequality.

5) The **Academies Programme** opened new schools in **disadvantaged areas** where existing schools were judged to be '**failing**'. They were run in partnership with local business **sponsors** to try to improve performance.

1) However, sociologists such as **Benn (2012)** have **criticised** New Labour because their policies aimed at **reducing** educational inequality seemed to be **inconsistent** with policies that threatened to **increase** it. For example, they introduced **university tuition fees** of £1000 per year in 1998, and increased them to £3000 in 2004. These fees are a **barrier** to higher education for many working-class students.

2) For Benn, therefore, **third-way politics** was **too contradictory**. She calls this the 'New Labour paradox'.

State Policy and Education

Privatisation and Marketisation Progressed under the Coalition Government

In the 2010 General Election, no one party won a majority of MPs in the House of Commons, so the Conservative and Liberal Democrat parties formed the **Coalition** government, led by Conservative Prime Minister David Cameron.

1) The Coalition government **changed** the **academies** programme. Any school classed as 'Outstanding' by Ofsted could apply to become an academy without a **sponsor**. Failing schools were made into **sponsored academies**. The increasing numbers of schools run by **private organisations** means that the **privatisation** of the education system has **advanced**.

2) They also introduced **free schools**, which are set up by groups of parents, teachers or religious groups and don't have to teach the National Curriculum. The government hoped that this would provide **more choice** in **disadvantaged areas**.

3) Under Education Secretary Michael Gove, there were also changes to the **National Curriculum**:
    *   A-levels were changed to a **linear** structure — all exams must be taken at the **end** of the course.
    *   In a similar way, **coursework** and **modular exams** were **removed** at GCSE.
    *   Far more **formal grammar** was included in the primary English curriculum.

4) The government also introduced the **pupil premium**, which provided **extra funding** for schools with students on **free school meals**. The funding was supposed to be spent on improving the educational experience of **these pupils**.

5) There are some **criticisms** of Coalition education policies:

    *   Critics say that, in some disadvantaged areas, the **academies** and **free schools** attract all the best teachers, which **undermines** other local schools.
    *   It is difficult to track whether **pupil premium** funding is actually being spent on **disadvantaged** pupils, or whether it is being **absorbed** into the whole school budget.
    *   The maximum **tuition fees** in higher education **increased** to £9000 per year. This can be seen as **socially exclusive**, because it's also increased the **loans** that most students need. This debt can be off-putting for working-class students.

Max was disappointed to find that his new 'free' school was not the lawless utopia he had imagined.

Education has been Affected by Globalisation

Globalisation is the idea that traditional national boundaries are **breaking down** across the world, as people become **more connected** by improved technology, multinational companies and increased migration.

It's tricky to study exactly how globalisation has **affected education**, but here are a few key ideas:

1) The British economy needs to be competitive in global industries like technology, so British workers need to be highly trained. This has an impact on education policy — e.g. computer programming has been introduced to the primary school curriculum.

2) Increased immigration to the UK has meant that there's a heavier focus on learning about other cultures. Schools also need to provide specialised support for pupils whose first language is not English. (In some areas of London, this applies to over 70% of students.)

In 2012, Finland ranked 5th in the world for science and 6th for reading. The UK ranked 20th and 23rd respectively.

3) Educational ideas are shared between nations. UK politicians have been influenced by countries such as Finland, whose education system is ranked very highly. However, Kelly (2009) has warned that as education systems become increasingly similar, they'll become less relevant to the needs of individual nations.

Practice Questions

Q1 What is 'third way politics'?

Q2 Give two examples of New Labour educational policies influenced by New Right thinking.

Q3 Give three educational policies of the Coalition government.

Q4 Explain one way in which globalisation has affected the UK education system.

Exam Question

Q1 How has government policy been designed to introduce market forces into education? Outline three ways.   [6 marks]

My education policy is to revise everything...

The New Right want policies that widen choice and give the market a chance to drive up standards. The left want the state to intervene in and have control over the education system. And New Labour wanted both. Make sure you learn about education policies for the exam (Sure Start, WISE, academies, tuition fees) — you might be asked to describe some of them.

Application of Research Methods to Education

In Paper 1, you'll be given a question that asks you to think about the advantages and disadvantages of using a particular research method to study a particular educational issue. Here are some tasty examples for you to digest.

> The advantages and disadvantages of all the various research methods can be found in Section One of this book (p.6-19).

Using *Unstructured Interviews* to Study *Anti-School Subcultures*

1) A **subculture** is a group who share **ideas** and **behaviour patterns** which are **different** from the mainstream culture (see p.23). So an **anti-school** subculture are a group who have a **negative idea** of education, and behave accordingly.

2) **Willis'** study of **pupil subcultures** (p.23) and **Labov's linguistic deprivation** study (p.25) both used unstructured interviews.

3) Here are some ideas about **unstructured interviews** that you could mention:

Advantages	Disadvantages
Students who are part of an anti-school subculture may **not want to talk** about their school lives. Using unstructured interviews would allow the researcher to build up a **rapport** with the students, potentially giving **greater insight** into their thoughts and feelings.	Unstructured interviews are quite **time-consuming**. This means that they tend to be used with **smaller samples** — the researcher may only be able to interview a **few** students from the subculture. This means the data wouldn't be very **representative**.
School may be a **sensitive topic** for students within an anti-school subculture. Unstructured interviews are good for investigating sensitive issues, because the researcher doesn't have to stick to a fixed **questionnaire**. They can change their approach to gain the **trust** of the students and make them feel more **comfortable**.	The interviewer could have an **effect** on the interviewee, making the data **less valid**. Students may give an answer they think the interviewer **wants to hear**, or an answer that **presents** their behaviour in a more **positive** light. These are examples of 'interviewer effects' (see p.15).
Unstructured interviews are likely to offer **greater validity** than questionnaires because they give the interviewer a chance to **adapt their questioning to the subject**. For example, if a student struggles to understand a question, the researcher can explain it.	The data collected from unstructured interviews is **qualitative**, so it would be harder to make **comparisons** between various students' ideas. It would also be harder to reproduce the data, making it **less reliable**.
Anti-school subcultures can cause **disruptive** behaviour in the classroom, as students **encourage** each other to misbehave. Using unstructured interviews would mean that students could be interviewed **away** from this **peer pressure**. This gives them more time to reflect on the issues and give a more **valid** response.	Students with a **negative attitude** towards school may also take a negative attitude towards the **interviewer**, seeing them as just another adult connected with school. This means they may not express their **true feelings**, or even deliberately **lie**, making the data **less valid**.

Using *Covert Participant Observation* to Investigate *Labelling*

> Labelling is covered on p.22.

1) In **participant** observations, the researcher **gets involved** with the people they're studying.

2) In **covert participant** observations, the people being studied **don't know** why the researcher is **really there**.

3) Here are some things you could talk about:

Advantages

1) Teachers often label students **without realising** they're doing it, so they may not mention it in an interview or questionnaire. Being a **participant** would allow the researcher to **observe** labelling in a **natural, real-life** setting.

2) Teachers probably wouldn't want to **be seen** to label their students, so they might **deliberately avoid** doing it if they knew this was the issue being studied. By observing **covertly**, the researcher could get more valid data.

Disadvantages

1) **Misleading** teachers counts as **deception**, which is arguably **ethically incorrect**. It may also be difficult to find a good enough cover explanation to gain **access** to a school, and **using a cover** would also be ethically questionable.

2) The researcher may become **too familiar** with the teachers and find it hard to analyse them **objectively**. The researcher may even start to label the students themselves, so they **stop recognising** that teachers are doing it.

3) The research couldn't be **exactly** repeated, so it isn't as **reliable** as questionnaires, for example. Covert participant observation also has to be conducted with a **smaller sample**, which makes the data **less representative**.

Application of Research Methods to Education

Using **Closed Questionnaires** to find out about **Parental Attitudes**

1) Parental attitudes to education can be **positive** or **negative**. (Have a look back at pages 24 and 27 in particular.)

2) Here are some things you could include in an answer:

1) Questionnaires can be used to collect a **large amount** of data very **quickly**. This means that lots of parents could be surveyed, which would make the results more **representative**.

2) Parents may be more **honest** about their attitudes towards education if they can complete a **private questionnaire**, rather than talking to an interviewer. For example, if their attitude towards education is negative they may be unwilling to speak about this **in person**.

3) The study could be easily **repeated**, making the data more **reliable**. This could be useful for investigating the **changes** in parental attitudes over time.

But...

1) Respondents can **easily lie** about their true attitudes. This makes the data **less valid**.

2) Using closed questions doesn't allow the respondent to **explain** their answer. It might not be a suitable method for researching **attitudes** to education, which are often **complex**.

3) If parents associate the questionnaire with the **school**, then the researcher may find that the questionnaire is mostly completed by those with a **positive** attitude towards education. This would **skew** the **sample**, making it **less representative**, so the data would be **less valid**.

7 out of 10 parents lie when asked if they've ever taken a silly photo of their child.

Using **Official Statistics** to Study **Mixed-Ability Teaching**

1) **Mixed-ability classes** are one of the three main ways to **organise teaching** in a school (alongside setting and streaming).

2) There are two **types** of statistics — **hard** and **soft** (see p.19). You should try to mention both of them in an answer.

Advantages

1) Using **hard** statistics would be a **reliable** source of secondary data, because they're **objective**. Schools can't adjust them to portray mixed-ability teaching in either a positive or negative way.

2) Statistics can be easily **compared** because they're a form of **quantitative** data. For example, the outcomes of mixed-ability classes could be compared for different genders, age groups and schools. They could also be compared **over time**.

Disadvantages

1) If **soft** statistics are used, the researcher would have to be careful that the data was **valid**. It could have been **adjusted** by schools, e.g. to **exaggerate** the successes of mixed-ability teaching.

2) Official statistics don't offer as much insight into the **reasons** behind achievement as other methods like unstructured interviews.

3) At **selective** schools, the variation in abilities in mixed classes would be less great than at non-selective schools, so this could **skew** the data.

Practice Questions

Q1 Why might covert participant observation be more useful than questionnaires for studying teacher labelling?

Q2 Give one disadvantage of using closed questionnaires to investigate negative parental attitudes to schooling.

Exam Question

Q1 Apply your own knowledge and material from Item A to evaluate the advantages and disadvantages of using overt non-participant observation to investigate institutional racism in schools.　　　　[20 marks]

Item A
Some sociologists claim that schools are institutionally racist. They suggest that some groups receive less teacher attention than their peers, and are punished more harshly. Sociologists have used overt non-participant observation to investigate this claim.

So many combinations, so little time...

There's no way you can prepare for every method-and-issue pair that might pop up in the exam (though for more examples, see Section One). The best thing to do is to make sure you know the methods inside out (they're all in Section One) — that way, you can apply them to any issue the examiner throws at you (Section One might help). Maybe you should revise Section One.

Different Types of Culture

In the UK, there's more than one type of culture and there are lots of ways to look at culture — folk vs urban, high vs low, popular culture, global culture...

Culture is a **Way of Life**

Culture means the **language, beliefs, customs, values, knowledge, skills, roles** and **norms** in a society. It's the way of life of a **society**. Culture is **socially transmitted**. That means it's **passed on** through **socialisation** (see p.40).

> **Norms** are ways of **behaving** and / or **thinking** that are seen as **normal** in society.
> **Values** are **beliefs** about what things are **important** and what things are **right** and **wrong**. Ideas like 'freedom of speech', 'respect for human life' and 'equality' are all **values**.

A **subculture** is an identifiable **group** within a culture whose members share **values** and **behaviour patterns** which are **different** from **mainstream norms**, e.g. youth subcultures like punks and goths. Subcultures can be a form of **resistance** to mainstream culture (see p.23).

Mass Culture replaces **Folk Culture**

Folk culture is the culture of **pre-industrial society**. It includes things like folk dances, folk songs, fairy tales, old wives' tales, traditional folk medicine and agricultural rituals. It's mainly passed on through word of mouth.

Sociologists have looked at the ways **culture changes** as people move from **villages** into **towns** and **cities**.

1) **Robert Redfield (1947)** said that '**folk societies**' were based on strong extended families, **supportive communities** and a **local culture**. In **urban** societies these were **not present**.

2) **Georg Simmel (1950)** argued that **urban societies** showed a **reduced sense of community**, and that urban people were more **individualistic** and **selfish**.

3) Theorists from the **Frankfurt School** (see p.38) said that this reduced sense of community was linked to the development of a **mass culture**. They said that the **media** had become a **strong agent of socialisation**, and it was wiping out the differences between local cultures. Instead, it looked more and more like there was just **one big culture**, shared by **everyone**.

4) These days, the term **mass culture** is used not just to describe the effects of the **media**, but also to refer to **fashion** and other types of **consumption**, e.g. if you eat lunch in a famous burger chain, you're taking part in mass culture.

Just try and tell me folk culture is dead... I dare ya, punk...

You can also **Divide** culture up into **'High Culture'** and **'Low Culture'**

The **elite** (better educated, with more money and power) tend to have a **distinct culture** from the **masses**.

1) Shakespeare, opera, sophisticated restaurants and arty French films are the type of things that are associated with '**high culture**'.

2) Meanwhile, the masses enjoy '**low culture**' — e.g. soap operas, reality TV, musicals, fast food and Hollywood films.

This is all linked to the ideas of 'class taste', cultural deprivation and cultural capital — see p.47.

3) 'High culture' is generally considered more **difficult to appreciate** and the audience is seen as **educated** and having '**good taste**'. Aspects of 'high culture' are seen as **good for society**, though they don't make much money compared to a lot of 'low culture', so the government often **subsidises** them.

4) In recent years a lot of **funding for high culture** has come from a 'low culture' source — the National Lottery®. Some customers have been hostile to the idea that the lottery is used to pay for 'arty' dance and theatre companies. They suggest it's **elitist culture** — most lottery punters **wouldn't get to see it** and probably **wouldn't like it** if they did.

Many sociologists say there's **No Such Thing** as **'Low Culture'**

1) The ideas of '**high culture**' and '**low culture**' are very **negative**. For example, **Bourdieu (1984)** says the **whole idea** of 'high culture' is to give **status** to **elite groups** — he says that status is maintained by passing on **cultural knowledge**.

2) Marxists argue that 'high culture' is just ruling-class culture, and that the ruling class have imposed their idea of culture on the rest of society, and defined it as 'better' than working-class culture. Some Marxists argue that so-called 'low culture' is just as **complex** and **sophisticated** as 'high culture'. For that reason, they prefer to use the term '**popular culture**', which is more of a positive idea.

Different Types of Culture

Popular Culture theorists emphasise that the Audience is Active

1) 'Mass' and 'low' culture are both concepts that are based on the idea of a **passive audience**. They assume that the audience is being **manipulated** by the media and doesn't have much control.

2) 'Popular' culture is a concept that is based on the idea of an **active audience**. This audience shapes and changes culture. The **Centre for Contemporary Cultural Studies (CCCS)** did a lot of research into the way this happens in youth fashions and subcultures. They analysed popular culture products like TV shows and magazines, finding **meanings** within them.

There's also a Global Culture

Giddens (1990) says that **technological change** has led to **globalisation**. Goods can be **transported** to anywhere in the world, and **information** can be quickly transmitted across the globe. This has meant that cultures that were once local have become global. For example, British and American pop music is everywhere. American and Indian films are popular internationally.

1) **Klein (2000)** and **Sklair (1995)** point out that a few large **transnational corporations** (TNCs), e.g. Coca-Cola®, NIKE and TimeWarner, are involved in the majority of cultural production, making cultural goods that are consumed all over the world. **Sklair** argues that TNCs and the global media have **more power** than individual **nation states**.

2) Critics of globalisation worry that these TNCs will replace the world's current **cultural diversity** (the differences in people's lifestyles because of the society they live in) with Western culture. They refer to cultural globalisation as **cultural imperialism**. **Klein (2000)** says there's already a trend towards **cultural homogeneity** (everyone having the same culture — wearing the same trainers, eating the same burgers, drinking the same fizzy drinks).

3) Supporters of cultural globalisation argue that it's a **two-way process**. Western culture is transmitted to new societies, and other identities and cultures get passed back to Western societies — e.g. through **Bollywood films** shown in Western mainstream cinemas. With the movement of people from different countries and cultures to other parts of the world, many countries are now **multicultural societies**. Postmodernists argue that this allows people to consume a **plurality** of cultures — this is called **multiculturalism**. They think that globalisation leads to **hybridity** (a **pick and mix**) of cultures rather than one culture being imposed on another.

Practice Questions

Q1 What is 'low culture'?
Q2 What do Marxists say about 'high culture'?
Q3 What is globalisation?
Q4 What is mass culture?

Exam Question

Q1 Apply your own knowledge and material from Item A to evaluate the idea that high culture is elitist. [20 marks]

> **Item A**
> Culture can be divided into 'low culture' and 'high culture'. High culture is often associated with the upper class, while low culture is consumed by the lower classes. Some sociologists argue that the upper classes use their knowledge of high culture to give themselves status and separate themselves from the lower classes.

If I watch X factor on top of Ben Nevis, does that make it high culture?

Culture is everywhere, apparently. Sociologists divide culture into different categories — unfortunately, they don't always agree on exactly how to do it. Some argue that using terms like 'low' and 'high' to describe culture isn't very helpful. You need to be familiar with the terms on these pages, because you'll need them to analyse different views of culture in the exam.

Theories of Culture

Marxism, functionalism, postmodernism — it looks brain-bursting at first, but once you get the key ideas it'll all fall into place.

Marxists Say Capitalism Creates **False Needs** and **Commodity Fetishism**

Marxists are pretty **pessimistic** about **low/mass** culture because they believe it is used to **control** the working class.

1) The Frankfurt School began as a group of **neo-Marxist** thinkers in 1930s Germany who combined Marxism and psychology. Frankfurt School sociologists **Adorno and Horkheimer (1944)** argued that mass culture encourages you to think you '**need**' to **buy things** which you don't really need, such as twenty pairs of shoes, or a TV. You don't need these things in the same way you need **food** and **oxygen**, but it's **good for capitalism** if you **think** you do. They're **false needs**.

2) **Commodity fetishism** is where false needs create **obsessions** and desires about consumer goods — '**must-have**' objects. An example of this is when a new mobile phone comes out and everyone wants it.

3) The Frankfurt School said that commodity fetishism was like a **religion** because **capitalism creates desires** that **only capitalism can satisfy**. This means we all end up thinking **capitalism** is **good**, because it gives us **what we want**.

Arnold misunderstood when they asked him to knead the bread.

Some **Neo-Marxists** Say the Working Class are **Oppressed** by **Capitalism** via **Culture**

1) The **Frankfurt School** decided that the main way of transmitting **capitalist ideology** was through the **media**.

2) They argued that mass culture **helped capitalism** to oppress the working class by **destroying community** and **individuality**. It also encouraged **acceptance of authority** and **discouraged** people from **thinking for themselves**.

3) The Frankfurt School argued that things like **newspaper horoscopes** were used to suggest that a person's life experiences were down to **luck** or **fate**, rather than social structures or personal actions. **TV and radio advertising** reinforced the values of **capitalism**, while **Hollywood films** distracted ordinary people from social issues.

4) In this way, capitalism used **mass culture** to **prevent revolution** from ever happening.

> So to sum up, the **Frankfurt School** took a **pessimistic** approach to mass culture:
> - Mass culture is used to **dull the minds** of the **working class**.
> - Mass culture promotes **capitalist ideology**.
> - The population are **passive victims** of mass culture.

Other **Neo-Marxists Disagree** with the **Frankfurt School**

1) The Italian thinker **Antonio Gramsci (1971)** said that the idea of a **single mass culture** was too **simplistic**.

2) **Gramsci** thought that capitalism creates a big **dominant culture**. He called this dominance **hegemony**.

3) Gramsci believed that **capitalism** had to **tolerate** some oppositional cultures, rather than stamp them out. By **allowing some opposition** to exist, he said, capitalism could create the **illusion** that it was a **fair** system.

4) He had a big influence on the work of Marxists like **Stuart Hall** of the **Centre for Contemporary Cultural Studies**. Hall says that **youth subcultures** help working class youths to **resist capitalist values**.

5) Hall, and other neo-Marxists who take a more positive, optimistic view of modern culture, prefer the term **popular culture** to mass culture.

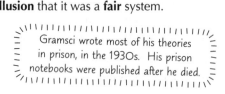
Gramsci wrote most of his theories in prison, in the 1930s. His prison notebooks were published after he died.

Functionalists See Culture as a Kind of **Bond**

Functionalists believe that **structures** of society are set up to allow society to **run as smoothly as possible**. **Durkheim's** functionalist theory of culture is also based on the idea of **social control**, but is more positive than that of the Marxists.

1) Durkheim's **functionalist** perspective describes culture as a kind of **social glue**. It bonds people together by creating shared interests and purposes.

2) Individuals **internalise** the **norms** and **values** (the rules and ideas) of society. This means those norms and values **become a part of who you are** — your personality and your **identity**.

3) The result is **consensus**, which means everyone sharing the **same norms and values** — Durkheim called the **shared norms and values** that **hold society together** the '**collective consciousness of society**'.

4) It also helps to **socialise** people into appropriate behaviour. This prevents society from breaking down into chaos.

Section Three — Culture and Identity

Theories of Culture

Postmodernism *Argues That* Culture *is* Diverse

1) **Postmodernists** say **functionalism is outdated** because it's based on the idea that there's only one dominant or shared culture. Instead they argue that **culture** is **increasingly diverse**.

2) Postmodernists **reject** the idea that culture helps to **unify** people in society.

Stuart Hall (1992) says that diversity results in fragmented identities. People can construct their identity from a range of different cultures. Layers of identity can include nationality, gender, ethnicity, religion and political beliefs. Hall links this with the rise of social movements such as feminism and black power. He also says people have constructed new identities such as 'Black British' and 'British Muslim' as a response to cultural globalisation.

Dominic Strinati (1995) agrees with some postmodern ideas, but he says that culture is also affected by structural factors like class — culture traditionally consumed by elites is seen as more valuable than that enjoyed by the working class.

Interactionists *Think That Culture is Determined by* Individuals

Many sociologists say that culture is actually determined by the **behaviour and interaction of individuals**. Theories like this are called **action theories** because they emphasise the **action** of individuals, as opposed to **structural theories** like functionalism and Marxism, which are all about the big structures of society.

1) **Interactionists** think that individuals can choose how to behave, and aren't simply responding to social forces — culture comes from **people's own ideas** of how people **interact** with each other.

2) They see culture as being partly developed from the **bottom of society** at the **individual** level — if people **change** the way they act in relation to each other, then **culture will change too**.

Goffman (1972) studied **pedestrian interaction** on busy Western city streets — he discovered that cultural **norms** associated with the **action** of walking through the streets prevented people from **colliding** with one another. **Unspoken rules** like not looking at people for a long time and avoiding conversation enabled people to walk freely.

Feminism *Links Popular Culture to* Socialisation *and* Patriarchy

During the 1970s and 1980s, many feminists researched the relationship between **popular culture** and **gender socialisation**. Most of these studies suggested that popular culture **stereotypes** women into roles — such as housewife or sex object. These roles are then **reinforced** in society.

1) **Ferguson (1983)** and **McRobbie (1978)** studied magazines, and found that they promoted traditional female roles.

2) **Radical feminists**, such as **Andrea Dworkin (1981)** in her study of pornography, suggest that many images of women in popular culture encourage and justify **violence** against women.

3) More recently, some feminists have argued that popular cultural representations of women can also be **empowering**. For example, **Camille Paglia** has written a lot about Madonna's public image as a strong female role model.

Practice Questions

Q1 How do the Frankfurt School view popular culture?
Q2 Define 'false need' and 'commodity fetishism'.
Q3 What did Stuart Hall mean by 'fragmented identities'?

Exam Question

Q1 Evaluate the idea that culture helps to unify society. [20 marks]

Capitalism didn't tell me to want a new phone — the TV advert did...

According to the Frankfurt School, I didn't really need that designer dress after all. If only Theodor Adorno could have texted me to tell me. Sigh. Anyway, make sure you know the nuts and bolts of these theoretical approaches, because you'll need them if you want to get top level marks. Without mentioning relevant theorists, you aren't going to win the examiner over.

Socialisation and Social Roles

Most sociologists believe you have to learn how to fit into society, e.g. learn how to behave. This process is called socialisation. It begins in childhood and continues throughout life. As usual in sociology, there are different views about how it all works...

Socialisation is the passing on of Culture

1) Culture is **passed on** through **socialisation** from generation to generation. Sociologists say that through socialisation the **norms and values** of society are **internalised** — they become part of everyone's way of thinking (see p.36 for more on norms and values).
2) **Laws** often reflect norms, but sometimes **law-breaking** is the norm. Making illegal CD copies is a good example of this.
3) **Culture, values and norms** are **not fixed**. They **vary** according to the time and place. For example, British culture is different from American culture, and today's culture is different from the culture of 30 years ago.
4) There are two kinds of socialisation — **primary socialisation** and **secondary socialisation**.

The Main Agent of Primary Socialisation is The Family

Primary socialisation comes first. In **early childhood**, individuals learn the **skills, knowledge, norms** and **values** of society. This all happens in three ways:

1) Children **internalise** norms and values by **imitating their parents / guardians**.
2) Children are **rewarded for socially acceptable behaviour**.
3) Children are **punished for socially 'deviant' behaviour**.

Children who are deprived of social contact during development often can't function as social adults. In 1970, an American girl known as 'Genie' was discovered. She'd been locked up by her father for her first 13 years and never managed to recognise even basic social norms.

There are many Agents of Secondary Socialisation

Secondary socialisation comes after primary socialisation and **builds on it**. It's carried out by **institutions** like these:

Education

The education system aims to pass on **knowledge and skills**. Learning these skills is a part of socialisation:
1) **Functionalists**, like Durkheim, believe that school **promotes consensus** by **teaching norms and values**. They also say children learn to value belonging to a **larger group** through things like school uniform and assembly. All this is important for **fitting into society**.
2) **Marxists**, such as **Bowles and Gintis (1976)**, reckon there are two sorts of curriculum at school — the acknowledged curriculum (maths, English, geography etc.) and the hidden curriculum (doing as you're told and not questioning authority). They believe that the **hidden curriculum** (p.22) socialises pupils into **ruling-class cultures** and encourages them to **accept exploitation**.

Peer Groups

Peer groups are made up of people of **similar social status**. The peer group can **influence norms and values**. This can be towards **conformity** or **deviance**. **Youth subcultures** sometimes encourage **deviant** behaviour, like joyriding.

Conformity means doing what society likes and deviance means doing what society doesn't like.

Religion

Religion often provides **social norms and values**. Most religions promote charitable giving and teach respect for elders.

The Media

The **media** are **powerful** in shaping norms and values in the audience. Some sociologists (e.g. Althusser) argue that the media have now **replaced religion** in secondary socialisation.

The Workplace

Workplace socialisation involves learning the norms and values that enable people to fit into the world of work, such as being on time and obeying the boss.

Socialisation and Social Roles

Individuals have Social Roles and Status

According to some sociological perspectives, an important result of socialisation is that each individual ends up with a number of **roles**. These are associated with different sorts of **status**.

1) Your **status** is your **position** in a **hierarchy**. You can have low status or high status. It's the respect and recognition others give to your position. Being the **monarch of the United Kingdom** is a **status**.

2) Your **roles** are the **behaviours and actions** you take on **because of your status**. In sociological terms, a role is a set of norms that go with a status. The UK monarch has to meet the public and show an interest, they have to speak to the nation on TV on Christmas Day, and they have to travel and meet leaders of other countries. These are all **roles**.

Status can be ascribed or achieved

Ascribed status is fixed at **birth**. For example, the King or Queen of the UK **inherits their status** from the previous monarch (normally their mother or father) when they die. Head teachers, on the other hand, have **achieved** status. This means they've **earned** it through **education** and **work**. This is a **very important difference** for sociological arguments about gender, class and ethnic identities.

Individuals can be Socialised into Socially Constructed Identities

Social constructs are ideas and behaviours that are **invented** by society rather than being dictated by the **laws of nature**. Everyone adopts social constructs and sees them as normal parts of the way society works. A person's **identity** (see p.44) is made up of several **socially constructed elements**:

Social Class	**Perceived differences** between members of the lower, middle and upper classes are related to things like money, family connections and the kind of jobs people have. These categories are **social** rather than **biological**.
Sexuality	**Sexual identities** are influenced by socially constructed ideas about what kind of sexual behaviour is **normal**.
Gender	**Gender identities** are based on **social expectations** about masculine or feminine traits and behaviours, rather than on **biological differences** between men and women.
Disability	Society often underestimates people with disabilities. **Socially constructed expectations** of disability can be a **bigger limiting force** than the actual impairment (the physical feature or characteristic).
Nationality	**National identities** involve the relationship between people and the nation they **belong to**. They are constructed around **social expectations** like being loyal to your country.
Ethnicity	**Ethnic identities** can either **complement or compete with** national identities and are constructed around things like **shared** languages and cultures.
Age	Different societies **construct childhood** and **old age** differently — for example, some cultures have more **age-based restrictions** than others.

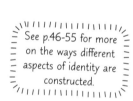
See p.46-55 for more on the ways different aspects of identity are constructed.

Practice Questions

Q1 What is a 'social construct'?
Q2 Name five agents of secondary socialisation.
Q3 What is a role?

Exam Question

Q1 Outline two aspects of identity that can be seen as being socially constructed. Explain each one. [10 marks]

And I thought socialisation was just something to do down the pub...

Socialisation is the process by which people learn to be members of society. The main things I remember learning when I was young are to only speak when spoken to, to always eat my greens, not to play football in the house, not to take sweets from strangers, not to pogo stick next to the cliff and not to offer myself as food to stray lions. I learnt that last one the hard way.

Theories of Socialisation

Sociologists have lots of theories about socialisation. Marxists, feminists and functionalists argue that socialisation leads to conformity. Interactionists and postmodernists think people have more choice when deciding which values to believe in.

Functionalists *Say That Social* Behaviour *is* Regulated *by* Social Control

1) Socialisation puts **limits** on people's behaviour. The functionalist Durkheim called this **constraint** (it's also known as **social control**). If it weren't for internalised norms and values, people would **do what they liked**.

2) Functionalists say that socialisation creates a **consensus**, where everyone has the **same values and norms**.

3) It's important for people to **conform** to the norms and values of society. When people conform to the expectations, they're **rewarded**. When people **don't conform** to social expectations, they're **punished**. Sociologists call these punishments **sanctions**. Sociologists call behaviour which doesn't conform to society's expectations **deviant**.

> **Parsons (1951)** argues that the **nuclear family** is key to primary socialisation of children. Parents shape a child's personality — Parsons calls the family a '**personality factory**'. As a result, children feel like they **belong** in society and subscribe to its **cultural consensus**. Children want to be like their **parent of the same sex**, which influences their behaviour.

Functionalists believe that **education** and **religion** function as key agents of **secondary socialisation**.

- **Durkheim** thought that institutionalised **education** is a **link** between the family and society as a whole. **Parsons (1961)** argues that **education** teaches children about **values** such as fair **competition**, striving for **success**, and **honest** conduct. Functionalists see this socialisation as important preparation for going to **work in adult life**.

- **Religion** produces codes of behaviour by giving **sacred status** to chosen **values** — adults socialise children to follow these codes, which promotes **social conformity**.

Marxists *Think Socialisation is* Designed *to Benefit the* Ruling Class

Marxists believe that the institutions of the **family**, **education** and **religion** are used to socialise the **working class** into **acceptance** of their own **exploitation** in capitalist society. They see the process of socialisation as a form of **indoctrination** (teaching people to accept a set of beliefs without **question** or **criticism**).

> 1) **Marxists** agree with functionalists that education promotes conformity. However, they think that the values transmitted by education, like obedience to authority figures and acceptance of failure, are designed to oppress the working class.

> 2) This kind of socialisation is good for the ruling class because it prevents aspiration and teaches the working class that obedience to authority is normal.

Neo-Marxists question the effectiveness of this indoctrination and accept that people are able to rebel against this kind of socialisation.

> 3) Religion is used to socialise the working class into accepting poverty and their own exploitation. Religion distracts people from their social inferiority by promoting the idea that suffering will be worth the reward of the afterlife.

Feminists *Also See Socialisation as a Form of* Indoctrination

Feminists believe that the socialisation of children is designed to pass on the ideals of the **patriarchy**. Socialisation in the **family** and in **wider society** promotes **conformity** to social expectations about **gender roles** and **acceptable behaviour**.

- **Oakley (1982)** argued that parents socialise their children to **conform** to **patriarchal ideals** by praising them for behaving in supposedly **gender-appropriate ways**. For example, they might direct children towards toys traditionally associated with their gender.

See p.48 for more on Oakley's theory of family socialisation.

- **Liberal feminists** argue that to **create gender equality** society needs to change the way children are socialised. They believe that **confronting gender stereotypes** will change **attitudes** to gender equality and create more equal **opportunities** for men and women.

- **Radical feminists** think that patriarchal ideals are **more deep-seated** in society. They argue that **revolutionary changes** to society's structure are needed to combat **patriarchal indoctrination**.

Theories of Socialisation

Interactionists see Socialisation as an *Active, Two-Way* Process

Interactionists believe that socialisation involves **two-way social interaction**. **Handel (2006)** argued that there are three key stages in **childhood development** that are important in the socialisation process:

1) In early life, children learn to **communicate** with others around them, but they have little understanding of **how others see them** and the **impact** of their own behaviour.

2) Later, a sense of **empathy** develops — children are able to understand the **feelings** of others around them.

3) Finally, children develop a **sense of self** — this means they are able to see themselves from the **perspective of another person** and **change their behaviour** so that others view them differently.

> **Mead (1925)** believed that play was important for developing a **sense of self**. Children learn to understand the **viewpoint** of other children and adults, and that they can **influence what happens** with their own **actions**.
>
> **Mead** accepted the functionalist view that **institutions** socialise people into **shared norms**. However, he said that **social control** depends on **how far** people take on the attitudes of others. Individuals can **rebel** against socialisation.

Interactionists believe that **indoctrination** is not the **only** way to socialise people:

• Interactionists point out that **peer group socialisation** influences the behaviour of children in society. Children put **peer pressure** on one another to **rebel** against existing rules or **conform** to alternative rules they have created themselves. **Adults** can also experience peer pressure while **socialising** and at **work**.

• Your **background** can influence the way you are socialised. Interactionists argue that parents are **free** to socialise their children however they like — they don't have to socialise their children into conforming to a **fixed set** of social norms.

> Some sociologists argue that interactionist theories of socialisation are too focused on the **minor details** of people's lives. They're also **criticised** for not paying enough attention to the impact of **social factors** (class, gender, ethnicity) and **institutions** (religion, education, the media) in the process of socialisation.

Postmodernists Argue That People Can *Resist* Socialisation

Postmodernists are big on the idea of **personal choice**. They say that in today's society people have a large amount of choice in their actions and behaviour — and in the values that they believe in.

1) **Lyotard (1979)** argues that there are lots of **competing versions** of knowledge and **truth** in postmodern society — people can **choose** who to listen to and what values to believe in.

2) **Lyotard** believes that even the most powerless person in society has **some control** over the kind of knowledge they are exposed to. No single institution has a **monopoly** on knowledge, so it's **harder** to convince people that they should stick to one way of living.

3) This **weakens** the effects of **secondary** socialisation in educational and religious institutions. There is no single, accepted version of the truth and **various** **cultural values** and norms exist — this helps people to **resist** socialisation.

The pro-leotard faction of the ballet were getting harder to resist.

Practice Questions

Q1 How do functionalists link religion to the process of socialisation?

Q2 Summarise the three stages of childhood development that interactionists believe are important for socialisation.

Q3 Why do postmodernists think socialisation is becoming less effective?

Exam Question

Q1 Analyse two explanations for how socialisation may benefit the ruling class. [10 marks]

Chocolate cake for breakfast — now that's a norm I can get on board with...

While sociologists disagree on the motives behind socialisation (shocker), most agree that successful socialisation helps society to agree on what is socially unacceptable. Socialisation is the reason you don't see people in business suits hopping to work on a pogo stick or galloping down the street like a horse (which, let's face it, would be a lot more fun...).

The Self, Identity and Difference

There are two main sociological approaches to identity — structuralist views (see p.3-4) look at how identities are caused by social structures. Social action views (see p.4) focus on the role of social interaction in constructing identities.

'Identity' is a Tricky Concept in Sociology

1) At a basic level, your **personal identity** is the sort of stuff that would appear on an identity card — name, age, physical appearance, distinguishing marks, place of birth. These are **easily checked**, hard to change **facts** about who you are.

2) In **sociology**, identity has a **deeper meaning**. It refers to the **way we see ourselves**, and the **way others see us**. This sort of identity comes from things that are more **complicated**, and sometimes **less fixed**, than the basic identity card stuff. Social class, ethnicity, friendships, work, gender, age and sexuality are all factors that contribute to your **social identity**.

3) Your social identity is often linked to **roles you perform** in society (e.g. daughter, student, volunteer, best friend) as well as the **social groups** you are a part of (e.g. female, middle class, Asian, teenager).

Structuralists Believe that Identity is Caused by Social Constructs

Structuralists agree that **institutions** socialise people into **shared identities** and **values**.
They disagree on which **values** are being upheld and **who benefits** the most.

Marxists

- Marxists think people's **identity** depends on their **class position** in the capitalist system. They argue that the cultural **values** and **norms** that influence identity are **created** and **maintained** by the **upper classes** with the aim of protecting capitalism.

- Socially constructed ideas about **cultural consumption** can cause people to develop different class identities — knowledge of **high culture** is considered to be a key part of **upper-class identity**, while consuming **mass culture** is part of **working-class identity** (p.36).

Functionalists

- Functionalism argues that **social institutions** allocate people different roles in society, based on the **best fit** for their talents and efforts. However, some functionalists argue that this isn't always **successful**.

- **Merton (1957)** said that all institutions have **manifest functions** (**intended** outcomes) and **latent functions** (**hidden** or **unintended** outcomes). For example, the **manifest** functions of the **education system** are providing **skills**, **knowledge** and **equal opportunities** to increase **social mobility**. However, the **latent** function is to maintain **socially constructed ideas** about the kind of future people can expect to have, based on their **social class identity**.

- **Trumpbour (1989)** found that **wealthier** university students expect education to prepare them for **professional** roles and leadership, while **poorer** pupils expect to be prepared for **lower status jobs**.

Feminists

- **Feminists** argue that the **patriarchal structure** of society has influenced **gender identity** by causing people to believe in gender **stereotypes** and socialising people to hold **sexist** views about male and female identity.

- **Marxist feminists** say that **capitalist** and **patriarchal** social structures have influenced female identity on a **subconscious** level. Some argue that patriarchal views have been a key part of female identity for a long time, which makes it difficult for women to **change the way they think about themselves** and their role in society.

- **Difference feminists** criticise these arguments — they think that women should be treated as a **diverse** group with **many identities**. The social forces that shape the identity of one woman **might not apply** to another.

Postmodernists say that We can Construct Our Own Identities

Postmodernists say **structures** like social class are no longer the most important part of the **construction of identity**.

1) Postmodernists argue that it's possible to **construct** a **unique** identity by drawing on **different cultural sources** — postmodern society allows you to **consume** food, clothes and other products from various cultures.

2) They argue that identity is becoming increasingly **unstable** because individuals can **choose** their own lifestyle and identity — this leads to **diversity**.

3) Critics of this argument point out that being able to buy and consume **whatever we like** depends on how much **money** we have and whether we have a steady **job** or **income** — these things are linked to our **social class**.

The Self, Identity and Difference

Goffman's Dramaturgical Model says Identity is Deliberately Constructed

Goffman (1956) says that you can **control** the way you present your identity during **social interaction**. You can **construct an identity** by controlling the **impressions** you give of yourself to other people — he calls this '**impression management**'.

1) Goffman saw **society** as a **big stage**. You behave differently when interacting with people depending on **where** social interaction is happening.
2) When you are in '**front stage**' environments (e.g. work, school, public places) you **carefully control** the **impression** you give to other people and **act out a specific role** (e.g. student, teacher, manager).
3) Once you are '**backstage**' (e.g. at home or with people you know very well) you **stop performing that role** and reveal the parts of yourself that you **hide** while playing a front stage role.
4) There is a **gap** between the **role** you play on the front stage and on the back stage — he called this '**role distance**'.

Cooley Wrote about Self-Image and Difference

Cooley (1902) argued that the way you **think** other people see you affects your **behaviour** and **self-image** — he called this the '**looking-glass self**'.

1) Cooley argued that you are always **unconsciously constructing** your identity. When you **imagine** yourself through the eyes of **other people**, you change your behaviour. You **become** the person that **you think they think you are**.

2) Cooley based his theory on the idea that **people are aware** of the ways that their personal behaviour and views are **different** from **social norms**. This helps you to define who you are in **opposition** to other people.

Nigel had taken the whole 'identifying with others' thing a bit too far.

Labelling Theory says We're Given Labels which Affect Our Behaviour

Labelling theory argues that the way **other people see and judge you** automatically **influences** who you are.

1) The **classic example** of labelling theory is the **self-fulfilling prophecy** of **educational failure** (see p.24). This is where a child is **labelled** as a bad student and actually **becomes** a bad student as a result.
2) Very **strong labels**, e.g. '**criminal**' or '**pervert**', can take on what's called **master status**, which means they replace an individual's other labels. As a result, people **change** their behaviour to fit the label that they've been given.
3) **Becker (1963)** said that people who are labelled as '**deviant**' become **outsiders** and their deviant label becomes their **main source of identity**. For example, once someone is labelled as a **thief**, this will always be their **master status**.
4) **Wilkins (1964)** discovered that people who have been labelled as '**deviant**' or **outsiders** often join a **subculture**. This makes them feel like they **belong**, but it also **creates more differences** between them and the rest of society.

Schooling can contribute to the **creation of differences** between **students** from different social classes. Some sociologists have found that teachers are more likely to label **working-class** pupils as **deviant**. Working-class pupils are often placed in **lower sets** as a result — this can lead to these students developing **lower self-esteem** and **aspirations** than their middle-class peers.

Labelling theory is a kind of interactionism — you can choose to accept or reject labels. Being called a failure will only turn you into a failure if you accept the label.

Practice Questions

Q1 Briefly explain two feminist theories on the construction of identity.

Q2 Describe Goffman's dramaturgical model.

Q3 Give two examples of labelling theories.

Exam Question

Q1 Evaluate the idea that social interaction contributes more to the construction of identity than social institutions.

[20 marks]

I was a pirate for Halloween once and now people keep asking me to parlay...

Structuralists think we've got hardly any say in who we are. Interactionists say what other people see is pretty important, and we can control how we're seen. Postmodernists reckon we can be whatever we want (like a fire-breathing unicorn... probably).

Class Identities

The following pages explore different aspects of social identity, starting with class.

Societies are Stratified — Divided into Layers

1) **Social class** is an important part of **identity**. Most societies are **stratified** by social class.

2) **Stratification** is the division of societies into **layers**. The **richest** and **most powerful** are at the **top**. The **poorest** and **most powerless** are at the **bottom**. In between are lots of **strata** (which means layers, like the layers in rock) organised in a **hierarchy**.

3) **Social class** is the main stratification system in **modern, Western capitalist societies**, such as the **contemporary UK**.

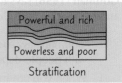
Powerful and rich

Powerless and poor

Stratification

There are Different Ways to Define Social Class

- Marx divided society into just two classes — the **proletariat** (the workers) and the **bourgeoisie** (the bosses).
- For the **UK census**, the **government** used to use a scale based on the **jobs** people do.
- Sociologists usually talk about just **four basic social classes**:

1) The **upper class** are **wealthy** and **powerful**. The original upper class were the **landowning aristocracy**. Their wealth is **passed on from generation to generation**. People who have made a lot of money from business or from the entertainment industry are also sometimes considered to be upper class.

2) The **middle class** earn their money from **non-manual work**. Teachers, doctors, managers and pretty much anyone who **earns their living sitting in an office** are middle class. The middle class is **getting bigger** because there are **more non-manual jobs** these days, and fewer manual jobs.

3) The **working class** make their money from **manual work**. Farm labourers and factory workers are working class. The working class have **poorer life chances** than the middle class.

4) The **underclass** get their money from **state benefits**. They include the long-term unemployed and the homeless. The underclass have **the poorest life chances**.

Class Culture Affects Identity

Sociologists often link **identity** to **social class**. **Who you are** is connected to your **class culture** and **class identity**.

1) **Barry Sugarman (1970)** argued that middle-class and working-class children are socialised into **different norms and values**. **Middle-class** children are encouraged to plan for the future (**deferred gratification**) whereas **working-class children** are encouraged to live for the moment (**immediate gratification**). Deferred gratification is a big part of studying and training for a **professional career**.

2) **Charles Murray (1994)**, a New Right thinker, suggested that **certain values keep people poor**, for example believing in the **acceptability** of living on **state benefits**. He argued these values are **passed on** from one generation to the next.

3) **John Scott (1991)** looked at the ways the **upper class** use the **public school system** (this means the **top private schools** like Eton and Rugby) to create **social networks** which then follow through into **high-status universities** (such as Oxford).

4) In the state education system, **middle-class children** tend to form **pro-school subcultures** (such as homework clubs) and are more likely to be placed in top sets. **Working-class children** are more likely to be **anti-school** and to find themselves in lower sets. (For more detail on this, see p.24-25.)

Negative Stereotypes About Social Class Can Influence Identity

Skeggs and **Loveday (2012)** studied the effects of **negative stereotyping** on **working-class identity** and sense of **self**.

- The study's participants felt like they were being held **responsible** for being born into a system with **structural inequalities**. They were being characterised as **selfish** or **greedy** individuals while other classes were allowed to **profit** from greedy behaviour.

- They identified strongly with values like **loyalty** and **caring for others**. They argued that people in the middle and upper classes don't value these things in the same way.

- The study found that **struggle** is a key part of the **performance** of working-class identity — the lower classes bitterly accept **class oppression** and **endure** poverty because they do not have the **power** to change their position.

- Skeggs and Loveday argued that members of the middle class often **negatively stereotype** people from lower classes, and use this form of **class oppression** to maintain their position by claiming **moral authority** over the lower classes.

Skeggs and Loveday argued that you need some kind of social, cultural or economic capital (see p.47) before you can present yourself as someone with social value.

Class Identities

Bourdieu said the Upper Class use Cultural Capital

Bourdieu (1984) argued that there are **different** kinds of **capital** in society:

> 1) **Economic capital** — your income or wealth
> 2) **Social capital** — being a member of a group or network of people
> 3) **Cultural capital** — the knowledge and skills you need to fit into the top level of society.

The competition to be Greece's Next Top Statue was getting a bit heated.

1) **Bourdieu** argued that the upper class **maintains its position** (on top, that is) by passing on **cultural capital**. It includes things like knowing **which knife and fork to use**, knowing the **'right' way to speak** and having an appreciation of **high culture** such as opera and ballet.

2) He also said that **middle-class** families try to **develop cultural capital** in their own children in order to **improve** their class position. These parents **encourage** their children to read 'good' books, experience theatres, go to art galleries and so on.

3) By contrast, he said that **working-class** families **don't develop** this form of **cultural capital**.

4) Bourdieu also argued that you need **social capital** to back up your **cultural capital**. **Middle-class children may be limited** by a lack of social capital, even if they've gained a lot of cultural capital.

Many Sociologists say Class Isn't the Most Important Influence any more

1) Most sociologists agree that identity used to be based on how and where people **earned their money** (social class). Many **postmodernists** say that these days identity is based on how and where people **spend** their money (consumption).

2) They also claim that people's **leisure activities** are **no longer class-based**.

3) Traditional **working-class** activities included things like **bingo**, **darts** and the **pub**. The **middle classes** were associated with **DIY**, **dinner parties**, **golf** and **bridge**.

4) Nowadays, lifestyles are based more on **individual choice** than class background. Middle-class people do traditional working-class leisure activities and vice versa.

> *Postmodernists also argue that there isn't any difference between high and low culture any more — globalisation means people have access to a range of media images in an instant, resulting in a mass culture (see p.36).*

New Right theorist **Peter Saunders (1990)** argues that today an individual's identity **isn't** based on social class. He claims that the old **divisions** between social classes have **disappeared** in our modern, **equal-opportunities** society.

Marshall (1988) suggests that the working class still see themselves as working class, but they are more **fragmented** than in the past due to the **loss of traditional industries**. This has meant that traditional working-class identities have weakened.

Bradley (1996) thinks class identity has become **less important** — social class used to determine a person's identity, but now it is **more common** for identity to be made up of **several fragments** based on ethnicity, gender and age, as well as class.

Practice Questions

Q1 What are the four social classes usually discussed in sociology?

Q2 What does the term 'immediate gratification' mean?

Q3 How does negative stereotyping influence the identity of the lower classes?

Q4 According to Marshall, why have working-class identities become fragmented?

Exam Question

Q1 Analyse two explanations for why different class identities exist in the UK today. [10 marks]

Some very classy pages to revise...

Most sociologists are keen on figuring out what makes the working class different from the middle class. Agents of socialisation like the family and social class (see p.1) are a common explanation. Postmodernists, on the other hand, argue that social class doesn't really exist in this twenty-first century world. I hope the Marxists don't hear them say that — things could get ugly.

Gender Identities

Gender is about masculinity and femininity (as opposed to straightforward biological boy/girl differences).

Sex *is* Not the Same *as* Gender

In sociology, **sex** means the **biological differences** between men and women. **Gender** means the aspects of **masculinity** and **femininity** that are **not biological** but **cultural**. They are **learned through socialisation**.

Sociologists focus on **gender**. One reason for this is that there are **gender inequalities** in education and employment that **can't be explained** by the **biological** differences between men and women.

The **Family** *is the Primary Agent of* **Gender Socialisation**

Ann Oakley's (1974) research led her to identify **four** ways in which **family life** usually teaches children the **norms** and **values** associated with **masculinity** and **femininity**:

1) **Manipulation** — parents **often encourage** 'normal' behaviour and interests for the child's sex and **discourage** what's seen as **deviant**. This **manipulates** the child's self-image — the child becomes interested in 'normal' behaviours. For example, girls are often dressed up in pretty dresses so that being pretty becomes important to them. Girls are sometimes told off for being 'unladylike' — shouting, playing loudly, getting mucky.

2) **Canalisation** — parents often **channel** their **children's interest** in particular directions. **Boys** may be given **construction toys** like LEGO® and **aggressive toys** like toy guns. **Girls** may be given **beauty toys** like toy jewellery and make-up, **mothering toys** like dolls and prams, or **housewife toys** like toy kitchens.

3) **Verbal appellation** — parents may **use language and names** to **define what's appropriate**. For example, 'you're an angel' (girl) versus 'you're a cheeky monkey' (boy), or 'what a beautiful little girl' versus 'what a big strong boy'.

4) **Different activities** — parents may involve children in **different aspects** of the **household**. For example, girls help wash the dishes, boys help wash the car.

School *is a* Secondary Agent *of Gender Socialisation...*

1) Girls and boys are treated **differently** in **education**. Sociologists say that education passes on **gender stereotyped assumptions** about how males and females should behave. Remember that gender stereotyped assumptions can **disadvantage boys** as well as girls.

2) There are still **gender differences** in **subject choice**. Boys are more likely to study physics and I.T. at A-level. Girls tend to dominate in art and English.

3) **Skelton (2002)** argues that schools both **create** gender stereotypes and **maintain** those learnt at home.

For more on the experiences of boys and girls at school see p.28–29.

...and so are the **Media**

1) The **mass media** help to build gender roles. For example, **females** in Hollywood films are often presented as **weak**, in need of rescuing by a strong male hero.

2) **Angela McRobbie (1978)** has argued that teenage female magazines **reinforce conventional notions of femininity**, emphasising the importance of getting and keeping a man, being 'beautiful' and so on.

Awww, kittens

3) **Wolf (1990)** suggests that **advertising** tends to present an unobtainable **'ideal image'** for women, reinforcing the notion that women should **look good** for **men**.

4) **Joan Smith**, in her 1997 book *Different for Girls*, also argued that **culture creates** and **perpetuates** gender differences.

Gender Stereotypes *can Affect* Employment Opportunities

1) **Traditional gender roles** can have an **impact** upon the **opportunities** and **experiences** of men and women in the workplace and at home. According to Social Trends 38 (2008), **19% of men** are employed as **managers or senior officials**, compared to **11% of women**.

2) It is still difficult for women to reach the **top levels** of traditionally **'male' professions**. For example, the majority of **judges** are male.

Gender Identities

Gender Roles are Changing — for Females...

1) In the **1970s**, when Sue Sharpe first researched **teenage girls' attitudes**, she found they valued **marriage** and **motherhood**. When she repeated the research in the **1990s**, she found that this generation of teenage girls stressed their **career ambitions**.

2) **Diana Gittins (1993)** looked at the **rising divorce rate** and said this was evidence that women's **attitudes to marriage** had changed a great deal. They were much **less willing** to **accept** relationships they weren't happy with. This was a sign that the old **passive female gender roles** were a **thing of the past**.

3) One important factor is the fact that more women **go out to work**, and earn good money. It is now more common for women to be the **biggest earners** or only earners in their household than it was in the past. The increase in office-based work is referred to as the **feminisation of the workforce**.

4) There has also been an **increase** in **female deviant behaviour** — for example girl gangs, as studied by **Ann Campbell (1984)**.

...And for Males

1) Research by **Jonathan Gershuny (1992)** shows that **childcare** and **housework** are **shared** between men and women much more than in the past. The so-called '**new man**' does the dishes and changes the baby's nappies. Statistics show an increase in the number of **househusbands** — men who stay at home, cook, clean and care while their female partners go out to work.

2) One cause of men staying at home might be the **loss of traditional jobs** and **roles** for men. **Heavy industry has declined** and the majority of jobs now require **traditionally feminine skills** such as communication. Boys aren't socialised to have these skills as much as girls are, and girls are now socialised to be ambitious and dominant — traditionally masculine traits.

3) **Máirtín Mac an Ghaill (1994)** says these changes have led to a **crisis of masculinity** where **men no longer know** what their role should be. This idea says that men are **shut out** from their **traditional** roles, and **not adequately socialised** to be able to **fit into new roles**.

Masculinity in the Media has Become Feminised

1) **Rutherford (1996)** points out that images of men in the media are now being used in traditionally female ways — e.g. to be ogled at. Male stripper groups like the Chippendales are a good example. He also looks at the marketing of **men's cosmetics and toiletries**. There are far **more** of these products now than in the past, and the images used to advertise them are often of **half-naked male models**. These are signs that men's roles have moved closer to women's. Rutherford calls this the **feminisation of masculinity**.

2) **Wilkinson (1997)** suggested that increasingly male and female **values** are **coming together**, with both men and women **creating** their **own identities**.

> Findings like this have led some sociologists to believe that **traditional ideas** of **masculinity** and **femininity** are now in **decline**. **Postmodernists** say that **both men and women** now see **consumption** and **leisure** as the **key factors** in shaping their **identity**, rather than masculinity and femininity.

Practice Questions

Q1 What is the difference between sex and gender?
Q2 Name two secondary agents of gender socialisation.
Q3 What did Rutherford mean by the 'feminisation of masculinity'?

Exam Questions

Q1 Outline two ways that agents of socialisation influence femininity. Explain each one. [10 marks]

Q2 Evaluate the idea that gender roles have changed over the last few decades. [20 marks]

I never liked pink much anyway...

With these pages, you need to learn about traditional masculinity and femininity AND how these gender roles are changing as society changes. As usual, those postmodernists claim nothing matters any more except shopping and leisure. Troublemakers.

Ethnic Identities

British society includes many different ethnic groups. Ethnicity can be an important part of identity. Not to forget gender, religion, class, nationality and occupation. One thing you can say for identity — it ain't simple...

Sociologists *Use the Term* Ethnicity, *not* Race

Race is a way of classifying people by **visible biological features**, like skin colour or bone structure. The idea of race is linked to **racism**, the idea that some races are inferior to others.

That's one reason most sociologists agree **ethnicity** is a better term to use when you're talking about society. People from the same **ethnic group share** the **same culture** and **socialisation**.

Ethnic Minorities *have* Different Cultural Features

Ethnic minorities in the UK are often people whose families came here from former colonies (like **Jamaica** and **India**) from the **1950s onwards**. The **2011 census** says that **14% of the population** of England and Wales are from ethnic minorities.

> Ethnic minorities have distinctive cultural features from their countries and cultures of origin. This means stuff like values, customs, religion, diet, language and clothing. These cultural features give each ethnic minority its ethnic identity.

It's a long time since the 1950s, so Britain's ethnic minorities have been through a lot of **changes**. The way **ethnic identity changes over time**, from one generation to the next, is something a lot of sociologists study (see below).

Culture based on **shared origin** is still an **important influence** on **ethnic identity** though. Some ethnic groups work hard to keep distinctive cultural features going. For example, **Modood et al (1997)** suggested that cultural origins still play a key role in influencing the behaviour of Asians, particularly the older generation.

Children *are* Socialised *into an* Ethnic Identity

Quite a few studies have looked at the way **parents pass on ethnic identity** to their children. This is **primary socialisation** — the socialisation that takes place as part of **family life**.

> **Rosemary Hill (1987)** found **the family** was very **important** in the Leicester Asian community. She also said that some children learned 'Western' ideas about marriage, education, work and so on from white peers. Hill thought this led to **generational conflict** between parents and children from ethnic minorities.

John's latest attempt to be more Western had failed to impress.

> **Roger Ballard (1994)** disagreed. He found that young Asians **negotiated** the two aspects of their lives (home and outside the home). That meant that at **home** they'd behave in **traditional** ways to fit in with their parents, but **outside** the home they'd '**act Western**'.

> **Shaun Hides (1995)** studied the use of **artefacts** in ethnic minority homes. He was interested in the way things like **furniture**, **pictures**, **ornaments** and **religious items** helped **reinforce** ethnic identity. Hides found that the wearing of **traditional dress** was a really important part of this. **Women** wore traditional dress **more often** than men, and Hides concluded that **women** had the most **important role** in keeping ethnic identity going.

Ethnic Identity *is Also Created by* Secondary Socialisation

1) **Racism** in British society can affect secondary socialisation. For example, studies by **David Gillborn (1990)** and **Cecile Wright (1992)** suggest that African-Caribbean pupils are often **labelled** as a **problem** by teachers. This can lead to a **self-fulfilling prophecy** where pupils form an **anti-school subculture** because that's what the school seems to **expect** them to do.

2) The **peer group** is important too. Academic **Tony Sewell** said in an interview in **2000** that he thinks young African-Caribbean males are too influenced by popular culture. He believes that they encourage each other to be interested in **expensive consumer goods** (e.g. cars, the latest mobile phones, clothes) instead of **education**.

Ethnic Identities

Some Sociologists Say that *Ethnic Identities* are a *Response to Racism*

1) When **African-Caribbean** and **Asian** families first arrived in Britain, they faced lots of **prejudice** from the white population.
2) Some people from ethnic minorities felt there **wasn't any point** trying to **integrate** into the mainstream.
3) One way minorities responded to **discrimination** in work, housing and education was to **hold on** to their **ethnic identity** and **resist** full assimilation into the mainstream.
4) **Cashmore and Troyna (1990)** show how people in ethnic minorities turned to **each other** for **support**, for example in religious groups like the (mostly black) **Pentecostal Church**.

New Ethnic Identities are Emerging

1) **Stuart Hall (1996)** talks about **new ethnicities** which are very **varied**. He says that the **old ideas** of condensing ethnicity to **white / black** are being **challenged**. There are lots of **different kinds** of Asian ethnicity and black ethnicity. Hall also points out that for ethnic minority people, **gender** identity, **class** identity and **sexuality** can actually be **as important** or **more important** than ethnic identity.

2) Many sociologists argue that **young people** from **ethnic minority** backgrounds are developing **hybrid identities** — based on a mixture of influences. **Paul Gilroy (1987)** examined how black and white culture has become mixed together. **Maria Gillespie (1995)** looked at how young Sikhs brought bits of **mainstream popular culture** together with **Punjabi traditions**.

3) **Modood et al (1997)** found that **ethnic identities** were **changing**. Things like wearing **ethnic clothes** were **less important** for young people than for their parents. **Younger** people were more likely to be **political** and **upfront** about their **ethnic identity**. On the other hand, second generation immigrants were **more likely** to **see themselves** as **British** or partly British than first generation immigrants.

4) **Basit's (1997)** study suggested that ethnic identities are **dynamic** and **changeable**. Basit's interviews with British Asian schoolgirls suggested that they **combine elements** of both British and Asian cultures. They created their identity based on their Asian culture's **ethnicity**, **language** and **religion**, but in the **context** of a **British society**. This made their identity particularly **unique**, as the girls' parents thought that their daughters would not feel as **comfortable** if they were to go to Pakistan or Bangladesh to live, because of the **impact of British culture** upon them.

Practice Questions

Q1 What's the difference between 'race' and 'ethnicity'?
Q2 What makes ethnic minorities distinctive from the mainstream population?
Q3 How can secondary socialisation affect ethnic identity?
Q4 Briefly outline the view that ethnic identities are a response to racism.
Q5 What are Stuart Hall's views about the emergence of new ethnicities?
Q6 What are hybrid identities?

Exam Questions

Q1 Outline two ways in which the family may influence ethnic identities. Explain each one. [10 marks]

Q2 Evaluate the idea that ethnic identities are becoming more diverse in modern UK society. [20 marks]

So many identities, so little time...
Sociology is full of these 'hot button' topics. Debates about racism, identity and multiculturalism come up in the newspapers and on the radio quite a lot. For you as a sociology student, the important thing is to know the main theories about how ethnic identity is learnt by socialisation. Make sure you can explain how modern life is changing the way identity is formed.

National Identities

Yup. Yet more aspects of identity.

National Identity is about Feeling you Belong to a Country and its People

Durkheim said that national identity (nationalism) has an important function. It makes **individuals** feel that they **belong** to a **larger group**. **Benedict Anderson (1983)** reckons that **nationalism has replaced religion** in giving people's lives meaning.

National identity can have **negative** effects. It can be used to **exclude** certain groups. For example, if someone defines being British as being **white**, then they are **excluding black and Asian British people**. When an organisation excludes ethnic minorities like this, it's called **institutional racism**.

1) **Symbols** and **rituals** are important to national identity. The symbols of a nation's identity include things like its **currency**, its **flag**, and its **national anthem**.

2) Every nation has its own **national rituals**. These are events when people are **expected** to **think** about what it **means** to be English or Scottish or French, etc. A good example from Britain is **Remembrance Sunday** when there are processions and ceremonies to remember British soldiers who died fighting in wars.

National Identity is a Product of Socialisation

Schudson (1994) says that individuals are **socialised** into a **national culture** and identity by agents of socialisation such as **education** and the **mass media**. For example, the National Curriculum says all children must learn about Shakespeare.

The **hidden curriculum** also contributes by having school celebrations for national events such as the **Queen's Jubilee**, or letting pupils watch 'important' national football matches at school.

The **media** are also very important in building up national identity. They do this by **broadcasting national rituals** — things like Royal funerals or the state opening of Parliament.

Stuart Hall (1992) writes about the way each country has its own collection of **stories** about itself. National identity is about **learning** and **sharing** these tales of **wars won**, **great sporting victories** and so on. These are **passed on** from one generation to the next.

Traditional National Identity is on the Decline

Some sociologists suggest that during the last 20 years, people have found it **harder** to **identify** with Britishness. British national identity isn't as strong as it was, and some would say it **doesn't exist** any more. There are a few reasons for this:

1) **Big business** is now **international**, and companies like the McDonald's fast food chain appear all around the world. People in Britain are often **working for companies** based in **Japan**, or **Germany** or the **USA**. Some **British companies** have been **bought by corporations** from **overseas**. Sociologists call this breaking down of national boundaries **globalisation**.

2) Mainstream **TV**, **fashion**, **music** and **film** are often dominated by **American products**. Many people think that the result of this is that Britain and other countries are **losing their own cultures**.

3) Britain today is **multi-ethnic**. It contains many **different** groups, religions and languages.

4) Britain has strong **regional differences**. Scotland, Wales and Northern Ireland have strong national identities of their own. Under the New Labour government, regional identities were given a boost by **devolution** — regions being given **more political power** by central government, e.g. the creation of the National Assembly for Wales in 1998.

New National Identities are Being Formed

The old 'Britishness' is partly being replaced by a **new multicultural national identity**. Things like food, fashion and music bring together **British traditions** with **multicultural influences** from **inside Britain** and **international influences** from the **rest of the world**. Our new 'national dish', chicken tikka masala, is an example of this.

There are some **obstacles** to the creation of this new British identity, one of which is **racism**. A lot of the traditional British identity was based on the idea that the British were **different from** (and **better than**) the rest of the world. Some people may prefer this traditional view of 'Britishness' and be **resistant** to the idea that British society and identity are changing.

Sexuality and Identity

Sexuality *is another part of* Identity

1) **Sexuality** means a person's **sexual orientation** — whether they are heterosexual, homosexual, asexual or bisexual. It can also imply **sexual desire**. It is something which **society** can seek to **control**.

2) **Attitudes** towards sexuality **vary** between different cultures and over time. **Jeffrey Weeks (1986)** argued that sexuality is a **social** and **historical construct** — taking on **different meanings** depending on the society and time period.

3) In the past in the UK, **monogamous heterosexual relationships** were the **norm** in **mainstream culture** — and people who tried to live differently were often treated **very negatively**. People with different sexual orientations sometimes formed **subcultures** — **alternatives** to the mainstream (see p.36).

4) **Agents of socialisation** such as religion, the media and the law can **pass on attitudes** about sexuality.

Religion passes on ideologies that control sexuality

1) Religion tends to **promote a norm** of **heterosexuality** and **marriage**. Many religions forbid homosexuality and sex outside of marriage, e.g. Catholicism.

2) **Feminists** argue that religion **oppresses female sexuality** by imposing a **strict norm** of staying a **virgin until marriage**, only having sex to have babies and being **sexually passive**.

3) **Functionalists** think that the **control** and channelling of **sexuality** is crucial to the continuation of society. They think it's important to have a **stable family** for kids to be born into, and a monogamous sexual relationship between husband and wife to keep society stable.

4) The **New Right** claim that a **moral decline** caused by **secularisation** has encouraged homosexuality, abortion and pornography. They say these are **threats to social order**.

5) **Postmodernists** think this is all old-hat and that religion doesn't have that big an influence on sexuality any more. They say individuals have choice in the **construction** of their **identity** — including **sexual identity**.

Representations of sexuality in the media can be stereotyped

1) **Homosexual** relationships and **heterosexual** relationships are often treated differently in the media. For example, very **few** main characters on TV and in film are gay.

2) **Early media reporting** of **HIV/AIDS** had a prejudiced aspect. It was initially openly characterised as a 'gay disease'. Some tabloid newspapers in the 1980s referred to AIDS as a 'gay plague'.

3) Increasingly though, the way that the **media** has **represented gay people** has been **more positive**, for example the television series *Queer as Folk,* and the films *Beautiful Thing* and *Brokeback Mountain.*

Social attitudes towards sexuality are reflected in the law

1) Homosexuality used to be **illegal** in the UK. It was **decriminalised** in England and Wales in **1967** — but the **age of consent was 21**, higher than for heterosexual people.

2) In 1988, **Section 28** came into force. It **prevented** local authorities from 'promoting' homosexuality, i.e. presenting gay relationships as acceptable. The scope of this law was ambiguous — but many **teachers** thought it meant they **weren't allowed** to **talk about homosexuality** with pupils.

3) Over the last few decades, there have been moves towards **equality**. For example, the **age of consent** for gay men was **lowered to 16** in 2000, Section 28 was scrapped in 2003, **civil partnerships** for gay couples were introduced in 2005, the **Equality Act (Sexual Orientation) 2007** made it illegal to discriminate against gay men and women in the provision of goods and services, and the **Marriage (Same-Sex Couples) Act 2013** legalised **gay marriage**. These all reflect **changing attitudes** in society.

Practice Questions

Q1 Give one example of a national symbol and one example of a national ritual.

Q2 Give three agents of socialisation that can pass on attitudes about sexuality.

Exam Question

Q1 Outline two ways in which national identity has changed. Explain each one. [10 marks]

I'm having an identity crisis...

People don't just have one identity — they have blimmin' loads. Class, gender, ethnicity, nationality, sexuality... and there's more over the page. So square your shoulders and chin up — another four pages and you'll have polished off this section.

Age and Identity

The identity topic rolls on... Two more aspects of identity are age and disability.

Attitudes about Age **Vary** between **Cultures** and **Change Over Time**

1) Views about age **aren't universal** — they **change over time**, and vary between **different societies** and cultures. **Age** can be seen as a **social construct**.

2) **Age** is part of social **identity**. People are **socialised** to accept the **norms** and **values** of the **society** they live in. So the way a society **views** certain **age groups** affects **people's behaviour** and **treatment of each other**.

3) People who are **similar ages** and have lived through the same **cultural and political events** are often referred to as being from the same **generation**. It can be part of an individual's **identity** that they **feel part of a generation** — e.g. the 60s generation.

Her cooking wasn't up to much, but if you're going to insist on hiring a two-year-old chef...

4) Assumptions about at **what age** someone becomes an '**adult**', or at what age someone is '**old**' can vary between different societies and cultures.

5) For example, in **modern, British society** children are treated **differently** from **adults**. They have to go to school, they aren't allowed to do certain activities (e.g. smoking), and they are viewed as needing constant protection and care. But back in 1800, many children in the UK were treated like **mini-adults** and **worked full-time** as soon as they were physically able to do so.

6) The **law** affects how different age groups are treated. For example, you **can't** get a UK **driving licence** until you're **17**, and people **over 70** have to **renew** theirs **more often** than everyone else.

Have a look at p.41 for more on social constructs.

7) **Bradley (1997)**, however, argues that age is **less important** to identity than other factors like class, gender and ethnicity. This is because people know that their age identity is **temporary** — they're not going to be a child, teenager or middle aged forever.

The **Media** sometimes present **Stereotyped** views of different **Age Groups**

1) The way the media represent different age groups can **influence** social attitudes — and **reflect** them.

2) Some sociologists have found evidence of **ageist** attitudes in media products. **Simon Biggs (1993)** studied the way older people are presented on television entertainment programmes. He found they were often in stereotyped roles, e.g. 'forceful', 'vague' or 'difficult' — especially in sitcoms.

3) **Lambert (1984)** found that **older men** were often portrayed in **positions of power**, e.g. newsreaders. But this was not the case for older women.

4) There are also media stereotypes of **young people**. Children are often represented as **innocent**. Teenage characters in TV soaps are often **a bit wild** — prone to drug-taking, petty crime, binge drinking and unplanned pregnancy.

Marxists think **Attitudes** to **Age** are influenced by **Capitalism**

1) Marxists suggest that age groups are defined by the **capitalist system**. For example, **adults** are people of **working age**, and the **elderly** are people who are **too old to work**.

2) **Phillipson (1982)** argues that capitalism views the **elderly** as a **burden on society**. This is because their **working life** has **ended**, and they usually have **less spending power**. Old age becomes a **stigmatised** identity.

Increasing Life Expectancy has changed attitudes to **Old Age**

1) The UK has an **ageing population**. **Social Trends 41 (2011)** said that between 1971 and 2009, the **percentage** of people in the population **over 75** rose from **4.7%** to **7.8%**.

2) This is partly because people are **living longer**. According to **Social Trends 33 (2003)**, between 1971 and 2001, **life expectancy** in the UK **increased** from 69 years to 75 years for men, and from 75 years to 80 years for women.

3) **Giddens (1986)** argues that **longer life expectancy** has an **effect on family life**. For example, people are more likely to know their grandparents or great-grandparents. Families continue for much longer after the children have left home.

4) **Postmodernists** argue that **attitudes** to old age are **changing**. **Featherstone and Hepworth (1993)** found that magazines aimed at older people portray an image of 'youthful' old age — enjoying holidays and sports, wearing fashionable clothes etc. They also argue that people can **mask their age** more than ever before, e.g. through cosmetic surgery.

Disability and Identity

Society puts Disabled People into a **Separate Category**

1) **Tom Shakespeare (1994)** argued that 'disability' is a label that society uses to **categorise people**. Being in the category of 'disabled' is often **more of a problem** than the disability itself. In this way, 'disability' can be seen as a **social construct**.

2) He argues that it's more useful to talk about **impairments** (the actual physical characteristics or symptoms). These don't make it **impossible** for people to do some tasks — they just make it **harder**. Since everyone's abilities are different, **everyone has some sort of impairment** — not just people traditionally defined as 'disabled'.

3) He also says that society should adapt so that **everyone** has access to the same services, regardless of how severe their impairments are.

There is sometimes **Prejudice** against **Disabled People**

There are **negative stereotypes** of disabled people as **weak** and **dependent on others**.

Scott (1969) studied the way that **blind people** were treated by **medical professionals**. He concluded that the blind people sometimes **learned helplessness** — they relied on sighted people for support because this was what the medical professionals **expected** them to do. Because they were **labelled** as dependent, it became a **self-fulfilling prophecy**.

Some people have challenged the idea that disabled people are unusual in being reliant on others. **Marsh and Keating (2006)** argue that everyone is dependent on other people to some extent.

Disabled People are Under-represented in the Media

1) There's very **little representation** of **disabled people** in the **media**. **Roles** for disabled people are **limited**. Research by **Cumberbatch and Negrine (1992)** looking at British television over six weeks found the roles for disabled people were based on **pity** or **comedy**. They found that **disabled actors** never appeared **just as actors** playing a person who **just happened to have a disability**, only in roles **particularly about disability**. However, there are some positive portrayals of disabled people in films and TV — e.g. in *X-Men* and *Glee*.

2) They also found that how people **interpreted** media messages about disability depended on their **personal experiences**. Those with real-life experience of disability were more likely to **reject unrealistic portrayals**, or to **reinterpret** them according to their own knowledge. This suggests that the media can only create **negative perceptions** amongst people who haven't already **formed their own ideas**.

Practice Questions

Q1 What characteristics have TV soap operas often given to teenage characters?

Q2 Give two examples of stereotypes about age groups that are sometimes presented by the media.

Q3 How do Marxists think that capitalism defines who society views as elderly?

Q4 What is Tom Shakespeare's view about how society should view disability?

Q5 How are disabled people usually portrayed in the media, according to Cumberbatch and Negrine?

Exam Questions

Q1 Analyse two explanations for why age might influence a person's identity. [10 marks]

Q2 Evaluate the idea that the media influence society's perception of disability. [20 marks]

You want to retire with a pension at 17? Oh, act your age...

Age is a flexible part of identity (my dad's been 21 for decades). Everyone gets older and society's views of age change, often due to changes in population within a single person's lifetime. On the other hand, disability is much more rigid — a person is unlikely to stop being disabled, and society often unfairly views a disability as the most important attribute of an individual.

Production, Consumption and Globalisation

In a postmodern world, identity is all about shopping...

Some Argue That **Identity** is Linked to **Work** and **Leisure**

In industrial society, traditional patterns of employment helped people to create a strong sense of shared identity through work, family and location. People often lived and socialised in communities close to their place of work. These communities were self-sufficient — they produced what they needed to survive. People were expected to stay in the same skilled or semi-skilled job for a lifetime, and work was closely linked to family and community traditions. This made it easier to build your sense of identity around your job.

In modern society, people have become more **geographically** and **socially mobile**, jobs are **less secure**, and families (traditional, extended and nuclear) are **less stable**:

1) Instead of **producing** everything themselves, people are increasingly **relying** on the work and services of **other people** to survive. More people are **defining** themselves based on what they **consume** (buy), **not** on what they **produce** — this means the identities people can build are more **varied**.

2) **Willis (1990)** suggests that work is now **less satisfying** because it often requires little **skill**. This leads to people using their **leisure time** to gain **satisfaction** and build their **identity**.

3) **Rojek (1995)** argues that work and leisure are often **combined** in **postmodern society** — lots of jobs exist in the **leisure industry** and more people are **turning their hobbies or passions** into **paid work**.

Social Class Affects the Link Between **Work** and **Leisure**

Parker (1976) looked at the link between **work** and **leisure**. He discovered **three** different patterns of **integration**:

> Bourdieu (1984) argued that there is a link between cultural consumption, class and identity (see p.47).

1) The **extension pattern** — leisure and work are **actively linked**.
2) The **neutrality pattern** — work and leisure may not be linked — their relationship is **not planned**.
3) The **opposition pattern** — leisure and work are **deliberately separated**.

1) Parker found that **upper-class** people with **high-status jobs** often follow the **extension pattern** — they spend leisure time **networking** (making social contacts) or doing other things that will help them advance in their working life.

2) **Middle-class** and **working-class** people in **jobs** that are **not stressful or rewarding** follow the **neutrality pattern**.

3) **Working-class** people in **tiring** or **dangerous jobs** follow the **opposition pattern** to get away from the stresses of work.

4) This theory has been **criticised** for ignoring the impact of **age**, **gender** and **personal choice** on leisure. For example, **Deem (1986)** argues that women who **work in the home** don't have **boundaries** between **leisure** and **housework** — these women are always '**on call**' to tackle any emotional and domestic issues. Women who have **paid work** can **separate** their work and leisure time **more clearly**, but they still often spend **free time** doing **domestic work**.

Postmodernists Say That **Class**, **Gender** and **Ethnicity** Don't Mean So Much

1) In recent years, sociologists have suggested that people do not feel constrained by **social class**, **gender**, or **ethnic** background, and are now much more likely to build their identities through **symbolic consumption** (see below).

2) An example of this is the 'new man', who is caring, sensitive and does the housework.

3) In these cases, individuals use **leisure time** and **products** from **culture industries** to build **identities** for themselves.

Symbolic Consumption and Consumer Culture

1) In our **industrial capitalist** society, we **buy goods** that have been made by the **cultural industries** (e.g. film, music, broadcasting). Buying goods has become part of modern, Western culture — it's known as **consumer culture**.

2) These industries create and sell things that fit into people's **cultural lives** — the stuff they **think about**, and **talk about**, and often the stuff that helps them to **define who they are**. This is called '**symbolic consumption**'.

3) When you choose a pair of trainers, you look for the **right brand** and the **right style**. You are buying what the shoes **stand for** — their '**symbolic value**'. What you're actually buying is part of your **identity**.

> Lury (2011) argues that shopping is becoming a more common way to spend leisure time — this is partly because there are more products to choose from and more ways to pay for things.

4) **Most industries** in the modern world have become **cultural industries**. Any industry that makes things with a **brand image** that **means something** to people, or **stands** for something, is involved in **cultural production**.

Production, Consumption and Globalisation

Pluralists say we have Power through Choice

In a **consumer culture**, people have **consumer power** (they can choose the products they buy). **Pluralists** argue that **cultural industries** make products based on what society **actively decides** to consume. It's the **consumers who shape popular culture** — not the other way round.

The chin-flator 5000. Surely a must-have?

1) Not everyone agrees with the pluralists. For example, **Ien Ang (1991)** suggests that the **opinions** of consumers are largely **ignored** by the cultural industry.

2) **Bauman** argues that **postmodern society** expects us all to play the **role of a consumer**, but that some people **can't** do this. Some people **want** to consume lots of cultural products, but their **freedom to choose** is limited by **lack of money**. They **can't use consumption** to create an **impression** of **who they are**. Bauman calls these people '**repressed consumers**'. (He refers to people who **can afford** to consume as much as they like as '**seduced consumers**'.)

3) Bauman also believes that consumer society gives you the **illusion** that your **identity** is flexible because you can change your way of living **at any time** by **changing what you consume**. However, consumer society still **forces you to make a choice** between the options that are on offer — this **limits** your power.

Clarke and Critcher (1985) argue that **capitalist society controls** the **choices** we make about **leisure consumption**:

- Leisure is **controlled by companies** who want to make **profit** — it's **cheaper** for them to give you a **limited number of popular choices** than to provide lots of different options. This means it's **harder** to create a **unique identity**.

- They argue that society encourages people to do **sports** so that there are enough **healthy people** to do the **work** that capitalist society is built on. This is a form of **manipulation** of leisure time.

Globalisation Has Influenced National and Individual Identities

Sociologists **disagree** over whether **globalisation** is having a **positive** or **negative influence** on national and ethnic identity.

Some think that globalisation is **bad news** for **ethnic identities** because everyone will experience the same, global culture — ethnic and national identities will **merge** and become **less distinct** and **less varied**. **Lemert and Elliott (2006)** and **Bauman** disagree with this — they say globalisation makes your identity **more unstable**, which creates **more** variety. You can try out lots of cultures and you **don't have to commit** to any part of your identity.

Some argue that globalisation **imposes Western culture** on other societies and **damages** traditional cultural identity. **Hall** disagrees and suggests that globalisation actually **strengthens national identity**:

1) **Hall (1992)** argues that both **ethnic minorities** and people in the **ethnic majority** group of a nation react to **globalisation of identity** by **emphasising** their own cultural roots.

2) Some people react by **breaking away** from the cultural identity **imposed** on them by their **nationality** or **ethnicity** — they create a **new identity** using lots of cultural influences.

Hall (1992) argues that **globalisation** means people don't have to construct their identity based on where they **live** — the growth of the **internet** means you can communicate with people across the world and **experience** different cultures. It's also getting easier to **travel** to other countries **cheaply**. Hall names this the '**cultural supermarket effect**'.

Practice Questions

Q1 Explain how identity and work were linked in industrial society.

Q2 What is 'symbolic consumption'?

Q3 Give two ways that globalisation has influenced identity.

Exam Question

Q1 Evaluate the idea that individuals in postmodern society build their identities through consumption. [20 marks]

It says it's about shopping but it looks like work to me...

Phew... It's the end of the section. There's been a lot of heavy theory in this section. The usual suspects — postmodernists, Marxists, functionalists, feminists and interactionists — have an opinion about everything (you might have noticed). If you can get your head around what they say about culture and identity, then you'll find it a lot easier to pick up marks in the exam.

The Nature and Role of Family in Society

The family is one of the most important social groups in sociology — almost all people live in a family for some of their life.

Families and Households are Not Necessarily the Same Thing

A **household** is a group of people who **live together** who may or may not have family or kinship ties. In 2010, there were **25.3 million households** recorded in the Great Britain. **Families** make up the **majority** of households, but there are other types, e.g. **students** or **friends** sharing a house or flat, or people living alone.

A **family** is a type of household where the people living together are **related**. Most commonly, a family is also a **kinship** group. Kinship means being related by **birth** or **blood** — parents, children, grandparents, cousins. Families also include **non-kinship relationships** — foster children, guardians, step-parents and stepchildren, mother-in-law etc.

Here are the main types of family:

1) **Nuclear family**: Two generations living together (parents and dependent children).

2) **Traditional extended family**: Three or more generations of the same family living together or close by, with frequent contact between grandparents, grandchildren, aunts, cousins etc.

3) **Attenuated extended family**: Nuclear families that live apart from their extended family, but keep in regular contact, e.g. via phone or email.

4) **Lone-parent families**: A single parent and their dependent children.

5) **Reconstituted families**: New stepfamilies created when parts of two previous families are brought together. For example, two new partners who bring children from former partners together to create a new family group.

My architect didn't quite understand when I asked him to extend my house.

Functionalists Emphasise the Positive Role of the Family

Functionalists see **every institution** in society as **essential** to the **smooth running** of society. A **key functionalist study** by **Murdock (1949)** concluded that the family is **so useful** to society that it is **inevitable** and **universal** — in other words, you **can't avoid** having family units in a society, and societies **everywhere** have family units.

Murdock (1949) looked at 250 societies in different cultures

Murdock argued that some form of the **nuclear family** existed in **all** of the 250 different societies he looked at. He argued the family performed **four basic functions** – sexual, reproductive, economic and educational (social):

Sexual	Provides a **stable sexual relationship** for **adults**, and **controls** the sexual relationships of its members.
Reproductive	Provides new babies — **new members of society**.
Economic	The family **pools resources** and **provides** for all its members, adults and children.
Educational	The family **teaches children** the **norms** and **values** of society, which keeps the values of society going.

In the 1950s, American sociologist **Talcott Parsons** argued that the family always has **two basic and irreducible** (vital) **functions**. These are the **primary socialisation of children** and the **stabilisation of adult personalities**.

1) **Primary socialisation** is the process by which children **learn** and **accept** the **values** and **norms** of society. Parsons described families as 'factories' where the next citizens are produced.

Remember: functionalists see the positive nature of the family as two-way — it's equally useful and beneficial to individuals and society.

2) For adults, the family **stabilises personalities** through the **emotional** relationship between the parents. The emotional relationship gives the **support** and **security** needed to cope in the wider society. It's a **sanctuary** from the **stress** of everyday life.

Some Say Functionalists Ignore the Negative Aspects of Family Life

1) The functionalist perspective has been **criticised** for **idealising** the family — focusing on the good bits and blanking out the bad bits. **Morgan (1975)** points out that Murdock makes no reference to **alternative households** to the family, or to **disharmony** and **problems** in **family relationships**.

2) The **functionalist** view of the family was **dominant** in sociology into the 1960s. Since then there's been **widespread criticism** that neither Murdock nor Parsons look at issues of **conflict**, **class** or **violence** in relation to the family. Some feminists argue that they also ignored the issue of **exploitation of women**.

3) The fact that functionalists **overlook negative aspects** of family life **makes their position look weak**.

The Nature and Role of Family in Society

Marxists See the Family as Meeting the Needs of the Capitalist System

Like functionalists, Marxists view the family as performing **essential functions** for modern industrial society.
The key difference is that **Marxists** argue that the family **benefits** the minority **in power** (the **bourgeoisie**)
and the economy, but **disadvantages** the **working class** majority (the **proletariat**).

1) **Engels (1884)** said the family had an **economic function** of keeping wealth
within the **bourgeoisie** by passing it on to the next generation as **inheritance**.
In other words, when a **rich person dies**, their **kids get their money**.

2) **Zaretsky (1976)** focused on how the family helped the capitalist economy.
He argued that the family is one place in society where the **proletariat** can
have **power** and **control**. When the **working man** gets home, he's **king of his
own castle**. This relieves some of the **frustration** workers feel about their low
status, which helps them to **accept** their **oppression** and exploitation as workers.

3) In capitalist society, a woman's role as **'housewife'** of the family means
workers are **cared for** and **healthy**. This makes them **more productive**
— a great benefit that the capitalist class (the employers) get for **free**.

4) The **family household** is a unit with the **desire to buy the goods**
produced by capitalist industry, e.g. washing machines, cars, fridges.
The family is a **unit of consumption**. The family buys the goods for
more than they cost to produce and the **bourgeoisie get the profit**.

When the time came for home
improvements, Steve decided
to interpret Zaretsky literally.

All in all, Marxists argue the family is a **very useful tool of capitalism**.

The Marxist View is Criticised for being too Negative

The Marxist view of the family is all about it being a **tool of capitalist oppression**,
and **never mentions nice things**, like bedtime stories for the kids, or trips to the zoo.

Criticisms of the Marxist view of the family

Marxist sociology is entirely focused on **benefits to the economy**, and benefits to
the working man's **boss**. It **ignores other benefits** to individuals and society.

Traditional Marxist sociology **assumes** that the worker is **male**, and that women are **housewives**.

There is **no Marxist explanation** for why the family flourishes as an institution in **non-capitalist**
or **communist** societies and there is little Marxist research on **alternatives** to the family.

Functionalists and Marxists both see the family as having a **key role** in society in **reproducing social structure**
and **order**. The **key sociological debate** between them is whether this is **positive** or **negative** and **who benefits**.

Practice Questions

Q1 What do sociologists define as a household?

Q2 What are the key functions of the family, according to Parsons?

Q3 Explain the ways in which functionalist and Marxist perspectives on the role of the family are similar.

Q4 Explain the ways in which functionalist and Marxist perspectives on the role of the family are different.

Exam Questions

Q1 Outline two ways that the Marxist view of the family might be criticised. Explain each one. [10 marks]

Q2 Evaluate the idea that the family performs the vital function of maintaining the existing structure of society. [20 marks]

Cog in society's machine or tool of capitalist oppression — you decide...

*If you're comparing functionalist and Marxist perspectives about the role of the family, make sure you cover the pros and cons
of each view — and most importantly, make sure you answer the question. Remember, functionalists believe that the family is
there to keep society chugging along smoothly, and Marxists believe it's there to help exploit the common worker.*

The Nature and Role of Family in Society

There are lots of different feminist theories about the family — these theories are mostly left-wing and anti-traditional. It's worth looking at right-wing pro-traditional ideas too. And at the postmodernists, who say everyone can do what they like. Hooray.

Most *Feminists* Believe the *Family Exploits* and *Oppresses Women*

1) From a **feminist perspective**, the **family** helps to **maintain the existing social order**. (If that sounds familiar, it's because functionalists and Marxists also talk about keeping up the existing social order.)

2) Feminists call the existing social order **patriarchy**. Patriarchy is the **combination of systems**, **ideologies** and **cultural practices** which make sure that **men** have power.

3) Feminist theory argues that the family **supports** and reproduces **inequalities** between men and women.

4) The idea is that women are **oppressed** because they're **socialised** to be **dependent** on men — and to put themselves in second place to men. The **family** has a central role in this socialisation — **male and female roles** and **expectations** are **formed in the family** and then **carried on into wider society**.

5) Feminist sociologists say that there's an **ideology** about men's **roles** and women's **roles** in the family.

> An ideology is a set of ideas about the way things are and the way things ought to be.

There are *Three Main Strands* of *Feminist Thought* on the *Family*

The three main strands of feminist thought are **Marxist feminism**, **radical feminism** and **liberal feminism**.

The distinction between the three theories comes from what they see as the **root cause of patriarchy**. For Marxist feminists it's the **capitalist system**, for radical feminists it's the **power dominance of men** and for liberal feminists it's **cultural attitudes** and laws that allow **discrimination**.

> All three of these theories generalise quite a bit.

Marxist feminism — key points

Marxist feminism sees the **exploitation of women** as essential to the success of **capitalism**. The family **produces** and **cares** for the next generation of workers for society at almost **no cost** to the capitalist system. It's cost-free because society accepts that **housework** should be **unpaid**. **Men are paid** for work outside the home, but **women aren't paid** for work **inside** the home. If this sounds outdated, remember evidence shows that even when women work outside the home they still do **most** of the domestic labour (see p.66). **Benston (1969)** points out that if housework were paid even at **minimum wage** levels it would **damage capitalist profits** hugely.

Radical feminism — key points

Radical feminist theory also highlights **housework** as an area of **exploitation of women**, but... and it's a big but... radical feminists don't see this as the fault of the capitalist system. Radical feminists see the exploitation of women as being down to the **domination of men in society**. Radical feminism believes that **men will always oppress women**. **Delphy and Leonard (1992)** are radical feminists who see the family as a patriarchal institution in which **women do most of the work** and **men get most of the benefit**.

Liberal feminism — key points

Liberal feminists emphasise the **cultural norms** and **values** which are reinforced by the family and by other institutions in society. The family is only sexist because it **supports mainstream culture** which is sexist. Liberal feminists believe **social change is possible**. They try to put pressure on institutions such as the **legal system** and **government** to change laws and social policies which **discriminate** against women.

Feminist Theory has been *Criticised*

1) All strands of feminist theory have been **criticised** for portraying women as **too passive**. It plays down the ability of individual women to **make changes** and **improve** their situation.

2) Feminist sociology **doesn't acknowledge** that **power might be shared** within a family.

3) Some feminist theory has been criticised for **not considering** the households in society which **don't** feature a **man and woman partnership**, e.g. **lesbian** and **gay** relationships and **lone-parent** households. The power structures in those families **don't get looked at**.

4) Some **black feminists** have pointed out that a lot of feminist theory doesn't address the fact that women from different **ethnic backgrounds** have different **life experiences**.

The Nature and Role of Family in Society

The *New Right* Believe the *Nuclear Family* is the *Bedrock of Society*

1) **New Right theory** gained influence in sociology in the **1980s**. It's based on the idea that the **traditional nuclear family** and its **values** (mum, dad and kids, parents married, dad in paid employment) are best for society.

2) New Right theorists reckon that **social policies** on family, children, divorce and welfare have **undermined** the **family**.

3) **Charles Murray** is a New Right sociologist who says the traditional family is under threat. **Murray (1989)** says that **welfare benefits** are **too high** and create a **'culture of dependency'** where an individual finds it easy and acceptable to take benefits rather than work.

There's more about the New Right on p.64.

4) New Right theorists are particularly concerned about giving lots of **welfare benefits** to **single mothers**. They also think that it's a very **bad idea** to have children brought up in families where adults aren't working.

5) New Right sociologists believe that the increase in **lone-parent** and **reconstituted** (step) families and easier access to **divorce** have led to a **breakdown in traditional values**. They say that this causes social problems such as **crime** to increase.

*Pine cladding — that's the *real* bedrock of society.*

6) Some politicians have made use of New Right theory. It's had an influence on **social policy** — making it **harder** for people to **get benefits**.

> New Right theory has been **criticised** for **'blaming the victim'** for their problems.

Postmodernists Say *Diversity* in Family Structures is a *Good Thing*

1) The **central idea** of **postmodern views of the family** is that there's a much **wider range** of **living options** available these days — because of **social** and **cultural changes**. There are **traditional** nuclear families, stepfamilies, cohabiting unmarried couples, **single people** flat-sharing, more **divorced** people etc.

2) Postmodern sociologist **Judith Stacey (1990)** reckons there's **such a diversity** of family types, relationships and lifestyles that there'll **never** be **one dominant type** of family in Western culture again. She says that family structures in Western society are **varied** and **flexible**. This means a person can **move** from one family structure into another, and not get stuck with one **fixed** family structure.

3) Postmodernists say the **key thing** is the idea that contemporary living is so **flexible** that one individual can experience lots of different types of family in their lifetime. Postmodernists see this **diversity** and **flexibility** as **positive** — because it means individuals can always **choose** from several options depending on what suits their **personal needs** and lifestyle. People aren't hemmed in by **tradition**.

4) Sociological **criticism** of postmodern theory **questions** whether this movement through different family types is really all that typical. **O'Brien and Jones (1996)** concluded from their UK research that there was **less variety** in family types than Stacey reported, and that **most** individuals actually experienced **only one or two** different types of family in their lifetime.

Practice Questions

Q1 Identify three different strands of feminist thought about the family.
Q2 Give two characteristics of patriarchy.
Q3 Name two things that New Right theorists blame for family breakdown.
Q4 Why do postmodernists think there will never be one dominant type of family in Western culture again?

Exam Questions

Q1 Outline two ways that men might benefit from existing family structures. Explain each one. [10 marks]

Q2 Evaluate the idea that the traditional nuclear family is under threat from a culture of dependency. [20 marks]

If this is too difficult to learn, blame your family. Or blame society...

Another couple of pages all about different views of the family. Feminist theory is complicated because there are different varieties of feminism. Which one you go for depends on exactly how unfair you think family life is on women, and exactly whose fault you think it is. Don't forget to learn the reasons why sociologists say each theory might be wrong, or flawed.

Changes in Family Structure

The average family today doesn't have the same structure as the average family 250 years ago.
Sociologists suggest various reasons for this, mostly to do with people moving to cities to work in factories.

Parsons said that Industrialisation Changed Family Structure

1) There are **two basic types of family structure** you need to know: **extended** and **nuclear** (see p.58).

2) There are **two basic types of society** you need to know:

> **Pre-industrial society** — society before industrialisation. It is largely **agricultural** and work centres on **home**, **farm**, **village** and **market**.
>
> **Industrial society** — society during and after **industrialisation**. Work centres on **factories** and production of goods in **cities**.

> *Industrialisation is the process by which production becomes more mechanical and based outside the home in factories. People travel outside the home to work and urban centres (cities) are formed. Industrialisation in the UK started in the 18th century.*

> **Talcott Parsons (1951) said that nuclear families became dominant in industrial society**
>
> In **pre-industrial** society, the **extended** family is most common. Families **live and work together**, producing goods and crops to live from, taking the surplus to market. This is where the term **cottage industry** comes from.
>
> In **industrial** society, the **nuclear family** becomes dominant. There is a huge increase in individuals **leaving the home** to work for a wage. The key social change is that industrialisation **separates home and work**.

Functionalists Say Industrialisation Changed the Function of the Family

Parsons was a functionalist — he thought that the **dominant family structure** changed from **extended** to **nuclear** because it was **more useful** for industrial society — i.e. the **nuclear family** is the **best fit** for **industrial society**.

1) Lots of **functions** of the family in **pre-industrial** society are **taken over by the state** in **industrial** society — e.g. policing, healthcare, education.

2) The nuclear **family** can focus on its function of **socialisation**. The family socialises **children** into the **roles**, **values** and **norms** of industrialised society.

3) Parsons said the industrial nuclear family is '**isolated**' — meaning it has **few ties** with local **kinship** and economic systems. This means the family can **easily move** to where the work is (this is called '**geographical mobility**').

> In short, **family structure adapts** to the **needs of society**.

Most functions of extended family taken over by state

Specialised for socialising children

Mobile

Nuclear family

Functionalists Say Industrialisation Changed Roles and Status in the Family

1) Status for an individual in **pre-industrial society** was **ascribed** — decided at birth by the family they were born into. Parsons reckoned that in industrial society an individual's status is **achieved** by their success **outside the family**.

2) The idea here is that the **nuclear family** is the **best** for allowing individuals to **achieve status** and position without **conflict**. It's OK for an individual to achieve higher or lower status than previous generations. This allows for greater **social mobility** in society. People can **better themselves**.

3) Parsons says that **specialised roles** for men and women develop within the family. He thought that men are **instrumental** (practical / planning) leaders and women are **expressive** (emotional) leaders in a family. As a **functionalist**, Parsons said these roles come about because they're **most effective** for society. **Feminists** and **conflict theorists** disagree — they say these roles come from **ideology** and **power**.

Other Sociologists say it's all More Complicated

Functionalists are **criticised** for seeing the modern nuclear family as **superior** — something that societies have to evolve into. They're also criticised for putting forward an **idealised** picture of history. **Historical evidence** suggests there was actually a **variety** of family forms in the past.

Sociologist **Peter Laslett (1972)** reckons that the **nuclear family** was the **most common** structure in Britain even before industrialisation. His evidence comes from **parish records**. Also, **Laslett and Anderson (1971)** say that the **extended family** actually was **significant** in industrial society. Anderson used the **1851 census** for evidence. He said that when people moved to the cities for **industrial** jobs, they lived with relatives from their **extended family**.

Changes in Family Structure

Willmott and Young Said Families Have Developed Through Three Stages

British sociologists **Willmott and Young (1960, 1973)** did two important studies looking at family structures in British society from the 1950s to the 1970s. They mainly studied families in different parts of **London** and **Essex**. Their work tested the theory that the **nuclear family** is the **dominant form** in modern industrial society.

You need to remember their conclusion, which was that **British families have developed through three stages**. (Initially, they set out four stages, but there wasn't a lot of evidence for the last stage, so they dropped it.)

Stage One: Pre-Industrial	Family works together as an **economic production unit**. Work and home are combined.
Stage Two: Early Industrial	Extended family is broken up as individuals (mostly men) leave home to work. Women at home have strong **extended kinship** networks.
Stage Three: Privatised Nuclear	Family based on **consumption**, not **production** — buying things, not making things. Nuclear family is focused on its **personal relationships and lifestyle**. Called '**the symmetrical family**' — husband and wife have joint roles.
Stage Four: Asymmetrical	Husband and wife roles become **asymmetrical** as men spend more leisure time **away from the home** — in the pub for example. *This stage got dropped.*

A key part of the definition of a **symmetrical family** is the idea that both partners **work** either part-time or full-time. The economic contribution of men and women is **equally important**.

1) **Helen Wilkinson (1994)** argued that increasing numbers of women are working because the economy has moved away from the historically male-dominated **industrial sector** towards the traditionally female-dominated **service sector**.

2) Women's **attitudes** towards work and family have undergone a '**genderquake**' — Wilkinson notes that, in the **early 1990s**, women between the ages of **16 and 35** saw **work** and **education** as more important than **having children**.

3) Women have gained **economic influence** in the family through **employment** — this changes the **structure** of the family because **traditional gender roles** within the family are **broken down**.

4) In **2012**, a survey of social attitudes found that 41% of women and 36% of men believed that the **ideal** way to structure a family with dependent children was for **men to work full-time** and **women to work part-time**. This structure was seen as **more desirable** than only having a male breadwinner.

Other Sociologists have Criticised Willmott and Young

1) Willmott and Young (and other functionalists) have been criticised for **assuming** that family life has got **better and better** as structure adapts to modern society. They're described as '**march of progress**' theorists.

2) Wilmott and Young **ignore** the **negative** aspects of the modern nuclear family. **Domestic violence**, **child abuse** and **lack of care** for **older** and **vulnerable** people are all problems in society today.

3) **Feminist** research (see p.60) suggests **equal roles** in the 'symmetrical family' don't really exist.

Practice Questions

Q1 Give an example of social change caused by industrialisation.

Q2 What roles did Parsons believe men and women had within the nuclear family?

Q3 What is meant by the term 'symmetrical family'?

Q4 Outline one criticism of Willmott and Young's 'march of progress' theory.

Exam Questions

Q1 Outline two ways that women's attitudes towards work and family have changed. Explain each one. [10 marks]

Q2 Evaluate the idea that industrialisation changed the function of the family. [20 marks]

My mum works at Sellafield — we're a real nuclear family...

OK — it helps to have a vague idea about history for this bit of sociology. You need to know what this 'industrialisation' business was. The idea is that when people went to live in cities to work in factories, society changed. Of course, it'd be far too much to expect sociologists to agree on all of this. Oh no. So you have another couple of pages of sociological debate...

Changes in Family Structure

Politicians sometimes try to promote certain family structures through their policies.

Governments try to Influence Family Structure through Social Policy

1) The UK government often makes **laws** that are designed to influence **family life** or **family structure**. These laws are part of **social policy**.

2) Social policy laws cover areas such as **divorce**, changes to the **benefit system** which affect family income, reforms to the **education** system, **adoption/fostering** and **employment**.

3) **Donzelot (1977)** argued that **social policy** can be used by the state to **control** families. He argues that **professionals** such as health care visitors can use their knowledge to **control** family behaviour.

Social Policy has Changed Over Time

1) The way that governments tackle social policy has **changed** since the Second World War.

2) In the 1945-1979 period, the state's social policy was quite **interventionist**.

3) **The Welfare State** (see p.87), which was set up by a **Labour government** in 1948, **supported families** through benefits, public housing, family allowances and free health care.

4) People paid into a **national insurance** scheme to pay for the welfare state. It was **universal** — everyone had the same benefits and services.

The NHS even covered floating baby syndrome...

The 1979 Conservative Government Believed in Reduced State Intervention

The **Conservative Party** was elected in 1979 with **Margaret Thatcher** as their leader. Reacting to several years of political instability, they set about **reforming** the relationship between society and the state.

1) The Conservatives were influenced by **New Right** ideology. They believed that nuclear families were the **cornerstone of society**, but also thought that society as a whole should be **freed from interference** by the state as much as possible. They thought the UK had become a **'nanny state'** with too much government control over individual lives.

2) They set out to make individuals more **responsible** for their own lives and decisions — the state would **intervene much less** in private matters. So benefits were cut and **taxes lowered**. **Means testing** was introduced for some benefits with the aim of helping only those in **genuine need**. (Means testing is when you only get a benefit if your household income is below a set level.)

3) Mothers were encouraged to **stay at home** through preferential tax allowances. Families were pushed to take on more responsibility for **older people** through benefit cuts.

> Mrs Thatcher's Conservatives echoed the concerns of Charles Murray, who first coined the phrase 'culture of dependency' (see p.61).

The Conservatives Legislated to Protect People in a Traditional Family

The Conservatives valued **traditional, nuclear families**. In 1988, **Thatcher** described the **family** as "the **building block** of society. It's a nursery, a school, a hospital, a leisure place, a place of refuge and a place of rest."

The Conservatives created several laws that enforced the **rights** and **responsibilities** of individuals in families.

1) The **Child Support Agency** was established in **1993** to force absent fathers and mothers to **pay** a fair amount towards the upkeep of their children.

2) The **Children Act 1989** outlined for the first time the rights of the child.

3) The Conservatives also considered a law to make **divorce more difficult** — a compulsory **cooling off** period of one year was proposed before a couple could divorce. In the end they **abandoned** this idea because they couldn't find a way to make it work in practice.

Changes in Family Structure

New Labour Promised a Compromise between the Old Ideologies

New Labour came to power in 1997 led by Tony Blair.

1) They based their ideology on 'The Third Way' — a middle ground between left-wing and right-wing politics. Their policies were designed to be more pragmatic and less ideological than either the 1979 Conservative government or previous Labour governments.
2) In their 1998 consultation paper 'Supporting Families', they made it clear that marriage was their preferred basis for family life.
3) However they showed an awareness of, and concern for, diversity of family life.
4) In 2005 they introduced civil partnerships, a union a lot like marriage that is available to gay couples.
5) They also introduced laws allowing any type of cohabiting couple to adopt children.
6) They adopted some New Right ideas about family policy — e.g. they cut lone-parent family benefits, supported means-tested benefits and were opposed to universal benefits.

The Coalition Government Promoted Family Stability

After the General Election in 2010, no single party won a majority — a coalition government of Conservatives and Liberal Democrats formed under Conservative leader David Cameron.

1) The Coalition promoted marriage as a stabilising force in family life. For example, they pledged to remove the 'couples penalty' that made those on benefits better off if they lived apart.
2) In 2014, they legalised same-sex marriage. However, not all Conservative politicians agreed — they thought that civil partnerships and same-sex marriage would damage family stability.
3) After the financial crisis of 2008, the Coalition introduced a policy of economic austerity, which aimed to reduce the amount of money the government was spending. This had an impact on family life in the UK.
4) In an attempt to reduce the welfare bill, the Coalition capped housing benefit in 2013 at £500 a week for couples and single parents with children — married couples were not prioritised in this policy.

In 2015, a Conservative government was elected. This government continued the Coalition policy of austerity and thought families should take more economic responsibility for their children.

1) In 2015, the Conservative government announced a cap on child benefit — they decided that families with three or more children would not receive an increase in child tax credits or housing benefit after their second child.
2) The Secretary for Work and Pensions, Iain Duncan Smith, suggested that limiting child benefit to the first two children would promote 'behavioural change' and discourage families from having too many children.

Practice Questions

Q1 What is social policy?
Q2 Give two examples of Conservative policies in the 1980s and 1990s that affected family life.
Q3 What was New Labour's attitude towards family diversity?
Q4 Give two criticisms of the New Right's attitude towards social policy.
Q5 Describe the attitude of the Coalition government towards marriage.

Exam Questions

Q1 Outline two ways that social policy has influenced family life in the UK since 1997. Explain each one. [10 marks]

Q2 Evaluate the idea that social policies in the UK since 1979 have favoured the nuclear family. [20 marks]

My social policy — Thursday is the new Friday...

Politicians usually want to support the traditional nuclear family, but since 1979 they've generally also wanted to reduce state intervention in people's private lives. The financial crisis in 2008 led to economic policies that have had an impact on family finances in the UK — this is a more indirect kind of intervention in family life. Think of a way to remember that if you can.

Roles and Relationships Within the Family

As well as studying the place of the family unit in wider society, sociologists also research what happens within the family. The key focus is on the different roles and expectations of men, women and children within the family.

The **Rise** of the **Nuclear Family** led to **Joint Conjugal Roles**

Conjugal roles are the roles of **husband and wife** (or partner and partner) within the home. **Elizabeth Bott (1957)** studied how **jobs and roles within the family** were **allocated** to **men and women** in modern industrial Britain.

Bott (1957) identified two ways household jobs can be shared	
Segregated roles	Husbands and wives lead separate lives with clear and **distinct responsibilities** within the family. The man goes out to work and does DIY. The woman stays home, looks after the kids and provides emotional support.
Joint roles	Husband and wife roles are **more flexible** and shared, with less defined tasks for each. Usually **leisure time** is shared. Responsibility for **making decisions** is also shared.

Bott's study is old, but it's a good foundation for the debate, so don't dismiss it — learn it.

1) **Willmott and Young (1973)** studied the changing structure of the British family from extended to nuclear (see p.63). They reckoned that the increase in the nuclear family meant that **joint conjugal roles** would develop. They predicted that **equal** and **shared responsibilities** would be the **future norm** in British families.

2) Willmott and Young's picture of **widespread equality** in marriage was **criticised** as soon as it was published.

3) **Oakley (1974)** pointed out that their study only required men to do a **few things round the house** to qualify as having joint roles. Their **methodology** overlooked the **amount of time** spent on housework — making 10 minutes washing-up equivalent to all the rest of the housework. Oakley's research found it was **pretty rare** for men to do a lot of housework.

Conjugal Roles are **Still Unequal**, although Most **Women** have **Paid Jobs**

Since the early studies by Bott, Willmott and Young, **new family structures** have developed. There are now lots **more families** where **both partners work outside the home**. Sociological evidence shows that an **equal share** of **paid employment** hasn't led to an **equal share** of **domestic labour**.

1) Edgell (1980) tested Willmott and Young's theory and found none of his sample families had joint conjugal roles in relation to housework. However, he did find increased sharing of childcare.

2) Oakley (1974) found that women took on a dual burden — taking on paid jobs and still keeping the traditional responsibilities for home and children.

3) Gillian Dunne (1999) studied lesbian households. She found that the distribution of responsibilities such as childcare and housework tended to be equal between the partners.

These are all **small-scale studies** — it's important to look at research using a much **larger sample**. The **British Social Attitudes Survey 2012** was a **large-scale study** that questioned about **3000 people** about **gender roles**. **Less than 15%** of those surveyed agreed that women should look after the home and family while men went out to work. There was also an **increase** in the number of people who thought that women with **school-age children** should **work full-time**.

Women Often Take Responsibility for the **Emotional Work** of a Household

Doing **emotional work** in a family means **reacting** and **responding** to other family members' emotions, **alleviating** pain and distress, and **responding** to and **managing** anger and frustration.

1) **Diane Bell (1990)** suggested that there is an **'economy of emotion'** within all families and that running this economy is the responsibility of women.

2) She says managing family emotions is a bit like **book-keeping** — women balance the family's **emotional budget**.

3) **Duncombe and Marsden (1995)** found that women in families are often required to do **housework and childcare, paid employment** and **emotional work** — amounting to a **'triple shift'** of work.

4) They found that married women were **happier** when their husbands **shared** some of the burden of emotional work, but women have the **main responsibility** for managing the whole family's emotions.

SECTION FOUR — FAMILIES AND HOUSEHOLDS

Roles and Relationships Within the Family

Industrialisation led to the Creation of the 'Housewife'

1) **Oakley (1974)** thinks that the role of the **housewife** was **socially constructed** by the **social changes** of the **Industrial Revolution**, when people started **going to work in factories** instead of working at home.

2) **Married women** were often **not allowed** to work in factories. A new role of **housewife** was created for them.

3) Middle-class households had female **servants** to do domestic work. Working-class women did it themselves.

4) The **cultural values** that said women should be in charge of housework were **so dominant** that domestic work came to be seen as '**naturally**' (biologically) the role of women.

Decision-Making and Sharing of Resources can be Unequal

As well as looking at the **division of labour** and tasks in the home, sociologists have researched how **power is shared** in the home. The traditional role of the **man** holding **power to make decisions** was **so widespread** that the phrase '**who wears the trousers**' is often used to mean who's in charge.

Alas, no one knows who was wearing these trousers. It's a mystery.

Edgell (1980) interviewed middle-class couples

He found that **men** had **decision-making control** over things both husband and wife saw as important, whilst **women** had control over **minor decisions**. This is linked to the fact that men often brought **higher earnings** into a household.

Pahl (1989, 1993) researched money management by 100 dual-income couples

She concluded that the most common form of financial management was '**husband-controlled pooling**', which she defined as money being **shared**, but the husband has the **dominant role** in how it's spent.

Other studies look at the **meanings** that couples and families attach to control over money. They discovered that control over money in a relationship is often more about **convenience** than **power**. This approach is called the **personal life perspective** — these studies do not use **traditional family norms** and **ideals** as a background to **judge** participants.

1) **Weeks et al (2001)** found that couples tend to **pool** money in a joint account while keeping some money back in a personal account — they have **sole control** over their **personal** spending money.

2) **Carol Smart (2007)** discovered that **same-sex** couples don't link control over money with **inequality** in the relationship — they organise their money based on what is best for them **as a couple**. She argued that same-sex couples don't have the same **ideas** about **gender** and **money** that heterosexual couples have **traditionally** held.

Practice Questions

Q1 What are 'conjugal roles'?

Q2 Describe the differences between joint and segregated conjugal roles.

Q3 What is meant by the 'dual burden' of women in modern society?

Q4 How was the role of 'housewife' socially constructed, according to Oakley?

Q5 Identify two areas of inequality in conjugal relationships other than household chores.

Exam Questions

Q1 Analyse two explanations for why conjugal roles are still unequal in modern British society. [10 marks]

Q2 Evaluate the idea that power is the key to understanding relationships within the family. [20 marks]

My husband just threw our money in the pond — he says he wants to pool it...

These pages are mainly about inequality in the family. You know, who does the housework and looks after the kids — that sort of thing. Some sociologists look on the bright side and say that things are getting more equal now that more women have paid jobs. Others say they still aren't equal enough. Remember to look at the possible causes and social construction of inequality.

Roles and Relationships Within the Family

These pages examine inequality within families and the dark side of family life — domestic violence and child abuse.

Explanations for Inequality are based on Theories About Power in Society

Guess what? There are **functionalist**, **Marxist** and **feminist** theories on power in society.

1) For functionalists, men and women still largely perform different tasks and roles within the family because it's the most effective way of keeping society running smoothly.

2) Marxist sociologists interpret the fact that men and women have different roles as evidence of the power of capitalism to control family life. They say women and men have unequal roles because capitalism works best that way. Even with more women working outside the home for equal hours to men, the capitalist class needs to promote women as 'naturally' caring and nurturing to ensure workers are kept fit, healthy and happy. This role for women is maintained ideologically through the media, e.g. in adverts.

Alice and Sam were awarded first place in the couples balancing competition.

3) From a feminist perspective, inequality in household roles demonstrates inequality in power between men and women. A patriarchal society will produce unequal conjugal relationships because society's systems and values will inevitably benefit men at the expense of women.

So, all explanations of conjugal **roles** lead back to **different theories** about **power in society**.

These explanations all agree that different roles for men and women in the family help to **maintain the status quo** (keep things the way they are at the moment) in society — the disagreement between them is over **who benefits**.

Some Sociologists See Child Abuse in Terms of Power

Sociologists study the issue of **child abuse** by parents and carers in terms of **power relationships**. You need to be able to **explain abuse** as a **form of power** rather than explore **details** of abuse itself.

- A parent or carer is able to abuse a child by **manipulating** the **responsibilities and trust** which go along with the role of parent or carer.
- Families are **private** and **separate** from the rest of society. This makes it **less likely** for children to **report** abuse.

> The year 2013-14 just means April 2013 to March 2014. This is because it's a financial year — these start in April in the UK, instead of in January.

1) **Social policies** have been **adapted** to give some **protection** to children. The **Children Act 1989** was set up so the state can **intervene** in families if social workers are **concerned** about children's safety.

2) In the year **2013-14**, almost **658 000** children were referred to **social services** in England. In **just under half** of these cases, the **main reason** for referral was because the child was thought to be at **risk** of **abuse** or **neglect**.

3) In the same year, social workers put **59 800** children in England under a **child protection plan** — this allows social workers to **monitor families** to **protect** children from **neglect** and **abuse**.

Domestic Violence Affects Many Families in the UK

Research by Professor **Elizabeth Stanko (2000)** found that:

> A lot of abuse goes unreported. Even though these figures are from a self-report survey (which is a more confidential method than interviews, for example), they still won't give the full picture.

- A woman is **killed** by her current or former partner **every three days** in England and Wales.
- There are 570 000 cases of **domestic violence** reported in the UK every year.
- An incident of domestic violence occurs in the UK every **6-20 seconds**.

1) The Home Office estimates that **16% of all violent crime** in the **UK** is domestic violence.

2) In the year **2011-12**, **7.3% of women** and **5% of men** in **England and Wales** had suffered from **domestic abuse**.

3) A **2012-13** survey found that **non-physical abuse** (**emotional** abuse or use of **financial** power to control a partner) was **more common** than **physical abuse**. This was true for both **male** and **female** victims.

Roles and Relationships Within the Family

Radical Feminists See Domestic Violence as a Form of Patriarchal Control

Radical feminist theory says **violence against women** is treated **differently** to **other violent crime**.

1) **Dobash and Dobash (1979)** found the **police usually didn't record** violent crime by husbands against their wives.

2) Since 1979, the police have set up **specialist domestic violence units**, but still the **conviction rate is low** compared to other forms of assault.

3) **Before 1991**, British law said a husband was **entitled** to have **sex** with his wife **against her will**. In 1991 **rape law changed** to say that a husband could be charged with raping his wife.

4) Evidence like that above is used by **radical feminists** to support their argument that **laws and social policies** in society have traditionally worked to **control women** and keep men's power in society going.

Radical feminists believe that **violence against women** within the **family** is a form of **power and control**.

1) The **social climate** helps to **maintain this situation** by making women feel **ashamed** and **stigmatised** if they talk about the violence. The shame and stigma are part of the **ideology of patriarchy** — the school of thought that says women should **know their place**.

Remember, not all feminists agree with the radical feminist view.

2) Shame also comes from the idea that women **should know better** — they shouldn't get involved with violent men in the first place. There's a tendency to **blame the victim**.

3) Dobash and Dobash found that most women who left violent partners **returned** in the end. This was because of **fear of being stigmatised** — and because they were **financially dependent** on their partner.

4) **Abusive partners** often **condition** their victim into thinking that nobody cares and there's nowhere to go. The pressure not to leave an abusive partner comes from the **relationship** as well as from society.

Radical Feminism is Criticised for Overemphasising the Power of Men

There are **two main criticisms** of **radical feminist** theory of the family:

1) It **overemphasises** the **place** of **domestic violence** in family life. **Functionalists** argue that most families operate **harmoniously**, while **postmodern theory** argues that individuals have much more **choice** and **control** to avoid, leave or reshape their family relationships.

2) It presents men as **all-powerful** and women as **powerless** when in reality women often hold some power over men. The journalist **Melanie Phillips (2003)** highlights the fact that **women abuse men too** and **male victims** are often **ignored** by society and the police. The pressure group **Families Need Fathers** campaigns for men to have **equal rights** in **family** and **child law**.

Practice Questions

Q1 What did the Children Act 1989 do?
Q2 What proportion of violent crime in the UK is estimated to be domestic violence?
Q3 What do radical feminists think is the cause of domestic violence?
Q4 Give two criticisms of the radical feminist view of domestic violence.

Exam Question

Q1 By applying material from Item A, analyse two explanations for why inequality of power in society is linked to inequality between men and women in the household. [10 marks]

> **Item A**
> Sociologists argue that power relationships that exist in society can be transferred to the household. Some say that inequality of power between men and women in wider society is responsible for unequal roles between men and women in the household. Others suggest that this inequality is necessary to maintain the status quo of society.

The roles in my family are always wholemeal...

When one person in a relationship has more power than another, there can be pretty serious consequences for the family. Make sure you can explain what Marxist, functionalist and feminist sociologists say about abuse of power in relationships.

Family Diversity — Changing Family Patterns

These pages are about which family types are getting more common, and which are getting less common.

Social Trends Indicate More Variety of Families and Households

Official government statistics clearly show that the **variety** of family types has **increased** in Britain since the **mid 20th century**. There's now no such thing as 'the British family' — there are several kinds of family structure out there.

Look at the evidence:

1) Two of the biggest **increases** in household type have been in **single-person** households and **lone-parent family** households. The vast majority of **lone-parent** households are **matrifocal** (families where **women** are the head).

2) **Single-person households** increased by 500 000 from 2003 to 2013 — this rise could be related to the increasing number of **divorced** people and a rise in people **over 65** living alone.

3) The **fastest growing** household type is **multi-family households** — these households **increased** by 56% between 2004 and 2014 to 313 000. This trend is partly linked to the growing number of **beanpole families** — grandparents might live with one of their **grown-up children** and some of their **grandchildren** in a multi-family household.

4) **Cohabitation** (living with a partner) **doubled** from 1996 to 2012 to 2.9 million couples — this number is still growing.

Increasing life expectancy means that children can become close to their grandparents, and even their great-grandparents in some cases. This creates a more 'vertical' family structure, with links between generations at different stages in their life-course (see below). Sociologists describe this as a 'beanpole family'.

There are two **overall patterns**:

1) There's been an **increase** in the **diversity** of families in the UK. There are more **different kinds** of family.

2) **The nuclear family** is still the most **common** type of family, though the **proportion** of nuclear families is going down.

Rapoport and Rapoport (1982) Identified Five Types of Family Diversity

Organisational diversity	**Differences** in the way families are **structured**, e.g. whether they're nuclear, extended, reconstituted or any other form.
Cultural diversity	Differences that arise from the different **norms** and **values** of **different cultures**.
Class diversity	Different **views** are often held by **different parts of society** concerning families. For example, more **affluent families** are more likely to send their children to **boarding** school than **poorer families**, leading to a different **relationship** between the parents and children.
Life-course diversity	**Diversity** caused by the **different stages** people have reached in their lives. E.g. **family relationships** tend to be different for newly-weds with children, childless couples, and people with grown-up children. *People can reach each stage of the life-course at different ages.*
Cohort diversity	Differences created by the **historical periods** the family have lived through. For example, children who reached maturity in the **1980s** may have remained **dependent** on their parents for longer due to **high unemployment**.

Increasing Individualism and Personal Choice is Linked to Family Diversity

Giddens (1992) argues that **individual choice** dictates family relationships — he calls this the **'individualisation thesis'**.

1) **Rigid class, gender and family roles** used to stop people from choosing their own **life-course** — he argues that these fixed roles **no longer exist** and people are free to make their own decisions.

2) People do not have to stay in relationships because of **fixed social expectations** — they are free to separate and go on to form **different types of families**, e.g. lone-parent families and multi-family households.

Postmodernists claim that there is no longer a **single dominant family structure** — postmodern society is **highly diverse** and its diversity is **increasing**. They see this diversity and fragmentation as the **new norm**.

- Improvements in **women's rights** and the availability of **contraception** have resulted in people having far more **choice** in their type of relationship.

- People now tend to create their relationships to **suit their own needs** rather than following the **traditional values** of **religion** or the **government**.

- Their relationships only last as long as their needs are **met** — creating even greater **diversity** and **instability**.

Postmodernists emphasise the rise of individualism as a crucial feature of postmodern society.

Family Diversity — Changing Family Patterns

Fewer People Marry and More People Live Together Instead

Marriage rates have **fallen** since the **early 20th century**. In 2009, the **lowest** number of **marriages** took place in the England and Wales since records began. However, the marriage rate began to **increase** again in 2010.

This does NOT mean a decline in family life, though:

1) While **marriage rates** have **fallen**, there has been an **increase** in the number of adults **cohabiting** in the last few decades. There were **nearly 1 million more** cohabiting couples in the UK **2014** than there were in **2001**.

2) **Duncan and Phillips (2013)** have discovered that the number of people who are in a **serious relationship** but who are **not** cohabiting or married may be as many as **half** of the single population of Great Britain. They are classed as **'living apart together'**.

3) **Social trends statistics** show that living with a partner doesn't mean you **won't** get married — it often just means a **delay** in tying the knot.

4) People are getting married **later** in life — between 1971 and 2011, the **average age** of men and women getting married in England and Wales **increased** by 8 years.

5) **Men tend to die** before women. **Widowed pensioners** make up a lot of **single-person households**. The **population** of the UK is **ageing** (see p.73), so this helps explain why there are so many single-person households.

The proportion of births outside marriage in England and Wales has increased rapidly since 1980 to 47% in 2013 — this change is largely due to the increase in cohabiting couples who are in serious relationships.

Divorce and Separation are Common in England and Wales

1) There's been a **steady rise** in the **divorce rate** in most **modern industrial societies**.

2) More than **40%** of all marriages in England and Wales end in divorce.

3) **Since 2000**, the percentage of marriages ending in divorce has **fallen** — this is related to people **marrying later** in their **life-course** and the increasing number of couples who **cohabit** before getting married.

4) **Serial monogamy** (having **several serious sexual relationships** one after another) is increasingly **common** in the UK — a significant number of divorces are granted to people who have been **married** and **divorced before**.

5) **Separation** often precedes divorce — in 2011, **32%** of divorces secured by **men** and **22%** by **women** followed **2 years** of separation. In the same year, **16%** of divorces for **men** and **9%** for **women** were granted after **5 years** of separation.

There are several **social**, **cultural** and **political** factors that explain why divorce is increasing in the UK:

- Divorce has become easier to obtain — it's now more **available**.
- Divorce is more **socially acceptable**.
- Women may have **higher expectations** of marriage, and **better employment opportunities** may make them less financially dependent on their husbands.
- Marriages are increasingly focused on **individual emotional fulfilment**.

Availability and acceptability are the buzz words in the debate on divorce.

The **link** between divorce and marriage breakdown isn't completely straightforward. You **can't** **assume** that **fewer divorces** in the past meant **happier marriages** — a marriage can break down but the couple still **stay married** and live together. This is called an **empty-shell marriage**.

Practice Questions

Q1 Which household types have increased in the UK in recent years?

Q2 Give five types of family diversity.

Q3 Why have single-person households become more common in the UK in recent years?

Exam Question

Q1 Analyse two explanations for why family diversity has increased since the mid 20th century. [10 marks]

86% of people get bored of reading about divorce statistics...

Sometimes I wonder what sociologists would do without all of those handy official government statistics floating around out there. Anyway, jot down your own list of trends in the size of the family, the number of single-person households, the number of divorces and the number of people who are cohabiting. You have to know which are going up and which are going down.

Demography and the Family

These pages will explore changes in the demography of the UK since 1900 and the impact of these changes on UK society.

Population Size is Affected by **Births**, **Deaths** and **Migration**

Demography is the study of the statistics that measure the **size** and **growth** of a **population** (e.g. birth and death rates).

1) A population generally **increases** when **birth** rates are higher than **death** (**mortality**) rates. **Low fertility** or **high mortality** rates lead to a **decline** in population, as too few children are born to **replace** those dying.

2) **Immigration** into a country causes the population to **increase**, while **emigration** away from a country **decreases** the population.

Birth and **Fertility** Rates Have **Decreased**

The **birth rate** has **fallen** since the **early 20th century**. In **2014** there were nearly **700 000** births in England and Wales — there were **1 million** in 1901. Fertility was **unusually high** after the **First** and **Second World Wars** and in the **1960s** — those born in these periods are called **baby-boomers**. The birth rate has **fluctuated** since the mid-1970s and is now **falling**.

• The **total fertility rate** (**TFR**) is the **average number** of children a woman would have if she followed the current fertility rates throughout her life. The TFR has generally **decreased** in England and Wales since the early 20th century — in **2014**, it was **1.83 children per woman**. There were unusual **peaks** in **fertility** during the **baby booms** of the 20th century.

• **Completed family size** (**CFS**) is the average number of children for a woman born in a specific year. In **England and Wales**, for example, a woman born in **1968** has a CFS of **1.92 children** compared to **2.34** for a woman born in **1941**.

People are Having **Fewer Children** and Having them **Later in Life**

Government statistics for **England and Wales** show that **childbearing trends** have changed in recent decades.

• People are having **fewer children**. The average number of dependent children per family was **2.0** in **1971**, compared to **1.7** in **2011**.

• Women are having children **later**. The average age of a woman at the birth of her first child was **24** in **1971**, compared to **28** in **2013**.

• More people are **not having children at all** — **9%** of women born in **1945** were childless at age **45**, compared to **20%** of women born in **1966**.

1) Social changes have influenced these trends. **Contraception** is more readily available and **women's roles are changing**. The emphasis on the **individual in post-industrial society** is a key factor.

2) Children are **expensive** and **time-consuming**, and couples may choose to spend their **time** and **money** in other ways. The **conflict** between wanting a **successful working life** and being a **mum** has made many women **put off having kids until later**.

Mortality and **Death** Rates Have Also **Fallen** Dramatically **Since 1900**

• Infant Mortality Rates, or IMR (the number of deaths of children aged 0 to 1 per 1000 live births), and childhood mortality dramatically improved in the first half of the 20th century. In 1901, 16.6% of boys and 13.6% of girls in England and Wales died before their first birthday — infant mortality is now less than 0.5%.

• Adult mortality has also fallen — the number of deaths per year has stayed roughly the same since 1901, but the increase in population in the 20th century means that the proportion of deaths has actually fallen.

1) **Medical advancements** in the second half of the **20th century** reduced mortality — the introduction of **vaccines**, **blood transfusions**, **antibiotics**, and better care for **pregnant women** meant that more people **survived serious illness** and **childbirth**. The creation of the NHS in **1948** made health care **free** and **accessible** to all.

2) The government **improved public health** by **regulating** food and drinking-water quality and enforcing **laws** to **improve cleanliness**. Improved public **awareness** of how infections are **transmitted** also led to a decline in disease.

3) **McKeown (1972)** thought that **better nutrition** was a major factor in improving mortality rates in the UK because people were more able to **fight off infection**. Critics of McKeown point out that cases of **some diseases** (like measles) **rose** as nutrition improved.

Demography and the Family

The Overall **Population** of the UK is **Ageing**

Life expectancy is the average length of time a person is expected to live. **Falling mortality** rates have led to **increased life expectancy** — 1 in 3 babies born in **2013** will have a life expectancy of **100**. **Falling infant mortality** is largely responsible for this improvement, but other factors linked to **public health** have also contributed to the trend.

The UK has an ageing population

A population **ages** when the **number** and **proportion** of older people increases. This causes the **median age** of the population (the age when **half** of the population is **younger** and **half** is **older**) to increase. A population needs a **TFR** of **2.1** to replace the **existing** population — this is called the **replacement level**.

1) The proportion of **over 65s** in the UK is **increasing** — almost a **quarter** of the UK population is expected to be **over 65** by **2035**. The proportion of **over 85s** in the UK has **doubled** since 1985.

2) Improvement in **mortality** rates and **increasing life expectancy** mean that more people now live **past the age of 65**.

3) When the **TFR** falls below replacement level, an **ageing population** develops. The **decline** in **fertility** rates since the **late 1970s** to below **replacement level** means that fewer children are being born.

> These trends have created beanpole families (p.70), which include several generations. Older generations of the family are living longer and there are fewer family members in each generation.

4) As a result, the **proportion** of young people in the UK is **decreasing** compared to older age groups. The **proportion** of older people in the UK is also set to **increase** as the **baby boomers** born after the **Second World War** reach their **late 80s** and the **1960s baby boomers** move into their **60s** and **70s**.

An **Ageing Population** Changes the **Burden of Care** in Society

1) Society has a **responsibility** to care for the **vulnerable** (e.g. children and older people) — this responsibility is called the **burden of care**, and it puts pressure on resources.

2) The burden of care shifts towards **older** people in an ageing population — at the same time, there is a decline in the proportion of **working-age** people. This **increases** the **dependency ratio** and the young **struggle** to **meet** the needs of older people.

> The dependency ratio is the number of people who are not of working age, compared to the number of working-age people who can support them (e.g. by paying taxes).

Hirsch (2005) suggests that people will either have to **work into their 60s and 70s** or **pay more taxes** during their working life to contribute towards the cost of **health** and **social care** in later life. He argues that **single pensioners** compete for housing with **single young people**. This makes house prices **rise**. Hirsch points out that older people often own their own homes, but young people have **fewer assets** (possessions and property), so they **lose out**.

In the **late 1980s**, the government commissioned **the Griffiths Report** on **care in the community**. The report looked at the **long-term care** of mentally ill, disabled and older members of society with the aim of making it **more efficient**.

1) Care of older people leaving hospital used to be carried out by various **NHS services** — this responsibility was shifted to **local council social services**. This was part of a movement away from **institutionalisation** (placing people in group homes, hospitals etc.) towards **care in the home**.

2) Delivering more minor **health** and **social** care in the **home** has improved the **independence** and **comfort** of older people who do not want to move into **retirement homes** or do not need **24-hour care**. However, since the **financial crisis** in **2008**, the government has given **less money** to local councils — this has resulted in **cuts** to **services**.

Poverty in Old Age is Linked to **Social Class**, **Gender** and **Ageism**

Ageism (discrimination against older people because of their age) tends to **increase** in ageing populations — the needs of older people are often seen as a problem. Ageism also involves underestimating the **value** of older people to society.

1) **Peter Townsend (1979)** studied **poverty** in the UK — he discovered that there was a **higher proportion** of older people in poverty compared to younger people. He argued that an **underclass** of pensioners developed because older people could no longer rely on **income from employment** (see p.83 for more on age and poverty).

2) People with **higher status** during their working lives were **less likely** to be in poverty in old age than people who were in a **low-status job** (who are **more likely** to have suffered **unemployment** and **illness** during their working life).

3) He linked this idea to **social class** — people who were in **poverty** throughout their working life were **less** likely to have **savings** and **private pensions** to support themselves in old age.

4) **Pilcher (1995)** argues that both **class** and **gender** affect income in retirement. Women often have **smaller** pensions because they might take time **away** from work while still of working age to care for children.

Demography and the Family

Net Migration Has Significantly Increased Since the Second World War

In the UK, **net migration** (the number of people **moving into** a country **minus** the number **moving away**) reached a high of **330 000** in the year 2014-15. The **foreign-born** population of England and Wales **nearly doubled** between **1991** and **2011**.

1) Before the Second World War, the **foreign-born population** of the UK was very **low**. After the war, a **labour shortage** prompted the government to encourage Polish soldiers to move to the UK.
2) The **British Nationality Act of 1948** made it easier for citizens of the **British Commonwealth** (countries that used to be part of the British Empire) to settle in the UK. This led to a wave of **mass immigration**.
3) Until the **1980s**, **emigration** from the UK to countries like **Australia** and **the USA** largely **matched** immigration into Britain. However, **mass immigration** in the 1990s **outstripped** emigration and **net migration** rose rapidly.
4) In the late **1990s**, **war** and **political conflicts** in South Africa, Afghanistan, Iraq, Somalia, Sri Lanka and Kosovo led to an **increase** in applications for **asylum** (protection) in the UK — applications **peaked in 2002** at just over **84 000**.
5) Between **2004** and **2007**, **new countries** joined the EU and **free movement** (allowing Europeans to move freely within the EU) was introduced. **New EU migrants** arrived in the UK and contributed to **rising net migration**.

Increasing Net Migration Has Affected the Structure of Society and Families

1) The impact of **low fertility rates** on population size in the UK is **outweighed** by the impact of net migration.
2) Migrants **decrease** the **average age** of a country, as they tend to be **young** and of **working age**. Immigration **decreases** the dependency ratio (p.73) by **increasing** the number of people able to **support** children and older people.
3) The fertility rate for mothers **not born in the UK** is **higher** than that of mothers **born in the UK**. While this **increases** the dependency ratio by increasing the number of **children** in the population, the impact is **temporary** because children of migrants will reach working age and go on to **decrease** the dependency ratio.
4) Increasing net migration has also led to an increase in **multi-family households** (see p.70 for more on this).

Globalisation Has Increased International Migration

Globalisation happens when nations become more **connected** and **barriers** separating societies are **broken down** — this leads to more **international migration** and more **diverse reasons** for migration.

1) Since the **1990s**, British society has become far more **ethnically diverse** — migrants have brought different **cultures** and **religions** to the UK, which has created a **multicultural society**.
2) Globalisation results in different reasons for migration — over half of the **visas** granted by the UK government between **June 2014** and **June 2015** were for **educational** purposes, while more than a **quarter** were granted to **economic migrants** (people moving for work).

Eriksen (2007) argues that migrants in a globalised world tend to form **transnational identities** — they do not belong to a **single** country but a **network** of countries across the world. They are less likely to **assimilate** (learn the **language** of a country or adapt to its **culture**) because they do not see it as a **permanent** home. Immigration becomes a **political** issue — governments have to decide whether to promote **assimilation** or accept **multiculturalism**.

Practice Questions

Q1 How have birth and death rates in England and Wales changed since 1901?
Q2 Name three things that have caused mortality rates to fall in England and Wales.
Q3 Give two main reasons why the UK population is ageing.
Q4 What is meant by 'dependency ratio'?
Q5 What is globalisation and how has it affected UK society?

Exam Question

Q1 Evaluate the idea that an ageing population has a negative impact on society. [20 marks]

Net revision = total time revising minus time spent watching cat videos...

You need to know how demographic trends have affected families and wider society. Net migration and the UK's ageing population have had a big impact. Make sure you know what sociologists have said about why these changes are happening.

Family Diversity and Social Change

Sociologists have different theories about family diversity — some argue that the nuclear family is still the most common family structure. Others think that your social identity (see p.1) influences the type of household you live in.

Functionalists *Think that the Growth in Diversity has been* Exaggerated

1) The functionalist **Robert Chester (1985)** admits that there has been **some growth** in family diversity, but believes that the **nuclear family** remains the dominant family structure.

2) He argues that statistics show a **greater increase** in diversity than is actually happening. This is because **UK society** has an **ageing population** (see p.73) — the proportion of older people is **increasing**. This increases the number of people who are at a stage in their life when they're **not in a nuclear family**.

Death rates have fallen for several reasons, e.g. improving standards of living, advances in health care and a decrease in manual, heavy labour jobs (Social Trends 38, 2008).

3) Chester has also suggested that nuclear families are becoming **less traditional** and **more symmetrical** (see p.63) to better fit modern living.

The New Right *think Family Diversity is* Caused *by Falling Moral Standards*

1) **New Right** theorists believe that family diversity is the result of a **decline** in traditional values. They see it as a **threat** to the traditional nuclear family and blame it for **antisocial behaviour** and **crime**.

2) **Murray (1989)** suggests that **single-mother** families are a principle cause of crime and social decay, because of the **lack** of a **male role model** and authority figure in the home.

The New Right have been criticised for their 'blame the victim' approach.

3) The New Right believe that **state benefits** should be **cut** and social policy targeted to **discourage** family diversity and **promote** marriage and the nuclear family.

The Sociology of Personal Life *Focuses on* Individual Families

The **sociology of personal life** looks at families from a different angle — it focuses on what the families themselves see as important in their lives rather than what sociologists **believe** is important.

1) The **individualisation thesis** states that people don't have to conform to **strict family roles** (see p.70). **Vanessa May (2013)** argues that it is based on an **idealised view** of freedom of choice. It **ignores** the differing levels of **choice** available to those who are not **white, middle-class males** — **social identity** affects ability to choose.

2) **Carol Smart (2007)** says that the term '**family**' is often linked to **traditional** ideas about family. She thinks the term '**personal life**' is better for studying family relationships, because it includes the **newer** kinds of relationships that exist in **postmodern** society.

3) Smart offers an **alternative** to the individualisation thesis — the **connectedness thesis** argues that individual choices are influenced by **relationships** and **past experiences**. **Class** and **gender** also influence our options where **structural inequalities** exist.

Alex couldn't escape his family's obsession with doing the conga.

4) Smart and May both accept that **family diversity** has increased, but they believe that the importance of **individual choice** is more **limited** than postmodernists suggest.

Ethnicity *Can Influence* Family Type *and* Household Structure

Immigration has had an impact on **family diversity** in England and Wales — the **2011** census found that a **higher proportion** of people who were **born abroad** lived in **multi-family households**, compared to people **born in the UK**. Also, in England and Wales, those born in **Bangladesh** or **Pakistan** were **most likely** to live in **extended families** with dependent children.

A study of ethnic minorities in the UK by Modood et al (1997) found that:

1) Whites and African-Caribbeans were most likely to be divorced. Indians, Pakistanis, Bangladeshis and African Asians were most likely to be married.

2) African-Caribbean households were the most likely to be lone-parent families — there is thought to be a higher proportion of matrifocal families (where women are the head) in African-Caribbean households in the UK.

3) South Asian families are traditionally extended families, but there are more nuclear family households than in the past. Extended kinship links stay strong and often reach back to India, Pakistan or Bangladesh.

4) However, there's diversity within each ethnic group.

Family Diversity and Social Change

Class and Sexuality Also Affect Which Types of Family You Experience

1) **Eversley and Bonnerjea (1982)** found that **middle-class** areas in the UK have a **higher** than average proportion of **nuclear families**. Inner-city **working-class areas** are more likely to have a higher proportion of **lone-parent households**.

2) **Weeks, Donovan et al (1999)** found that there had been an increase in the number of **gay** or **lesbian** households since the 1980s. This is due to changes in **attitudes** and **legislation**.

3) **Fertility treatments** have allowed **gay and lesbian** couples (and **single** and **older women**) to have children when they wouldn't have been able to before. This means that **family structures** exist that were **impossible** in the past.

Some Sociologists Say You Can Choose Who to Include in Your Family

The postmodernist **Beck** (1992) believes many people now live in '**negotiated families**' — family units that vary according to needs of the people in them. Negotiated families are **more equal** than nuclear families, but **less stable**.

Some sociologists argue that groups who do not fit the **traditional structure of a nuclear family** can often **decide** who they consider as family — **same-sex couples** and **lone-parent families** can choose **supportive people** to be part of their family.

Stacey (1998) has highlighted the existence of the '**divorce-extended family**' where mostly female members of an extended family stay connected by **choice** after divorce. A woman may **choose** to stay connected with her former **mother-in-law** or form a new relationship with her **ex-husband's new partner**. This is a result of **greater individualism** among women — they are able to form a **new family structure** based on their own **needs**.

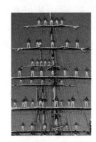

Once you start building a negotiated family, it can be pretty hard to stop.

Weeks, Donovan et al (1999) suggested that family commitment is now viewed as a matter of **ongoing negotiation** rather than something that lasts forever once entered into. **Weeks (2000)** believes that personal **morality** has become an **individual choice**, rather than a set of values influenced by **religion** or dictated by **society**. He sees modern **liberal attitudes** towards marriage, divorce, cohabitation and homosexuality as a major cause of **irreversible** diversity.

Weston (1992) has observed that **same-sex couples** often form a 'family of choice' by surrounding themselves with **supportive** members of their friends and family.

Practice Questions

Q1 Why do functionalists think that the growth in family diversity has been exaggerated?

Q2 On what grounds do New Right theorists oppose family diversity?

Q3 How has immigration contributed to changing family structure in the UK?

Q4 Give two examples of 'negotiated families'.

Exam Questions

Q1 Outline two ways that social identity contributes to family diversity. Explain each one. [10 marks]

Q2 Apply your own knowledge and material from Item A to evaluate the idea that family diversity is a result of weakening traditional values. [20 marks]

> **Item A**
> Sociologists have many theories about the causes of family diversity. Some sociologists argue that family diversity is a result of people abandoning traditional morals, with increasing acceptance of divorce and cohabitation. Immigration has also been highlighted as a contributing factor, as family types vary by ethnic group. Alternatively, some sociologists argue that family diversity has been exaggerated because the nuclear family is still the most common family type in the UK.

Have you met the nuclear family? They make you feel right at-om...

The New Right think family diversity is the result of falling standards, Carol Smart reckons class and gender are more important than personal choice when it comes to family type, and Jeffrey Weeks thinks everyone just makes their own mind up. At least everyone agrees that diversity is increasing. Well, except functionalists. They say that families are just more symmetrical. Weird.

Childhood

These pages examine the social construction of childhood, the position of children in today's society, and the future of childhood.

Childhood is Partly a **Social Construct**

1) Sociologists say **childhood** is not only a **biological stage of development** but a **social construct** as well. The idea of how children are **different** from adults in their **values, behaviour** and **attitudes** isn't the same **everywhere** in the world, and it hasn't been the same for all **times**. In other words, it's **not universal** — different societies, with different **cultures** and **values**, can view childhood in different ways.

2) An example of this is how the age that you can **leave education** in Britain has moved from 12 to 18 in the last century. It would now be not only **socially unacceptable**, but also **illegal**, to leave school and **work full-time** at the age of 12.

3) The minimum legal age for **marriage** in Britain rose to **16** in **1929** — before that, girls could be married at **12** and boys at **14** (although in England and Wales they needed **parental permission**). Effectively, the age at which **childhood ends** and **adulthood begins** has moved in line with social attitudes.

4) **Jane Pilcher (1995)** highlighted the **separateness** of childhood from other **life phases**. Children have different **rights** and **duties** from adults, and are **regulated** and **protected** by special **laws**.

Ariès says a **Cult of Childhood** Developed After Industrialisation

Sociologist Philippe Ariès' work on the **construction of childhood** is a classic study.

> ### Ariès (1962) looked at paintings
>
> Ariès said that the concept of **childhood** in Western European society has only existed in the **last 300 years**. Before this, in **medieval** society, a child took on the role of an adult as soon as it was **physically able**. Children in medieval paintings look like **mini-adults**.
>
> With **industrialisation**, social attitudes changed and people began to **value** children as needing **specialised care and nurturing**. The importance of the child reinforced the importance of the role of the **housewife** — it was the housewife's job to look after children.
>
> This '**cult of the child**', as Ariès referred to it, first developed in the **middle classes** and over time has become a part of **working-class values**.

Although Ariès' work is very important, he has been criticised — e.g. **Pollack (1983)** says that Ariès' work looks **weak** because it uses paintings for its **main evidence**.

Functionalists See the Position of Children in Society as a **Sign of Progress**

Some functionalist sociologists, including **Shorter (1975)**, make the '**march of progress**' argument:

1) Society has a functional need for **better-educated** citizens and **lower infant mortality rates**.
2) So school leaving ages have **gone up** and child protection has **improved**.
3) That means that the current position of children is the result of **positive progression** from the past.

The **Status** of Children Has **Changed** — Society is More **Child-Focused**

1) **Donzelot (1977)** has observed that theories of **child development** changed in the **19th century** — they began to argue that children needed to be **protected** and **supervised**. He linked this to **growing medical interest** in childhood development.

2) **Infant mortality** has dramatically **decreased** since the **early 20th century**. In **1901** just over **150** children aged under one died per 1000 children, but in **2012**, this rate had fallen to **3.9** deaths per 1000 children.

3) Families are also getting **smaller**. Fewer children die in infancy and families are **having fewer children** on average. **More attention is devoted** to each child and **more money is being spent** on their development, both within the family and wider society.

4) This is linked to the '**march of progress**' argument, which suggests that families are increasingly **child-focused** — parents want a **better life** for their children than they have experienced themselves.

Harry's family found an alternative to surrounding him in cotton wool.

Childhood

Children are Protected by *Special Laws*

1) Children are subject to laws that restrict their **sexual behaviour**, their **access to alcohol and tobacco**, and the amount of **paid work** they can perform. These laws act **in addition** to the laws that affect adults.

2) Children are offered **additional protection** by the **Children Act 1989**, which allows them to be **taken away from their parents** by the state if it judges the parents to be **incapable** or **unsuitable**.

3) But organisations such as the **National Society for the Prevention of Cruelty to Children** (the **NSPCC**) argue that they need greater protection. An NSPCC report by **Cawson et al (2000)** said that **16%** of children aged under 16 have experienced **sexual abuse** during childhood, and **25%** of children have experienced **physical violence**.

Child Liberationists Believe that Society *Oppresses* Children

Some see the increased **protection** of children and their **separation** from adult life as **oppressive**.

Diana Gittins (1985) argues that there is an 'age patriarchy' — adults maintain authority over children. They achieve this using enforced dependency through 'protection' from paid employment, legal controls over what children can and can't do, and in extreme cases abuse and neglect.

Hockey and James (1993) noted that childhood was a stage that most children wished to escape from and which many resisted.

Childhood *Varies* according to *Class*, *Gender* and *Ethnicity*

Some sociologists suggest that the **experience** of childhood varies depending on class, gender and ethnicity:

1) Children living in **poverty** tend to suffer **poorer health**, a lack of **basic necessities**, **lower achievement** in school, poorer life chances, and higher incidences of **neglect** and **abuse**. Children from low-income, **working-class families** are more likely to live in poverty — in **2013-14**, **17%** of children in the UK were living in **low-income households**.

2) **June Statham and Charlie Owens (2007)** found that **black** and **dual-heritage** children were **more likely** to end up in **care** than white or Asian children.

3) **Ethnicity** may **influence** where a child **lives**. For example, in England and Wales in **2011**, **22%** of **white British** people lived in rural areas, compared to **1%** of **Bangladeshis** and **Pakistanis**.

Households earning less than 60% of the median income.

4) **Julia Brannen (1994)** said that **Asian** families were much **stricter** with their **daughters** than their **sons**.

5) **Hillman et al (1990)** studied children aged 7 to 15 and found that parents generally give **boys** more **freedom** than **girls** to travel around their local areas **unaccompanied**, **cross roads**, and go out **after dark**.

6) **Bonke (1999)** has discovered that **girls** perform more **household chores** than boys — this trend is particularly true in **lone-parent** households.

Ideas of Childhood are *Different* in Different *Cultures*

Wagg (1992) argues that the construction of childhood **varies** across different **historical** and **cultural** societies. Because of these **cross-cultural differences**, children are not always seen as **vulnerable** and can have a **similar status** to adults.

Punch (2001) found that children growing up in the countryside in Bolivia were given responsibilities and work to perform at the age of 5. This contrasts with Western attitudes towards child labour that have developed since industrialisation.

Katz (2004) has found that Sudanese children have far more freedom to explore and travel around their local area than children in Western societies.

Children in less industrialised societies are often treated differently to children living in Western societies. Some argue that ideas of **Western childhood** are **projected** onto different cultures.

Judith Ennew (1986) argued that **humanitarian** and **welfare work** is often based on the belief that Western childhood is the '**correct childhood**'. The idea that childhood should be a **separate**, more **innocent** stage of life can be projected through this work onto cultures that may have **different views** on the needs of children.

Childhood

British Society Today is More Child-Focused than Ever

1) Children are now recognised as having unique **human rights**. The **United Nations Convention on the Rights of the Child** was ratified (agreed to) in 1990 by all the UN members (except the USA and Somalia).

2) In Britain, the **Child Support Act 1991** established the **Child Support Agency**. This gave children the legal right to be **financially supported** by their parents, whether the parents are **living with the child or not**. This Act also made courts have to ask for the **child's point of view** in custody cases and take the child's view into consideration.

Advertisers recognise the **financial power** of children — this is often referred to as **'pester power'**. They advertise a product to children because they know the children will **pester** their parents to buy the product.

Sociologists Have Looked at the Impact of Postmodern Society on Childhood

1) **Jenks (2005)** argues that the **20th century** was focused on the **'futurity'** of the child — children symbolised **future potential** and were the main concern of society. Adults **sacrificed** their needs to **protect** and **nurture** children.

2) Jenks believes that adult relationships are now **less dependable** due to **divorce** becoming more common — adults prioritise their relationships with children instead of **investing trust** in relationships with **friends** and **partners**.

3) Adults see children through a lens of **nostalgia** — children **represent** a lot of the things that **society has lost** over time (like **innocence**). This has led to increased **protection** and **surveillance** of children.

4) Critics of Jenks' theory say he makes too many **generalisations**.

5) **Palmer (2007)** believes children are now experiencing **'toxic childhood'** — children's lives are more **violent, stressful,** and **sexually active**, which leads to **teenage pregnancy, obesity, self-harm** and **addiction** to alcohol and drugs. She also argues that children's **development** has been **damaged** by the increasing speed of **technological advancement**.

Sociologists Disagree over the Future of Childhood

1) **Neil Postman (1994)** believes that childhood is **disappearing**.
2) Children grow up **very quickly** and experience things only available to adults in the past.
3) This is due to a **shift** from **print** and literary culture to **visual** culture. Lack of **literacy** is no longer a barrier to the adult world — children can access it through **watching TV**.
4) He argues that our definitions of 'childhood' and 'adulthood' will need to be **changed** soon.

1) **Nick Lee (2005)** disagrees with Postman.
2) He agrees that childhood has become an **ambiguous** area, but argues that parents have **financial control** and children can only spend as much as their parents allow.
3) So the **paradox of childhood** is one of **dependence** and **independence** at the same time.
4) **Opie (1993)** argues that **childhood culture** still exists **independently** of adult influence.

Practice Questions

Q1 Explain the view that childhood is partly a social construct.
Q2 Describe how functionalists see the role of children in society.
Q3 How do class, ethnicity and gender influence a person's experience of childhood? Give examples.
Q4 Give two ways in which 21st century British society could be said to be more child-focused than before.
Q5 What arguments have been put forward to support the view that childhood is disappearing?

Exam Questions

Q1 Outline two reasons for the change in status of children since industrialisation. Explain each one. [10 marks]

Q2 Evaluate the idea that cross-cultural differences affect experiences of childhood. [20 marks]

Here's looking at you, kid...

It's all a bit dramatic really. Toxic childhoods. Disappearing innocence. Evil parent overlords ruling children. Ahem... sorry... got a bit carried away there. The main ideas on these pages are that childhood is partly socially constructed and that theories about it are not universally accepted. It's not enough to say that something is a 'social construct' — you need to say how and why.

Definitions of Poverty

Poverty is basically about not having enough money. However, sociologists don't all agree on exactly what constitutes poverty, and how badly off you must be to be 'in poverty'. There are quite a few definitions...

Absolute Poverty is a Lack of the Minimum Requirements for Survival

1) An individual is in absolute **poverty** if they can't afford the basic necessities — **food**, **warmth** and **shelter**.

2) **Rowntree (1871-1954)** set up the first major studies of poverty in the UK in **1899** and measured it in absolute terms. He made a **list of essentials** needed for life and recorded how many families could **afford** them. Those whose income was **too low** were classed as **in poverty**. People were shocked that a large proportion of **York** was in poverty.

3) There are criticisms of Rowntree's study. His definition of poverty didn't allow for any wasted food and it assumed the **cheapest** options were **always available**. The lists were compiled by **experts** and **didn't match the lifestyle** of the folk he surveyed. He did listen to his critics though, and for two further studies (published in 1941 and 1951), he **added more items** to the list of essentials. By this time, **more people** could afford the basics on the list. His conclusion was that **poverty was disappearing fast** in 20th century Britain.

4) Another **study of poverty in absolute terms** is **Drewnowski and Scott (1966)**. They devised a **"level of living index"** which worked out the income needed for **basic needs**, adding **cultural needs** to the list. However, it's debatable whether cultural needs like TV should be included in a study of **absolute** poverty.

> Measuring absolute poverty means making assumptions about people's basic needs. It also assumes that everyone has the same basic needs. It disregards information about occupation, gender and age that might be relevant to deciding someone's basic needs.

Bradshaw (1990) Devised the Budget Standard Measure of Poverty

1) **Bradshaw (1990)** used an approach similar to Rowntree's idea of **absolute poverty**. He studied the **spending patterns** of the least wealthy and used those patterns to calculate an **adequate budget**. Anyone earning less than the adequate budget was classed as **"poor"**.

2) The main difference between the approaches was that Bradshaw studied how people **actually spend their money** whereas Rowntree assumed people weren't poor if they earned more than the **usual total cost of essential items**.

3) Because Bradshaw's test isn't relative (see below), it gives clear and unambiguous statistics that are easy to **compare** between different studies. However, critics have argued that Bradshaw set a **very low 'adequate budget'**, so his conclusions are not a **true reflection of deprivation** in society.

Relative Poverty is a Comparison with the Average Standard of Living

1) Many sociologists favour the **relative** definition of poverty. This considers whether an individual is rich or poor in **relation** to **other people** in their society, rather than whether people have the basics like food and shelter.

2) The **downside** of relative poverty is that some people will always **appear to be "poor"**. Also, if the rich get richer **more quickly** than the poor get richer, then relative poverty will **increase** even though the lives of the poor **improve**.

Townsend (1979) Introduced the Concept of Relative Deprivation

1) **Townsend (1979)** devised a **"deprivation index"** — a list of 60 things **central to life** in the UK. The list included **social activities**, such as inviting other people over for meals, and **possessions**, such as owning a refrigerator.

2) From his list of 60 things, he selected **12** that he thought were **equally essential to the whole population**.

3) He then gave each household a **deprivation score** based on whether or not they had the items on his shortlist of 12 items.

4) Looking at his statistics, he found that the deprivation score **went up rapidly** after wealth dropped **below a certain threshold**. The threshold was about 150% of the 1979 basic supplementary benefit levels (now called income support).

5) So he said all households **earning below the threshold** were **"suffering from poverty"**.

6) Townsend calculated that **22.9%** of the population were suffering from relative poverty.

Barney was well stocked in all his essential life items.

- **Piachaud (1987)** has argued that Townsend's deprivation index is too **subjective** and **culturally biased**, citing shortlist items such as having **cooked breakfasts** and **Sunday joints**.

- **Wedderburn** also criticised Townsend's method for creating the deprivation index. She argued that he should have carried out **research** into the customary behaviour of people in society. It seemed to her as though he had just picked items based on his own **cultural opinions**.

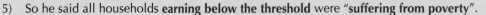

Definitions of Poverty

Mack and Lansley (1985) Measured Poverty using a Consensual Approach

1) Mack and Lansley (1985) measured poverty in a similar way to Townsend, but acted on some of the criticisms his work had received. They defined poverty to be "an enforced lack of socially perceived necessities".

2) They used a survey to determine which items to include on their list of perceived necessities. They asked respondents what they considered to be the necessities. Any items that were classified as essential by over 50% of the respondents were added to their list. They ended up with a list of 22 items.

3) They then surveyed households to find out what they lacked. Households could answer that they had the item, didn't want the item, or wanted but couldn't afford the item. Only those who said the latter were considered deprived. Mack and Lansley therefore argued that their figures would only reflect involuntary deprivation.

4) If a household involuntarily lacked three or more items from the list of necessities then they were classified as poor.

5) Mack and Lansley reported that 14% of the British population were living in poverty in 1983. When they repeated the study in 1990, they found that this figure had risen to 21%. In 2012, a Poverty and Social Exclusion (PSE) report found that 33% of the population were living in poverty according to this method.

6) The list of necessities changes over time — e.g. a telephone was considered a necessity in the 1990 study whereas it hadn't been in the 1983 survey. Critics have argued that because the surveys didn't produce the same list of necessities, the results are not directly comparable.

Subjective Poverty — whether people Think they're in Poverty

1) **Subjective poverty** is based on **how** poor people **feel**. It's their **own evaluation** of how much money they **need** to live a decent life. It all depends on their **expectations**.

2) Subjective poverty studies ask **questions** such as 'What **income** do you think is **necessary** to keep a household such as yours out of poverty?', and 'How far **above or below** that level is your household's income?'.

3) The Poverty and Social Exclusion Survey (2000) found that the proportion of people who consider **themselves** to be in poverty was **similar** to the 'scientific' consensual poverty figure. This means subjective poverty is a **good way** of assessing how **widespread** poverty is (although the **same people** aren't necessarily 'in poverty' according to **both** measures).

Social Exclusion — when people Can't Participate in Society

1) Social exclusion is about a much **wider range of deprivation** than just being short of money. It involves not being able to **participate** in **normal activities**, whether economic, social, cultural or political, as well as not being able to **access services**.

2) The **government** said social exclusion can occur when "people or areas suffer from a **combination** of **linked problems** such as unemployment, poor skills, low incomes, poor housing, high crime environments, bad health and family breakdown."

3) Factors such as **age** and **disability** contribute to social exclusion, but the Poverty and Social Exclusion Survey (2000) found that **poverty** has the **biggest effect**.

4) These problems trap people in a "**spiral of disadvantage**" (Department of Social Security, 1999) and **limit their opportunities**, as well as those of their children. For example, low income may mean having to live in an area with poor schools, reducing their children's later chances.

Practice Questions

Q1 What is absolute poverty?

Q2 Outline how Townsend measured relative poverty.

Q3 List three problems that can combine to cause social exclusion.

Exam Question

Q1 Outline two reasons why sociologists disagree about whether someone is in poverty. Explain each one.

[10 marks]

Poverty is a bad thing, no matter how you measure it...

Many people think that absolute poverty isn't much of a problem in the UK. However, the dramatic rise in the number of people needing to use food banks over recent years may suggest otherwise. Learn the three definitions of poverty, and make sure you know that social exclusion is what happens when different problems all join forces to damage people's well-being.

The Distribution of Poverty, Wealth and Income

Wealth isn't equally distributed. In fact, the richest 10% of UK society own over half the country's wealth, whereas the poorest 50% have only 6% of the wealth. Also, people belonging to some social groups are much more likely to be poor than others...

Wealth and Income are Different

1) Wealth is defined in official statistics as the **value of all the possessions** of an individual **minus** any **debt**. It includes houses, land, money in the bank, shares and personal goods.

2) **Wealth** largely results from ownership of **business** and **property**. Most of this gets **passed down** to the **next generation**, so wealth **stays in the same families** for years. However, lots of the richest people in Britain have generated their own wealth.

3) The vast **majority** of the British population **doesn't have significant wealth**. For most individuals their money comes from an **income**. Income is defined as the **personal funds an individual receives** on a **monthly / yearly basis**. This is usually from a **job** but can be from **benefits**, or **interest** on a savings account.

£9.18 a month just doesn't go as far as it did in my day.

Recent Changes in Society Have Increased the Gap between Rich and Poor

1) Household **disposable income per head** has **grown steadily** in the UK since the early 1980s. This reflects **overall growth in the economy**, and could be said to show that **everyone is getting richer** to some extent.

2) On the other hand, the **gap** between **rich and poor** has **widened** in recent years (according to the Social Market Foundation, an independent public policy think tank). This means that the rich are getting richer whilst the poor are getting **relatively** poorer. Ahhh... the stuff sociology is made of...

- The gap between the income of the rich and the income of the poor went down in the 1970s. Under the Labour government (1974-1979), benefits given to the poor went up and taxes paid by the rich were very high.

- In the 1980s, under the Conservative government, the gap widened. The top rate of tax went down so the rich kept more of their earnings. Taxes that everyone pays like VAT and fuel tax went up. The economy did well, so rich people earned more money on their investments. Benefits went down.

- Adonis and Pollard (1997) reported that the gap continued to widen into the 1990s. In addition to policies introduced during the 1980s, they identified the increase in private education as a factor affecting wealth distribution.

- An Office of National Statistics report by Penny Babb (2004) based on the 2001 census suggested that the gap between rich and poor continued to grow under New Labour. A Centre for Welfare Reform report by Simon Duffy (2014) suggests that the Coalition's VAT increase and benefit cuts hit the poorest section of society the hardest.

- There has been an increase in the number of lone-parent households, who tend to have less money (see the next page). This means the statistics show more poorer households.

- There are also more dual-income households — e.g. families where both parents work. Income is measured by household, so a household with two people in good jobs is relatively rich. This contributes to the statistics showing an increase in rich households.

Some Social Groups are More Likely to be Poor Than Others

The government measure of poverty in the UK is an income of **less than 60% of the median income**. (The **median** income is the **middle** income. **Half** the population **earn more** than the median, **half** of them **earn less**.)

It's a measure of **relative poverty** — it **changes** in line with the incomes of the rest of the population.

Social Class affects Wealth, Income and Poverty

1) This isn't surprising. The factors determining social class, such as type of **job**, are **closely linked** to **economic well-being**. People in unskilled, manual jobs tend to have **lower wages** and **less job security** than those higher up the socio-economic scale.

2) People in higher social classes are more likely to get **better qualifications**, leading to better-paid jobs. **Smith, Smith and Wright (1997)** suggest that a reason for this is that **market-driven educational reforms** (p.33) favour middle-class children.

3) Middle-class people can continue working for longer because they tend to have **better health**.

Have a quick look at p.96 for the reasons behind this.

The Distribution of Poverty, Wealth and Income

Income *Also Seems to be Related to* **Ethnicity**

1) Census data shows that **White British** and **Indian** people are **much more likely** to be in **paid work** than **Bangladeshi**, **Pakistani** and **Black African** people. The difference for **women** is **much greater** — probably due to **cultural** reasons, e.g. women in some cultures are traditionally expected to stay at **home** to look after the children.

2) Studies have also shown that Bangladeshis, Pakistanis and Black Africans are generally **less well paid**.

3) **Family structure** also has an impact — the ethnic minorities which tend to have **more children**, or a greater proportion of **lone-parent families** (see below), are likely to be less well off.

4) **Racism** and **discrimination** are also thought to **limit the opportunities** of people from some ethnic groups. Also, if **English** is not someone's **first language**, this might pose another barrier.

Lone-Parent Families *are More Likely to be Poor*

1) Raising children is **expensive**, so families **with children** are **more likely** to be in **poverty** than families without them.

2) **Lone-parent families** are **more likely** to be poor than **two-parent families**. In 2015, the **Department for Work and Pensions** (DWP) found that **41%** of children in **lone-parent families** live in **relative poverty** — about **double** the proportion of children in **two-parent families** that do. It's hard to get **good work** and **look after kids** at the same time.

Women *are* **Slightly** *More Likely to be* **Poor** *than Men*

1) This difference is partly because women are **more likely** to be **lone parents** than men, and **female** lone parents tend to be from **less affluent** backgrounds in the first place. **Working mums** are more likely to be in **part-time jobs** that fit in with childcare, but that pay less.

2) **Single female pensioners** are **more likely** to have **low incomes** than single male pensioners.

Age *is a Factor too*

1) **Children** in the UK are statistically **more likely** to live in low-income households than the population as a whole. DWP (2010) data has shown that unless an adult in their family **works full time**, there's a **high chance** that a child will be in **relative poverty**.

2) **Pensioners** are now **less likely** than non-pensioners to live in **poverty**, even though the opposite was true until about 15 years ago. This could be due to **more generous benefits** for pensioners.

These benefits include things like payments to help with winter fuel bills.

Disabled *people are More Likely to have* **Low Incomes** *too*

1) Disabled adults are **twice as likely** as non-disabled adults to live in low-income households. This is because disabled adults are **more likely** to be **low paid** or **not in work**.

2) They often either **can't work** or face **discrimination** in the job market. They may have also had poorer access to **education**, making them **less qualified** on average than other people.

Practice Questions

Q1 Give three reasons why the gap between rich and poor has widened since the 1980s.

Q2 Explain why a person's social class affects their chance of being in poverty.

Q3 Give two reasons why disabled people are more likely to be in poverty than others.

Exam Question

Q1 Outline two arguments which support the view that a lone-parent family is more likely to be in poverty than a dual-parent family. Explain each one. [10 marks]

Disposable income — money you can throw away...

Remember that the gap between rich and poor went down, then up again. It's mainly related to tax and benefits — fun stuff. It's also important to remember that the information on these pages is all based on statistics. It doesn't mean that every single person in these groups is going to be living in poverty, just that they're a bit more likely to be — some over-65s are loaded...

Explanations of Poverty

Unsurprisingly, different schools of sociological thought have different explanations of why poverty exists.

Early Theories *Blamed the Poor for Being Poor*

1) The first theories of poverty **blamed the individual** for the poverty they were in.

2) The **19th century** sociologist **Herbert Spencer** said the **poor** were those in society who had **failed** to do the best for themselves. He suggested that they were **immoral**, **lazy** and more interested in **booze** than an **honest day's work**.

3) Spencer said the **state shouldn't intervene** to help the poor because the poor are a useful **example to others** not to follow that way of life.

Rich footballers are always impeccably moral and teetotal.

Oscar Lewis *said* Culture *was the* Cause of Poverty

Lewis (1959, 1961, 1966) studied the poor in Mexico and Puerto Rico

Lewis thought that the **values**, **norms** and **behaviour** of the **poor** were **different** to the rest of society and these values were passed on from generation to generation. He said individuals **learn** how to be poor and learn to **expect** to be poor through the subculture of poverty they're socialised into.

He reckoned that this **culture** of resignation, apathy and lack of participation in wider society initially starts as a response to poverty but then becomes a culture which keeps people in poverty. He called it a **'design for life'**.

1) Lewis's work was controversial and criticised from the start. Similar research done at the same time found highly organised community facilities and political involvement.

2) Schwartz (1975) concluded that the poor weren't culturally different from the well-off.

1) Situational Constraints theory says that the poor have the same values and norms as the rest of society and any difference in the behaviour of the poor is because they're limited by their poverty. For example, unemployment restricts lifestyle options.

2) Coates and Silburn (1970) studied poor areas of Nottingham. They found that some people in poor areas did feel resigned to being poor, and that it wasn't worth trying to get out of poverty. But... they said this was a realistic assessment of an individual's situation. It wasn't proof of some kind of alternative value system.

3) Coates and Silburn's research supported the idea that poverty leads to other forms of deprivation which can trap people into a cycle of deprivation. This means poverty is practically hard to get out of, not culturally hard to get out of.

Functionalists *Say* Unequal Distribution *of* Wealth *is* Good *for Society*

1) Functionalism says that some people are richer or poorer than others because **society functions that way**. It says that there needs to be a way of allocating people to **suitable roles and jobs**. The **top jobs** need to be **rewarded more highly** than others to motivate **intelligent people** to train for them.

2) American sociologist **Herbert J. Gans (1971)** identified many **functions of poverty**, for example:

- Poverty makes sure that there are people willing to do **dirty, dangerous or menial jobs** for low wages.
- Poverty **creates jobs** in occupations serving the poor, e.g. social workers.
- Poor people make the rest of the population feel **more fortunate**. It's also easy to **blame** this section of society for social problems. Alternatively, **helping** the poor (e.g. through donating to **charity** or **volunteering**) provides people with an opportunity for **'emotional satisfaction'**.

3) Functionalist arguments have been **criticised** — they assume the best jobs are allocated on the basis of **talent** when in reality **discrimination** by social class, age, ethnicity and gender often influences who gets the top jobs.

Explanations of Poverty

Marxists Blame Capitalism for Inequalities in Wealth and Income

1) According to Marx and his followers, **capitalism thrives** on **inequality of income** — if wealth was distributed equally there wouldn't be any profit for the capitalists. The capitalist class **needs profit** to maintain its **power in society**.

2) Marxism says **exploitation** is an **essential part of capitalism**, and inequalities in **wealth** and **income** are a central part of that exploitation.

3) **Kincaid's (1973)** explanation of **why poverty is needed** goes like this:

As you may have noticed, the Marxist explanations are quite similar for most things. Capitalism, exploitation, etc., etc...

- The low-paid provide a **cheap labour supply** for the **capitalist class**, which keeps **profits high**.
- The varying pay levels within the working class keep individuals **competing** against each other to get the best jobs. This **divides the working class**. Marxism says that if the working class all **united together** they'd be a **threat** to capitalism — so it's in the **interests of capitalism** to keep the **working class divided**.
- Kincaid believes poverty is **not an accident** — he thinks it's an **inbuilt part** of the capitalist system.

Marxist Explanations of Poverty Have Been Criticised

1) Marxist explanations of poverty **don't explain** why some groups are more likely to experience poverty than others. Marxists treat poverty as a **characteristic of capitalism**, and as something that the **working class as a whole** suffers. They don't look for much **detail** about the experience of poverty for **individuals** or **groups**.

2) Marxism **ignores** the effects of **gender** and **ethnicity** on poverty. It doesn't explain why **women** are more likely to be poor than **men**, or why **Bangladeshi** households are more likely to be poor than other households.

3) **Capitalism** creates **wealth** in the economy. Increase in wealth contributes to the **reduction of absolute poverty**.

Weberians Say Distribution of Wealth is Based on Market Situation

1) Weberian sociologists (followers of **Max Weber**) say that the distribution of wealth and income is based on what they call **market situation**.

2) An individual's market situation is how **valuable** their **skills** are for society and how **scarce** their skills are. It's about **supply and demand** of skills. High demand for your skills makes them worth more.

3) For example, currently **plumbers** can earn **higher wages** than other skilled manual workers, because there's a **shortage** of plumbers and people **need their skills**. So plumbers have a good market situation at the moment.

4) Weberians say **poor people** have a **poor market situation**.

5) There **isn't always the same demand** for the **same skills** — the same people don't always have the best market situation. This means there's always some **movement of wealth in society**.

6) **Dean and Taylor-Gooby (1992)** think that **changes in the UK labour market** have led to increased poverty. There are more casual and temporary jobs, but less job security and far fewer "jobs for life". Dean and Taylor-Gooby say this means more people are likely to experience poverty at some point.

7) Individuals **compete** to improve their market situation:

- **Powerful people** like judges, politicians and the directors of big companies can **do the most** to keep themselves in a good market situation.
- **Low-status** workers don't have much power to improve their labour market situation. **Townsend (1970, 1979)** believes that this is the key **explanation for poverty**.

The Feminist Perspective says that Things are Worse for Women

1) The official figures say that women in the UK are only **slightly more likely** to be in poverty than men, and that this is due to women being more likely to be **lone parents** or **single pensioners** (see p.83).

2) However, feminists say that the **real situation** is far more **unequal**. They claim that because lots of poverty research focuses on the **formal economy** and **work**, the experiences of women's **domestic lives** are often ignored.

3) For example, some studies have shown that:

- in **couples**, men tend to have **more money** to spend on **themselves** than women.
- women are more likely to make **sacrifices**, such as going **without food**, to provide for their children.

Explanations of Poverty

New Right Theorists Blame Dependency on Welfare for Poverty

1) **Charles Murray (1993)** said there's a sector of society who have a **culture of dependency** on the **state** and an **unwillingness to work**. He called this group the **underclass**.

2) Murray identified the **rising number** of **lone-parent families, rising crime** and **attitudes** of **resistance to work**. Murray accepts that **not all** poor people are work-shy but he thinks a **significant group** just don't want to work.

3) In Murray's opinion, **Welfare State benefits** are **too high**. He says this means there's not much encouragement to get off welfare and get a job.

4) Another right-wing sociologist, **Marsland (1989)**, thinks that the **level of poverty** is **exaggerated** by other writers. He says society should **keep a small level of poverty** to **motivate** others to work. Marsland agrees with Murray that the **Welfare State is too generous** and encourages a **culture of non-work** amongst some groups.

Tinkerbell and Lewis were unwilling to work.

Sociological **criticism** of Murray says his **evidence** for the existence of an underclass is **too weak**. **Walker (1990)** found very little evidence of **different values** and **behaviour** among the poor. His opinion was that **blaming** the poor **distracts** from the **real causes** of poverty such as the **failure** of **social policy**. It also ignores factors such as **unemployment** and **disability** that individuals can't control.

Social Democrats Blame Poverty on Structural Causes

1) Social democrats believe that the **capitalist system** and the way **society** is **structured** will always mean that some groups hold a **weak economic position** in the labour market (e.g. the disabled).

2) They believe **inequality** in **wealth and income** is the root cause of poverty, so they want government policy to **redistribute wealth** and **resources** from **rich** to **poor**.

3) The big idea is that the state **can** work to stamp out poverty — and that the state **should** work to stamp out poverty.

> Social democratic theory believes that inequalities can be addressed by the state through increased welfare spending.

Practice Questions

Q1 Why did Spencer argue that the poor are good for society?

Q2 What did Lewis (1959, 1961, 1966) mean by the term 'design for life'?

Q3 Give an example of how poverty is helpful to the capitalist class, from a Marxist perspective.

Q4 How does an individual's market situation affect their wealth?

Q5 According to Murray (1993), what are the characteristics of the 'underclass'?

Exam Questions

Q1 Outline two reasons why inequality of wealth distribution may be considered beneficial to society. Explain each one. [10 marks]

Q2 Apply your own knowledge and material from Item A to evaluate the idea that structural factors are to blame for poverty. [20 marks]

> **Item A**
> Some sociologists argue that poverty is an inevitable result of our society's structure. They point to inequality of income as the main cause of poverty, rather than the actions or attitudes of those who are actually in poverty.

Blame the victim or blame the system...

It's not as easy as you might think to explain why people get stuck in poverty. Each of these theories makes some sense, but they don't account for all the factors. When you're answering questions about why poverty exists, remember the downsides of each theory, and that there are lots of different groups in society — the reasons why they experience poverty may differ.

Social Policy and Poverty

Welfare means all the institutions that look after people — whether they're state-provided or not.

Four Sectors provide Welfare — Public, Private, Voluntary and Informal

Public (or State) Welfare

The **British Welfare State** was set up in the 1940s and was designed to wipe out the **social problems** of society, such as **poor health**, **poor housing** and **poverty**. It provides **services** which are **funded**, **regulated** and **run by the state**, e.g. the **NHS**, the free **education system** and the **benefits system**. The idea was that people **in work** would pay into a **national insurance scheme** which would pay for the Welfare State, making it **free** at the point when you actually **need it**.

This system is **still in operation**, but there are also **three other sectors** providing welfare.

Private Sector

These services are **run by companies for profit**. They often offer **alternatives** to state services — e.g. **private hospitals** and **schools**. They're not state-funded but they have to **meet state regulations**. The individual **pays for these services directly**.

Voluntary Sector

These services are provided by **charity**. They often provide **extra** facilities and services beyond what the state provides, e.g. the **hospice** movement and **Age UK**. They have to **conform to state regulations**. Voluntary services **may get some state funding**. The individual receives these services **free** or at a **subsidised low cost**.

Informal Sector

This means services and help provided by **friends and family**. The informal sector often provides services **in addition to state services** or when there **isn't enough state provision**. Examples: **family carers, family childminders**. There's **little** or **no state funding** or **regulation**. It's usually **free** to the individual but **costs the provider money**.

Benefits can be Universal or Means-Tested

Universal benefits are paid to everyone regardless of wealth.
Means-tested benefits are targeted at those **most in need**, such as those on **lower incomes**.

	Universal benefits	Means-tested benefits
Advantages	• Simple and cheap to administer. • No stigma attached to them. • Promote idea of citizenship.	• Less money is paid out, reducing welfare spending.
Disadvantages	• Wastes money, as many recipients don't need them.	• Costly to administer. • People in need might not claim them due to social stigma or because they don't know about them. • People whose income is just above the threshold may be left in need.
Examples	Winter fuel payments for pensioners	Free school meals, child benefit

The New Right believes in the Reduction of the Welfare State

1) The **New Right** thinks that a **generous welfare state** actually **makes people poorer**.
2) British New Right thinker **Marsland (1989)** thinks all **universal benefits** should be abolished because they **encourage dependency**. He says that **means-tested benefits** should be used to support those in the most desperate need for the shortest possible time. He argues that this will encourage people to "stand on their own two feet".
3) **Right-wing policy** encourages **business** so that **wealth will be created**. Right-wing politicians would prefer everyone to make their own money and decide how to spend it, instead of paying lots of tax or getting benefits from the state.
4) American sociologist **Murray (1993)** recommended a "**moral**" benefits system to discourage people from forming **lone-parent families**. He thought that unmarried mums should get no benefit at all.

Some **criticisms** of the **New Right solutions**:
1) Means-testing benefits cause a '**trap**' — getting a low-paid job may mean you **lose the benefit** and are **no better off**.
2) Poor people may end up with **second-class services** if other people are expected to use **private providers**.

Social Policy and Poverty

State Welfare Provision has been Declining

1) The British system is based on **welfare pluralism** (the combination of all four types of welfare provision). Since the 1979 Conservative government, there has been a **steady growth** in **private**, **voluntary** and **informal sector welfare** and a **relative decline** in **public sector welfare**. For example, local authority care homes have been closed and replaced by private care homes, and housing associations (many of which are charities) have taken over many council houses.

2) The shift from **public sector** to **private sector welfare** is supported by New Right sociologists such as **Marsland** and **Bartholomew**. They reckon the **free market economy** is the **best way** to ensure services are provided at the **lowest prices** and the **best quality**. This is because **private welfare providers** have to compete, giving individuals **choice** and **value**. They suggest that if the tax burden was reduced, most people would be able to be **self-reliant** (e.g. by buying health insurance) and welfare could be focused on those in **dire need**.

3) The '**Big Society**' was a **key element** of the Coalition government's policy (2010-2015). It aimed to encourage **businesses** (private), **charities** (voluntary) and **informal providers** to take over a **greater share** of welfare provision from the state. Some people argue that the 'Big Society' gives communities and organisations the **freedom** to develop their **own responses** to problems at a **local level**.

4) It was also an **austerity measure** to reduce state spending. Although the government would provide **grants** and **loans** to the private organisations and charities, they believed it would still be **cheaper** than the state intervening directly.

5) Not everyone is convinced that this is a **good solution**:

> • Some people argue that the private and voluntary sector won't be able to provide such **comprehensive welfare** as the state. State welfare has **greater funding** and can **guarantee** to provide assistance.
>
> • *Whose Society? The Final Big Society Audit* (2015) by the think tank Civil Exchange found that the Big Society had **failed** to do what it set out to. It said that a '**big society gap**' had opened up in **deprived areas** which have **lower levels** of **charitable giving** and **volunteering**.
>
> • **Informal carers** are saving the government a **huge amount** of money. However, despite many carers being eligible for **carer's benefits**, many people feel that the system **doesn't** meet their needs and carers may end up **workless, isolated** and in **poverty** themselves.

Social Democrats Believe Social Policy Reforms Could Solve Poverty

1) Social democratic theory says **increasing welfare provision** will help to **solve poverty**.

2) **Mack and Lansley (1985)** suggest a big increase in benefits. They conducted a public opinion poll in which British people said they were **prepared to pay higher taxes** to get rid of poverty.

3) **Townsend (1979)** sees the solution to poverty in the **labour market**. He says **social policy** must have the job of **reducing inequalities** in the labour market.

4) The poor are most often unemployed or low-paid. This means **policies** are needed to **improve wages** and conditions and to **protect workers' rights**. The **National Minimum Wage** and **Working Families' Tax Credit** brought in under the New Labour government are examples of this kind of intervention.

5) British sociologists **Walker and Walker (1994)** argue for an "active employment strategy" where the government would actually **create work** for the unemployed.

> Social democratic theory has been **criticised** by people on the **right wing** and on the **left wing**.
>
> 1) **New Right** theorists say the social democratic policy of **strengthening the Welfare State** and increasing the power of social policy would be an **absolute disaster** in terms of solving poverty. The New Right say these things led to the increase in poverty in the first place.
>
> 2) Left-wing **Marxists** say the **state** will always **serve the interests** of those in **power**, which means that nothing the government does can make a big difference to poverty in capitalist society.

Edwin's attempt to parallel park had been an absolute disaster.

Social Policy and Poverty

There's also the 'Third Way' Approach

Recent governments have used a philosophy which **combines** both the **New Right** and the **social democratic** approaches — it is called '**the third way**'.

New Labour (1997-2010)

1) When New Labour took power in Britain in 1997, they claimed their social policies would reduce poverty significantly. The theme was that the poor need **"a hand up not a handout"**. The "hand up" part means the state should have **social policies** which **help the poor** — rather like the social democratic theory. The "not a handout" part means people **shouldn't depend** on benefits — rather like New Right theory.

2) They said the state has a responsibility to **help people in real need**, but individuals have a **responsibility to help themselves**. The **"New Welfare Contract"** of 1998 said that the **government** had to **help people find work**, make **work pay**, help with **childcare**, help the **poorest** old people and help those who really **can't work**. In turn, **individuals** had to look for work, be as **independent as possible**, support their own family, save for retirement and not defraud the taxpayer by claiming benefit when they shouldn't.

> **New Labour Reforms aimed at making sure working pays more than benefits:**
> - **Working Families' Tax Credit** — tax reductions for the **low-paid who are working**.
> - **National Minimum Wage** — to ensure every employer **pays more than benefit levels**.
> - **Income Tax cuts** — they halved the **starter (lowest) rate**, meaning poorer families **keep more** of what they **earn**.

The Coalition Government (2010-2015)

1) The **Coalition government** continued the Third Way approach. The 'Big Society' (p.88) was part of this.

2) They introduced **changes** to the benefit system so that people moving into work didn't **suddenly** see all of their benefits stop — their aim was for people to be able to see that the **more they worked**, the **better off** they were.

3) They also introduced '**sanctions**' for people who repeatedly **refused work** (they lose their benefits for some time).

Marxists say Nothing Will Work Except the Overthrow of Capitalism

1) Marxists believe that the root cause of poverty is the **inequality** central to the **capitalist system**. Therefore, the Marxist solution to poverty is the **removal** of the **capitalist system**.

2) Marxists say that while the capitalist system keeps on going, poverty will still be around — **no matter** what **social policy** you throw at it. **Westergaard and Resler (1976)** think no big **redistribution of wealth** can happen until capitalism is overthrown and replaced by a **socialist** society where **wealth is communally owned**.

3) The most **common criticism** of the Marxist approach is the **evidence** that **socialist** and **communist societies haven't eradicated poverty**. People were poor in Soviet Russia and there is poverty in Cuba.

Practice Questions

Q1 Give two reasons why non-state welfare providers may perform better than the state welfare sector.

Q2 What's the difference between universal and means-tested benefits?

Q3 Why do the New Right think that the Welfare State can be too generous?

Q4 How do Marxist theorists believe poverty could be eradicated in Britain?

Exam Question

Q1 Evaluate the idea that reducing welfare provision will reduce poverty. [20 marks]

Sounds great on paper — but will it work in real life?

Although the theories here are different, they all make some kind of sense on paper. It'd probably be great if everyone earned enough money to buy the best kind of private welfare. It'd probably be great if the state provided really good public welfare for everybody. In real life it's hard to make things work. At the moment, the jury's still out on the Third Way idea.

The Labour Process

These two pages are about labour, as in work — not the Labour Party (we want no confusion here).

Division of Labour — Breaking Down Work into Very Specialised Tasks

1) **Specialisation** is a common way to **organise** a work force. We've always needed people to **specialise**, because **no one person** can learn **all** the skills a society needs.

2) In **pre-industrial** agricultural societies, villages would **divide up** the work according to **individual strengths** — this led to the creation of **craft jobs** such as woodworker, cook, blacksmith and farmer. These craftsmen were **skilled** and carried out a **range of tasks** within their jobs, e.g. a blacksmith would make **all kinds** of metal objects and tools, carrying out **all the steps** in the process himself.

3) However, during the **industrial revolution**, the **division of labour** became more **extreme**. In factories, it was far **more efficient** for workers to learn how to do a **single task**. They'd do this **over and over again** and could do it very **quickly**.

> For example, in 1776 the economist Adam Smith wrote about pin-making factories, in which some workers made the pinheads and others the points. Nobody made a whole pin, or even knew how to. This allowed many more pins per worker to be produced each day.

Marx and Durkheim saw the Division of Labour Differently

Karl Marx saw the organisation and control of labour as exploitation… but Emile Durkheim took a different view.

Marx argued that the whole capitalist system exploits the working class

1) Marx said that the rich **control the means of production and distribution** (e.g. factories and shops). This means that the working class have **no choice** but to work for the rich.

2) This means that the rich can pay the working class **whatever they like**, so workers aren't paid the **full value** of their labour.

3) Work becomes **meaningless** and **empty** for the working class, which leads to **alienation** (where the worker becomes **detached** from **society** and **themselves** due to a **lack of control** over their own future).

4) According to Marx, **division of labour** in a factory **increases alienation**. The work is broken into small, easy, repetitive tasks that don't have any **meaning** on their own. This process is called **deskilling**.

Durkheim was far more positive about the division of labour

1) He saw it as **constructive** because it exists in **all societies**. The **more progress** a society makes, the **more specialised** its members become.

2) Durkheim also claimed that the division of labour is a **natural law**. This argument is based on **biology**. Each part of a living creature has a **specialist purpose** — e.g. the heart pumps blood, the stomach digests, etc. Durkheim argued that **society** should be based on the **same idea**.

3) In **contrast** to Marx's idea of **alienation**, Durkheim thinks the division of labour creates **social solidarity**. His argument is that it makes people **depend on each other more**, so they **value** each other more **highly**.

These viewpoints make more sense if you remember that **Marxism** is a **conflict theory**, and **functionalism** (**Durkheim**) is a **consensus theory** (see p.3).

Taylor and Ford encouraged the Division of Labour...

1) In the early twentieth century, **F.W. Taylor** (an American engineer) promoted the idea of '**scientific management**'. He argued that it was **most efficient** to **remove** the need for **knowledge** and **decision-making** from workers' jobs and give each person a **very simple task**. All **planning** and **creative work** should be done by **managers**.

2) When the industrialist **Henry Ford** designed his first **car assembly lines**, he based them on Taylor's ideas. Every worker did **one small job** towards building each car, and nobody needed to be a **skilled mechanic**. This is known as the **Fordist model**.

...But Others have Criticised it

American Marxist **Harry Braverman**, criticised **scientific management**. In 1974 he wrote that the **deskilling** in the Fordist model made workers feel like they were **no more than machines**. It also **took power away** from workers, by making them **easier to replace** if they threatened to go on **strike**.

The Labour Process

Technology can Deskill Workers

1) **Modern technology** makes life **easier** for workers in many ways, but it also means **people** are **less vital** to production. Workers on **production lines** being replaced by **machines**, processes becoming more **automatic**, and the more widespread use of **ICT** mean more and more tasks can be done by **technology**, not **people**.

2) Some sociologists argue that technology has led to **upskilling** (where workers learn **additional skills**) or **reskilling** (where workers learn **new skills**) to cope with the new technology. However, others have argued that only workers who are **highly skilled** in the first place will be able to upskill or reskill, while the rest are **deskilled** or **replaced**.

1) **Braverman (1974)** looked at new technology from a **Marxist** perspective. He argued that technology **further deskilled** workers, who were already deskilled by the Fordist model. He also said it **reduced** workers' **bargaining power** even more — machines would never strike for more pay or better conditions.

2) **Andrew Friedman (1977)** criticised Braverman's analysis — he found that workers in British car factories **did** still **strike** for **better conditions**. However, Friedman also said **union power** had a lot to do with **economic factors**. The workers were **stronger** when general unemployment was **low**, but **weaker** when unemployment was **high**.

High unemployment means it's difficult to get another job, so workers might not want to risk losing their current one.

3) **Michael J. Piore (1986)** had a different view — he argued that technology actually makes a workforce more **flexible**. When machines can be programmed to do **different tasks** (e.g. 3D printers can print different prototypes), the workers need to be able to **adapt** as well. Their work is more **diverse**, so they **reskill**, and there is less of a **gap** between the **workers** and the **management** (as well as better communication between them).

Shoshana Zuboff said Technology increased Managers' Control

1) **Zuboff (1988)** studied **office work** in the 1980s. She found that **technology** was used to **increase** the bosses' **power and control** over workers.

2) Her study showed that computers were being used to **take jobs away** from **human beings** and to **increase surveillance** of **office staff** — for example by **keylogging** (recording what you type).

Zuboff said that there are **three laws of information technology**:
1) **Everything** that **can** be **automated will** be **automated**.
2) **Everything** that **can** be **informated** (turned into information) **will** be **informated**.
3) **Every** digital application that **can** be used for **surveillance** and **control will** be used for **surveillance and control**.

Ruby had gone to great lengths to prevent keylogging.

Practice Questions

Q1 What is the division of labour?
Q2 Give an advantage and a disadvantage of the division of labour in industrialised society.
Q3 Describe the Fordist model.
Q4 What is reskilling?
Q5 What did Zuboff's (1988) study discover about the use of technology in offices?

Exam Questions

Q1 Outline two ways in which technological change has affected the workforce. Explain each one. [10 marks]

Q2 Analyse two explanations for why the division of labour may be a cause of conflict in the workplace. [10 marks]

Don't leave Windows® open — your computer will get cold...

Is division of labour a good thing? Well, it depends on your sociological viewpoint. It's probably no surprise what Karl Marx had to say about the matter, but make sure you know other sociologists' views too. And remember, technology has come a long way since most of these studies were done, bringing about even more changes in the way we live and work.

Work and Life Chances

The job you do (and whether you have a job at all) influences many other aspects of your life (so say the sociologists).

Your **Work** Affects Your **Life Chances**

> In sociology, **life chances** are the **opportunities** an individual has to get all the things their **society values**, such as money, security, status and comfort.

Peter and Jamie's life chances were looking pretty sweet.

1) The **sort of work someone does**, or if they have a job **at all**, affects their **life chances**.

2) Here are some examples of how the **opportunities** of a **low-paid manual worker** may **differ** from those of a **high-paid skilled worker**.

High-paid skilled worker	Low-paid manual worker
• Can afford **good quality**, **comfortable** housing in a **safe area**.	• Lives in **poor quality** housing in an area with a **high crime rate**.
• Can afford to **eat better** and access **better health care**, so generally **healthier** and **lives longer**.	• Eats **less well** and **can't** always access **health care** easily. Is **less healthy** and **dies younger**.
• Treated with **respect** due to **high-status job**.	• Gets **little respect** due to **low-status job**.
• Passes **advantages** on to **children** by supporting their **education** financially.	• Likely to pass **disadvantage** on to **children**, e.g. can't support them through **higher education**.

3) The examples in this table are **generalisations**. There's a lot of **variation** — e.g. some **high-paid workers** are so **stressed** that they smoke or drink heavily and **die young**. On the other hand, some **low-paid workers** live happily within their means in an area of the country with a low cost of living.

Work Satisfaction *is Important*

1) In general, higher-paid jobs involve **control** and **variety** for **workers**, leading to **work satisfaction** and **job fulfilment**. **Lower-paid jobs** tend to be more **routine**, leading to **poor work satisfaction** and **alienated workers** (who are purely doing the job to **get paid**).

2) **Robert Blauner (1964)** argued that **how technology is used** is the **key factor** in **work satisfaction**:

> • Blauner studied **car assembly line workers** and also **machine operators** in a **chemical factory**. Both of these sets of workers had **similar pay and status**.
>
> • He found that car assembly line workers were **bored, dissatisfied and alienated**, whereas the chemical factory machine operators had **high levels of work satisfaction**.
>
> • **Both** jobs involved **machinery**, but on the car assembly line the workers used the machines to do the **same task over and over**. They **could not control** the **speed** of their work — it was determined by the speed of the assembly line. They were also **isolated** from other workers.
>
> • In **contrast**, the machines used in the chemical factory relieved workers of the **monotonous, repetitive tasks**, leaving them with the more interesting **decision-making** to do, such as when **maintaining** the machines. They also worked **in teams**, each with a responsibility for a **whole process**.

There's more on technology in the workplace and worker alienation on p.90-91.

3) Recently, employers have begun to see **boredom and demotivation** in the workforce as a **problem**. They try to **improve conditions** by **rotating jobs** and giving employees **different responsibilities**.

4) However, **Marxists** see **all** working-class labour as **alienating**, and a cause of **misery** — whether the worker realises it or not. So, from a Marxist perspective, these changes are just ways to **distract** the workers from noticing that they're being **exploited**.

Work *is associated with* Social Identity

1) **Giddens (2009)** wrote about the **importance of work** in people's lives. He pointed out that for most people work is **not** just drudgery. It takes up a **large proportion** of their **time**, and when people find themselves **unemployed**, it's usually very distressing.

2) This is not only because of the **loss of income**, but also because we see our **social identity** (p.1) as closely tied to the **job** we do. It gives us a **routine** to follow, a **set of people** to socialise with and a **sense of purpose**.

Work and Life Chances

Worklessness can be Very Bad for Individuals

1) Unemployment is **stigmatised** by society — unemployed people are often considered **lazy** and **unskilled**.

2) Long-term unemployment can lead to **poverty**. Studies also show that the **social effects** of unemployment can be very **damaging**. For example, in areas where there is high unemployment, social problems like **crime**, **violence**, **vandalism** and **drug use** tend to be more common.

3) Many sociologists have investigated the **effects of unemployment**:

   - **Fagin and Little (1984)** found high levels of **illness** among **unemployed men**. They concluded that the sickness was a **strategy** for coping **psychologically** with feeling **rejected** by society.
   - In 1997 a study by the **Joseph Rowntree Foundation** showed that long-term unemployment caused feelings of **isolation** and **low self-esteem**.

4) People who are **unable to work**, e.g. those with **disabilities**, can also suffer from **poverty** and **isolation**.

5) **Underemployment** is also a problem. This is when people who want **full-time**, **permanent** work are only employed in **part-time** or **temporary jobs**. The pay they receive might not be **enough** to keep them out of **poverty**. Underemployment also includes **highly-skilled** workers in jobs which **don't** utilise their skills, e.g. someone with a **law degree** working as a **bartender**. This may lead to a **lack of job fulfilment** and **low self-esteem**.

Retirement can have Similar Effects to Unemployment

1) **Cumming** and **Henry's** Disengagement Theory (1961) suggested that worklessness in old age led to **isolation**, **detachment** and **unhappiness**.

2) **Hockey and James (1993)** wrote that retired people are **not treated like adults** by carers and family members. This is because **without a job** they have the **status of children**. This can lead to **low self-esteem**.

3) Although some people **enjoy** the increased **leisure time** that retirement brings, others still **want to work**. This can be because they're **bored**, they're **lonely** or their **pension** isn't enough to live on — or sometimes because they miss the feeling of **job fulfilment**.

Globalisation is Changing Employment in the UK

No unions means that companies can get away with poorer working conditions.

1) **George Ritzer (1993)** wrote about **McDonaldisation**. He argued that an increasing number of jobs are like working in a **fast-food restaurant**, where every aspect is **standardised**, **predictable** and **controlled**. It's like an **extreme** version of **scientific management** (see p.90). This has come about as a result of globalisation (see p.1).

2) **Naomi Klein (1999)** describes how the **transnational corporations** (TNCs) have all moved their factories to **developing countries**, where wages are **cheap** and there are **no unions**. Mostly these are 'McJobs' — **low status**, **badly paid** and offering **poor job security**. Meanwhile, in **developed countries** like the UK, TNCs mainly employ people in jobs such as **sales** and **marketing**.

Practice Questions

Q1 What are 'life chances'?

Q2 How can technology affect work satisfaction?

Q3 What is underemployment?

Q4 Describe one way in which globalisation has affected employment in the UK.

Exam Questions

Q1 Outline two ways in which work can affect an individual's life chances. Explain each one. [10 marks]

Q2 Analyse two explanations for why worklessness may cause problems for individuals. [10 marks]

Fagin (1837) says that picking pockets is a suitable form of employment...

In the future, even more jobs could become automated — e.g. driverless cars may make taxi drivers obsolete some day. However, as Blauner found, technology doesn't always mean doom and gloom for employees — it depends on how the workers are using it. I'm all for new technology, personally — my state-of-the-art typewriter has made my job much quicker.

Definitions of Health

Sociologists see health as more than just not feeling poorly. Well, they do like to complicate things.

The Biomedical Model *says Health and Illness are* Natural, Physical Things

The **biomedical model** (favoured by scientists and health professionals)
says that health and illness are caused by factors **within** the body.
This model has **three** key characteristics:

Key characteristics of the biomedical model

1) Health is seen as the **absence of biological abnormality**.

2) The human body is likened to a **machine** in that it needs to be **repaired** by treatment when it breaks down.

3) The health of society is regarded as dependent on the **state of medical knowledge**.

Related to this is the **biomedical view of disability**:

The biomedical model **looks in** at the patient and
tries to **fix** the disability through medical practice.

Medical practice is **interventionist** —
it's something that's **done to** the patient.

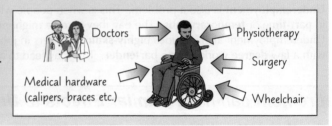

Doctors → Physiotherapy

Surgery

Medical hardware
(calipers, braces etc.)

Wheelchair

The Biomedical *Model has been* Criticised

1) Some sociologists, e.g. **McKeown (1976)**, say that **improved nutrition and hygiene** have been more important in improving health than **developments in medicine** — starting with 19th and 20th century public health reforms.

2) **Marxist sociologists** in the 1970s accused biomedicine of distracting attention away from what they see as the real causes of illness — the **social causes**.

3) The biomedical approach can be viewed as **stigmatising** people who have an illness or disability — it views illness or disability as something **abnormal** that should be **fixed**.

4) **Tom Shakespeare (2000)** said that traditional approaches **individualise** and **medicalise** disability. They deal with the symptoms of each case and **ignore** social patterns.

5) **Ivan Illich (1975)** and others have argued that modern medicine actually **creates disease**.

Medicalisation is when human conditions start to be treated as medical problems and studied, diagnosed and treated medically.

Illich *Says the* Medical Elite *Actually* Cause Bad Health

1) **Illich (1975)** defines **health** as the **capacity** to cope with the **human reality** of **death**, **pain** and **sickness**. This is a very different definition to the mainstream biomedical definition.

2) Illich believes that medicine has **gone too far**, and that the **medical elite** (**doctors**) have started to 'play God' — trying to **wipe out** death, pain and sickness. OK so far... he then says that **trying to control death and illness** is a bad move which **turns people into consumers** or even objects. In his opinion, this messes up people's natural capacity for health and **makes people ill**.

3) Illich uses the word **iatrogenesis** to refer to this kind of illness that's caused by modern medicine. He says there are **three types of iatrogenesis**:

> 1) **Clinical iatrogenesis** — the **harm** done to patients by **ineffective** treatments, **unsafe** treatments or getting the **wrong diagnosis**.
>
> 2) **Social iatrogenesis** — the idea that **doctors** have **taken over control** of people's lives, and individuals can't make decisions about their problems. More and more of people's problems are seen as **suitable for medical intervention**. This is called the **medicalisation of social life**.
>
> 3) **Cultural iatrogenesis** — the **destruction** of **traditional ways of dealing** with and making sense of **death, pain and sickness**.

4) According to Illich, dying has become the ultimate form of **consumer resistance** (when you're dead, you can't buy any more Nike trainers, I'd imagine). **Death** isn't seen as something normal. It's become a **taboo**.

Definitions of Health

The **Social Model** says that Health and Illness are **Social Constructs**

1) The **social model** (favoured by **sociologists**) says that health and illness are caused by factors **outside** the body.

2) The **medical elite** haven't always **dominated** the definition and treatment of illness — it's a modern phenomenon, e.g. in the **1700s**, **mental illness** was often thought to be caused by **evil spirits** — a **religious** thing, not a **medical** thing.

3) In modern society illness is only recognised as serious if it has been **diagnosed** by the medical elite. The **social model** says **definitions of health and illness** are 'social constructs' — not actually always related to **real physical symptoms**.

> A **'social construct'** is an **idea that's created by a society** — as opposed to an idea that's based on objective and testable **facts**. It's specific to the **values and behaviour** of that society — it's not universal.

4) The **social model of health** looks to see which **environmental, social and behavioural factors** have contributed to make someone ill. **Social factors** (such as diet, housing or stress) make some people more likely to become ill than others.

A social view of disability:

- The social model looks outwards from the individual to the environmental and social factors which disable an individual, e.g. lack of access, rights and opportunities.

- A person using a wheelchair might feel more disabled by the lack of a wheelchair ramp than the fact that they can't use their legs to walk.

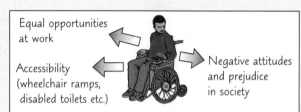

Equal opportunities at work

Accessibility (wheelchair ramps, disabled toilets etc.)

Negative attitudes and prejudice in society

The **Social** Model has been **Criticised** too

1) Illness is often **not subjective**, and **isn't** affected by changes in the social environment.

2) The social model of disability **ignores impairments**, such as **pain**, which cause the disability.

E.g. Whether or not you have food poisoning is not subjective.

> An **impairment** is a **physical feature** or **characteristic** (e.g. **blindness**), whereas a **disability** is an **inability** to do something because **society** hasn't made a **provision** for it (e.g. a blind person using a **cash machine**). Impairments **don't always** cause disability, but disability is **always** due to impairment.

The **Body** is a **Social Construction** Too

1) The **ideal** body **size and shape** is socially constructed, e.g. today's **media** often portray a very **slim ideal** for a woman and a **muscular ideal** for a man. However, in the **past**, being thin was associated with not having enough to eat and **indicated poverty**, so a more curvaceous figure was more desirable.

2) The **typical body shape** of a society is also a result of the **dominant cultural attitudes** to diet and lifestyle, e.g. the **fast food culture** of the US is linked to **increased obesity**.

3) However, the ideal body **isn't just** a social construction. A high body mass index (BMI) is **objectively linked** to increased risk of a range of diseases.

Practice Questions

Q1 What is the difference between the biomedical model and the social model of health?

Q2 What does 'iatrogenesis' mean?

Q3 Explain the difference between an impairment and a disability.

Exam Question

Q1 Outline two ways that the body may be viewed as a social construct. Explain each one.   [10 marks]

All I care about is why I feel ill...

Hmm... the social model of illness seems a bit odd at first — how can it be society's fault that I've got a sore throat... But when you look into it, you have to admit that things like clean water, proper sewers and a good diet are at least relevant to health. As always, you're expected to know the key points of each theory, as well as their faults and pitfalls.

Inequalities in Health

*Your chances of staying healthy, and of recovering if you do get ill, depend on which social group
you belong to and where you live. Sociologists have given various explanations for this.*

Health Inequalities are Strongly Linked to Social Class

1) Most sociologists **agree** that **economic deprivation** is probably the **major factor**
   causing health inequalities, even if they don't agree exactly **why**.

   - The working class in England and Wales have a higher infant mortality rate than the UK national average.
     The wealthiest social groups have lower infant mortality rates than the national average.
   - Working-class people are statistically more likely to suffer from
     serious medical conditions such as heart disease, strokes and cancer.
   - Working-class people are more likely to die before retirement age than the national average.

   Social Trends 33 (2003) report, Office of National Statistics.

2) A major government survey, '**Inequalities in Health Working Group Report (1980)**'
   (also known as the **Black Report**) confirmed that the poorer you are, the less healthy
   you're likely to be. It also found that those with the **most** need for health care get **least**,
   and those with the **least** need get **most**. This is called the **Inverse Care Law**.

Cultural Explanations Blame Bad Health on Variations in Attitude

Some sociologists attribute **differences in health** to the **values** held and choices made
by **different social groups**. These are called cultural explanations. **Cultural deprivation
theory** is a cultural explanation that looks at differences between social classes.

1) **Cultural deprivation theory** says that the **working class** lead **relatively unhealthy lifestyles** with relatively **poor diets**,
   more **smoking**, less **exercise** and more **drinking** — these are known as **behavioural factors**, as well as cultural ones.

2) It also says that the working class are less likely to take advantage of NHS
   public health measures such as **vaccinations**, **health screening** and **antenatal care**.

3) **Howlett and Ashley (1991)** found that **middle-class** people are better **informed** about health,
   with more **understanding** of health issues. Therefore, they tend to follow **healthier lifestyles**.

   Cultural deprivation theory suggests that society needs better **health education** to make
   people more **aware** of health issues. It's resulted in lots of **government initiatives** through the
   Health Education Authority — trying to get people to give up smoking, eat less fatty food, etc.

Structural Approaches link Health Inequalities to Deprivation

Many sociologists, such as **Shaw et al (2008)**, **disagree** with cultural explanations. Instead they believe
that **differences** in health and illness are caused by the way **society is structured**. The **middle class** is
healthier than the **working class** because society gives the poor **less chance** to keep healthy.

1) Healthier diets can cost more, and gyms are often very expensive.
2) Smoking and drinking may be related to stressful lives, not cultural values.
3) Working-class people are less likely to be able to afford private health care.
4) Living in poor housing can cause health problems, e.g. damp housing contributes to child respiratory problems.
5) Living in high-crime areas can contribute to stress, as can worrying about bills and making ends meet.
6) The fact that working-class people often don't take advantage of public health facilities has also been
   blamed on feeling intimidated by health care and health care professionals. Health care professionals
   are mostly middle class and health care in general can seem like it's set up to suit middle-class people.

The **Black Report (1980)** concluded that **material factors** were the **major cause** of health inequalities.

Inequalities in Health

There are *Gender Differences* in Health and Mortality

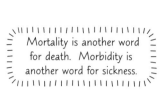

Mortality is another word for death. Morbidity is another word for sickness.

1) On average, **women** live **four years** longer than men in the UK. **Men** are more likely to **smoke** and **drink heavily** and are more likely to have **physical, dangerous jobs**. They also take more **risks**, leading to an increased risk of accidental death (e.g. in road accidents or through drowning) — this is a **behavioural** factor. All these factors may contribute to their **lower life expectancy**.

2) However, data shows that women have **more morbidity** throughout their lives. They also spend a greater proportion of their life with a **disability**, and **go to the doctor** more often.

3) The differences may be caused by **biology**, e.g. due to pregnancy and childbirth. Women also suffer more from **mental health issues**, such as depression and anxiety. However, **Hilary Graham (1984)** also suggested that women are more likely to go without **food** and **heating** to save money in times of **financial difficulties**, which could contribute to their increased health issues.

Brad and Tony were fairly sure they knew how to swim.

There's a *Relationship* Between *Ethnicity* and Health Too

1) The rate of **heart disease** is significantly higher in men and women of **Indian** origin.
2) **African-Caribbean** people have a higher incidence of **stroke, HIV/AIDS infection** and **schizophrenia**.
3) **Suicide** rates are **relatively high** amongst **Asian** women.
4) **Sickle-cell anaemia** is most common in people of **African** origin.

1) **Cultural factors** might have an impact too, e.g. research found that **British Chinese people** were **less likely** to seek help for **mental health problems** because of **social stigma**.

2) Some ethnic groups are more heavily concentrated in the **lowest social classes**. This is a **material factor**, and is likely to be the **most significant factor** in deciding the health of different ethnic groups.

Where you live in the UK is Also Important

1) **Morbidity** and **mortality** rates vary between different **regions** of Britain:
   - People in **Scotland** are more likely to die of lung cancer than people in **England**.
   - People in the **south of England** live more of their lives without a **disability** than people in the **north of England**.

2) There are also differences on a **smaller scale** — neighbouring areas of a city can have very **different** health statistics. There are thought to be **two factors** contributing to this:

   - **Social class** — there are **local variations** in income and deprivation.
   - **Social capital** — this refers to the existence of **social networks** and a sense of **community spirit**. Research has shown that where these things exist, people are **more likely** to have **better health and well-being**.

Practice Questions

Q1 What is the Inverse Care Law?
Q2 Describe the mortality and morbidity gender trends in the UK.
Q3 Why are people in some ethnic groups likely to have higher rates of morbidity than others?

Exam Questions

Q1 Outline two arguments that support the idea that social class can affect health. Explain each one. [10 marks]

Q2 Evaluate the idea that cultural variations by social class are the most important factors in determining health. [20 marks]

Apparently it's not all down to deep-fried chocolate bars then...

It's mostly down to the good old class system — and once again, it's the working class that suffers. They really do get the rough end of the deal. I reckon Marx would have something to say about that — it's a shame he doesn't pop up on these pages. Ah well, I'm sure we'll hear from him again at some point. What's a sociology section without a good bit of Marxism?

Access to Health Care

The National Health Service was set up to give free and equal health care for all. It was mostly a success. Mostly.

There are **Inequalities** in the Health Care **Provided** by the **NHS**

The **NHS** was set up in 1948. It aimed to provide **free** and **equal** health care for **everyone** in the country. Unfortunately, although the NHS was **generally a success**, it **doesn't give 100% equal health care** to all.

There are **Regional Inequalities...**

1) The NHS in England is split up into **regional 'trusts'**, each with responsibility for their own **budget**. This means that money is **spent differently** in different areas of the country, so some regions have access to **different levels** of care.

2) **Specialist** hospitals, e.g. heart hospitals, **aren't spread out equally** across the country either.

... as well as **Social Class Inequalities**

1) NHS hospitals are now carrying out an increasing number of **private treatments and operations** to raise funds. Some sociologists and politicians claim that this is creating a **two-tier system** in the NHS — people who can **pay** get seen **more quickly** and may get **better treatment**, whilst those who can't are left **waiting**.

2) **Working-class people** are **less likely** to attend screening programmes, e.g. for cervical cancer. A Cancer Research survey found that people from deprived backgrounds are less likely to be **aware** of the screening offered, as are people with **lower literacy levels**. Other reasons may be **practical**, such as **childcare problems**, or not having **paid time off work**.

The **Inverse Care Law** can be Applied **Today** to **Inequalities** in **Health**

Remember the Inverse Care Law from p.96.

The **Inverse Care Law (Tudor-Hart, 1971)** states that people whose **need** for health care is **greatest** are actually **least likely** to get it.

Working-class areas tend to have the worst health facilities, the **fewest doctors** and the **fewest hospitals**.

Julian Le Grand's survey (2003)

- Le Grand's conclusion was that the middle class get far more benefit from the NHS than the working class. The benefit the middle classes got wasn't in proportion to their actual health needs.

- Le Grand found that the working class were 20% less likely than the middle class to get a hip replacement despite being 30% more likely to need one.

- Even with something as simple as consultation times in GPs' surgeries, Le Grand found that professionals were likely to get on average two minutes more of a doctor's time than working-class patients.

This evidence supports the idea that the health care system is biased towards middle-class people.

Research by **Cartwright and O'Brien (1976)** suggests that **middle-class patients** tend to have a **better relationship** with their **doctor** than working-class patients. Working-class patients said they **felt** like the **doctor doesn't listen**.

Your **Age** can Affect Your **Access** to Health Care

1) Research has shown that **older people** often **don't** get the **same treatment** as younger people suffering from the same problem. This is sometimes due to **health care rationing** — there isn't enough money to treat everyone so the people who'll get the **most benefit** get **priority**. There may also be a **greater risk of complications** for older people undergoing operations.

2) In a survey of older people, **over half** agreed that their symptoms were often **dismissed** as '**just old age**'. Older people may also put their own symptoms down to old age and **not bother** going to a doctor.

Access to Health Care

The *Inverse Care Law* Could Also Apply to *Ethnic Minority Groups*

1) **Ethnic minority** health needs were identified as **relatively high** in a report published by the **Department of Health in 1992**. Remember, "relatively high" doesn't mean "shockingly sky-high" or "loads higher than the white population". It means anything from a **tiny bit more** to a **lot more** than the **average population**.

2) Some sociologists think that **ethnic minorities** have **relatively poor health** because they're **less likely** to get the **full benefit** from NHS services. **Various possible reasons** have been suggested for this:

   1) The cultural values of the NHS might be different from those of some ethnic groups. Some advisers say the NHS needs to adapt to fit the cultural values of ethnic groups.

   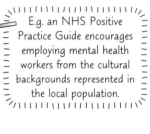
   E.g. an NHS Positive Practice Guide encourages employing mental health workers from the cultural backgrounds represented in the local population.

   2) Some people from ethnic minorities, especially older people, might not speak enough English to communicate well with health care staff.

   3) There's some evidence that discrimination and racism affect access to health care. For example, research in the 1980s found that Asian women in family planning clinics experienced racism.

   4) Some ethnic minority groups tend to see illness and disease as a part of life you can't do much about — and don't bother to go to the doctor.

Women go to the Doctor *More* than Men

1) Women traditionally look after the **health of the family**, e.g. they take the children to the doctors. They also tend to use the NHS **earlier in life** than men, because of **contraception**, **pregnancy** and **childbirth**. This may make them **more comfortable** consulting a doctor than men.

2) Research suggests that to **achieve equality**, policies for different health issues should be **gender-sensitive**. They should take into account how conditions **affect** men and women differently, as well as differences in how men and women **seek treatment**. For example, a report found that locating **mental health services** in bars and clubs was more successful in **meeting the needs** of **young men**.

Rex had left it a little late to go to the doctor.

People with *Disabilities* face *Barriers* to Health Care

1) Research has found that **barriers exist** that prevent some people with disabilities from **accessing health care**. For example, **physical barriers** can make it difficult to use doctors' or dentists' surgeries, or they might have **communication difficulties** that make it hard to book appointments.

2) **MENCAP (2004)** found that people with **learning difficulties** often suffered from **discrimination** from health care professionals — they were sometimes **denied** treatments that would be offered to a non-disabled person. The study also found that **communication** was difficult, both in terms of the **patient** trying to describe their **symptoms** and the **doctor** trying to explain the **solution**.

3) Physical symptoms are sometimes **mistakenly** attributed to the person's disability, even when they are **completely unrelated**. This is called '**diagnostic overshadowing**' — it means people don't always get the treatment they need.

Practice Questions

Q1 Describe the 'two-tier' system in the NHS.

Q2 Why might older people not have the same access to health care as younger people?

Q3 Give three barriers that might prevent someone with disabilities from accessing health care.

Exam Question

Q1 Outline two arguments that support the idea that an individual's ethnicity might affect their access to health care. Explain each one. [10 marks]

Doctor, doctor — the NHS is biased against me...

Unfortunately, the NHS doesn't help everyone equally. People are at an advantage if they can read health literature, are able and willing to make an appointment, and are then able to talk to health professionals about their symptoms. Remember that social class, age, ethnicity, gender and disabilities can all affect a person's access to and understanding of health care.

Mental Illness

These pages cover different perspectives on mental health in the UK.

Mental Illness in UK Society is Unequally Distributed

Sociologists and psychiatrists can't agree whether mental disorders have **physical causes** or **social causes**.
Sociologists have tended to favour the view that there is a **social basis** for mental illness. Given the **social inequality** in who has good or bad mental health, maybe the sociologists have a point. For example:

1) **Working-class** people are statistically **more likely** to be diagnosed with mental illness than **middle-class** people.

2) Women are statistically more likely to be diagnosed with **depression** or **stress** than men.
They're also much more likely to be on **drug treatments** for **mental illness** — antidepressants etc.

3) **African-Caribbean individuals** are more likely to be 'sectioned' under the Mental Health Act (**admitted against their will**). They are also more likely to suffer from **schizophrenia**. This is despite being **less likely** to suffer from **common** mental health problems than other people from minority groups.

Mental Health is Often Treated using the Biomedical Approach

1) The biomedical approach to mental illness focuses on the **abnormal individual** rather than the **environment** that the individual lives in. It concentrates on the **physical symptoms** of mental illness. For example, a **biomedical approach to schizophrenia** might say it's caused by a **chemical imbalance in the brain**.

2) The biomedical approach is **cure-orientated**. It emphasises the importance of treatments involving **drugs or surgery** for depression.

3) The biomedical approach suggests that treatment is best carried out in the **medical environment** (e.g. a hospital rather than the community) and should always be carried out by the **medical elite** (doctors).

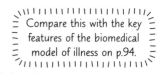
Compare this with the key features of the biomedical model of illness on p.94.

> 1) In the 1930s, mental disturbance was sometimes treated surgically. Doctors actually severed neural connections between certain parts of the brain. This is called a lobotomy. It often had unwanted side effects, such as adverse effects on the patient's intellect. Lobotomies aren't done any more, although more refined brain surgery is sometimes used in extremely severe cases.
>
> 2) In the 1940s, electroconvulsive therapy (ECT) was used to treat depression. It's still sometimes used to treat very severe depression. In ECT, an electric current is passed through the patient's brain, to create a seizure a bit like an epileptic fit.
>
> 3) Drugs are used to treat all sorts of mental illness. Some drugs have severe side effects.
>
> 4) Mental illness is also treated by psychotherapy, where the patient talks to a therapist who tries to get them thinking in a more healthy way.

Poverty and Low Social Class have Links to Mental Illness

1) There are **structural explanations** for the link between mental health problems and **low social class**. For example, **unemployment**, **social exclusion**, **poverty** and **stress** may make mental disorders more likely.

2) It's a **vicious cycle** too — people suffering from **poor mental health** are more likely to become **unemployed** and **socially excluded**, which may make their **mental health worse**.

Feminists see Women's Mental Illness as a Result of Patriarchy

Joan Busfield (2001) thinks that women might be diagnosed with more than their fair share of mental health problems because of **sexism** in the **male-dominated medical elite**. She thinks that doctors **label** and **interpret** behaviour differently depending on whether it's a man or a woman doing it. For instance, an **angry, stressed, upset woman** might be labelled **mentally ill** but an **angry, stressed, upset man** might just be 'overworked'.

1) **Marxist feminists** think that women's mental illness is caused by their 'dual oppression' as **housewife** and **worker**.

2) **Radical feminists** suggest mental illness in women is a consequence of **patriarchal society** in which women have **low social status**, the **stress** of **housework** and **childcare** and the stress of **social isolation**.

3) However, **women** are also more likely to **seek medical help** than men (see the previous page), which may account for some of the difference in statistics.

Mental Illness

Inequalities in Ethnicity and Mental Health have Different Explanations

1) Some sociologists use **interactionist thinking** to explain inequalities in **ethnicity and mental health**. **Littlewood and Lipsedge (1982)** found that psychiatric doctors and nurses were more likely to use sedatives with **black** patients. They suggested that this was because the medical staff were **mostly white** and did not understand how to speak to patients who were **culturally different**. They looked to drugs as an **easy solution**.

2) Others have offered **structural** explanations. **James Nazroo (1997)** found that ill health in ethnic minorities in general was linked to **poor housing**, **stress**, **low status** and **poverty**. Mental health differences could be part of the **same pattern**.

The Interactionist Approach Sees Mental Health as a Social Construct

Thomas Szasz (1971) reckoned that **mental illness doesn't really exist**.

1) He thought that what we call 'mental illness' is really just another '**social construct**' — a **label** society uses to **control non-conformist behaviours**. He said that people who behave in a way that the rest of society sees as **unacceptable** or **dangerous** are defined as 'mentally ill'.

2) Szasz compared **sectioning** (see p.100) to the **persecution of witches** in the Middle Ages.

3) Szasz prefers a **system** where individuals are **free** to get psychotherapy **if they want to**. He says it's important that there's **no threat of force**, coercion or **loss of liberty**.

R.D. Laing was a psychiatrist who wrote in the late 1960s. He believed that 'mental illness' is really a natural response to being in an unbearable situation. He also thought that mental illness needn't always be a negative thing. He had an idea that **mental breakdowns** could turn into **mental breakthroughs**.

1) **Erving Goffman (1961, 1970)** saw mental illness as a **stigma** caused by **negative labelling**.

2) Goffman was particularly **harsh** on the **role of mental institutions** in reinforcing these labels.

Goffman (1961) studied patients and staff in psychiatric institutions

Goffman described three stages that patients tend to go through in response to being labelled 'mentally ill'.

Withdrawal	Patient doesn't communicate with other patients — doesn't believe he / she belongs with them.
Rebellion	Patient refuses to cooperate with staff.
Cooperation	Patient plays along with the staff idea of how a mental patient behaves. Patient starts to act crazy.

The staff respond to the patient's 'crazy' behaviour by **punishing** the patient — they take away the patient's liberty and privacy and they don't let the patient make choices. This is called '**mortification of the self**'. It ends up with the patient losing their personality.

The patient becomes **institutionalised**, which means they can't manage on their own outside the institution. After this, the staff can start from scratch, building up a 'sane' conformist personality.

If a patient said, "I don't belong here — I'm not mad", the staff might think, "that's just what a mad person would say — you must be mad".

Practice Questions

Q1 Which social groups are statistically most vulnerable to mental illness?
Q2 What is the biomedical approach to mental health?
Q3 According to Szasz, what is mental illness?

Exam Questions

Q1 Analyse two explanations for why feminists blame the patriarchy for women's mental heath issues. [10 marks]

Q2 Evaluate the idea that mental illness is a social construct. [20 marks]

If you say you're sane, it's proof you're not...

There's a lot of stigma attached to mental illness. Some charities, such as Mind, are campaigning to end the stigma and discrimination that people suffering from mental illness face. Things are improving, but there's still a way to go. Anyway, learn about which groups are most likely to suffer from poor mental health — but remember, they're all generalisations.

The Role of Medicine and Health Care Professionals

Sociologists have differing views on the purposes that doctors and other health care professionals serve.

Functionalists *See Illness as* Deviant — *Doctors* Control *this Deviance*

1) According to **functionalists** like **Talcott Parsons (1951)**, doctors have an **important function in society** — they control the amount of time people take off **work** and **family duties**.

2) Illness is **'deviant behaviour'** which **disrupts** work and home life — you're not supposed to take time off sick.

3) Parsons said that sick people take on a **"sick role"**. While a person is sick, they're allowed to stop functioning in their **normal role**. They don't have responsibility for making themselves better — but they are **expected** to **want to get better**, and to do whatever the doctor tells them.

4) Doctors have the **power** to **confirm** that the patient is **actually ill**. Doctors **allow** the sick person to take limited time off, and **make them better** by using their **expert medical knowledge**. Parsons thought that doctors always put the patient's needs before their own needs.

Critics of Parsons say the medical profession don't always put patients first — they say private medicine is proof that doctors are self-interested. However, it **can't be denied** that doctors really do give people **sick notes** so they can take sick leave.

Interactionists *Look at* Doctor-Patient Interactions

Interactionists (also called interpretivists) focus on the **social interactions between individuals** (see p.4). Research by **Szasz and Hollender (1956)** found there were **three types of interactions** between a patient and a doctor, which don't all match Parsons' 'sick role' concept.

Relationship	What happens	Example of condition
Activity/passivity	The doctor **does something to** the patient.	An operation such as a liver transplant
Guidance/co-operation	The doctor **tells** a **co-operative patient** what to do.	Acute conditions such as bronchitis
Mutual participation	The doctor **helps** the patient to administer **self-care**.	Chronic conditions such as diabetes

Marxists *see* Medicine *as an* Institution *which* Supports Capitalism

Marxists believe that the medical profession only do good for the **capitalist** class — they **keep class inequalities going**. Marxists say that medical professionals are in a position of **power** and have a **conservative** role in society.

1) Doctors keep the workforce **healthy** and **productive**. **Healthy** workers can **work harder** and won't have to take **time off sick**. This means **more profits** for the capitalist class.

2) Doctors **check** that **workers** aren't spending **too much time on sick leave**.

3) Marxists believe that doctors **hide the real social causes of illness** (poverty, class inequality etc.) by focusing on the individual and their physical symptoms.

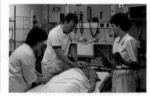

Donald had been deemed fit for work.

Some Marxists think that **doctors** are **agents** of **large drugs corporations** — they exist to produce **profits** for the pharmaceutical industry...

The Global Pharmaceutical Industry *has been* Criticised

1) The **global pharmaceutical industry**, sometimes nicknamed **'big pharma'**, grew through researching and producing medicines that successfully cure and treat serious diseases. However, drug companies always want to make a **profit**...

2) Writers such as **Jacky Law (2006)** say that the industry has too much **power**, and accuse it of:

- **Controlling** which 'illnesses' are **publicised** and **researched** — these being the ones that'll make them **most money**. They're even accused of identifying and promoting **new conditions** for the medicines they already have.

- **Hiding drug trial results** that show the drugs **don't** work very well.

- Providing **incentives to doctors** to endorse or prescribe their products.

> E.g. some people claim drug companies have caused the rise in ADHD, by persuading adults that if they're easily distracted then they have ADHD and need drugs.

3) The pharmaceutical industry has also been accused of making life-saving drugs too **expensive** for the people who need them. On the other hand, there are some companies that aim to provide **free** or **affordable** drugs to developing countries — for example, to cure **malaria** in **Africa**.

The Role of Medicine and Health Care Professionals

Feminists *see the* Medical Profession *as serving* Patriarchal Interests

1) Some feminists say that most **contraceptive methods** (e.g. the pill and IUDs) are designed for men rather than women. This doesn't mean men are supposed to use them — it means they have **significant health risks** for women that **men would never put up with**.

2) **Oakley (1984)** has said that the process of childbirth has been "**medicalised**". In other words, women giving birth are treated like there's **something wrong with them**. **Control** over giving birth is taken away from women and given to **men**. Male doctors are often in charge, not midwives or the women who are actually giving birth.

3) Women tend to have **subordinate** roles in medicine — **nurses** and **auxiliaries** tend to be **women**, while **consultants** tend to be **men**. Some feminists think that the role of being a nurse has been made to look like being a '**doctor's handmaid**' — a female servant **obeying** the male doctor.

4) **Cosmetic surgery** is criticised by some feminists as the 'medicalisation of beauty', and also as a **social control** over women.

5) Feminists see the diagnosis and treatment of **depression** in women as another kind of **social control**.

Weberians *see the* Medical Profession *as Self-Serving*

1) Weberians think that doctors **arrange** things so that they **keep** their **power** and **high status** in society.

> A Weberian is a follower of German sociologist, historian and economist Max Weber (1864-1920).

2) They suggest that the medical profession is **self-serving**. They argue that the medical profession has managed to **shut out** other forms of healing such as homeopathy, aromatherapy, faith healing and other types of **alternative medicine**. This gives modern medicine a monopoly.

Postmodernists *Believe the* Power *of the Medical Profession has* Reduced

Postmodernists **don't** accept that the other sociological views explain the role of health care professionals **today**.

1) Traditionally, doctors held **all the knowledge** about medical conditions and treatments — this gave them **power**. Postmodernists say this has changed. The **internet** means people **empower themselves** by doing their **own research** and **diagnosing themselves**. However, some doctors complain that this often misinforms patients, causing **unnecessary worry** and leading them to **demand inappropriate treatments**.

2) Postmodernists believe that health care is now part of our **consumerist society**, e.g. patients can **choose** which NHS hospital to be treated at, based on mortality rates, etc. They can also **pick** from a range of **complementary and alternative treatments**, such as acupuncture or homeopathy (although not necessarily funded by the NHS).

3) Postmodernists also believe that society has become **medicalised** so that normal **life changes**, such as the **menopause** and **old age**, are treated as medical conditions. This transfers power from health professionals to both the **drug companies** (who advertise their products as **wonder cures**), and to the patient **consumers**.

Practice Questions

Q1 What is the 'sick role'?

Q2 According to Marxists, how does medicine support capitalism?

Q3 Give two reasons why the medical profession could be seen as patriarchal.

Q4 What is the postmodernist view on the power of the medical profession?

Exam Questions

Q1 Outline two arguments that support the idea that pharmaceutical companies can influence global health care. Explain each one. [10 marks]

Q2 Evaluate the idea that the medical profession has a lot of power in today's society. [20 marks]

'Big pharma' — making up diseases and convincing us we have them...

It all sounds like a conspiracy theory to me. But that doesn't mean it isn't true. Look back at the stuff on iatrogenesis on page 94, as that's relevant here — some people have accused the big pharmaceutical companies of this. Make sure you know all the different sociological viewpoints on these pages — some of them aren't that surprising. But who likes surprises?

Consensus Structuralism

> For papers 1 and 3 of the **full A-level exams**, you need to make sure that you've revised the content in **Section One — Sociological Methods** as well as the content in this section.

Structural Theorists see Society as a System Of Parts

1) **Structural** theories analyse society as a **whole system** made up of **different parts** that **mesh together**.

2) Structural theories can be either **consensus** or **conflict** based. The main **consensus** theory is **functionalism** (which you already know about). It stresses the **consensual** nature of society, something Durkheim called "social solidarity".

Functionalists use the 'Organic Analogy' to describe the Nature of Society

1) The **organic analogy** is used by **Talcott Parsons (1951)** to show how society acts like a **living organism**. An organism has a series of **organs** that are **interconnected** and **interdependent**, and Parsons says that likewise **society** is a set of parts that are all **interconnected**, and all **interdependent**.

2) Functionalists describe change as 'evolutionary', which means that if there's a change in one part of society, other parts will **slowly evolve** to adapt to this change.

3) **Social ills** (such as excessive crime) have a **disabling** effect on certain parts of the organism (society), and they can gradually 'infect' other parts.

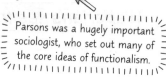
Parsons was a hugely important sociologist, who set out many of the core ideas of functionalism.

Functionalists say that Society is Based on Conformity

1) According to functionalism, interrelations between the various parts of society can only happen because all members of society **agree** on **values** and **norms**. This is called **value consensus**.

2) Individuals **receive** these agreed values and norms in two ways:

- They are **passed down** from generation to generation through the process of **socialisation**.
- They are reinforced through **social control** — **conformity** is **rewarded**, and **non-conformity** is **sanctioned**.

3) Functionalists argue that if society **changes too quickly**, norms are lost before new ones can be created. **Durkheim** called this **anomie** — a state of moral confusion and social instability that's bad for individuals and society.

Functionalism says Society's Needs are met by Four Major Subsystems

Functionalism says all members of society have **needs** and **desires** that the **social system** must cater for. These needs can be broken down into **instrumental** needs and **expressive** needs.

Instrumental needs are **material** — e.g. the need to be fed, the need to have a home. These needs are supported by:

Expressive needs are **emotional** — e.g. the need to **belong**. These needs are looked after by:

| the **political subsystem** (political parties, trade unions) | the **economic subsystem** (industries) | the **kinship subsystem** (marriage and family) | the **cultural subsystem** (e.g. schools, churches) |

Functionalism tries to Explain Everything

1) Functionalism, through the work of **Comte, Durkheim and Parsons**, was the first real attempt to create a theory to explain the operation of the **whole of society**. This kind of theory is called a **macro-theory** — i.e. a **large-scale theory**, as opposed to a **micro-theory** or **small-scale theory**.

2) It's useful in showing how all the main institutions of society, such as the **education** system and the **family**, are **linked** to each other.

3) It helps to explain activities and actions that superficially seem **unusual** or strange. An example of this is **Durkheim's** study of **suicide (1897)**. In this study, Durkheim argues that **social structure** and problems in the modern world cause people to commit suicide. In this case, what seems to be an **individual act** is actually part of a **wider social picture**.

Functionalism says that this hairstyle has a purpose in society.

Consensus Structuralism

Functionalism is *Criticised* for *Ignoring Conflict* and *Maintaining Inequality*

1) Functionalism is criticised for its focus on **harmony** and **cooperation**. It fails to take into account the **differences** and **conflicts** between groups in society. For example, **Merton (1968)**, who is actually a functionalist himself, argues that some things that are functional for one group may cause problems for another, e.g. **poverty** may benefit the rich and cause problems for the poor (see p.84).

2) In seeing all individuals as products of society, functionalism doesn't allow for the **free will** of individuals to make their own choices. This is a criticism from **action theorists** (p.108-109), such as **Dennis Wrong (1961)**. He argued that functionalists give too much importance to the role of society in determining people's **behaviour**.

3) Functionalists try to see a **positive purpose** in **all aspects of society** (even aspects which many people would view as harmful and negative). Durkheim claimed that if a **social phenomenon** didn't fulfil a **function**, it wouldn't **exist**.

4) According to functionalists, **conflict** in society is **minimal** because people **accept** that **inequality** is **inevitable**. **Conflict theorists** (see p.106-107) disagree with this, and see functionalism as a **conservative** approach to society that **upholds inequality** and injustice. They argue that the problems suffered by the working classes, women and ethnic minorities have not been **adequately explained** and justified by functionalism.

5) Functionalists such as Parsons talk about "**meritocracy**", which is the idea that people succeed or fail based on their **own merits**. This suggests that society is **already fair**, so it's pointless to try to make things more equal.

6) **Postmodernists** argue that today's society is too **diverse** for functionalism to be relevant. They say that the idea of value consensus cannot account for the **variety** of lifestyles and values in postmodern society (see p.110-111).

The *New Right* is also a type of *Consensus Structuralism*

1) Like functionalist sociologists, New Right sociologists believe that **traditional institutions** and **values** in society are what maintain **social order**.

2) According to New Right thinkers, the **family** is one of the most important social institutions. The family **socialises** children into traditional norms and values, and **reinforces the traditional roles** of 'male breadwinner' and 'female housewife' — they believe these roles are essential for society's stability. Unsurprisingly, therefore, New Right sociologists **favour the nuclear family** and see **marriage** as **crucial** (see p.61).

3) The New Right believe that **society** is **breaking down**, and that this has come from a **decline in traditional moral standards**. They blame changes in **family structures** (see p.62-63), an **over-generous welfare state**, and too much **sexual freedom** (such as the legalisation of homosexuality — see p.53) for society's problems.

The *New Right* has been *Criticised* by *Feminists*

1) Feminists criticise New Right theorists for wanting women to focus on **marriage** and **children** and **not work** outside the home. Feminists see this as **harmful** to **women's rights**.

2) **Abbott and Wallace (1990)** argue that New Right theorists are wrong to **prioritise marriage so much**, because some women feel **trapped** in **unhappy** or even **abusive** marriages.

3) Feminist theorists argue that New Right thinking is an attempt to **justify** a **patriarchal** society.

See p.107 for more on feminism.

Practice Questions

Q1 What is the 'organic analogy'?

Q2 What are the four main subsystems in society, according to functionalists?

Q3 Why do New Right theorists believe that the family is important for maintaining social order?

Exam Question

Q1 Evaluate the idea that the functionalist approach is the best way to understand society. [20 marks]

I'm barely functional before my first cup of tea...

You'll probably be at least a little bit familiar with these theories from earlier sections. It helps to have it all here, so that you can revise what you need to know for the sociological theory and methods questions without getting it mixed up with other stuff. Make sure you can describe the ideas of both functionalism and the New Right — and know the main criticisms of both.

Conflict Structuralism

Time to say goodbye to all the nice harmonius stuff on the previous pages and say hello to OPPRESSION and EXPLOITATION.

Conflict Structuralists *say that the* Different Parts *of* Society Clash

Like consensus structuralists, **conflict structuralists** look at society as a **system of parts**. However, they believe that there's a **conflict of interest** between different **groups** in society. **Marxists** and **feminists** are conflict structuralists.

Marxism *says* Capitalist *society has created* Two Classes *with* Different Needs

1) **Marx (1867)** said there are **two conflicting classes** in **capitalist society**. The ruling class (the '**bourgeoisie**') owns and controls the means of production (e.g. factories and machinery), and the working class (the '**proletariat**') works for them.

2) According to Marx, the means of production make up the economic **base** of society. This base then **determines** the **superstructure** (the **institutions** in society, e.g. religion, the education system). This is called **economic determinism**.

3) In Marxist thought, the job of the superstructure is to **legitimise** the position of the ruling class — institutions are set up to **stop** the working class gaining **power**, and to make it seem **okay** for the ruling class to own and control everything.

4) Marx claimed that these messages lull the proletariat into a **false consciousness**, which means they aren't fully aware of the **oppression** they suffer and how to **break free** from it. Marx argued that **revolution** was the only way for the proletariat to recognise how they have been oppressed, and that a socialist/communist society would then emerge.

Neo-Marxism *focuses on* Ideology

In the Western world, Marx's revolution **has not happened** (though it did in some parts of the world, like Eastern Europe). Therefore, in the twentieth century, **Neo-Marxists** developed new models of Marx's theories to make them relevant to the modern world. There are **two** important models:

Ideology is a set of ideas and beliefs about the way things should be.

Humanistic Marxism *was Developed by* Gramsci

1) **Gramsci (1971)** focused on **hegemony** (the **domination** of ruling class **ideology** in society). He argued that social control doesn't just come from **economics** — it also comes from **ideas**.

2) For Gramsci, because the ruling class controls the means of **producing ideas** (e.g. the press and the education system), their ideas become **dominant**, and the working class **consent** to them. Gramsci argued that, in the modern world, **consent** is a crucial way of **maintaining power** — more so than **coercion** (using the police, army etc.).

3) Gramsci said that people could **never** rise up because of **economic position** alone. They would have to rise up **intellectually**, by working out a '**proletarian hegemony**' with a completely new **idea** of how to organise society.

Althusser *is an Important Figure in* Structuralist Marxism

1) According to **Althusser (1970)**, people **can't** come up with **new ideas** about society — this ability is a **lie** created by society's **ideological state apparatuses (ISAs)**. These ISAs (elements such as the press, religion and the education system) are closely controlled by the **state**.

2) **Marx** believed that **economics** determined **everything**. Althusser said that there are also **two other** important structures in society — political and ideological. Each of these structures is **partly independent** from the other two. Althusser believed that capitalism would be **overthrown** when these three structures **contradicted** one another.

Marxism *is criticised for its* Structural Focus *and* Determinism

1) Marxism is **deterministic** — it assumes that oppression is **inevitable** for the working class, until a revolution happens.

2) **Traditional** Marxism sees everyday life purely in terms of '**class conflict**'. **Ethnicity** and **gender** are largely **sidelined**.

3) Additionally, the fall of Communism in Eastern Europe has been used as **evidence** for **flaws** in Marxist theory. However, many people argue that Eastern Europe didn't have **true Communism** anyway.

4) The **increased affluence** and **consensual nature** of many Western societies highlights the **lack of conflict**.

Weber was Critical of Marxism

Weber said that there could be **conflict** between **all kinds of social groups**. He **rejected Marx's idea** that **owners vs. workers** was the **only important division**, and said that people were also divided by **class**, **status** and **political** grouping.

Conflict Structuralism

Feminist Theory aims to explain the causes of Gender Inequalities

1) Feminists believe that society is **patriarchal** — institutions are run by, and in the **interests** of, **men**.

2) Feminist theory aims to **unmask** patriarchy and to **empower** people to campaign against it.

3) Feminists also believe that **traditional sociology** and its theories and methods are often patriarchal and male-orientated. They are often interested in studying issues which have been **ignored** in traditional sociology, for example **domestic violence**, power relationships within the **family**, and gender inequalities in **education**.

4) There are many **different strands** of feminism, including **liberal** feminism, **radical** feminism and **Marxist** feminism.

Liberal Feminists want Equal Rights for Women

1) **Liberal feminists** believe that the main cause of inequality is a lack of legitimate opportunities for women in education, employment and politics.

2) They think that the best way to bring about greater gender equality is to work within **existing power structures** to create **equal opportunities**.

3) An example of this is the introduction of laws that prevent sex discrimination, such as the **Equal Pay Act (1970)**.

4) Liberal feminists have been criticised by radical feminists for failing to recognise that **patriarchal values** are rooted in other areas of social life such as the **family**, as well as in formal institutions.

After completing her degree in engineering, Phyllis was delighted to find work within existing power structures.

Radical Feminists want to Change Society Itself

1) **Radical feminists** argue that the very **structure** of **society** is based on the **oppression of women**. **Revolutionary change** is needed to bring about **new 'gender roles'** and **real equality**.

2) **Kate Millett (1970)** argued that **patriarchy** was the **first** and is the **most fundamental** form of **inequality**. She argued that, **regardless of class**, **all women** are expected to be **subservient** to **all men**. While it may be **difficult** to **change** your **class**, historically at least, it has been all but **impossible** to **change** your **sex**.

3) Millett argued that there's a form of **politics** in all **relationships** featuring an **imbalance** of **power** — such as **at work** and **in the home**. Sexual politics for Millett was the **working** of that **power** to keep **women** in **subordinate roles** in:

   • **the family** — women are brought up to **expect** and **assume subordinate roles**.

   • **education** — women **aren't expected** to **study subjects** which **lead** to **high powered** or **highly paid jobs**.

   • **religion** — which uses its **authority** to **strengthen patriarchy**.

4) Millett believed that women largely **internalise patriarchy** and come to **see themselves** as **inferior** — but that the **final guarantee** of **male dominance** is **force** and the **threat of violence**.

Marxist Feminists believe that Capitalism is Partly to Blame

1) For Marxist feminists, **capitalism benefits** from the **exploitation** of women. Within families, women look after homes and raise children **for free** — at no cost to the **state**.

2) **Ansley (1972)** claims that women also bear the brunt of their husbands' work **frustrations**, which would otherwise be directed at their **capitalist employers**.

Practice Questions

Q1 What is the main difference between neo-Marxism and traditional Marxism?

Q2 Name two models of neo-Marxism and a key sociologist for each.

Q3 Name three strands of feminism.

Exam Question

Q1 Evaluate the idea that Marxist approaches are the best way of understanding society. [20 marks]

Patriarchy — the more you write it, the less it looks like a real word...

I like feminism — it's a theory that has clear ideas about the things to be researched (women, gender, etc...), and has a history of getting things done. Nice and efficient. Make sure you know the different strands, though — not all feminists are the same.

Action Theories

Action theories are pretty much the same thing as interactionism and interpretivism, which you've come across before.

Action Theorists *see individuals as* 'Social Actors' *who* Act *rather than* React

1) Unlike structuralists, **action theorists** say that people **make their own choices**, and take their own **action** — rather than being **controlled** by **social structure** or **reacting** to it. They see people's actions as key to studying society.

2) Action theorists claim society is **constructed** from people's meanings, interpretations, behaviours and negotiations.

3) Action theories can be called **micro-theories**, because they look at **individuals**, rather than the big structures of society.

Action Theories see Social Order as a Social Construction

1) Action theorists argue that social order isn't something generated by **institutions**, either through consensus or conflict. Social order is **part of everyday life**, and they see everyday life as a series of **interpretations**.

2) They say social order is a social construction — a **product** of individuals' minds. They say people want to **believe** that there's order in society so they behave towards others in a way that **convinces** them that there **is** order. For example, they **follow social norms**, e.g. being **polite** to each other, **not stealing** from each other.

Action Theories reject the idea that Sociology is Objective

1) If you believe that people put their **own meanings** and **labels** on the world, you also have to accept that they can all put **different labels** and **meanings** on the **same action**. Every person will **interpret** an action (e.g. drinking alcohol regularly) slightly differently to others depending on the meaning they attach to it, e.g. one person might think it's a **normal** part of relaxing after work, and another person might think it's the first sign of **alcoholism**.

2) This means that sociologists **can't predict** people's behaviour as easily as structural approaches would suggest. People don't passively react to external stimulation in exactly the **same way** every single time. They act differently according to the **circumstances**, and according to their own **personal opinions**.

3) In other words, action theories say that sociology **isn't an objective science**. It's all very, very subjective.

Action theories are **criticised** for their **subjective** and **relativist** nature. Critics worry that if the world is seen as subjective and based on assumptions and interpretations, then **nothing is true or false** — this would reduce sociology to a **mess of individual opinions**.

There are Three Important Action Theories

Social Action Theory *Started with* Max Weber

1) Weber argued that a sociologist needs both **structural** approaches (like Marxism) and **action** approaches in order to understand society. He said that human behaviour needs to be described on **two levels**:
   - **The level of cause**, which explains how behaviour is shaped by **objective structural factors**.
   - **The level of meaning**, which looks at the **subjective meanings** that people attach to their actions.

2) For example, same-sex marriage was legalised in England and Wales in 2014. At the **level of cause**, Tim and James get married because the **law** now allows it. At the **level of meaning**, Tim and James get married because of the love they **feel** for one another. You need to think about **both** levels to properly **understand** the couple's behaviour.

3) Weber tried to **categorise** all these different possible meanings into **four types of action**:
   - **Instrumentally rational action** is based on the most efficient means of achieving a goal, e.g. Sue builds a bridge to get across a river.
   - **Value-rational action** is taken because something is important for its own sake, e.g. Mary builds a bridge because she thinks bridges are beautiful.
   - **Traditional action** is based on habit, e.g. Mel builds a bridge because her family have always built bridges.
   - **Affectual action** is based on emotion, e.g. Paul builds a bridge because his wife died trying to cross the river.

Social Action Theory is Criticised for being so Subjective

1) Weber has been criticised for focusing too much on **individual** meanings, and not explaining how we develop **shared** ones — e.g. everyone knows that standing up when someone enters a room is a sign of **respect**.

2) It can also be **difficult** to **classify** actions into **just one** of the four types. For example, you might build a bridge to get across a river, but you might **also** try to make that bridge beautiful.

Action Theories

Symbolic Interactionism focuses on How We Relate To Others

1) **Mead (1934)** claimed that most human interaction is **symbolic** — e.g. when you wave at a friend across the road, a **symbol** (the wave) conveys the **meaning** of your action (a greeting).

Language is the most important 'shared symbol'.

2) There is a **gap** between your friend **seeing** your symbol and them **responding** to it, during which they **interpret** your action. To do this, they must put themselves in **your position**. This is called '**taking the role of the other**'.

3) According to Mead, we learn to interpret symbols through **social interaction**, and it's this knowledge of **shared symbols** and their meanings that allows us to function as members of society.

4) **Blumer (1969)** added more detail to Mead's ideas, and divided interactionism into **three key ideas**:

   - Actions **aren't instinctive** (as with animals). They're based on the **meanings** we attach to the world around us.
   - These meanings come from the ways in which we **relate** to others, so sometimes they can **change**.
   - More specifically, we **mostly relate** to others by **taking the role of the other**.

Ethnomethodology argues that 'Society' is only a Construct

1) The biggest name in ethnomethodology is **Harold Garfinkel (1967)**. Unlike functionalists, Garfinkel sees **society** as something that's created from the '**bottom up**'. It's not an objective structure, but something we all **construct ourselves** through our **behaviour**.

Testing your reflexivity can be a dangerous business.

2) **Ethnomethodology** studies the **methods** we use to create meanings. For ethnomethodologists, meanings are always potentially unclear, because they are dependent on their context — they call this **indexicality**.

3) To stop this lack of clarity from causing **chaos**, we all engage in **reflexivity** — using our **common sense** to determine the meanings of behaviour and communication, so we can maintain social order.

Structuration combines Structuralism and Social Action

1) Structuration theorists such as **Anthony Giddens (1984, 1987)** believe that sociologists should look at both the **interactions between individuals** and the **social structures** that influence these interactions.

2) Like structural theorists, structuration theorists say that individuals have to conform to the **rules** of **social structures** and **social systems**. A lot of **actions depend on these structures**. Giddens used the example of **language** — you have to stick to the **rules** of a language to **communicate** with others.

3) But... Giddens also argues that the **structures** are **dependent** on people **living by them** — e.g. a language only survives if people **use it**. Structuration theorists also say that social structures can be **changed** by the actions of individuals (e.g. new words can be **added** to a language). This is more like what action theorists say.

4) Individuals also **respond** to the structures in **different ways**. Individuals have an **awareness** of the social rules and structures and have **some level of choice** about how to react to them.

This is a simplified version of Giddens' theory. The real thing is pretty abstract.

Structuration theory assumes that if people want to change the world, they can manage it **fairly easily**. This is something that Marxists and feminists would **disagree** with.

Practice Questions

Q1 Name the two levels that Weber used to understand human behaviour.

Q2 What does 'taking the role of the other' mean to social interactionists?

Q3 How does structuration combine both structuralism and action theory?

Exam Question

Q1 Evaluate the idea that action theories provide the best way to understand society. [20 marks]

Now, how many of these words can you actually spell...

Joking apart, make sure you know how to spell these terms — no one wants to read about endomethnodology. Also, make sure you know the difference between action theories and structural theories. Action theories focus on how society is created through people's actions (see what they did there). Structural theories see society as something that's already constructed.

Modernity and Postmodernity

Modernity and postmodernity may sound similar, but they're very different perspectives. Modernists believe that we can discover truths about our society through rational thinking. Postmodernists say that 'truth' doesn't even exist. Tricky.

Modernity refers to the Modern, Industrial, Ordered world

1) Modernity refers to the **industrial world** that began to emerge in Western Europe in the late eighteenth century.
2) This saw the rise of **mass production**, **urbanisation** and **state bureaucracy** — **states** are crucial to modern society.
3) Modernity refers to a period of time when studies of the world were guided by **ordered**, **rational scientific** thinking. **Science** was seen as the answer, rather than the **traditional** sources of knowledge, such as religion.

1) **Modernist sociological theories** study **modernist societies**. They aim to investigate the world scientifically, and explain why societies have evolved to be the way they are, and why they're arranged in the way they are.
2) The modernist theories are the **structuralist** theories of **Marxism** and **functionalism**. These are also called **'grand narratives'**, which is a fancy way of saying **'big stories'**, and **'metanarratives'**, which is a fancy word for 'stories that make sense of other stories'. They're **big**, **all-encompassing theories** that try to find **certain answers** to questions.
3) Modernist theories like Marxism claim a **monopoly of truth** (they claim that they're **objectively right** about society).

Postmodernism argues that Society has Progressed from Modernity

Postmodernists say that society today has **moved on** from the ordered world of **modernity** because of various **changes**:

1) **Work** has become more **flexible**, and service industries have partly taken over from manufacturing industries.
2) There's an emphasis on **consumption of cultural products**.
3) There's **pluralism of culture**, and **pluralism of roles**. People interpret society, and their own identities, in different ways according to the circumstances they're in (e.g. the same woman could have labels and roles of 'mother', 'wife', 'friend' and 'employer').
4) **Globalisation** has affected both **production** and **communication**, which has made the boundaries between states less important:
   - There's been globalisation of **consumption** and **culture**.
   - **Technology** has improved **communications** between countries.
   - There is a more **global economy**, with many transnational corporations (TNCs).

Work had become increasingly flexible for Jeffrey.

See p.156-157 for plenty more on globalisation.

1) **Postmodernists** argue that sociology has moved into a time when **metanarratives** (like functionalism) can't answer all the questions about the social world. Postmodernists say that there's a whole range of **competing theories** out there, which all have **something** to say about society. They argue that no one theory can claim a monopoly of the truth. All versions of the truth are true for the people who believe in them — this is a **relativist** position.
2) **Lyotard (1979)** argues that this has important consequences for our understanding of **language**. Instead of one overall language of words and their **set meanings**, there is just a series of **'language games'** — the meaning of a word depends on the way someone **uses it**. Meaning is something we **construct**.

Baudrillard said we're living in a Hyper-reality

A signifier is something you can see or hear, e.g. a red traffic light. The signified is what this represents, e.g. stop your car. The sign is these two elements linked together.

1) For **Baudrillard (1981)**, postmodern society is more about **consumption** than production, and he focuses on how we consume **signs**.
2) Baudrillard argues that, in postmodern society, signs don't actually relate to any **real things**, because we have **no agreed definition** of what is real any more. We consume these signs (he calls them 'simulacra' — one is called a 'simulacrum'), even though they're actually **meaningless**.
3) Baudrillard calls this situation **'hyper-reality'** — a complete inability to tell what is real from what is not, so that **simulacra** take over from **reality**.

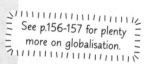
E.g. a child buys a poster of his favourite film character, but this signifier (the poster) represents something that isn't actually real (the character).

Baudrillard is pretty negative about society

- Baudrillard is very critical of the **media**. He says that **television** is one of the main causes of hyper-reality, confusing what is real with **representations** of reality.
- He argues that since we've lost our ability to tell what's **real**, we've also lost our ability to **improve** society.

Modernity and Postmodernity

Postmodernism is Criticised by Structuralists, Action Theorists and Others

1) Postmodernists emphasise the role of **culture** and the **media** in driving the creation of **identities**, **norms** and **values**. People no longer seek one answer to life but are happy to **pick** and **choose** values and identities.

2) This approach largely ignores the interactions between **individuals**, which **upsets action theorists**. It also ignores the relationships between **social institutions**, which **upsets structuralists**.

3) It annoys **Marxists**, because it ignores inequalities, e.g. Baudrillard's idea that television is a cause of hyper-reality **ignores** its function as a way of maintaining hegemony (see p.106).

4) **Harvey (1989)** also says that Baudrillard is **too pessimistic** about our inability to change society for the better.

5) Postmodernist theories (like Lyotard's) seem to **contradict** themselves — postmodernism claims that no one theory can claim a monopoly of truth, so postmodernist theories surely **can't do that either**.

Late Modernity is an Alternative Theory to Postmodernism

1) Some sociologists **disagree** with the claim that we're living in a postmodern society. **Giddens (1990, 1991)** argues that we're actually in a state of '**late modernity**' (or '**high modernity**') — a **continuation** of modernity, not a break from it.

2) In **late modernity**, the **changes** to work, consumption, culture and so on are **accelerated**. Giddens says this is due to two things:

   - **Reflexivity** — we constantly **reflect** upon ourselves and our actions, and **modify** them accordingly.
   - **Disembedding** — we **interact** with one another without meeting **face to face**, e.g. via internet chats.

   For Giddens, these two things have combined to **constantly change culture**, making it **unstable**.

3) **Late modernity** is a state with **high risks** — of war, economic collapse or environmental disaster. Giddens sees high modernity as like a **juggernaut** — a massive force which we can collectively try to direct, but which could go **out of control**.

4) Crucially, Giddens **disagrees** with postmodernists about our ability to **solve** these problems. As a modernist thinker, he believes that we **are** capable of **rational thinking**, which we can use to **make plans** and **reduce risk**.

   1) **Beck (1992)** argues that we are becoming **more individualised**, and therefore we're becoming **even more reflexive**, because we have to take **more responsibility** for our **own actions** and their consequences.

   2) As we do this, we seek to **minimise** the **risk** of bad consequences — Beck calls this '**risk consciousness**'.

   3) For Beck, **society can be improved**, because we can minimise risks on a **political scale**. For example, we try to **monitor** and **minimise** the risks of using **nuclear power**.

Practice Questions

Q1 List three ways in which society has progressed from modernity, according to postmodernists.

Q2 In what way can postmodernist theories be said to contradict themselves?

Q3 Which theory is more optimistic about our ability to improve society, postmodernism or late modernity?

Q4 What is 'disembedding'?

Exam Question

Q1 Apply your own knowledge and material from Item A to evaluate the idea that postmodernist theories provide the best way of understanding today's society. [20 marks]

> **Item A**
> Postmodernists argue that today's society is far too flexible and varied to be understood by one overarching sociological theory. They point to today's plurality of cultures and lifestyles, and claim that theories such as Marxism and feminism are too narrowly focused to explain the workings of a globalised world.

When crossing the road, look both ways for the juggernaut of modernity...

Postmodernism is a lot easier to understand when you look at modernism. Modernism has all these ideas about how the world should be, and how sociology should be, and postmodernism decides to do the opposite. Remember that you can be asked about the usefulness of social theories to explain society, and that includes all the theories on the last eight pages.

Sociology and Science

Depending on your view, sociology may or may not be a science. Of course that also depends on what science actually is.

Science uses Experiments and Observation to Test Theories

1) Scientists collect data through **experiments**, **observation** and **measurement** in order to **test hypotheses** (a hypothesis is an unproved theory).

2) Science values **objectivity** (an unbiased viewpoint). Scientific statements are **based on evidence** which has been collected using **systematic**, **logical methods**.

There is more about theories of science on p.140-141.

There are Different Philosophies of Science

Obviously, it couldn't all be that simple. There are **different views** about **what science is all about**.

Logical positivists believe that scientists go off in search of scientific laws

1) The researcher **observes** something, and decides it needs to be **explained**.

2) The researcher thinks up a **hypothesis** to **explain** the observed phenomenon.

3) The hypothesis is **tested** by **experiments**.

4) If the experiments **agree** with the hypothesis, then the hypothesis becomes a **scientific law**. Scientific laws are **universal** — they explain all phenomena which are similar to the one which was observed in the first place.

This process is called verification, which means checking that something is true.

Popper (1959, 1963) argued that experiments should try to prove the hypothesis wrong — this is called "falsification"

1) The idea is that you can't ever **prove** a hypothesis **100% correct**, no matter how much evidence you've got — but you can prove it **wrong** with just **one** piece of evidence that **contradicts** it.

2) For example, the hypothesis 'all swans are white' isn't proved correct by seeing one flock of white swans. You'd have to look at **every single swan in the universe** and see that they were all white to do that. But if you see just **one black swan**, that proves that 'all swans are white' **isn't true**.

3) Popper believed that it wasn't possible to know **absolute truth**, because you can't prove things are correct.

Popper's view has been **criticised** by later philosophers of science who point out that an experimental result might disagree with a hypothesis because of **experimental error** and **silly mistakes**. In chemistry practicals, you may not get the **predicted result**, but that doesn't mean you've **proved chemistry wrong** — it usually means you've made a **mistake**.

Thomas Kuhn (1962) disagreed with both the logical positivists and Popper

1) Kuhn believed that science uses an **accepted body of knowledge** to solve puzzles. He called this 'normal science'. He was pretty **critical** of it...

2) He thought that scientists took a lot of **assumptions** about the world **for granted**. This assumed **way of looking at the world** is called a 'paradigm'. He said that what scientists do is **constrained** by the **paradigm** they take for granted. For example, for hundreds of years people thought that the Sun went around the Earth, and astronomical observations were **interpreted** according to the paradigm that the Sun went around the Earth.

3) Kuhn argues that **big leaps** of scientific progress come about when **evidence** which **doesn't fit the paradigm** builds up to the point where it **can't be ignored**. Then, scientists come up with a **new paradigm**. This process is called **scientific revolution**.

Paul Feyerabend (1975) went even further, and claimed that there **weren't** any **hard and fast rules** of scientific method. He argued that scientists make all kinds of **tweaks** to theories to make them work. He also disagreed with the idea that science tests hypotheses according to whether they fit observed facts, claiming that already-accepted theories **influence** the way scientists actually **observe** facts.

There's Disagreement about whether Sociology is Scientific

1) **Popper** (see above) said that some sociological concepts **weren't scientific** as they couldn't possibly be **proved wrong**. Sociology could only be a science if it made **hypotheses** which could be **falsified**.

2) **Kuhn** argues that sociology **doesn't have a paradigm** — there isn't a consensus as to what it's about and how it's done. So in his view, it doesn't count as a science.

Sociology and Science

Sociology is More Subjective than Traditional Science

1) **Objective knowledge** is the **same** no matter what your **point of view** is. **Objective** methods provide **facts** that can be easily **verified** or **falsified**. Objective research is also **value-free** (see p.114-115), and doesn't have any **bias**.

2) **Subjective knowledge** depends on your **point of view**. **Subjective** methods give data that **can't** be easily tested. Subjective research requires **interpretation**. Sociology is **more subjective** than the physical **sciences**.

3) Some **postmodernists** like **Lyotard (1984)** claim that it's **impossible** to be objective at all. Lyotard sees **knowledge** as something that people **construct**, not something that people **discover**.

Positivist Sociologists try to be as Objective as Possible...

1) **Positivists** think sociology should be **scientific** and **analyse social facts**. Positivists define social facts as things that can be **directly observed and measured**, e.g. the number of followers of Christianity in Britain. Positivists claim that social facts are **external** to individuals, and constrain their behaviour.

2) Positivists look for **correlations in data**, and **cause and effect relationships**. To do this, they use **quantitative** methods like **questionnaires** and **official statistics**, which are **objective** and **reliable** (see p.8).

...but Interpretivists take a more Subjective approach

1) **Interpretivist sociologists** (or **interactionists**) try to understand human behaviour from the point of view of the **individual**, so they use **qualitative methods** that let them discover the **meanings**, **motives** and **reasons** behind **human behaviour** and **social interaction** (see p.8).

2) **Weber** said it's important to use **empathy** to figure out **why** an individual is doing what they're doing. He called this "**Verstehen**". Interpretivists do this a lot — it's like putting yourself in **someone else's shoes**.

Realist Sociology argues that Sociology can be Scientific

The term 'realism' means different things in different contexts. Here, we're talking about different realists from the ones in 'Crime and Deviance'.

1) **Realists** believe that sociology can be **scientific** — but they divide science into two types:

- The study of **closed systems** — subjects like chemistry where the **variables** can be **closely controlled** and laboratory experiments can be done.
- The study of **open systems** — subjects such as meteorology where the variables are **difficult** or impossible to **control**. Scientists can't make very accurate predictions and can't easily test them experimentally.

2) **Sayer (1984)**, a realist, argued that sociology is the scientific study of an **open system**. Society, like the weather, is **too complex** a system to lend itself to accurate predictions and experiments, but that doesn't mean sociology's not a science.

3) Realists use **qualitative** as well as **quantitative** methods. Individual human motivations — which are investigated by qualitative methods — can't be **directly observed** or **measured**. **But** realists argue that science has a long and **successful history** of **researching** things that can't be **directly observed** (or couldn't at the time), e.g. **black holes** in space.

4) Realists argue that science isn't fundamentally defined by the **collection** and **recording** of **observable data** — for them it's the **search** for the **underlying causes** of **things**, even if those causes aren't directly observable. Realists believe that the **mechanisms** behind social trends and phenomena are **real** and can be **scientifically studied**.

5) They argue that sociology **can't** be entirely **value-free**, but researchers must try to **collect** and **present data** in a **clear** and **neutral** way.

Practice Questions

Q1 What is a hypothesis?
Q2 What, for realists, is the difference between an open and a closed system?

Exam Question

Q1 Outline two reasons why some sociologists say that the study of sociology is scientific. Explain each one. [10 marks]

Don't even get them started on "What is art?"...

If you're flagging, remember that sociology can lead to all sorts of good jobs — researcher, writer, lecturer, civil servant, NHS manager, housing officer, social worker... If you want to be a lion-tamer though, you're in the wrong book.

Sociological Theory and Methods

Sociologists are only human, so they make value judgements about things. The question is whether they should (or can) keep these judgements separate from their research. It's a question that's been asked since the dawn of... sociology.

The **Classical Sociologists** disagree about **Values** in Sociology

Everyone has **values** — general beliefs about what's **important** in life, and what is **right** or **wrong**. Whether or not values **can** or **should** be **separated** from research is a topic of great debate, which began with the founders of sociology.

Comte (1798-1857), Marx (1818-1883) and Durkheim (1858-1917) thought that **sociology** should aim to discover **social facts** about how society **works**. They believed that society is shaped by **big value systems**, and that all the **meanings** and **values** we attach to things are actually **determined** by these **systems** — they aren't really to do with **individuals** at all. This means that sociologists can study society **without** worrying about personal **value judgements**.

Max Weber (1864-1920) **disagreed**. He argued that there was a crucial **difference** between the **facts** discovered by research, and the **value judgements** attached to those facts. For example, you can prove the fact that net migration has increased, but you can't prove the value judgement that immigration controls should be tightened.

Weber argued that values are **needed** when:

- choosing which **area** to study (see p.11).
- **interpreting** data, but these values must be clearly stated.
- choosing how to **use** the findings (and taking **responsibility** for their use).

But Weber believed that the **research process** itself must be kept **value-free**...

Value-Free Research Isn't Influenced by the Researcher

1) **Value-free research** doesn't make **judgements** about whether the things that are researched are **good** or **bad**.
2) It doesn't let the **researcher's own ideology** (ideas and beliefs about how society should be) get in the way. For example, questionnaires mustn't ask questions that **lead** the respondent towards a particular answer (p.14).
3) In order for the idea of **value freedom** to work, the researcher must **interpret** all data **objectively**.
4) Value freedom means that the **end use** of the research **shouldn't matter**. Research should come up with **knowledge**, and how that knowledge is used **isn't** up to the researcher.

Weber argued that the researcher **is** responsible for this.

There's **Debate** over whether **Research** can be **Value Free**

20th Century Positivists believed their Research was *Value Neutral*

20th century positivists argued that their research could be **value neutral** for two reasons.

1) Because they viewed sociology as a **scientific** discipline (see p.112-113), **positivists** believed that it was concerned with **social facts**, not with values about those facts. Their role was to discover **truths** about society, not to judge society.
2) Sociologists were increasingly sought out by **governments** to solve **social problems**. In theory, sociologists could **walk away** after handing in their research findings. This would mean that the sociologist's **own** values were **unimportant** during the research, and that they would **not be responsible** for how their research was used.

Together, Giles and Winette had uncovered the truth. They were donkeys.

Positivists argue that, in general, **quantitative** research methods are **more value-free** than **qualitative** methods (see p.8). Qualitative methods, such as unstructured interviews, mean the researcher is **more involved**, so there's **more risk** their attitudes will **influence** the respondents. Quantitative methods, such as closed questionnaires, allow the researcher **less opportunity** to influence their respondents. They allow the researcher to **keep their distance**.

Look at p.14-15 for more on interviews and questionnaires.

Sociological Theory and Methods

Some sociologists say sociology *Can't* be *Value Free*

1) The decision to research in the first place is **value laden** — someone has to decide that the research is worth spending money on. Some say that research which the **state** or **businesses** want to see is most likely to get funding.

2) It's difficult to **completely avoid bias** and interviewer effects (see p.15). Researcher bias may interfere with structured questionnaires as it's still the researcher who chooses the questions respondents answer.

Other groups of sociologists argue that sociology *Shouldn't* be *Value Free*

Some sociologists argue that we shouldn't try to remove values from sociology. They are called **committed sociologists**.

1) Some Marxist and feminist sociologists **deliberately choose research** with an **end use** that they **approve** of. They believe that sociology **should** make **value judgements** about society and **suggest** ways it could be **better**. For example, **feminists** have researched how the **police** respond to sexual abuse and used it to try to **change policy**.

2) According to **Gouldner (1975)**, value-free research is both **impossible** and **undesirable**.

   - It is **impossible** because you **cannot separate** value judgements from the work. He points to the reasons above, such as value-laden research choice and interviewer effects.

   - It is **undesirable** because sociologists **should** use their values to guide them **morally**. They **have** to take responsibility for the uses of their work in wider society.

Becker (1970) wants sociologists to take the side of the underdogs in society

- Becker says that if research is committed, then that means **taking sides**.
- He believes that it's a **good thing** if sociologists **take sides** with the **less powerful groups** in society, such as **criminals** and the **mentally ill**.
- Becker has been **criticised** for being too focused on powerless groups. **Gouldner** says that it's more important to help those who are actively trying to **fight back** against their powerlessness.

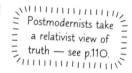

This kind of research would suit interpretivist (or interactionist) research methods (such as participant observation), which produce qualitative data and help the researcher to understand their target group's motivations and feelings.

There are *Other Factors* which make *Values Important* in *Research*

1) The way in which a research project is **funded** and the **career** of the sociologist can also **introduce values** into research. For example, if the research is funded by a charity that helps homeless people, the research data may be **interpreted** in a way that suggests homeless people need more support from the government.

2) Every culture in society has its **own values** and **beliefs**, and each culture thinks that its values and beliefs are **true**. From a **relativist** perspective, this means that there is **no objective way** of saying what is **true** and what is **not**. This also applies to **research** — no one researcher can provide an **objective** picture of society, because their research always depends on what **they think** is true.

Postmodernists take a relativist view of truth — see p.110.

> All of these factors are covered in more detail in Section One of this book — you need to revise that for your exam too. (Sorry.)

Practice Questions

Q1 Name two classical sociologists who felt that sociology was about facts, not values.

Q2 Give two reasons why 20th century positivist sociologists felt that their work was value neutral.

Q3 According to Gouldner, why is value-free research both impossible and undesirable?

Exam Questions

Q1 Outline two ways that sociology can be seen as value free. Explain each one. [10 marks]

Committed sociologists probably make great life partners...

I know it seems unfair — you're nearly at the end of a section, and then a little box pops up telling you to go and revise another one. Well, life's not fair, but Gouldner says that it's a sociologist's job to conduct committed sociological research that does something about that. Look how I seamlessly integrated a learning point into that sentence. See, I'm quite nice really.

Sociology and Social Policy

Social policy focuses on social problems and how social institutions respond to them. Social policy analysts use sociological research to inform governments and other organisations, and influence their response to social problems.

Giddens claims the study of sociology gives Four Practical Benefits

Anthony Giddens (2001) believes that sociological research has four practical purposes:

1) An **understanding** of the world.
2) A heightened awareness of the needs of **individual groups**.
3) An assessment of "**what works**" (**evidence-based policy**).
4) An increased **personal knowledge** of ourselves and others.

Social Policy is the area of Government that tries to Help People

1) **Social policies** are **government** policies that deal with the **well-being** of **citizens** — pensions, health, education, etc. **Social Policy** has also become the name of the **academic subject** that **studies** this area of government.

2) New ideas for social policy are generated by **governments**, **political parties** and **pressure groups**. Social policy **varies** with the **party** in power — in the UK most likely either **Labour** or the **Conservatives**.

3) Most **research** into social policy issues is carried out by **government agencies** such as the departments for **education** and **health**, but some is done by **charities**, such as the **Joseph Rowntree Foundation**, and **university departments**.

4) Governments use **quantitative statistical social research** to **discover** basic **social trends**, e.g. levels of population growth, unemployment and income. More in-depth, **qualitative social research** can give governments an **insight** into the **causes** of social problems such as **poverty** and **crime**, and can **help** in the search for **policies** to tackle them.

The link between sociology and social policy was particularly close in the case of the sociologist **Frank Field**. Between 1997 and 1998, he was a **minister** and **policy-maker** in the Labour government.

Sociological Research gives Policy-Makers insight into Poverty and Inequality

1) The creation of the **Welfare State** after the Second World War gave many the **impression** in the late 1960s that **poverty** had been largely **eradicated** from the UK.

Empirical evidence means data that's from observation and experience.

2) However, **empirical evidence** from **Peter Townsend (1979)** and **Mack and Lansley (1985)** showed that poverty was a hidden problem. Sociologists then did more research to come up with theories of **why** certain groups were **more vulnerable** to poverty. **Social Democrats** blamed an **inadequate** welfare system, the **New Right** (e.g. **Marsland (1989)**) blamed **reliance** on an over-generous welfare system, and **Third Way** thinkers emphasised **citizenship** (two-way responsibility between the citizen and the state).

3) These theories, plus **empirical data**, guided **social policy** about welfare, poverty and inequality.

Weber believed Sociology shouldn't tell decision-makers How to Fix Society

1) Weber believed that sociology **shouldn't make value judgements**. It shouldn't tell policy-makers **how to fix society**.

2) Weber argued that sociological research can **tell** decision-makers whether a particular policy is likely to have the **desired result**, and what **social costs** the policy will incur. Weber thought that the **policy-maker** should come up with the **policy first**, and **then** the researchers should go away and **find evidence** to work out the **best way** of doing it.

3) Weber thought it was important to have **good methodology** to give the most **useful information** to policy-makers.

4) Critics of this view say policy should come **after evidence gathering**, not before. There's a danger that only evidence which **backs up** the policy will be found. Evidence which might suggest a **much better policy** might be ignored.

Postmodernists have Diverse Views on the link between research and policy

1) Postmodernist **Zygmunt Bauman (1990)** believes that sociology **should** inform social research, and worries that society may **get worse** if sociological theories about **poverty** and **welfare** aren't listened to. He argues that **postmodern consumer society** is **marginalising** the Welfare State, and believes this to be a bad thing.

2) However, **Lyotard** is worried that '**scientific**' methods of sociological research could be used to construct **oppressive metanarratives**. **Lyotard** sees **modernist metanarratives** (see p.110) as leading to **strict doctrine** and **oppression**.

Sociology and Social Policy

Marxists think sociology is Too Close to the Capitalist System

1) **Marxists** believe that sociology is **too closely intertwined** with the **capitalist system** to make a difference to society. Since Marxists believe that **capitalism** is inherently **flawed** and **oppressive**, they suggest that sociological study is a **tool** used to **justify unjust social policy**.

2) Marxists believe that research is **controlled** by **ruling-class interests**, which prevents it from being used to change the system to socialism. They point to the amount of **funding** for sociological research which comes from the **state** and from **industry** — they claim sociology is being **bought**.

Some Feminists believe Sociology Can't affect Gender Inequality

Feminists **disagree** about whether or not sociological research can **improve** the lives of women in a **patriarchal society**.

1) Liberal feminists believe that sociological research and analysis has influenced governments and had beneficial results for women's lives. For example, the UK has developed social policy designed to improve the status of women and make them equal in all spheres of social life including employment and benefits.

2) However, radical feminists argue that liberal feminist sociology can't make much difference to the lives of women because society is inherently patriarchal. Radical feminists such as Shulamith Firestone (1971) believe that patriarchal society must be dismantled before women's lives can ever be improved.

3) Socialist feminists claim that social policy oppresses women in particular. They argue it undervalues women's labour (e.g. in the voluntary and informal welfare sectors) and assumes they will bear a dual burden of work and housework. Socialist feminists propose changes to social policy based on their own research and ideology.

Some believe the Link between Sociology and Social Policy isn't very strong

Governments take account of research, but they're **constrained** by **other factors**.

1) Firstly, governments often seek to implement social policy that's **popular** with the **electorate**. It's argued that policies which aren't clear **vote-winners** don't get implemented.

2) Some groups in society may be marginalised because they **don't vote** in **large numbers**. Even if sociology focuses on these groups, they may still find themselves neglected if they don't have **electoral power**.

3) Governments must consider the **financial implications** of any policies they introduce. If a policy is **too expensive**, then no matter how persuasive the sociological research behind it is, it **isn't going to happen**. Also, **expensive policies** tend to make **voters worry** that **taxes** might have to **increase** to pay for them.

4) Sociologists try to solve **sociological problems**:

> Sociological problems are issues that need explaining, even if they don't have negative consequences. For example, which toys boys choose to play with.
>
> Social problems are defined by Worsley (1977) as issues that cause 'friction' or 'misery' and need solving. For example, why boys don't achieve as well as girls in education.

If a **sociological problem** is **also a social problem**, the research will be **useful** for policy-makers. But if it's **not** also a social problem, the research **won't be relevant** to policy-makers.

Practice Questions

Q1 What four practical benefits does sociology have for society, according to Giddens?

Q2 How do Marxists criticise the link between sociology and social policy?

Q3 What other factors affect government decisions on social policy, other than sociology?

Exam Question

Q1 Evaluate the idea that sociology has no effect on social policy. [20 marks]

Sociology, eh — what's it all for...

In an exam, remember that all arguments in this topic are broken into three camps: 1) sociology should actively try and influence policy, 2) sociology should try to change and replace the system, and 3) sociology shouldn't influence social policy. Some people criticise sociologists such as Giddens for overstating the ability of sociology to influence government decisions.

Defining Crime and Deviance

Before you start looking at all the gory details of crime and deviance, you need to get to grips with what they actually are.

Here are some **Definitions** of **Crime** and **Deviance**

Crime = behaviour which **breaks laws** and is **punished** by the **legal system**.	**Deviance** = behaviour which goes against the **norms**, **values** and **expectations** of a **social group** or **society**.

Crime is mostly deviant, but **not all deviance** is **criminal**. Think about it — it's hard to think of a criminal act which isn't also viewed as deviant, but it's easy to make a long list of **non-criminal deviant behaviour** — picking your nose in public and eating it, barking like a dog during a job interview, swearing at the referee, cheating at poker, etc.

Crime and **Deviance** are **Socially Constructed**

1) Crime and deviance are **culturally determined** (though what's seen as deviant **varies** more than what's seen as criminal).

2) In the 1970s, **Michel Foucault** wrote about how definitions of **criminal** deviance, **sexual** deviance and **madness** have changed throughout history, e.g. 100 years ago in the UK it was deviant for **women** to wear **trousers**, but today it's **acceptable**. **Deviance changes** with **time** and **place** as values, norms and social expectations change — it's **relative**.

3) **Plummer (1979)** made a distinction between **situational deviance** and **societal deviance**:

Situational deviance means acts which can be defined as deviant or normal, depending on the circumstances
- Being **naked** — OK in your **own home**, deviant on the **high street**.
- Wearing **chainmail** and carrying a **sword** — OK at a **fancy dress party**, deviant at **work**.

Social rules can be temporarily rejected.

Societal deviance means acts which are seen by most of society as deviant, in most situations
- **Swearing** at an **authority figure** — even people who do it know it's deviant.
- **Kicking a dog** — just about everyone would be shocked by this.

4) Also, what's **deviant** for some groups in society is **conformity** for others. **Subcultures** (see p.120) have **different norms** to mainstream society.

Social Order and **Social Control** create a **Consensus** of how to behave

1) By definition, **most behaviour** in society isn't **criminal** or **deviant**. **Social order** and **social control** create **consensus** for how to behave. People are **socialised** to follow social norms.

2) Some norms become **second nature** — e.g. not standing too close to someone when having a conversation.

3) Other norms are followed because we're **consciously aware** that they're a norm — e.g. stopping at a red traffic light.

4) **Sanctions** are **rewards** and **punishments** that **reinforce** social norms:

	Positive sanctions — **reward** people for **conforming** to a norm	Negative sanctions — **punish** people for **deviating** from a norm
Formal sanctions — carried out by an **official agency**.	• A medal for bravery in the armed forces. • A cup for winning a sporting final.	• A fine for speeding. • A yellow card from the referee.
Informal sanctions — carried out by the **public**.	• A pat on the back. • Saying "well done" for good behaviour.	• Deliberately ignoring someone. • A telling-off for bad behaviour.

Practice Questions

Q1 What is situational deviance?

Q2 Give an example of a formal negative sanction and an example of an informal positive sanction.

Exam Question

Q1   How might crime and deviance be socially constructed? Outline two ways.   [4 marks]

Crime and Deviance — Dostoyevsky's less successful sequel...

Deviance isn't just limited to crime (even if that's what first springs to mind). It actually covers all behaviour that doesn't conform to social norms. Conformity is rewarded and deviance is punished — and some deviance depends on the situation.

Functionalist Theories of Crime

Some theories say that the cause of crime lies with the individual, whereas other theories say that the cause of crime lies within society. If only sociologists would all sit down together and work it out over a nice cup of tea.

Functionalists say Crime and Deviance are Useful and Necessary in society

You might well wonder how on earth crime can be useful. Functionalists say it's because it has a **function** in society:

1) Crime and deviance reinforce the consensus of values, norms and behaviour of the majority non-deviant population — people can join together in outrage. As a result, the differences between deviant behaviour and non-deviant behaviour are reinforced — this is known as boundary maintenance.

2) Durkheim (1897) said deviance allows for social change to occur. Durkheim and the functionalists who came after him argue that all societies need some change to remain healthy and stable. If society reacts positively to deviant behaviour, it starts the process for that behaviour to be seen as non-deviant in the future.

3) However, Durkheim said crime becomes dysfunctional when the level of crime is either too high or too low:
   - Too high, and it threatens social order.
   - Too low, and there's no social change.

Cohen identified Two Ways that deviance maintained Social Order

1) **Albert Cohen (1966)** argued that forms of deviance such as **prostitution** provide a **safety valve** for releasing tension without threatening social stability.

2) Secondly, he argued that deviant behaviour (e.g. civil disobedience, protests and truancy) is used as a **warning device** by society to **identify** emerging **social problems**, which can then be dealt with.

Merton said Crime is a Response to Failing to Achieve society's Cultural Goals

1) Functionalist **Robert Merton (1968)** concluded from his **American** study that the vast majority of individuals share the **same goals** but don't have **equal access** to the means of **achieving** those goals.

2) He identified the **main cultural goals** in **American** society as **success** and **wealth** — this is known as the **American Dream**. He said that the main (institutionalised) means of achieving those goals was through the **education system**. When individuals **fail** or are **excluded** from this system, this creates **anomie**.

3) When an individual is **unable** to achieve society's cultural goals due to factors **beyond their control** (e.g. **discrimination** or **deprivation**), it causes a **strain** which leads to **deviant behaviour**. This is known as **strain theory**.

anomie = a lack of values, and a feeling of normlessness.

4) Merton identified five **adaptations to strain**:

When Nigel felt he couldn't achieve society's goals, he retreated into his shell.

Conforming	Innovating
People who **still try** to achieve the main cultural goals through **legitimate** means are said to **conform**.	People who **fail** at the **standard route** to success **innovate** to find **alternative** and **deviant** means of reaching success and wealth — e.g. **crime**.

Ritual	Retreating	Rebelling
People who cannot achieve society's goals and have **stopped trying** may still **act legitimately** because they're used to the **ritual**.	People who **reject** the main cultural **goals** and the **means** of achieving them may **retreat** from society — e.g. by **dropping out** of school, **drinking** to excess or taking **drugs**.	Instead of retreating, people may **rebel** against society, and engage in **protest** and revolution to try to change it.

Differential Association Theory says that people Learn Deviance from Others

1) **Edwin Sutherland (1939)** argued that **deviance** is **learned** — criminals learn **criminal behaviour** from other **criminals**. This may be within the **family**, if the **parents** are criminals, or through **friends**, **associates** or **gangs**.

2) This is known as **differential association theory**, as deviance (including criminal **attitudes**, **values** and **techniques**) is **passed on** through **association** with other deviants.

Functionalist Theories of Crime

Cohen said Working-Class Boys experience Status Frustration

Subcultural theories say that the **cultural values** of some **groups** (or **subcultures**) actually **encourage deviance**. Some deviance is **conformity** to norms and values — just **different** norms and values to **mainstream society**.

> Cohen said delinquent gangs provide prestige for adolescents frustrated at their lack of status in society

Albert Cohen (1955) said that working-class boys have a lack of opportunities to succeed in mainstream society, largely due to cultural deprivation. This leads to dissatisfaction with their social position. He called this status frustration.

This tension is released by joining or creating groups which have alternative values for achieving status. These values tend to be the reverse of those of mainstream society — behaviour deviant in society becomes normal and valued in the subcultural group. For example, petty crime or drug-taking might be valued by the group.

Cloward and Ohlin identified Three Subcultures that lead to Deviance

1) **Cloward and Ohlin (1960) combined** the ideas of **Merton** (see previous page) with the ideas of **Cohen**. They believed there was a **legitimate opportunity structure** (passing exams and getting a job, as Merton said), and an **illegitimate opportunity structure** (being in a gang and committing crime).

2) They also argued that **access** to the **illegitimate** opportunity structure could be **unequal**, just like access to the **legitimate** system. In some areas, there are **criminal gangs** which provide adolescents with a deviant route to success, and in some areas there aren't. This explained why **not all** frustrated working-class boys turned to **crime**.

3) Cloward and Ohlin came up with **three different subcultures** which encourage different types of **deviance**:

Criminal subculture	Conflict subculture
Some areas have an **established criminal culture**, where young people can be taught by **adult career criminals**. Crime in these areas is usually **utilitarian** (crimes that **make money**, such as **robbery** and **selling drugs**). Areas controlled by a **mafia** or **mob** have a criminal subculture.	In areas that **don't** have an established criminal culture (often due to factors such as a **rapidly changing population**), young people organise themselves into **gangs**. Their crimes tend to be **non-utilitarian** — e.g. **violence** or **vandalism**. They often engage in '**turf wars**' with other gangs.

Retreatist subculture

Young people who have failed in both the legitimate opportunity structure and the illegitimate opportunity structure retreat from society and turn to drink or drugs.

The subcultural theories have been criticised for **assuming** that the majority of people aspire to the **mainstream goals** of success and wealth. **Taylor, Walton and Young (1973)** point to deviant groups, such as **hippies**, who **don't** share these goals. Also, subcultural theories often **assume** that there is **no overlap** between these three types of subculture. For example, you can be part of a retreatist and a criminal subculture at the **same time**.

Practice Questions

Q1 Why did Merton think people committed crime?

Q2 What are Merton's five adaptations to strain?

Q3 What is meant by 'status frustration'?

Exam Questions

Q1 How might criminal subcultures and conflict subcultures encourage deviance? Outline three ways. [6 marks]

Q2 Evaluate the functionalist idea that crime and deviance are necessary in society. [30 marks]

I did it for the good of society...

Unlikely to stand up in a court of law, that one. I wouldn't recommend defending yourself by quoting Durkheim. It didn't work for me after all that unpleasantness with the goat smuggling. Anyway, I'm not going into all that now. Make sure you know Merton's five adaptations to strain, and Cloward and Ohlin's three criminal subcultures, and you'll be well on your way.

Labelling Theory of Crime

Interactionists (also known as interpretivists) say deviance is actually defined by social reaction. Great.

Interactionists *say that* Deviant *folk are not that* Different *from everyone else*

Interactionist (or interpretivist) study of crime and deviance says that deviants are **not characteristically different** from the rest of the population. They stress that **deviance varies** over time and place because it is **socially constructed**.

1) **Becker (1963) challenged** the assumption that sociologists should focus on what **causes** people to act in deviant ways.
2) Instead, interactionists like Becker studied how an act or behaviour comes to be **labelled as deviant** by the rest of society, and the consequences of that label or reaction.
3) The **same behaviour** gets **different reactions** depending on the social situation (see p.118). Becker thought there's therefore nothing **intrinsically deviant** about the act itself.
4) The **reaction** of those around you is what makes you **recognise** your behaviour as deviant.

Being Labelled *as* Deviant *can* Affect Future Behaviour

Interactionists argue that we form our identity by **interpreting** how others respond to us. A **label** can have a **positive** or **negative** effect and helps us define ourselves in our **own eyes** as well as in others' eyes. Becker calls this a '**self concept**'.

1) Becker argued that a **self concept** of being deviant can **increase deviant behaviour**. If a person is **shamed** by the reaction of others who know they have been in trouble with the police, they may **return** to criminal activity to **escape** the feeling of rejection. This **reinforces** the label of criminal. Becker called this process the **deviant career**.
2) The **label** of **criminal** is **not easily removed** by society — it becomes an individual's **master status** (see glossary). On release from prison many individuals find it hard to obtain work, because of their status as an **ex-offender**.
3) **Jock Young (1971)** studied **drug users** in Notting Hill. They developed a **deviant self concept**, which became their **master status**. Society responded **negatively**, their drug-taking became more **significant** to them, and the drug-taking **increased**.
4) **Goffman (1961)** wrote about a deviant career in **mental illness**. He said the **negative label** of being **mad** is **imposed** on the patient by society and psychiatry, and the patient must eventually **conform** to it.
5) **Braithwaite (1989)** argued that the effects of **negative labelling** (or **shaming**) actually depend on **how** the label is applied. **Disintegrative shaming** labels both the **crime** and the **person** as deviant — this causes **social exclusion**. **Reintegrative shaming** only labels the **crime itself** as deviant, so the **person** has a chance to **rejoin society**.

Lemert (1951) *distinguished between* Primary *and* Secondary *deviance*

1) Lemert argued that **most people** commit some acts of **primary deviance** in their lives, but that this is of little **significance**.
2) However, when there's a **societal reaction** to an act (either from society as a whole or groups within society, e.g. family, peers, police and the media), the individual is **labelled** as **deviant**.
3) Lemert argues that when an individual **feels the weight** of the label 'deviant' or 'criminal', they sometimes commit **more** of the deviant behaviour. Lemert called this **secondary deviance**.

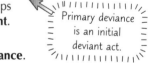
Primary deviance is an initial deviant act.

Similar to this is the idea of '**deviance amplification**', which says that **social control** can **cause** more **deviance**.
1) A common **response** to deviance is to **increase** social control. This can lead to **more deviance**, which provokes **more extensive** social control. The result is **even more deviance**, and the **cycle** continues.
2) The **media** often play a role in deviance amplification, as they can influence **reaction** to deviant acts (p.132).

Practice Questions

Q1 Give a definition of the term 'self concept'.
Q2 Explain the concept of secondary deviance.

Exam Question

Q1 Evaluate the idea that being labelled a criminal makes an individual more likely to commit a crime. [30 marks]

I did it because everyone called me a criminal anyway...

Once someone has been labelled as deviant, public reaction can be very powerful. Sometimes, individuals commit suicide once their deviance has been discovered by the rest of society, as they are scared of the way they will be treated by the public.

Marxist Theories of Crime

Deviance is controlled by society, and kept to a low level so we can all get on with important stuff like working to keep the capitalist system going. Sadly, social control also stops you doing radical things like wearing fluffy pyjamas to school. Boo.

Social Control *keeps* Order *in* Society

Functionalist sociologists argue that deviance must be kept to a **low level**. They say that a small amount of deviant activity can actually help **maintain** social order because it **unites** the rest of society in **disapproval** of the deviant behaviour. Functionalists say social control **benefits everyone** in society.

Take a look at p.119 for more on this.

Marxist sociologists agree that social control is essential to keep **order**. However, they say capitalism is an **exploitative** system which requires systems of social control over the population to **prevent rebellion and revolution**. Marxists say social control **benefits the ruling class** and works against the interests of the majority working class.

The **neo-Marxist Gramsci (1971)** said that **hegemony** (the dominance of ruling class ideology) is used to maintain **social control**. **Institutions**, such as the **legal system**, socialise everyone into **accepting** ruling-class **ideas** — see p.106.

Marxists *Argue that Capitalist Society* Causes *Crime*

Marxists say that **capitalist society** is 'crimogenic' — in other words, it **leads to crime**.

1) Capitalist society works at the **expense** of the **working class**. This can cause **poverty**, which may **force** working-class people to commit crimes so they can **afford** to **pay rent** and **buy food**. Working-class **frustration** can lead to **violence**.

2) The constant desire to make **more money** can also lead to criminal behaviour (e.g. fraud, blackmail) among **professional workers** and the **ruling class**.

Marxists *say the* Capitalist State *passes* Laws *which benefit the* Ruling Class

1) According to Marxism, laws **aren't the will of the people**. They're a reflection of **ruling-class interests**, as the ruling class are responsible for **law-making**.

2) Other than the most **serious** crimes of murder, rape and violence, the vast majority of law in the UK is **property law**. **Chambliss and Mankoff (1976)** wrote that most of this law serves to keep **working-class** people **away** from the property and land of the rich. The ruling class uses the law to protect **private property** because **capitalist exploitation** is built upon it.

Hugo invested in quality camouflage to protect his property from the riff-raff.

3) Most of the population have **no power** or **say** in the creation of **laws** and **punishments**.

4) Canadian sociologist **Laureen Snider (1993)** argues legislation regulating **large companies** is **restricted** in capitalist societies because it could **threaten ruling-class interests**. For example, health and safety, pollution and fair trade legislation is passed to a **minimum level** and often **weakly enforced**. **Tobacco companies** have put huge **pressure** on governments **not to pass laws** making them **legally responsible** for the deaths of smokers.

5) **Pearce (1976)** suggested that even the laws which supposedly **protect** the working class (e.g. health and safety laws, consumer laws) are really in **ruling-class interests**. He said the system needs healthy, safe and loyal workers.

Marxists *say* Ruling-Class *lawbreakers are* Less Likely *to be* Punished

Marxists also say the law is not enforced **equally** in capitalist societies.

1) **Laureen Snider (1993)** argues that **working-class crimes** such as **burglary** don't cause as much harm in society as **corporate crimes** such as breaking health and safety law.

2) Marxists suggest that **ruling-class ideology** presents the burglars as a **threat to society**, largely through the **media**. Meanwhile **corporate lawbreakers** get **little media condemnation** and are treated more **leniently** by the legal system.

3) Also, if company bosses are charged they have the **money** to buy the **best legal advice**.

4) The work of **Chambliss (1978)** is good evidence for this. He studied crime in the American city of **Seattle** and found those in **power** were able to use their power to **conduct criminal activity** and to **avoid prison**. He found an **organised crime syndicate** which included **elite businessmen** and **politicians** who used money and influence to **bribe officials**.

Gordon (1976) argues **selective enforcement** of the law and **selective reporting** in the media gives the impression that criminals are largely **working class**. He thinks this not only **diverts attention** from ruling-class crime but also **divides the working class** because the working-class criminal becomes the **target of anger**, rather than the system itself.

Marxist Theories of Crime

Traditional Marxists are Criticised for overlooking Other Effects on Crime

1) The assumption that capitalism is **crimogenic** is **rejected** by many. There's **crime** in **socialist societies** like Cuba, and **some capitalist societies** have very **low crime rates** (such as Switzerland).

2) **Feminists** accuse traditional Marxist theory of **ignoring** the role of **patriarchy** in rule creation and social control.

3) More recent Marxist-influenced theory such as **left-realism** (see next page) reckons traditional Marxism focuses too much on **corporate crime**. They dispute the argument that other crimes, such as burglary, don't cause much harm, especially as the **victims** are usually **working class**.

Critical Criminology argues criminals Choose to break the law

Taylor, Walton and Young's *The New Criminology* (1973) says crime is a choice

Background:	'The New Criminology' was an attempt to present a thorough and considered Marxist analysis of crime, largely because Taylor, Walton and Young thought other Marxists, including Marx, had failed to do so. The main aim of 'The New Criminology' was to move the sociology of crime on from the idea that society should be trying to remove deviant behaviour to a need to understand and accept it.
Theory:	Taylor, Walton and Young argued that criminals were not passive individuals unable to control their economic situation as traditional Marxists had stated. Instead, crime was a conscious, meaningful and deliberate choice individuals made to try and change society.
	Much crime is a deliberate fight against capitalism. Taylor, Walton and Young point to political action groups such as the Black Panther Movement, who use criminal means to agitate the system. Robbery is also seen by the new criminologists as a potential means of redistributing wealth. (Robin Hood, anyone...)
Conclusion:	Sociology needs a "fully social theory of deviance". Deviance needs to be explained from different viewpoints, which consider how society is organised and at the same time how and why individuals choose to be deviant.

Taylor, Walton and Young's 'fully social theory of deviance' analyses deviant acts in terms of:

1) How **wealth** and **power** are **distributed**.
2) The **unique circumstances** of each **deviant act**.
3) The **nature** of the **deviant act** itself.
4) **Reactions** of the **rest of society** to the deviant act.
5) Who has the **power** to **make rules** about the **treatment** of deviance or **response** to deviance.
6) The **effect** being **labelled deviant** has on an individual.
7) How all these factors **interlink**.

This approach is known as critical criminology.

In **1978**, **Hall et al** applied the 'social theory of deviance' to media reports of large numbers of muggings involving black muggers. They analysed the situation in terms of:

- **Social, economic** and **political conditions** — The country was in **economic crisis**. Unions and militants were **threatening state power**.

- **Motivations of the state** — The government wanted to feel in **control** of the situation.

- **Motivations of the media** — The press and broadcasters wanted a **dramatic story**.

- **What happened** — The police **arrested more people**. The media reported this and presented the muggers as a **threat to society**, creating an unjustified **moral panic**.

Practice Questions

Q1 Give one difference between functionalist and Marxist views on social control.

Q2 Why do some sociologists reject the Marxist idea of crimogenic capitalism?

Q3 According to Taylor, Walton and Young, why do people commit crime?

Q4 Why did the public overreact to black muggings, according to Hall et al?

Exam Question

Q1 How might the law benefit the ruling class? Outline two ways. [4 marks]

It's not my fault — capitalism made me do it...

Again, not recommended as a defence in a court of law. It didn't work for me when I insisted on running through the streets wearing only a tutu. Marxist theories of crime aren't that surprising really — they blame capitalism and the ruling class (shocker). There are a lot of studies, but if you can work them into your answer in the exam, then you'll be on to a winner.

Left and Right Realist Theories of Crime

Two theories focused on finding a solution to crime have had a big influence on social policy in Britain and America — left realism and right realism. No prizes for guessing which is more right wing and which is more left wing.

Left Realists *said policy must accept that crime is Real and Rising*

Lea and Young (1984) produced a **new theory** of crime and how to reduce it. They criticised other **left-wing writers** (especially Marxists) for overlooking the **reality** of crime in Britain by focusing on the problems within **capitalism**.

Lea and Young said left-wing sociological debate and social policy on crime must accept that:

- Crimes **other than white-collar crimes** are a **problem**.
- There has been a **rise in crime** in Britain since the Second World War.
- Being a **victim** of crime is a very **significant event** in an individual's life.
- **Fear of crime** is a real factor in shaping modern urban lifestyles, especially for **women**.

Left realists think society is unfair, and reform is the solution (not revolution, like Marxists).

Kinsey, Lea and Young (1986) *recommend changes in Policing Policy*

1) **Kinsey, Lea and Young (1986)** say that British policing policy needs to be centred on **creating** and **maintaining good communication** between the **police** and **local communities**.

> The public **report most crimes** to the police.
> The public **provide most evidence** to solve crimes. = The police **need** the public.

2) Kinsey, Lea and Young say the public should have a **key role** in deciding **police policy**. They propose having **democratically elected Police Authorities** that will develop policing policy and direct police action.

3) This would create **consensus policing** where police act on the **local community's instructions**, rather than in **isolation**.

4) Kinsey, Lea and Young say the key role of the police should then be "**full and proper investigation of crime**", which they reckon has been reduced in recent years.

5) They say the police need to improve their **detection** rates (how many recorded crimes are successfully cleared up by the police). Even today, only **29%** of crimes are detected in England and Wales.

Left realists say *Relative Deprivation causes Subcultures and Crime*

1) **Lea and Young (1984)** argue that a sense of **relative deprivation** is a major factor leading to crime. When an individual feels **deprived** in relation to **similar social groups**, they can turn to crime to 'solve' the problem and acquire the **resources** to remove the feeling.

2) It's not actual deprivation but the **feeling of being deprived** relative to someone else that triggers this response. This explains why crime occurs in **all social groups** — the **rich** can feel deprived next to the **super-rich**.

3) **Lea and Young** say these feelings of deprivation are compounded by the **consumer culture** of modern Britain, which makes people more **individualistic** — **advertising** and the **media** present individuals with images of what **they could have** and what others have got. Therefore, a rising **standard of living** can lead to a rising **crime rate**.

4) Left realists think that **criminal subcultures** (see p.120) are a **result** of, and a way to **combat**, relative deprivation.

5) They say that any **marginalised** (isolated or excluded) group could turn to **violence** to tackle **inequality**.

Left realists say *Social Inequality must be fought in order to Reduce Crime*

Left realists say that in the long term, **social order** will come from a **fair** and **just** society. They stress the need for **all social agencies** to have a direct aim of removing inequality, including the general public.

> Left realists use the 'square of crime' to show the **interactions** between **four elements** which affect crime — the state, the public, the offender and the victim. Left realists argue that all four elements should **work together** to understand and reduce crime.

Left realist work influenced the 1997-2010 **Labour** government's **social policy**. Tony Blair's phrase "tough on crime, tough on the causes of crime" sums up the left realism theory pretty well.

The Left Realist Square of Crime

state (formal control) ↔ public (informal control)

CRIME

offender ↔ victim

Left and Right Realist Theories of Crime

Critics *say that if Left Realism was* Correct *there'd be* More Crime

1) **Hughes (1991)** says the left realists haven't explained why **some people** who experience **relative deprivation** see **crime** as a **solution** and others don't. He argues there would be a lot **more crime** if **relative deprivation** was the main cause.

2) Critics also say that **Kinsey, Lea and Young** didn't collect enough **data** to develop a **full theory** of crime. Their theory only focuses on **property crime**.

> *These left and right realists aren't the same realists as the ones who talk about sociology being a science in Section Seven.*

Right Realists *think there are* Three Main Causes of Crime

Right realists believe that there are **three main factors** that cause crime: **biology**, a lack of **socialisation** and **rational choice**.

1) Wilson and Herrnstein (1985) claim there's a biological predisposition to crime in some individuals, but the right socialisation can train them away from it. They argue that lone-parent families are more likely to have 'criminal children' because their socialisation hasn't been complete.

2) They also say that people have free will and are able to think rationally and reason things out. Therefore crime is a decision they make — they consider the rewards of crime to be greater than the risks, and choose to commit the crime. This is why Murray (1997) claims that the higher the risk of going to prison, the less likely people are to commit crime.

Right Realists' Solutions to Crime *have influenced* American Social Policy

1) **Wilson (1975)** believes individuals commit crime because the **gains outweigh** the chances of being **caught and punished**. In order to reduce crime, Wilson says it's necessary to issue **harsh punishments** for the smallest crimes, as a **deterrent** to future offenders.

> *Wilson was a social policy advisor to the Reagan government of the USA in the 1980s.*

2) This has been put into action in the social policy of **Zero Tolerance**, first in America and now in parts of the UK (e.g. Middlesbrough).

3) **Wilson and Kelling (1982)** say that damage to a neighbourhood has to be put right **straight away**, or problems of crime and delinquency quickly get **out of hand**. This is called the **'One Broken Window'** idea — their article says that tolerating just one broken window sends the message that you can **get away** with crime.

4) Wilson and Kelling actually advocate **taking resources and police supervision away** from areas where law and order has **broken down** — this sounds wrong, but Wilson says that once **social order** has gone it's almost **impossible** to regain it. He recommends **focusing police efforts** on areas which **aren't too far gone**.

Right Realism *has been* Criticised *from* Many Angles

1) The idea that criminals are **biologically different** is **rejected** by many, as it comes from discredited theories.

2) Critics also say that **Zero Tolerance** policies have led to a big rise in the **US prison population** — e.g. the **'three strikes and you're out'** policy which means three serious offences automatically result in **life imprisonment**.

3) **Matthews (1992)** didn't find any evidence that tolerating **broken windows** leads to crime.

4) **Jones (1998)** questions the assertion that **resources** put into run-down areas are **wasted**. He argues that investment in these areas makes a **positive difference** to the communities who live there.

Practice Questions

Q1 Give two causes of crime, according to left realists.

Q2 Give two examples of things that right realists say would reduce crime.

Q3 Give one criticism of left realism and one criticism of right realism.

Exam Question

Q1 Analyse two explanations for how different policing strategies could reduce crime. [10 marks]

I've run out of excuses...

Both these new approaches are quite different to the old sociological theories, which tend to blame society. The left realists are quite harsh on Marxism, and say that it ignores the effect of crime on ordinary people. Right-wing politicians and right realists have been quite firm in their claim that prison works, but just like everything in sociology, there's no broad agreement.

Crime, Ethnicity and Social Class

Sociologists look for crime patterns in ethnicity and social class data, and try to find explanations for them.
It's all a bit inconclusive though — and it's tricky to get hold of reliable statistics.

Crime Statistics can be Unreliable

1) Police statistics show that **ethnic minorities** in general, and **black people** in particular, are **more likely** to be **stopped and searched**, **arrested** or end up in **prison**. For example, black people only make up **3.3%** of the population of England and Wales, but **14.2%** of stop and searches, **8.3%** of arrests and **13.5%** of the prison population.

2) Whilst sociologists have tried to **explain** these trends (see below), it has been argued that these statistics are not actually **representative** — they are **skewed** by other factors than ethnicity, such as **age** and **gender**. For example, the majority of **all** stop and searches are carried out on **young males**. There is a **high proportion** of young males in the **black population**, so **black people** end up being **over-represented** in stop and search statistics.

> Having said that, once factors like this have been taken into account, black people are still more likely to be stopped and searched — it's just that their over-representation is not quite as significant as the statistics suggest.

3) Also, only **29% of reported crimes** in 2013-14 were **solved** — i.e. someone was convicted or warned for the offence. The social profile of who committed the **unsolved** and **undetected** crimes could change these patterns considerably.

4) In fact, all crime statistics should be taken with a pinch of salt — these **official** statistics **differ** from **victim surveys** (where people are asked if they've been the victim of crime) and **self-report studies** (where people are asked to admit to the crimes they've committed).

Sociologists try to Explain the Trends

1) Some sociologists, such as **Bowling and Phillips (2007)**, have argued that **police racism** results in higher suspicion against black people in general.

> The Macpherson Report (1999) concluded that the police were **institutionally racist**. The court system has also been accused of automatically favouring **white middle-class defendants**. There are relatively few black people in the **police** or the **legal system**.

> Arguably, this means ethnic minorities have less faith in the police.

2) **Neo-Marxists** such as **Hall et al (1978)** and **Gilroy (1987)** argue that young black people **don't actually commit more crime** than other ethnic groups. They've been **labelled** as criminal by modern British society.

- Hall et al argue that black youth have been used as scapegoats to distract society from social issues caused by capitalism, especially in the 1970s. They also say that high levels of unemployment among young black men lead some of them to opt out of mainstream society and turn to crime.

- Gilroy argues that black people are victims of racist stereotypes that paint them as more criminal than other groups. The criminal justice system subscribes to these stereotypes and convicts a high proportion of black people as a result. Gilroy also points out that ethnic minorities may use crime to fight back against inequalities caused by capitalism — it's a kind of resistance. (This is a bit like critical criminology — have a look at p.123.)

> Similar in some ways, but Hall blames the system and left realists blame the person.

3) **Left realist** sociologists favour a **subcultural** explanation for the differences (see p.120). They believe that ethnic minorities **are** more likely to **commit crimes**, but this is because of factors **other** than their ethnicity. They argue that **relative deprivation** and **marginalisation** (p.124) are more **common** within ethnic minorities, so they are more likely to form **criminal subcultures**.

Ethnic Minorities are More Likely to be Victims of Crime

1) **Ethnic minority** households are **more at risk of crime** than other households — the Crime Survey for England and Wales found that they were more likely to be **mugged** than white groups, and slightly more likely to be victims of **vehicle theft**.

2) People from **mixed ethnic groups** are **more** at risk of being **victims** of crime than **black** or **Asian groups**.

3) Some of these incidents are **racially motivated** (i.e. the victims were targeted because of their race), but others are **intra-ethnic** (i.e. the criminals and the victims are of the same ethnicity).

4) The survey found ethnic minority respondents were also **more worried about crime** than white respondents — this could be partly due to their **lack of faith** in the **police** and **criminal justice system**.

Crime, Ethnicity and Social Class

Most criminal convictions are of people with a **Working-Class Background**

There are more **working-class** people in **prison** than any other social class.
The majority of people who appear in **court** are working class, regardless of whether they're found guilty or not.

1) A lot of **working-class crimes** are either **violence** or **theft/burglary** —
   they receive **publicity** because the public feel sorry for their **victims**.

2) **Left realists** such as **Young (2002)** believe that the **media** allows the working class to see how many possessions other people have, which increases their feelings of **relative deprivation**, making them more likely to turn to **crime**.

3) **Marxists** argue the system of law and order is run by the **ruling class**, against the interests of the working class.
   They say parts of the working class are **criminalised** by a biased criminal justice system — see p.122-123.

4) **Subcultural theorists** argue the high **working-class crime rate** is because of
   working-class subcultures (see p.120), which often **accept** or **reward** crime.

- **W B Miller (1962)** said that general **lower working-class culture**, not subcultural gangs, was what encouraged lawbreaking behaviour. Values passed from generation to generation encourage **working-class men** to break the law. Delinquents are simply conforming to the **focal concerns** of their culture.

- Miller's ideas have been supported by recent **New Right** sociologists. **Charles Murray (1990, 1993)** believes that there's an **underclass** in both British and American society with a **distinct culture** and **value system** which **encourages** deviant behaviour.

  'Focal concerns' are the main things that are valued in that culture, e.g. exciting thrills and macho toughness.

- Miller was **criticised** right from the beginning. **Bordua (1962)** said that the idea that the working class live their lives **isolated** from the rest of society is **flawed to begin with**.

'White Collar' Crime is often treated **More Leniently**

'White collar' refers to the white shirts usually worn by business people.

Roger was guilty of pink collar crime.

Edwin Sutherland (1939) defined white collar crime as a criminal act committed by a person of **'high social status'** through his or her **job** — in other words, **corporate crimes** (usually involving **money**) such as **fraud** and **embezzlement**.

1) These crimes are usually **non-violent**, so are often treated more **leniently** by **society** and the **justice system**.

2) They're also sometimes viewed as **'victimless crimes'** by the public, as they don't target **individuals** (e.g. they steal from **large corporations**). However, **large-scale corporate crimes** actually have **many victims**, and do damage to **society** as a whole.

3) White collar crime is also more likely to go **unreported** or **undetected**, and sometimes companies **cover up** the fact that they've been victims of it to avoid the **negative publicity** (especially if it undermines their **security**). This partly explains why there are **fewer** middle-class or upper-class people in **prison**.

4) Recently, there has been more **public interest** in white collar crimes — for example, the **tax evasion scandals** (involving **large businesses** and **celebrities**) received a lot of **media attention**. However, the **punishments** for these offences have been relatively **minor** — some celebrities seem to have got away with just **apologising**.

Practice Questions

Q1 Give one reason why crime statistics might be unreliable.

Q2 What did the Macpherson Report (1999) conclude?

Q3 Give one example of a stereotypically working-class crime and one example of a white collar crime.

Exam Question

Q1 Evaluate the idea that racial stereotyping is the main factor in high rates of crime among ethnic minorities. [30 marks]

No one ever solved the mystery of my missing custard cream...

Crime statistics are pretty tricky — official statistics only refer to reported crimes, victim surveys don't cover more serious crimes, and self-report studies depend on people actually confessing to their own crimes. I'm not sure I'd like to take part in a self-report study, myself — I've a whole collection of not-entirely-legally-obtained traffic cones stashed under my bed...

Crime and Gender

Statistics show that there are far more men in prison than women, and suggest that men commit more crimes than women. There are different sociological explanations for why this is the case — and of course you have to know them all.

Men are Convicted of More Crime than Women

All the statistics below are for England and Wales from **2010-11** or **2011-12**.

- **Women** made up only **5%** of the prison population.
- **16%** of those arrested and **24%** of defendants in court were **women**.
- When found **guilty**, women were more likely to be **fined** than men, but less likely to be **sent to prison**.
- When given a **custodial** (prison) sentence, women were generally given **shorter sentences** than men.

Men are **suspected**, **charged** and **convicted** of crime of **almost all types** more than women.

This pattern crosses **all other social factors** such as age, class, ethnicity and region.

There are Different Explanations for these Figures

1) The subcultural theories of **Miller (1962)** and **Merton (1968)** argue that the **culture** and **lifestyles** of **young men** encourage and lead to crime (remember, most crime is committed by the young).

2) **Ian Marsh (1986)** reckons that men commit more crime because they have more **opportunities** to do so. For example, women have **fewer opportunities** to commit **white collar crime**, because there are **more men** in **powerful positions** in corporations (where this crime may be committed).

3) **Marsh** said that where females have **similar opportunities** to males they seem **as likely** to break laws. An example of this is **shoplifting**.

Other sociological theories have been developed to explain why these differences have formed.

The Chivalry Thesis

1) Sociologists such as **Pollak (1950)** put forward the **chivalry thesis**, which argues that men are **socialised** to be protective of **women**.

2) As the majority of the **police force** and the **criminal justice system** are male, their **chivalry** means that women are **less likely** to be **arrested** and are treated more **leniently** if they **are** arrested.

3) This can lead to an **underestimation** of female crime in official statistics. The chivalrous behaviour works as a form of **sexism** against male offenders, which allows female criminal activity to go **unchecked**.

4) **Campbell (1981)** did a **self-report survey** which unearthed a lot **more female crime** than the official statistics. (However, she did include more **trivial** crimes than the official statistics do.)

5) The chivalry thesis has been **criticised** though — some sociologists argue that women's crimes are generally **less serious** (for example, they are less likely to be **violent**), which is why they are **punished less harshly** than men.

6) Also, women often show **remorse**, which means they are more likely to be treated **leniently**.

Tom's sense of chivalry was getting out of hand.

Sex-role Theory

1) **Sex-role theory** suggests that **girls** are brought up to be **passive** and **conformist** so are less likely to commit crimes.

2) In contrast, **boys** are brought up to be 'tough' and 'manly'. Feminist **Frances Heidensohn (1986)** says that this can make them more **aggressive**, and more likely to commit violent crime.

In other words, boys and girls are socialised differently.

3) **Heidensohn** also says that **women are socialised into not being criminal** in the same way as men are socialised into seeing criminal activity as **acceptable**. For women, criminal behaviour would be seen as **highly deviant** (as well as illegal).

Pat Carlen (1997) found that the **courts** treated women differently depending on how they conformed to **gender roles**. For example, women who were deemed to be **good mothers** were **less likely** to be **jailed** than women **without children** or with children **in care**. In other words, women who did **not** conform to society's **gender ideals** were punished more **harshly**.

Crime and Gender

Other Theories have Also come from Feminists

Feminist sociologists have put forward **other explanations** for this.

Social Control

1) **Abbott and Wallace (1990)** argue that young women are more **closely watched** by their families and given **less freedom** outside the home, reducing their **opportunities** for crime.

2) Even **outside** the home, there are levels of control in action. Women are encouraged to **dress** and **behave respectably** to avoid being **judged** by society. In the **workplace**, **managers** and **bosses** are often male.

3) **Heidensohn (2002)** agrees with Marsh that women have less 'opportunity' to commit some types of crime. She argues that this is because of a **patriarchal, male-dominated society**. For example, you can't commit **financial fraud** unless you're in control of large sums of money. The crimes women do commit tend to relate to their role in the **home** as a **wife** or **mother**, e.g. **shoplifting**.

Freda Adler thinks that **female crime** is **increasing** because society is becoming **less patriarchal**:

The Liberation Thesis

1) **Freda Adler (1975)** developed the **liberation thesis** — the idea that as women become **more liberated** and society becomes **less patriarchal**, women's crime rates **increase**.

2) This also leads to an increase in women committing previously **male-dominated crimes**, such as **violence** and **armed robbery**.

3) Her ideas are supported by a **rise** in the **female crime rate**, and an increase in **violent girl gangs**.

4) **Westwood (1999)** suggests female **identities** are changing and women are adopting more typically **male behaviour patterns**. This could be linked to an **increase** in **female crime**.

5) The liberation thesis has been **criticised** — the **rise** in female crime actually began **before** many women became **liberated**. Also, **working-class** women benefit **least** from women's liberation, yet they commit the **majority** of female crimes.

Committing crime can be a form of **liberation**. **Carlen (1988)** interviewed **working-class women** with **criminal records**. She found that most of the women had made a **rational choice** to turn to crime — many lived in **poverty** and felt **unrewarded** by **society** and **family life**. They felt **powerless** to change their situation without breaking the law.

Practice Questions

Q1 Are men or women more likely to be sent to jail if found guilty of a crime?
Q2 Give one reason why women are less likely to commit financial fraud than men.
Q3 Briefly explain the chivalry thesis.
Q4 What is sex-role theory?
Q5 Give one criticism of the liberation thesis.

Exam Question

Q1 Apply your own knowledge and material from Item A to evaluate the idea that women are socialised not to commit crimes. [30 marks]

> **Item A**
> Some sociologists argue that, from a young age, women are socialised to be caring and passive, and to view crime as highly deviant. They are brought up to conform to gender roles, such as housewife or mother, rather than to seek high-powered corporate careers. These roles often confine them to the home.

I'd like to be liberated from sociology exams...

So, to sum up — theories... ooh, that's a shiny sword... more theories... FREEDOM. At least the statistics are pretty conclusive for this topic — there's no denying that there are fewer women in prison than men, regardless of age, class or ethnicity. There was a lot to take in on these two pages — I think it's time you rewarded yourself with a cup of tea and a pink wafer biscuit.

Recent Issues in Crime and Deviance

A global crime is one that affects national and international economies, politics or security. Globalisation has meant that countries are now connected economically, culturally and environmentally, which has had an impact on the nature of crime.

Globalisation *has led to* Transnational Organised Crime

1) **Held at al (1999)** argued that **crime** has become **globalised**. The nature of globalisation has also allowed **transnational organised crime** to **grow**.

2) **Transnational organised crime** is crime committed by a **global criminal organisation** (e.g. a **mafia**) that operates in **more than one country**. These crimes include things like drug trafficking, money laundering, smuggling human organs and the sex trade, and also **new types** of crime (e.g. **cybercrime** — see below).

3) Global criminal organisations can have **thousands** of members across the world.

4) Globalisation has changed their **structure** — they used to have a clear **power hierarchy**, but now they tend to have **small**, **almost independent networks** in different countries. **Hobbs and Dunningham (1998)** described this structure as '**glocal**' — **local networks** with **global links**.

5) The **global criminal economy** is worth **hundreds of billions** of pounds per year.

- **Globalised crime** can be hard to **police**, as it **crosses borders** — it's not always clear whose **responsibility** it is to police it. It's also **hard** for the police to pin down members of **global criminal networks**, as they're highly **secretive**.

- It's also harder for **sociologists** to **study** globalised crime. The secretive nature of global criminal networks often means that sociologists would have to use **covert participant observation** (see p.17) to study them effectively.

Trading in illegal Drugs *and* Arms *causes huge* Social Problems

1) Criminals make **hundreds of billions** of dollars each year from the **global trade** in **illegal drugs**.

2) **Karofi and Mwanza (2006)** have outlined the **negative impact** of the trade in illegal drugs. They pointed to the consequences for **health**, the changes in **social behaviours** and the **funding** of **terrorism** and **war** with the profits.

3) Global **communications** and relatively **unregulated** financial markets have made the illegal trade in **arms** easier to carry out and harder to trace. **Karofi and Mwanza** highlight its role in **destabilising societies** (violent crime) and making existing conflicts worse.

Human Trafficking *creates modern-day* Slavery

1) **Human trafficking** is the **illegal movement** of **people** for **exploitation**. Victims are taken with **force** or **deception**.

2) Human trafficking is one of the **fastest growing global crimes**. **Millions** of people across the world are currently in **forced labour** as a result of **human trafficking**.

3) It's a **global problem**, involving global criminal organisations, and has a **devastating effect** on its victims.

Cybercrime *is crime that uses the* Internet

1) Globalisation has seen a massive increase in computer use and internet use, giving rise to '**cybercrimes**' such as **data theft**, **fraud**, **credit scams**, **email scams** and **illegal pornography**. Because cybercrime breaches **national borders**, existing criminal law is often **powerless** to tackle it.

2) The extent of cybercrime is difficult to assess accurately, but some observers have suggested that it will soon **rival** the **drugs trade** in terms of **profits**.

Maureen and Brenda were two of the FBI's most wanted cybercriminals.

The **globalisation** of **communications** and the media has also aided the growth of **international terrorism**. Terrorists can now access a global audience for their **propaganda**, and are able to create **online networks** for their organisations.

Recent Issues in Crime and Deviance

Environmental or Green Crimes are those which Harm the Environment

1) **Green crime** might be something as small-scale as **fly-tipping**, but on a global scale it includes the illegal trade in **environmentally sensitive substances** like **CFCs** (banned substances that can harm the ozone layer), the illegal trade in **protected animals** and products derived from them, and illegal and unregulated **logging** and **fishing**.

2) The **environmental impact** of green crimes can be huge — e.g. illegally traded **CFCs** significantly contribute to **ozone depletion**. There are also severe **financial costs** — the World Bank estimated in 2004 that **illegal logging** costs timber-producing countries around **10-15 billion dollars** per year in **lost revenue**.

3) **Developed** countries sometimes **exploit developing** countries' lack of **safety and environmental regulations** to dispose of **toxic waste** cheaply. Also, the **effects** of environmental damage are often felt in **neighbouring countries** (not the country that actually committed the green crime) — e.g. **industrial pollution** and **nuclear accidents**.

4) **Beck (1992)** argued that we are living in a '**global risk society**' because the **risks** associated with green crimes are often on a **global scale**. For example, green crimes that contribute to **global warming** are a global issue.

5) Many activities that **harm** the environment aren't actually **against the law**, which can make them difficult to prosecute. Also, what is **illegal** in one country may be **legal** in another, so companies could simply **move** operations abroad. And, as governments **make the laws**, they can choose **not** to **criminalise** activities that make them **money**.

6) **M J Lynch (1990)** introduced the idea of **green criminology**, which has been built on by others, e.g. **White (2008)**.

> **Green criminology** looks at actions that cause **harm** to **people**, **animals** and the **environment** (unlike **traditional** criminology, which only considers actions that are **against the law**).

Secondary green crimes are more indirect.

7) **South (2008)** splits green crime into **two** categories:

Primary green crimes have an **immediate impact** on the environment, e.g. **water pollution**, **deforestation** and committing acts that threaten the **survival** of **species**.	**Secondary green crimes** are committed when individuals, companies, or governments **break laws** that are meant to **protect** the earth from **environmental emergencies**, e.g. **BP** pleaded guilty to **environmental crimes** after causing a giant **oil spill** in the **Gulf of Mexico** in 2010.

Ian Taylor argued Economic Liberalisation has caused an Increase in Crime

1) **Taylor (1997, 1998)** argued that **economic deregulation** had given some people more **opportunity** to commit crimes like **fraud**, **money laundering** and **tax evasion** (these are known as '**crimes of the powerful**'). And, as it is those in **power** who make the **laws**, their crimes are more likely to go **unnoticed** or **unenforced**.

2) He also argued that **globalisation** and **deregulation** have made employment less secure and increased economic instability by **reducing** the **control** states have over their economies. **Increased unemployment** and **cuts** in **welfare** have led to a **rise in crime** as people don't believe they will be able to secure a **reliable income**.

3) **Global capitalism** has arguably created even more **exploitation** of workers by **transnational corporations** (p.171).

4) Taylor also blamed **marketisation** for rising crime. This is where **economic considerations** begin to **dominate** in the way people think of social life. Success becomes equated to owning **expensive consumer goods** — some people turn to crime as a way to achieve this, e.g. by stealing an expensive car.

5) Taylor argued that it's **too late** to turn the economic clock back completely, but believed that attempts should be made to **recreate** shared **values** of community and civility to **counteract** the process of marketisation.

Practice Questions

Q1 What is meant by the term 'transnational organised crime'?

Q2 What is cybercrime and why is it difficult to police?

Q3 What is 'green criminology'?

Exam Question

Q1 How might globalisation cause crime? Outline three ways.   [6 marks]

I committed a green crime — I stole some manure...

If you're thinking we need some kind of superhero to save the planet from green crimes, you're absolutely right. In fact, there already is one — he's called Captain Planet, and he was the star of an awesome 90s animated TV series (with a brilliant theme tune). Your homework tonight is to watch an episode of Captain Planet and analyse how he tackles environmental crime.

The Media and State Crime

I'd better warn you now — these next few pages aren't going to be very pleasant. It's all about the atrocious things that governments have got away with. This first page is a little less depressing though (and it's got a picture of a rabbit on it).

The **Media** plays a powerful role in **Amplifying Deviance** in society

1) **Interactionists** (also known as interpretivists) such as **Stanley Cohen (1972)** argue the media helps to **create** the **deviance** it predicts or anticipates.

2) This is part of the interactionist idea that attempts to **increase social control** can actually **cause more deviance** (see p.121). Here's how it works:

> ### The Amplification of Deviance
>
> 1) The media presents a distorted view of the level of crime.
> 2) This distorted view creates public concern.
> 3) Related incidents of crime and deviance are over-reported and given more prominence than they'd otherwise have.
> 4) This keeps the issue or problem high on the public agenda.
> 5) The public want something done about the problem.
> 6) The police are more aware or sensitive to the problem, so they discover more crime.
> 7) Police records reinforce the idea that there is more crime and deviance.

LOCAL RABBIT
RANSACKS
VEGETABLE BASKET

The **Media** can be viewed as a **Cause of Crime**

1) Some sociologists think that the **media** may actually be a direct **cause** of crime — especially for those who are more **easily influenced** (e.g. **young people**).

2) They believe that **violent TV shows or films**, **computer games** and even **music** (e.g. **rap music**) can have an effect on their viewers (or listeners) and make them think that violence is a **normal**, **everyday occurrence**.

> • Young people might view the violent characters on screen as role models, and try to imitate their behaviour.
> • They might also learn how to get away with crime from watching detective programmes such as CSI.
> • Being frequently exposed to violence and criminality can also desensitise people, which may make them more likely to carry out violent or criminal acts.
> • The media have also been accused of presenting crime as exciting.

Take a look at p.186 for some examples of sociological research into the effects of violent media on audiences.

3) The media can also increase the public's **fear** of crime — if people **see** a lot of crime on TV (even on fictional programmes), they believe that it's more **common** in **real life**.

4) However, other sociologists think that the **influence** of the media on violence has been **exaggerated**.

5) For example, if the media **did** cause violent crime, then we would expect **all** people who play violent computer games to **re-enact** onscreen violence in real life. Evidence of a **connection** between media and violent behaviour isn't very **reliable**.

6) These sociologists believe that there must be **other factors**, not just the media.

The **Media** can be Seen to **Cause Crime** in **Less Direct** Ways

1) **Left realists** argue that the media bombard society with images of **luxury products** that most people **can't afford** to buy. The media make it obvious that other people **can** afford to get these products, which increases feelings of **relative deprivation**. As a result, people may **steal** what they **can't afford**, or **resort** to **crime** to make money to **fund** a more luxurious lifestyle (see p.124).

2) **Yvonne Jewkes (2003)** has argued that newer forms of media, such as the **internet**, have made some **crimes** (such as **child pornography**) more **accessible**. The internet has also led to **new crimes** that weren't possible before — **cybercrimes** (see p.130). **Cyber bullying**, 'trolling' and 'revenge porn' have all been made possible by the **growth** of the internet.

The Media and State Crime

The *Media* can create *Moral Panics*

1) The **perceived risk** of being a **victim** of crime is **amplified** by **over-reporting** by the media. This creates a public response of **panic** or **outrage**. **Cohen (1972)** refers to this as a **moral panic**.

2) **Cohen** developed his idea about moral panics from a study of conflicts between **Mods and Rockers**, two groups of **working-class youths** who clashed in the **1960s**. The media **exaggerated** the extent of the violence between them, **predicted** more of it and **negatively labelled** the symbols of each group (e.g. the mods' scooters and the rockers' motorbikes). This all combined to create a **moral panic**.

3) There are plenty of **new** examples of moral panics, especially with the increased power of the media — e.g. **gun crime**, **student drinking** and **benefit fraud**. Some sociologists have also suggested that **fear** of **global terrorism** following the 9/11 attacks on New York in 2001 triggered a moral panic, and that the **terrorist threat** has been **exaggerated**.

> **Example — Poor behaviour** among small groups of **students** is often reported in the media.
> 1) When **isolated** examples of **bad student behaviour** are discovered, the media reports the stories as if they're part of a **pattern** of bad behaviour. They **exaggerate** the extent of the problem.
> 2) This leads to **all** students being **labelled** as a **threat** to social order. They are **stigmatised**.
> 3) **Some students** may react **negatively** to this label, which results in a **self-fulfilling prophecy** — if society already **believes** that students are a menace, students may as well **behave** that way and **join in** with the deviant behaviour. The level of deviance **increases**.
> 4) The public **panics** about how **widespread** student misbehaviour has become.

4) The state response to a moral panic in society is often to introduce **stricter** forms of **social control** through legislation. **Functionalists** think this is a good way to **reinforce** social norms — society defines itself in **opposition** to the deviant groups (p.119). However, **left realists** argue that **marginalising** deviant groups in this way actually **increases** the level of deviance (p.124).

5) **Hall et al (1978)** claim that national concern about **mugging** in the 1970s was a **moral panic**. The media claimed that mugging was a new kind of crime, but Hall et al point out that **violent street robbery** had been a **long-term problem**, and wasn't rising particularly fast at the time.

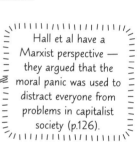
Hall et al have a Marxist perspective — they argued that the moral panic was used to distract everyone from problems in capitalist society (p.126).

6) However, other sociologists such as **McRobbie and Thornton (1995)** think that the public are now **getting used to** moral panics, so people aren't as **likely** to panic as in the past.

State Crimes are committed by Governments

1) **State crimes** are acts committed by **governments** (or **agents** acting for governments) that break **national** or **international criminal law**. State crimes include:

- war crimes
- genocide
- links with **organised crime**
- the funding of **terrorism**
- **corruption** or **censorship**
- use of **torture**
- **assassination**
- **imprisonment** without **trial**

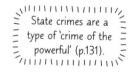
State crimes are a type of 'crime of the powerful' (p.131).

2) A state can make **laws** that **persecute** its citizens — e.g. the **Nuremberg laws** that persecuted **Jews** in **Nazi Germany**. **Kristallnacht** in 1938 saw widespread attacks on **Jewish homes**, **businesses** and **synagogues**, as the police **looked on** (having been ordered **not** to **intervene** by Nazi officials).

3) State crimes are often carried out on a **large scale** due to the **power** of the state. In **Cambodia** in 1975-78, **2 million civilians** (**20%** of the population) were killed by the **Khmer Rouge government**.

4) Whilst acts of **genocide** are often carried out by **dictatorships**, governments in **democratic** countries (including the UK and USA) can also be guilty of state crimes, especially **torture**, **corruption** and **illegal imprisonment**.

5) **Eugene McLaughlin (2001)** divides state crimes into four different types:

> 1) **Politically** motivated crime — e.g. **rigging elections**
> 2) Criminal activity in the **police** or **security forces** — e.g. **assassination** of prisoners
> 3) Crimes with **economic** motives — e.g. cooperating **illegally** with **TNCs**
> 4) Crimes of a **social/cultural** nature — e.g. **vandalism** of cultural sites and works

6) As states themselves define what is **illegal**, it can be difficult for **international bodies** like the **UN** to **stop** state crime, or to bring states to **justice**. Governments can also use their power to **cover up** or **deny** their crimes (see next page).

The Media and State Crime

Not all **Human Rights Abuses** are **Against the Law**

1) **Herman and Julia Schwendinger (1970)** believed that any actions that **violated human rights** should be classified as **crimes**, regardless of whether they were **against the law** or not.

2) Whilst there is **no conclusive definition** of human rights, most sociologists agree that there are **two main categories**:
   - **natural rights** come from simply being human — e.g. the right to **life** and **liberty**
   - **civil rights** are made by humans — e.g. the right to **education**, a **vote** in elections or a **fair trial**

3) By the Schwendingers' definition, therefore, countries that deny **women** the right to **vote** should be seen as **criminal**.

4) This view has been **criticised** by sociologists such as **Cohen (1996, 2001)**, who argue that just because something is **morally wrong**, it doesn't make it **criminal**. Also, as there is no **definitive list** of human rights, it's difficult to decide exactly what would count as a **violation** of them.

5) However, Cohen admits that states often try to **deny** or **cover up** their **abuses of human rights**. There are **two key ways** that states try to do this — **'the spiral of denial'** and **'neutralisation theory'**.

The Spiral of Denial

This often follows a **3-step process**:

1) States **deny** that human rights abuses ever happened (this is more likely in a **dictatorship**).

2) Someone proves that it **did** happen, so the state claims that things **aren't as they appear**.

3) It's **proven** that things **are** as they appear, so the state **claims** their actions were **justified**.

Neutralisation Theory

Sykes and Matza (1957) said that there are **five different ways** that **deviants** try to make their actions seem **reasonable**, rather than denying them — this is called **neutralisation**. **Cohen** says that **states** also use these **methods of neutralisation**.

1) **'The Denial of Injury'** — they are just **fighting back** against someone who made the **first aggressive move**.

2) **'The Denial of Victims'** — the **target** of their abuse or criminal activity is **not a victim**. They are **violent** and **their behaviour is much worse** than the state's behaviour.

3) **'The Condemnation of Condemners'** — the criticism is **unfair** — **other states** have committed **worse crimes**.

4) **'The Appeal to Higher Loyalties'** — they have a **bigger reason** for committing the act than **personal** gain (e.g. nationalism, defence of freedom of speech, to preserve national security).

5) **'The Denial of Responsibility'** — they are acting on the **orders** of **someone else** or just doing their **duty**.

Practice Questions

Q1 What is 'amplification of deviance'?
Q2 Give three examples of moral panics.
Q3 What is state crime?
Q4 Give four different examples of state crime.
Q5 Describe three methods of neutralisation used by states, according to Cohen.

Exam Question

Q1 By applying material from Item A, analyse two explanations for why the media can be considered to be a cause of crime. [10 marks]

Item A
The media often contains violent content. Children are exposed to fictionalised violence while playing computer games and watching films. New media, such as the internet, also allow people to communicate quickly and easily, and can be difficult to police. Some sociologists also argue that media advertising makes society more materialistic and increases desire for luxury items.

The TV's broken — PANIC...
The idea of crime gets a bit confusing when those who make the laws start breaking them. State crime is a bit like a referee who goes around kicking all the players at a football match. Another rather unhappy page for you to learn (sorry about that).

Victims, Prevention and Punishment

This fine trio of pages opens with some thrilling theories about how people become victims of crime, ramps up the fun with a look at ways of preventing crime, then concludes with a spectacular grand finale on punishment.

Some **Facts and Figures** about **Victims***

* from 'Crime in England and Wales 2009/10'

- **Men** are **more than twice** as likely to become **victims of violence** as women.
- Young **men aged 16-24** experience the **most** violence.
- However, more **women** are **afraid** of becoming victims of crime.
- Women are more likely than men to be victims of **domestic violence** — 7% of women were affected but only 4% of men. People who suffer domestic violence are likely to experience **repeat attacks**.
- People from **ethnic minority groups** are **twice as likely** to be victims of **robbery** than **white** people.
- Those from **mixed ethnic groups** are **most likely** to be **victims of violent crime**.
- Those from **high-income households** are more likely to be **victims of credit or debit card fraud**.
- People from **lower-income households** are most likely to experience **domestic violence**.

Repeat victimisation happens when **individuals** or **households** fall victim to the **same type of crime** on more than one occasion. Some types of crime are **more likely** to involve repeat victimisation than others.

1) For example, **only 14%** of victims of **burglary** in the year **2012-13** experienced this type of crime **more than once** in that year. Victims of this kind of **theft** can take steps to **improve** the protection of their property.

2) It's a different story for **violent crime** — **27%** of victims of violent crime in the year **2013-14** were victimised **more than once** in that year and **13%** of victims were victimised **three times or more** in that year.

Yet again, Fleur fell victim to one of her owner's weekly photo shoots.

Victimology Theories *try to explain* How *people become* Victims

Christie (1986) believes that a 'victim' is a **social construct**, and that society is **more willing** to see certain people as victims, e.g. an **old man** who has had his walking stick stolen.

'**Positivist victimology**' and '**critical victimology**' are sociological theories that try to explain how people become victims of crime.

1) According to **Miers (1989)**, **positivist victimology** is interested in how some people are **more likely** to become victims than others — either because of their **actions** (e.g. leaving valuables on display in a car) or because of their **characteristics**.

2) This approach has been criticised for '**blaming the victim**'. Positivist victimologists have tended to focus on '**visible**' crime, such as **reported robberies** and **assaults** — they've been criticised for ignoring issues such as **state crime** (see p.133).

3) **Critical victimology** is influenced by **Marxism** and **feminism** — it says that groups who are more likely to be **oppressed** (such as the **working class** and **women**) are also more likely to be **victims**. **Mawby and Walklate (1994)** described this as '**structural powerlessness**'.

4) Critical victimologists such as **Tombs and Whyte (2007)** argue that those in power can fail to **label** sufferers as **victims**. This means that they **refuse to acknowledge** that harm has been done, or even **blame the victim** for their own situation.

Feminists *say* Women *become* Victims *because of* Patriarchal Attitudes

1) Feminists argue that **domestic violence** is the result of an **unequal power relationship** between men and women.

2) Some feminists argue that **fear of crime** is used to **control women**. **Stanko (2000)** suggests that women have to **restrict** their behaviour by taking care not to be too **provocative**, e.g. in their appearance.

3) Many feminists believe that the **law is biased against women**. They say that crimes against women have been **ignored**. **Heidensohn (2002)** says crimes by **men** against women (e.g. rape and abuse — '**gendered crime**') often go unreported.

See p.129 for more about feminist theories of crime.

4) **Radical feminists** see domestic violence as a form of **patriarchal power and control**. **Marxist feminists** say domestic violence can be explained by the frustration and **lack of control** that men experience in the **capitalist workplace**.

Victims, Prevention and Punishment

There are Different Approaches to Crime Prevention

Right realism theorists favour the **situational approach**.

1) **Situational crime prevention** involves **changing the physical environment** of an area to make it **harder** for people to commit crimes. Changes could include creating **gated communities**, putting up more **surveillance cameras** or improving **lighting** in streets and car parks.

2) The situational approach is based on **rational choice theory**, which argues that criminals **won't try** to commit a crime if it's **likely** that they will **fail**.

Some have criticised situational crime prevention...

- Critics such as **Chaiken et al (1974)** argue that situational approaches don't always **reduce** crime — they just **move** it to a less well-protected area (this is known as **displacement**).

- This strategy is heavily focused on crimes such as **vandalism**, **theft**, and other types of **disorder** in local neighbourhoods. It **doesn't** deal with crimes committed by **professionals** and **governments**.

- Some sociologists also point out that situational crime prevention only deals with the **symptoms** of criminality, rather than tackling the **factors** that **cause** people to **resort** to crime.

Environmental crime prevention tries to stop specific areas from becoming **vulnerable** to crime. There are **two main** elements to this approach:

1) This approach involves keeping an area's **environment clean** and in **good repair** to make it obvious that people **care** about the area. For example, **fixing vandalised property** and **clearing away rubbish** quickly prevents an area from **falling into decline** and becoming a **target** for criminal activity.

2) **Wilson and Kelling (1982)** put forward the idea of **zero tolerance policing** — where antisocial behaviour is tackled **swiftly** and **strictly**. They argued that **serious crime** can be prevented by combining **good policing** with the **maintenance** of **environments**.

See p.125 for more on Wilson and Kelling's solutions to crime.

Social and community approaches try to **remove** the **social conditions** that might force people to **resort** to crime.

1) **Structuralists** argue that crime is caused by **inequalities** in wealth and income. They say the only way to reduce or prevent crime is to address **social inequalities**. Subcultural, Marxist and left realism theorists are structuralists.

2) **Individualist** or **interventionist** theorists argue that some groups of people are more likely to commit crime than others. They say the best way to prevent crime is to **change the behaviour** of these 'criminal types', e.g. by targeting children from a disadvantaged background.

3) **Social** and **community** approaches require **long-term commitment**, as they try to address criminality **before** it actually develops. Situational and environmental approaches are more **reactive** (they tackle existing criminality).

Surveillance is used to Detect and Prevent Crime

Surveillance is a type of situational crime prevention.

1) **Surveillance** is used to **detect** and **prevent** crime. **Physical surveillance** methods, such as **CCTV cameras**, are used to **watch** over neighbourhoods. They are designed to **deter** criminals, as it **increases** the chance that they'll be **caught**.

2) **Technological surveillance** involves screening **online communications** and **phone calls**, and collecting **personal data**. **Governments** and the **police** use this information to keep track of **known criminals** and to **detect criminal** or **terrorist activity**. Arguably, this makes it **harder** for criminals to **organise** their activities online.

3) Some people argue that **accessing personal data** and **online communications** gives the government **too much power** over individuals who **haven't** committed any crimes. They may also see surveillance as a **breach of privacy**.

4) **Surveillance** is also used to **deter** bad behaviour in **prisons**.

Jack and Harry worried that their cover had been blown.

Some sociologists say that surveillance has now spread into all areas of our lives — they say that we are living in a 'surveillance society'.

Michel Foucault (1977) argued that **prisons** exert their **disciplinary power** by using **surveillance**. Whilst this idea includes physical surveillance (e.g. **CCTV** or patrolling guards), much of it is **internal** — this is known as **self-surveillance**. He believed that if prisoners know that they **might** be being observed, they will behave **all the time**, just in case.

Victims, Prevention and Punishment

Society tries to Control Crime through Formal and Informal Agents

1) The **police** are a **formal** agent of social control, responsible for **enforcing the law**.

   In theory the **police** should be **impartial**, but have sometimes been accused of **institutional racism** and **sexism**:
   - The **Macpherson Report (1999)** said that the police showed clear signs of **racism**.
   - **Black men** are more likely to be **stopped and searched** than white people (see p.126).
   - **Graef (1989)** said the police have a 'canteen culture'. He thought the majority of police officers, who tend to be white males, adopt racist and sexist attitudes as a way of fitting in.

2) Other formal **agents** include **Parliament**, which passes laws to say what behaviour is criminal, the **Crown Prosecution Service**, which decides who should be taken to court for a particular crime, the **courts**, which determine any punishment, and the **Prison Service**, which imposes custodial punishments (e.g. prison sentences).

3) There are also agents of **informal social control**. These include the **family** unit, the **education** system, **religion** and the **media**. All these channels help to reinforce a general sense of what behaviour is considered non-deviant.

Criminals are Punished for a number of Reasons

Most societies around the world have systems for **punishing crime**.
Sociologists (unsurprisingly) have different views on the **purpose** and **importance** of punishment.

1) **Functionalists** argue that punishment **keeps society going**. If crimes went **unpunished** the result would be **anarchy** and society would **collapse** — the public needs to see that there is **retribution** for the crime. **Durkheim** said that **public punishment** of criminals was **good for society**. He thought it helped create **unity** and **consensus** as people came together to condemn the criminal — in other words, a **public hanging** was good for society.

2) **Marxists** say punishment serves the needs of capitalism by **keeping the workers under control**. They argue that the police are used to **enforce social control** in **poorer areas** whilst the **rich** get away with crime **unchallenged**.

3) The **interventionist** camp see prison as a **deterrent** — the very fact it **exists** should put people off committing crimes. The evidence suggests that this theory does not work **in practice**.

4) Some sociologists see punishments as a way to **rehabilitate** criminals — they **reform** criminals so that they can become **respectable** members of society when they are released. Rehabilitation involves things like **education** or **counselling**.

Some Sociologists Argue that the Role of Prisons is Changing

1) Prison can be a way of **removing** criminals from the streets so they cannot commit any more crime. However, **David Garland (2001)** argued that **zero tolerance attitudes** and policies that **crack down** on crime have led to **mass incarceration** — since the 1970s, the number of people in prison in the UK and USA has **increased dramatically**.

2) Bodies that are associated with **criminal justice** and **welfare** are increasingly working together. **Prisons** are taking on more of a **welfare role** than they have before.

3) However, this can lead to more '**transcarceration**', where **vulnerable individuals** are constantly **moved** between different kinds of **institutions** (e.g. prison, mental institutions, young offender facilities) that **control** their lives. Today's **prison system** has arguably become part of this **network** of institutions.

Practice Questions

Q1 Describe two victimology theories.
Q2 Give two main features of situational crime prevention.
Q3 What is the functionalist view on punishment?

Exam Question

Q1 How might punishment deal with crime? Outline three ways. [6 marks]

Prevention is better than cure, they say...

Unfortunately, by the time all the sociological theorists have finished debating how we become victims and the best ways of preventing and punishing crime we'll all be... no, what am I thinking — sociologists will never stop debating. The best policy for you as a conscientious sociology student is to learn what the main arguments say, and draw your own conclusions.

Theories of Ideology

*These pages are about the many different ways people have used the concept of **ideology**. It's an important concept in sociology — but unfortunately it doesn't have one agreed definition. So there's lots to learn.*

The term 'Ideology' has several meanings

Antoine Destutt de Tracy first used the word **ideology** in 1796 to describe what he called a new '**science of ideas**' which he saw emerging after the French Revolution.

Since then the term has been used in several different ways.

Ideology has been defined in a large variety of ways

1) As a set of **political beliefs**, e.g. socialism, liberalism.
2) As the **ideas** and **beliefs** of a **particular social class**.
3) As the **dominant ideas** and **beliefs** of the **ruling class**.
4) As the **official beliefs** of a **political system**, e.g. in totalitarian (dictatorial) regimes like Hitler's Germany.
5) As a set of beliefs that represent a **total view of reality**, e.g. religious fundamentalism.

It's not easy to **pin down** just one workable definition for 'ideology' — but it's important you understand how the word has been used by some **prominent thinkers**.

Your *Social* and *Political* perspective *Influences* how you define *Ideology*

When someone uses the word 'ideology' their **perspective** will give you a clue as to what they mean. E.g.

Marxists	See ideology as the set of ruling ideas that **keep workers in their place**.
Feminists	See ideology as both the set of ideas that **keep women oppressed** (patriarchal ideology), and a potentially **liberating set of beliefs** (feminism).
Liberals (pluralists)	Tend to see ideology as **totalitarian** and **oppressive** — e.g. Stalin's Russia and Hitler's Germany both had official ideologies which were repressive. Pluralists **reject** the idea that there can be a **monopoly of truth**.

Karl Marx said *Ideology* was a *False Picture* imposed by the *Ruling Class*

1) **Karl Marx** believed the most important force in society was **class conflict** between the workers and the ruling class.
2) Marx and **Friedrich Engels** said that the **ideas** that a society **lives by** are the ideas of that society's **ruling class**.

1) In capitalist societies, workers are employed to **produce goods** which are sold by their employers to **make money**.
2) Only a **bit** of this money ends up in the **workers' wages** — most of it's **kept** by the employer.
3) Marx said if workers were allowed to notice the **unfairness** of this they'd **revolt**.
4) Ruling ideas (or **ideology**) are needed by the ruling class to make a grossly unfair system **appear fair** and **legitimate** and therefore keep it going.
5) Marx claimed that **ruling-class ideology** creates a **'false consciousness'** for the workers. It gets them to **believe** that the system and their **position** within it are both **fair** and **just** by **mystifying** and **falsifying** their picture of reality.
6) The function of ideology for Marx then was to keep the workers in their place and **stop them rebelling**.
7) According to Marx only the ruling class has an ideology because only they have the need to **create illusions**.

In his false consciousness, Jeremy was a horse.

Theories of Ideology

The *Marxist* view of *Ideology* was developed by *Gramsci*

Antonio Gramsci was a Marxist who called the domination of ruling-class ideology in society '**hegemony**'.

1) Hegemonic ideas don't just rule — they **dominate**. Other values and ideas still exist in society, but **don't** get taken **seriously**. Ruling-class ideas become '**the common sense of the age**'.
2) Nobody questions 'common sense' and so **nobody questions** the **ruling class's right to rule**. Gramsci argued that the ruling class's ideology becomes **entrenched** in all areas of social life — e.g. religion, art, law, language, education. This makes it difficult to challenge.
3) The **struggle** against hegemony for Gramsci had to be an **intellectual** one, with socialist thinkers developing an alternative '**proletarian hegemony**' (proletarian = working-class).

Gramsci wrote most of his theories in prison, in the 1930s. His prison notebooks were published after he died.

Althusser argued there were *Ideological State Apparatuses*

1) The neo-Marxist **Althusser** argued that elements of society like the education system, mass media and religion were **Ideological State Apparatuses** (ISAs).
2) The ISAs are a tool of capitalism used to **justify**, **maintain** and **reproduce** class inequalities.
3) For example, according to Althusser, education **transmits** and **reproduces** an ideology about what it means to be working class, what it means to be middle class, and what everyone's **place in society** ought to be.

Karl Mannheim identified *Two* types of *Ideology*

Mannheim (1929) argued that ideology can be defined in two ways.

1) A set of beliefs used to **justify** and **perpetuate** an existing social order (a ruling-class ideology).
2) A **utopian** set of beliefs about how the world **could be organised** in the **future**. Utopian ideologies tend to be formed by **oppressed groups** who want **radical change**.

According to Mannheim both types of ideology **distort reality** — the former is a distortion to create the illusion of **fairness** in society, the latter is just a '**wish image**' of what the future might be like.

- **Marxism** could be seen as a **utopian ideology** with its vision of an ideal future society after the ruling class has been overthrown. The ideal vision is used to **criticise existing society**.
- **Functionalism** (see p.104) could be seen as a **ruling-class ideology** as it seeks to **justify existing society** with its emphasis on **agreement**, **consensus** and **stability**.

Benji's idea of rebranding their petrochemical business as "Benji's Bag o' Fun™" was little more than a wish image.

Practice Questions

Q1 List four different ways in which the word ideology has been used.
Q2 According to Marx, what is the purpose of ruling-class ideology?
Q3 Explain what is meant by false consciousness.
Q4 Why aren't hegemonic ideas challenged in capitalist society, according to Gramsci?
Q5 What two types of ideology does Mannheim identify?

Exam Question

Q1 Evaluate the idea that Marxism is a utopian ideology. [20 marks]

Explain the different theories — and get top Marx...

The trick is to remember that ideology doesn't have just one definition that you can reel off, but is used in lots of different ways by different sociologists depending on their... er,... ideological perspective. My own ideology mainly consists of tea and cake.

Theories of Science

*These pages examine theories of science in relation to other types of **belief system**, and discuss the debates surrounding their similarities and differences.*

The **Traditional View** is that **Science** is **Objective** and **Evidence-Based**

Critics of religion claim there is a clear **distinction** between **science** and other ways of viewing the world. They believe that science is based on **theories** that are backed up by **evidence**, whereas **religion** (for example) is based on the interpretation of **religious texts** and **holy books**. They argue that in religion, what's written in the holy books is regarded as **absolutely true**, and if evidence **contradicts** it, it is the **evidence** that is seen as **wrong**, not the holy book.

> **The traditional view of science**
>
> 1) **Science is objective** — the scientist is **neutral**.
> 2) Scientific enquiry is **evidence-based** — conclusions are based on evidence, not **preconceived ideas**.
> 3) Scientific enquiry is **'open'** — ideas which are **tested** and proved wrong are rejected and **more accurate** ideas replace them.

It may not have been holy, but Rita was convinced that *Alice in Wonderland* was absolutely true.

This **Traditional View** of science has been **Challenged**

Michael E. Lynch argued that science is **far less objective** than scientists claim.

1) In 1985, he published a study of the **interactions** between scientists experimenting on lab rats. He concluded that the scientists were more **influenced** by their **existing theories** than may have been expected.
2) When **'anomalies'** occurred — i.e. results they were not expecting — the scientists often put them down to **errors** in the images they were studying, rather than seeing them as **evidence** towards a new theory or hypothesis.

Science can be viewed as a **Belief System** like **Religion**

Polanyi (1958) suggested that a **belief system** was made up of **three factors**. Science can be viewed as fitting this model.

> 1) **A circularity of beliefs** — each idea within the belief system is explained in **relation to others**. If one is challenged or fails it is **defended** by reference to another, to **avoid changing** the belief system.
> 2) **Supporting explanations are given for difficult situations** — if any **evidence** is shown to **contradict** the belief there will be a reason to explain it (as with the anomalies in the experiments Lynch observed).
> 3) **No alternative belief systems can be tolerated** — a sweeping rejection of religion could be seen as an example of this.

The postmodernist **Lyotard (1984)** argues that science can be seen as another kind of **metanarrative** (p.110) — it claims to have a **monopoly of truth** and to **explain** how **everything** works. In this way, it's just another **ideology**. Also, some **Marxists** and **feminists** argue that **scientific knowledge** may be used to strengthen **capitalist** and **patriarchal ideologies**.

Sociology can be treated as a **Science**

Positivists like Comte believe that sociology is scientific. It consists of **gathering information** about the social world, **classifying data**, and **drawing conclusions** about **'the social laws'** which govern human society.

The positivist **Durkheim** claimed that by using the technique of **multivariate analysis**, 'social facts' could be uncovered.

1) Multivariate analysis is the attempt to **isolate** the impact of **independent variables** (the factors affecting something) on the dependent variable (the thing being affected).
2) For instance, the level of working-class achievement in school might be the **dependent** variable, and material deprivation and teacher labelling the **independent** variables.
3) Durkheim believed that by complex, in-depth **statistical analysis** the independent variables could be measured and a **social law established**.

The early positivists used an **inductive** approach. This means they first **collected data on their topic**, which they **studied** and **analysed**. From this they composed a **theory** or **hypothesis**. They then **tested** their hypothesis and drew **conclusions**. If their results were **repeatable** (i.e. if people repeated their experiment and got the same results), the hypothesis was considered a **social fact**.

Theories of Science

Popper said scientists should use the Deductive Approach and Falsification

The **deductive approach** is similar to the inductive approach, only in reverse — it starts with the theory, which then leads to the investigation. **Karl Popper (1959, 1963)** argued that theories or hypotheses could spring from anywhere, such as **flashes of inspiration** ('eureka moments') or even from **dreams**.

Popper said the positivists were **wrong** in their belief that theories could be **proved** to be **true**. He had a different idea of scientific method:

1) Popper rejected the idea that there are **permanent social laws** governing human behaviour. He claimed that any 'law' could at some point be **falsified** (proved wrong), no matter how many times it has been 'proved' correct in the past.

2) The famous example he gave was the hypothesis '**all swans are white**,' which can be 'proved' thousands of times until you encounter a **black swan**.

3) Popper said the aim of science and social science should be to constantly **strive to falsify** theories. This 'falsification' of theories arguably distinguishes science from religion and other supernatural belief systems.

Don't believe the hype.

Gomm argued that scientists' work should be viewed in its Social Context

Roger Gomm (1982) argued that the theories scientists produce are in part a product of their **social context**, and that scientists tend to try and **prove** rather than falsify their theories. Gomm gave the example of **Darwin** and his **theory of evolution** to explain this.

1) Gomm suggests Darwin's theories of natural selection and the competitive struggle for the survival of the fittest were not supported by all of the evidence.

2) Darwin therefore missed the opportunity to 'falsify' aspects of his theories. Gomm suggests the reason for this was ideological rather than scientific.

3) Gomm argued that the 'survival of the fittest' theory slotted neatly into the Victorian capitalist ideology of free-market economics, individualism, and the minimalist approach to welfare of the time. Gomm therefore emphasised the importance of placing 'science' in its social context. Science can be seen, at least in part, as a social construct, because it is researched and interpreted by people who are influenced by existing social values.

Kuhn challenged the idea that science is Objective

Thomas Kuhn (1962) introduced the idea that scientists, at certain times in history, work in a **paradigm**.

1) A paradigm, according to Kuhn, refers to the **framework** of **accepted ideas** in which scientists operate. It might include ideas on **truth**, **validity** and **methodology**.

2) Kuhn argued that scientists will tend to work within the paradigm and so seek evidence which **supports** it. This will continue until **anomalies** ← are so strong as to trigger a **paradigm shift** or **scientific revolution**.

Working within the paradigm can be seen as similar to Polanyi's first factor of a belief system — circularity of beliefs (see p.140).

3) When this happens, a new '**normal science paradigm**' is established and the process begins again.

Practice Questions

Q1 Describe the traditional view of science.

Q2 What is the difference between an inductive and a deductive scientific approach?

Q3 What is meant by falsification?

Q4 How does Gomm think social context affects scientific theories?

Exam Questions

Q1 Outline two arguments which support the view that science is a belief system. Explain each one. [10 marks]

Q2 Evaluate the idea that science operates within a paradigm. [20 marks]

Study this page — it'll help you do your experiments Popper-ly...

You see, science is a funny thing — you think it's a clean break from the superstition and mummery of the past, and yet it all turns out to be the product of inspiration and whimsy and elves. Well, maybe not that last one. No elves on this page.

Theories of Religion

Sociologists disagree about religion. Some think it's great and stops society descending into chaos — others think it's just there to oppress people. God doesn't seem to have much to do with it.

Religion *is hard to* Define

1) The **definition** of religion is very hard to pin down — some definitions can either **exclude** belief systems commonly thought of as religions, or fail to **distinguish** between **religious** and **secular** organisations.

2) Some people define religion as **belief in God** or a **higher power** (this is known as a **substantive** definition because it's to do with the **substance** or **content** of a religion). However, this definition excludes belief systems such as **Buddhism**, which do not worship a god. Defining religion as a **system of faith** is a little more inclusive.

3) A different view is the **functional** definition — it is based on what the religion actually **does** (either for an **individual** or for **society** as a whole). It focuses on the idea of **community** and **integration**, which is where problems can arise — an organisation that gives a sense of community (such as the **Young Farmers**) isn't necessarily a religion.

4) **Social constructionists** concentrate on how **individual** members of society define religion. This attitude is very **inclusive**, but also makes it virtually **impossible** to come up with a **general** or **universal definition**.

Functionalists *see religion as* Maintaining Harmony *and* Social Cohesion

Functionalists see religion as something that **inhibits change** and helps **keep society as it is**.
But they think this is a **positive** role, which creates **social order** based on **value consensus**.

1) **Durkheim** studied **Aboriginal** society and suggested that the **sacred worship of totems** was equivalent to **worshipping society itself**. Durkheim said that sacred religious worship encourages shared values.

2) **Malinowski (1954)** looked at how religion deals with situations of **emotional stress** that **threaten social order**. Unpredictable or stressful events like births and deaths create **disruption**. Religion **manages** these **tensions** and promotes stability.

   Religions have ceremonies for dealing with birth and death.

3) **Parsons** wrote in the 1930s and 1940s that religion provides **guidelines** for human action in terms of "**core values**". Religion helps to **integrate** people into a value consensus and allows them to **make sense of their lives**.

4) Functionalist **Bellah (1967)** suggested the idea of **Civil Religion**, which is when secular (non-religious) symbols and rituals create **social cohesion** in a similar way to religion. **Flags**, famous **political figures** and even **royal deaths** bring about some kind of **collective feeling** that generates **order** and **stability**.

Functionalism ignores **dysfunctional** aspects of religion. There are **religious conflicts** all over the world (see p.144). Religion can be a source of **oppression**. Religion can also bring about **change**, and functionalism ignores that as well.

Feminists *point out the* Sexism *in* Religion

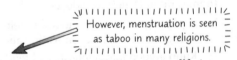
However, menstruation is seen as taboo in many religions.

1) Women's capacity to **have babies** gives women an **important role** within religion, in terms of bringing **new life** into the world. Women's role as **primary caregiver** is seen as **important** by traditional religion — it's the job of a mother to raise her children to **believe in God** and worship God. Feminists say this **traps** women in **traditional** roles.

2) Because women are **sexually attractive** to men they're perceived to be **distractions** from worship. Many religions believe in giving worship to God through a denial of sexuality (e.g. priests in the Roman Catholic Church have to be **celibate**). Religions have historically seen women as '**temptresses**' of men — think of Eve and the apple.

3) Women are **excluded from power** in many religious organisations.

4) Feminists argue that religious texts **transmit messages** to readers through stories that reflect and uphold a **patriarchal** society. This patriarchal ideology says that women are part of the profane and imperfect, and maintains the **conformity** and **submission** of women.

   profane = not sacred or holy

5) **Simone de Beauvoir (1953)** saw religion as **exploitative** and **oppressive** towards women. She thought that religion promotes the idea that if women **suffer** in their present lives, then they'll receive **equality in heaven**, which allows women to **put up with** being treated as **inferior** to men in the hope of gaining in the afterlife.

The relationship between religion and patriarchy is more complicated than the feminist view suggests

1) Religion may transmit **patriarchal ideals**, but there is a **bigger picture**. Other **social** and **cultural** influences (e.g. **socialisation** within the family and in education) contribute towards the creation of patriarchal society too.

2) Some women may also **actively resist** religious oppression by fighting against the **limitations** it places on them, e.g. in **Afghanistan** under the Taliban it was **forbidden** for girls to go to **school**, so women educated girls **in secret**.

Theories of Religion

Marx said Religion helps to Oppress Workers and Inhibits Social Change

1) Karl Marx said that in **capitalist** society there was a **conflict of interests** between the **ruling class** and the **working class** because the ruling class **exploit** the working class to get the most profit out of them (see p.138).

2) But — there's **something stopping** the working class from **uniting** and **overthrowing** the ruling class. Marx argued that the working class are in a state of **false consciousness**. This means they're **not aware** of **how unfair** society is.

3) This is where **religion** comes in. Marx is **very critical** of religion. He said it's one of the things that **keeps** the working class in a state of **false consciousness**. He described religion as "**the opium of the people**". This means that it **dulls the pain** of oppression like **opium** — a **drug** which kills pain. It doesn't take the oppression away, though.

> ### Marx said that religion is used to justify social inequality
>
> 1) People have the afterlife to look forward to if they're good, so they don't break the rules and don't challenge the capitalist system.
>
> 2) Religion consoles people with the promise of life after death and so they put up with their suffering here on Earth more easily.
>
> 3) Religion often tells people that their position is decided by God. This encourages false consciousness by blaming God instead of blaming capitalism.
>
> 4) If God is all-powerful he could do something about the suffering if he wanted to. He doesn't do anything — so people think this must be how society is meant to be.

Marx believed religion was both a way of oppressing people and a way of cushioning the effects of oppression.

4) Marxism says that religion **passes on beliefs** that **oppress the working class**. It argues that religion is a **conservative** force (see next page) which prevents revolution — it keeps things the same. The **rich stay rich** and the **poor** keep on working. It's a neat **social control**.

5) **But...** there are **problems** with applying this Marxist view to **today's society**. **Fewer people** go to a **place of worship** than in the past — if people **don't go to worship**, it's **hard** for them to be duped by formal religious ideology.

6) Also, traditional Marxists tend to ignore the fact that religion can bring about **social change** (see next page). **Neo-Marxists** do accept this, and agree that this social change can actually **help** the working class. This is known as the **dual character** of religion — it can both **hinder** and **benefit** the working class.

Postmodernism says that Religious Beliefs are Changing to Reflect Society

1) Postmodernism argues that people no longer believe in '**metanarratives**' (see p.5) — **all-encompassing stories** that present '**universal truths**' (e.g. in religion or politics). Because of this, people don't necessarily accept **traditional religions** just because their **parents** followed them.

2) Instead, they can make their **own choices** and create their own **individual belief system**. People can choose to **reject** the values of organised religion, so it plays a **less important role** in the development of **social values** and **beliefs**.

3) In a postmodern society, the role of the church is **less direct** — people no longer go to **church** just because it is **expected** of them. This has led to a **decrease** in **church attendance** (see p.150). However, this does not mean there has been a decrease in **faith** — people may be choosing to celebrate their faith **privately**, or in **non-traditional ways**.

Practice Questions

Q1 What is the role of religion, according to functionalists?
Q2 Give three examples of feminist views of sexism in religion.
Q3 In what ways does Marx say religion is used to justify social inequality?
Q4 What are metanarratives?

Exam Questions

Q1 Analyse two explanations for why Marx believed religion is oppressive. [10 marks]

Q2 Evaluate the idea that there is sexism in religion. [20 marks]

The function of religion is to give you someone to pray to before exams...

There's an awful lot to learn here, I'll be honest. To make it easy on yourself, take each kind of theory individually. Once you've read it through, what functionalists, feminists, Marxists and postmodernists think about religion probably won't come as a big surprise to you. The next step is to learn the key names and studies. Work on it until you can remember the names and ideas.

Religion and Social Change

Religion can both cause and prevent social change. Have a read through the next two pages and it should all become clear...

Religion can be seen as Conservative...

1) Religion is often seen as **traditional** — it encourages traditional **values** in things like **morals, roles, family life** etc. It also has various **ceremonies** and **customs** that follow **established patterns**.

2) Religious **attitudes** to matters such as **abortion** and **homosexuality** can also be quite **old-fashioned**.

3) Religion also tends to **keep things as they are**. For example, the **caste system** in India (which divides people based on inherited status) prevails because of the **Hindu** belief in **reincarnation**.

4) **Marxists, feminists** and **functionalists** all agree that religion is conservative. Marxists and feminists view this as a **bad thing**, as they believe that it allows **repression** of the **working class** and **women** to continue unchallenged. Functionalists, however, see it as a **good thing** as it provides **stability** (see p.142-143 for more on these viewpoints).

... but it can also Encourage Social Change

1) Marx's good pal **Engels** reckoned that in **some circumstances** religion could actually be a **revolutionary** force. Sometimes **religion** is the **only means of change** because all other routes have been blocked.

2) **Early Christian sects** opposed Roman rule and brought about change. **Jesus** himself encouraged social change.

3) In the 1960s and 1970s, **Catholic priests** in **Latin America** criticised the bourgeoisie and preached **liberation theology** — using religion to free people from oppression. This led to **resistance** and **social change** — in 1979, revolutionaries threw out the oppressive government in **Nicaragua**.

4) Reverend **Martin Luther King** and the **Southern Baptist Church** resisted oppression and segregation, bringing about **political** and **social rights** for black people in **1960s America**.

5) In Iran, **Islamic fundamentalism** encouraged **social change**. In 1979, there was a **revolution** against the Shah, led by followers of the Shia Ayatollah **Khomeini**. Khomeini set up a **religious government** that followed Sharia law.

6) **Fundamentalism** (see p.153) tries to provoke social change, often through a **regression** to more **traditional values**. It tries to change people's **religious practices**, but is often met with **opposition**, and sometimes leads to **violence**.

Weber said that Religion can Create a Capitalist Work Ethic

Weber looked at how the **religious** ideas of **Calvinism** led to social change. He spotted **two important things** in Calvinism:

1) **Predestination:** This is the idea that your life and whether you're going to heaven are **predetermined** by God. Calvinists believed only a **few** were **chosen** for heaven. This created **anxiety** — no one knew if they were chosen.

2) **Ascetic Ideal: Working hard** in your job was a **solution** to this anxiety. Success might be a sign that you were chosen for heaven. Early Calvinists lived a **strict** and **disciplined** life of hard work and simple pleasures.

Weber claimed that the ascetic ideal helped create an ethic of **disciplined hard work**. This is the **spirit of capitalism**. Not only was there a build-up of **capital**, there was the right **work ethic** for capitalism. Religion **indirectly** brought about change. However, **Eisenstadt (1967)** contradicts Weber's theory by claiming that capitalism occurred in **Catholic** countries like Italy **before** the **Protestant Reformation happened** and before the ideas of **Calvin ever came out**.

Religion can bring about Stability or Conflict

1) **Functionalists** believe that religion brings **stability** (see p.142). By giving a society **common values** and **morals**, it can create and maintain **harmony**. A **unifying** religion can **bring people together** and help them **function** better as a community.

2) However, one **criticism** of the functionalist view is that religion only creates stability **within** a religious community, not **between** different religions.

3) In fact, in these cases, religion can actually **create** conflict (and has done so throughout history) — the **Crusades** of the Middle Ages pitted **Christians** against **Muslims**, whereas more recent history in **Northern Ireland** saw the struggle between **Catholics** and **Protestants**.

The nuns of St Hilda's had excellent stability.

4) **Samuel Huntington (1993)** describes a **'clash of civilisations'**, where conflicts are caused by the **different cultures** and **religious beliefs** of different civilisations (e.g. **Western** and **Islamic**). However, **critics** of Huntington argue that his view is **unfair** on the **majority** of a religion (e.g. only a few **fundamentalist** Muslims are involved in conflicts), and that he ignores any conflicts **within** 'civilisations' (e.g. between **Catholics** and **Protestants**).

Religion and Social Change

Religious Beliefs and Practices change as Society changes

1) Social changes such as **urbanisation** (in the UK) and **globalisation** have **changed** the nature of religious belief.
2) Urbanisation has meant that **religious communities** that were **small** have become **larger** and more **spread out**, so the **bonds** that held them together, which were created by **shared religious beliefs**, are **weaker** and **less effective**.
3) Globalisation means there are people from **diverse backgrounds**, with **different religions**, all living in the **same area** (this is known as **multiculturalism**) — so there is no **single unifying religion** as there may have been in the past.
4) Social change has led to an increase in **secularisation** (see p.150) — religion has less of an **influence** over society, so **traditions** and **practices** associated with religion are declining.
5) All of these factors have led to a **decline** in **church attendance**. However, in an increasingly **digital** society, **online chatrooms**, **prayer groups** and **religious TV channels** provide new ways for people to worship.

Social change can lead to New Religious Organisations

Sometimes **new religious organisations** come into existence as a **direct result** of social change.

The **Methodist** church was formed partly as a result of the **Industrial Revolution**. A large number of people moved from **country villages** into the **city** to work, and as a result lost much of their sense of **community**. The Methodist meetings provided a renewed sense of **community** and **friendship**, which appealed to the **working class**.

More recently, sociologist **Roy Wallis (1984)** identified three types of **new religious movements** (NRMs):

- **World-rejecting movements**, which require **total commitment** and **cut themselves off** from society (e.g. the **Unification Church**, also known as the 'Moonies').
- **World-affirming movements**, which are more like **self-help** or **therapy groups** and are **tolerant** of other religions (e.g. **Transcendental Meditation**).
- **World-accommodating movements**, which are more **traditionally religious** (e.g. **Pentecostalism**).

The **growth** of NRMs is thought to be partly a result of the **uncertainties** caused by **social change**:

1) Marginality — inequality, immigration and racism may marginalise some groups. So some new religious movements may help marginalised people make sense of their situation, and may promise a better life after death as compensation. Weber called this the "theodicy of disprivilege".
2) Relative deprivation — the concept of marginality doesn't explain why white, middle-class groups join new religious movements. Although they aren't absolutely poor or deprived, some middle-class people may see themselves as deprived in comparison to their peers.
3) Modernity and post-modernity — the alienation of capitalism, the increasing amount of red tape, bureaucracy, and disillusionment with work may create uncertainty. The choice people have in constructing their identity may create uncertainty and a crisis of identity.

Practice Questions

Q1 In what ways can religion be considered conservative?
Q2 Give three examples of how religion has brought about social change.
Q3 Explain how Calvinism is said to have created capitalism.
Q4 Give one criticism of Huntington's idea that conflicts are caused by a 'clash of civilisations'.
Q5 How has social change affected religious beliefs?
Q6 Name the three types of new religious movement (NRM), according to Wallis.

Exam Question

Q1 Analyse two explanations for why social change can lead to religious changes. [10 marks]

Create the right work ethic for revision and you'll be sorted...

Don't worry, you don't need to know all the specific details of the new religious movements, just how they've been brought about by social change. It works both ways — social change can bring about religious change, and religions can bring about social change. It's a never-ending cycle, like the circle of life, the water cycle, the carbon cycle, the bi-cycle...

Religious Organisations

Religious groups organise themselves into different forms. They differ in leadership, relationship to the state and politics, how they worship and who they appeal to. Sociologists have put forward different classifications of religious organisations.

A **Church** is a well-established **Religious Organisation**

Sociologists often use a **typology** (a set of '**ideal types**') to categorise and analyse religious organisations, e.g. 'church', 'sect' and 'denomination'. It is important to remember that these are **ideal** types — perfect **pure** models. **Real** religious organisations may include features of **more than one type**.

Social historian **Ernst Troeltsch (1912)** distinguished between different types of religious organisation, and used the word **church** to mean a **large religious organisation**. He said churches usually have four main features:

1) A church claims **monopoly over the truth** — it says its claims are **absolutely true** and others are **false**.
2) Churches have a **complex rigid hierarchy** and a **bureaucratic structure** with lots of **rules and regulations**.
3) Churches often have a **close relationship** to the **state**. Some nations have an official national religion (e.g. Islam is the national religion of Egypt) — Weber used the term "**ecclesia**" for this.
4) They are closely integrated into **mainstream society**. Churches act as a **conservative** force, resisting change. This is why the **upper classes** are more likely to join, even though churches are **universal** and **inclusive in principle**.

Examples of churches include the **Roman Catholic Church**, the **Church of England** and the **Episcopal Church**.

Troeltsch studied churches in **16th century** Europe. **Steve Bruce (1995)** says that Troeltsch's points don't always apply to today's churches because there's **religious pluralism** these days. Nowadays, the Church of England doesn't claim a monopoly over the truth and it isn't always conservative.

Religious pluralism = lots of different types of religious groups.

Sects are **Small, Radical Religious Movements**

Troeltsch defined sects as being almost the **opposite of churches**. Few religious groups fall into the category of sect.

People who are **dissatisfied** with mainstream religion can be attracted to a sect. Sects are often formed by people **splitting off from a church** because they **disagree** with the church's **practices** or **theology**.

1) Sects claim a **monopoly over the truth** and are intolerant towards other religious organisations.
2) Sects have **no complex hierarchy**. They often have a **charismatic leader** who **persuades** members to **follow his or her teaching**.
3) Sects are **small**. Their members follow with **total commitment**, and they can be **manipulated** by the sect's leader.
4) Sects are separate from the state — they're in **opposition** to mainstream society. Sects can sometimes offer an alternative way of life for **deprived** and **marginal** groups.

Examples of sects include the **early Methodists** and **Calvinists** (although over time these have become more mainstream). This category also includes **extremist** groups like the **People's Temple** in America who were led to mass suicide by Jim Jones, or the **Branch Davidians** led by David Koresh.

These extremist groups are often called cults, but watch out — in sociology, 'cult' means something else (see below).

Denominations are **Subsets** of **Churches**

Troeltsch **originally classified** religious organisations into **churches** and **sects**. The term '**denomination**' was added later.

1) Denominations don't usually claim **a monopoly over the truth**. They see themselves as a **possible route to the truth**. They are **tolerant** towards other religious organisations.
2) Like a church, they have a **hierarchy** and **bureaucratic structure**, but it isn't as complex.
3) They have a reasonably **large membership**, but not as large as an established church.
4) Members of denominations are usually **not as loyal** as members of churches.
5) Denominations **aren't closely connected to the state**. They get involved in society and **comment** on **current events**.

Examples of denominations are **modern Methodists** and **Baptists**.

Cults are **Mystic Movements** — often **Wrongly Defined**

Bruce (1995) defined cults as movements without a fixed set of beliefs. They emphasise the **inner power** of the **individual** and **mysticism**. Cults are usually loosely knit and don't have a hierarchy.

Religious Organisations

New Age Movements are Cultural

1) **New Age movements** are close to cults and world-affirming movements (see p.145). New Age ideas often aren't linked to an organisation, but spread through a **culture**, e.g. **dowsing**, **feng shui**, **crystal healing**, **neopaganism** and **reiki**.

2) **Heelas (1996)** claims that New Age followers focus on "**self-spirituality**" and the development of the self.

3) **Bruce (1995)** highlights **three themes** to New Age movements: **New Science** rejects many claims of traditional science, **New Ecology** is concerned for the environment, and **New Psychology** sees the self as sacred.

New Age Movements appeal to people already Examining their Identity

1) New Age beliefs appeal to people who have **turned away from traditional religion**. New Age beliefs say that people can find salvation, peace or perfection **inside themselves**. Modern society is more **individualistic** than before — **individual beliefs** are **trusted more**, and authority is **trusted less**.

2) New Age movements help some people cope with the **uncertainties** of modernity. In the modern world, people have a lot of **different roles**. New Age beliefs can help people find a sense of **identity**.

3) New Age beliefs often appeal to middle-class people working in '**expressive professions**' — actors, writers, social workers, counsellors, therapists etc. New Age beliefs appeal to **women** more than men, and the **middle class** more than the working class.

4) New Age movements may also reflect a **cultural change** in mainstream society. People are surrounded by non-conventional ideas like horoscopes, feng shui and homeopathy. **Mass communication** gives us an awareness of different movements.

5) The New Age is quite a **postmodern** thing. In a **postmodern** society of **choice** and **diversity** people can **pick and mix** from all kinds of New Age philosophies to help them construct their own identity.

Christmas: one of the busiest periods for spiritual shoppers.

> There are more and more belief systems in society. '**Spiritual shoppers**' are people who **sample** different systems of belief to find the **best fit**. This is an **individualistic** and **consumerist** attitude.

Religious organisations Grow or Decline for different reasons

1) **Social change** can bring about changes in religion (see p.144-145) — this often leads to a **decline** in **churches**, but **growth** in **denominations** or **sects**.

2) **Churches** tend to **grow** in countries with a **strong link** between church and **state**, but in other countries, the **competition** between churches and **denominations** can lead to a **decline** in churches (but often a **growth** in denominations).

3) **Sects** can **grow rapidly** as a result of a **charismatic leader** or a **religious schism** (when a sect breaks away from the church). However, if the leader **dies**, or the sect's **promises** do not come true (e.g. the world doesn't end when they said it would), the sect can **decline** as rapidly as it began.

4) If sects **don't** die out but **grow** over time and become more **accepted** and **respectable**, they sometimes become **denominations**.

5) **Cults** demand **less commitment** than sects, so can become more popular in a **modern**, **busy** world.

Practice Questions

Q1 Explain the differences between a church and a denomination.

Q2 Give two examples of a sect.

Q3 Give the key characteristics of a cult.

Q4 What three themes did Bruce identify in New Age movements?

Exam Questions

Q1 Outline two arguments which support the view that New Age beliefs are becoming more popular in modern society. Explain each one. [10 marks]

Q2 Evaluate the idea that the very nature of a church is the reason for its decline. [20 marks]

Lots of religions don't condone sects before marriage...

Don't assume you already know what a church is, what a sect is, etc. Sociological definitions can be a bit different from the everyday definitions. Obviously, not all religious groups will fit neatly into one of these categories — but most will.

Religion and Social Groups

How religious a person is (or says they are) is related to age, gender, ethnicity and social class.

Religiosity and Religious Belief are different things

1) **Religious belief** is believing that the world is controlled by **supernatural forces** (usually a **god**, or **group of gods**).
2) **Religiosity** is the **level** of an individual's connection to **all aspects** of religion — **how** religious the person is.

Religiosity varies by Age

1) The 2011 census found that **22%** of **Christians** in England and Wales were **over 65**. In contrast, just **3.9%** of Muslims were **over 65** (and **88%** of them were **under 50**). This means **Christianity** has a far **older age profile** than **Islam**.
2) People who said that they had **no religion** also tended to be **younger** — more than a third were **under 25**.
3) **Middle-aged** groups are more likely to get involved in **world-affirming movements** (see p.145).
4) **Sects** and **cults** (see p.146) are more likely to be populated with **young adults**.

- **Sects** often appeal to young adults by messages of **friendship** and **companionship** — this can be attractive to those who are experiencing forms of **anomie** (lack of social/moral standards) and **detachment** from the world, and those who have few responsibilities (e.g. marriage).
- **Cults** appeal to the **inner thoughts** and **feelings** of young adults who are often alienated from the primary cultures of society. **Cults** are attractive to individuals who are often already engaging in **counterculture** activity.

Religiosity varies by Gender

1) **Women** are **more likely to attend church**, and more likely to say they belong to a religion. This has often been explained by women's traditional role as **primary caregiver**. Going to **church** and **raising children** to be **religious** is traditionally seen as an **extension** of that role.
2) **Differential socialisation** is also a factor. The argument goes that girls are socialised to be **passive** and to **conform** — which fits in with the behaviour of more **traditional** and **conservative** religious groups.
3) Another argument is that **women** simply **live longer**. More women are on their **own** as they get older, and they may **turn to religion** for a sense of community. **Older** people are often **more religious** anyway.
4) More **men** than **women** have **turned away** from organised religion in the 20th century.

Feminists' views of religion

1) **Beauvoir (1949)** claimed that the **images of gender** in Western religion deceive women into thinking they're **equal** when they're not. Women are sometimes portrayed as **'nearer to God'** than men by religious imagery and so are **duped** into believing their **sufferings** on Earth will be rewarded with **equality** in Heaven (see p.143).
2) **Jean Holm (1994)** outlined how many contemporary religions both **exploit** and **subordinate** women and give men **dominant organisational roles**. She suggested this secondary status has its origins in **biology** and **sexuality** — things like **menstruation** and **childbirth** are often seen by religions as being **'polluting'**.

Women often have Significant roles in New Religious Movements (NRMs)

1) Women generally **participate** in **sects** more than men, and many sects and NRMs were **established** by **women**, e.g. the Seventh Day Adventists and the Christian Science movement.
2) **Glock and Stark (1965)** have argued that the gender difference in membership of NRMs is because **deprivation** (social, physical and mental) is **disproportionately** experienced by **women**.

esoteric = elitist and specialist

3) **Bruce (1995)** suggests that men are more interested in NRMs that advocate **esoteric knowledge** — women are more interested in subjects that can be classified as **New Science**, **New Ecology** and **New Spirituality**.
4) Some sociologists claim that **New Age** movements appeal more to women because they emphasise **'feminine'** characteristics such as healing, caring and cooperation.

Remember, some NRMs have **narrow beliefs** about **women's role** in society, and therefore may **not appeal** to women. For example, some new evangelical right-wing Christian movements believe that women shouldn't work outside the home.

Religion and Social Groups

Religiosity Varies by Ethnicity

The 1994 PSI Fourth Survey of Ethnic Minorities (**Tariq Modood et al**, published **1997**) found that, in England and Wales, nearly all **ethnic minority groups** are **more religious** and participate more in religion than white groups.

1) Religion maintains a sense of **community** and **cultural identity** within ethnic minority groups.

2) **Johal (1998)** claims that in a multi-faith society such as the UK, **religious identity** has become of key importance to members of ethnic minorities.

3) **Davie (1994)** argued that identification with a **religious organisation** was important to South Asians such as Indians, Pakistanis and Bangladeshis in the UK because it gave a sense of cultural identity and a feeling of **belonging**.

- **Modood et al** found that Pakistani and Bangladeshi Muslims in the UK identified themselves primarily as **Muslim**.
- Many young Muslims have a deeper **knowledge of Islam** than their **parents** do.
- Many Muslim girls feel more **liberated** by wearing headscarfs and dressing modestly because they are not subjected to the same **stereotypes** and values as non-Muslim girls.

i.e. rather than British, Pakistani, or Bangladeshi

4) **African Caribbeans**, who are mainly Christian, attempted to incorporate themselves into the established churches of the UK but found **racism** within many congregations. One way to tackle this was to develop their own churches and ways of worshipping — e.g. Pentecostal churches.

5) **South Asians**, however, had to establish their faiths in a country with **radically different** systems of belief. Religion acted as a **support mechanism** for new immigrants, allowing them to share their culture. South Asians **quickly established** religious organisations — mosques, Sikh gurdwaras, etc. **Bruce (2002)** calls this **cultural transition**.

6) **Modood et al** found some evidence for a decline in religious practice among **Asian men** in the UK — for example, **younger** Sikh men are **less likely** to wear a **turban** than **older** Sikh men.

Religiosity Varies by Class

1) The **middle class** is disproportionately **Anglican** and **Quaker** compared with a more **Roman Catholic** or **Methodist** working class (this can be partly explained by their popularity in **Victorian industrial areas**). This pattern can be seen across many countries, including the **US**, and this would seem to back up **Marx** and **Weber's** opinions on **Protestantism** and **capitalism**.

2) Religious participation is greater in the **middle classes** (**62%** of regular church-goers are middle class), partly because religious affiliation is seen as a **desirable** social characteristic. Church is an opportunity for **social networking**.

3) Some argue that participation in **denominations** and **sects** is based on **class position** — they claim that there are middle-class denominations and working-class denominations.

4) **Bruce (1995)** found that **cults** are primarily **middle class** — in his opinion because they fulfil **spiritual needs** for people who have little **financial pressure**.

The sauna: another excellent opportunity for social networking.

Practice Questions

Q1 Suggest why young adults participate more than other age groups in sects and cults.

Q2 What role does religion play in upholding patriarchy, according to feminists?

Q3 Suggest why middle-class people participate more in cults.

Exam Questions

Q1 Outline two arguments which support the view that there are gender-based differences in religiosity. Explain each one. [10 marks]

Q2 Evaluate the idea that religious identity is of key importance to ethnic minorities. [20 marks]

"Ah no, this is the women's church. The men's church is next door"...

Well, obviously it's not quite like that. The examiners will expect you to know how religion relates to age, gender, ethnicity and class, and also how religious participation relates to those things. You should mention a few studies too — no, don't kid yourself that you can remember them all — what did Glock and Stark argue? What about Johal? Davie? Bruce? Ha!

Religiosity in the Contemporary World

As the world changes, so too do religions and patterns of religiosity.

Secularisation Theory says Religion has Lost Its Influence Over Society

> **Bryan Wilson (1966)** defined secularisation as the **decline** of the "**social significance**" of **religious beliefs, practices** and **organisations**. Secularisation is said to be a result of the social changes brought about by **modern, urban, industrial society**. There are lots of **different explanations** and **theories** for why secularisation happens.

The 'founding fathers' of sociology **predicted secularisation**.

1) **Auguste Comte** claimed that **science** was the **final stage** in the **development of human thought**. He said modern society would be dominated by **science** and not religion.

2) **Max Weber** believed that **modern society** would be the age of **technology**, **rationality** and **bureaucracy**. He said rationality and efficiency **sweep away magic**, **myth** and **tradition**.

Church Attendance and Membership is in Decline in the UK

Recording the number of people who **attend church** gives **supporting evidence for secularisation**:

1) **UK church membership** has gone **down** — it fell by over 1 million from 1992 to 2013.

2) Attendance at church ceremonies such as **baptisms** and **marriages** has also dropped since **1980**. Many parents are now opting for a non-religious '**naming ceremony**' instead of a baptism, and some couples prefer **cohabiting** (living together) or having a **civil marriage** (that doesn't take place in a church) rather than a church wedding.

Gretchen was well excited about her baptism.

Measuring secularisation by church attendance has **limitations**:

1) People may **attend church** but **not believe in God**. They might attend a service, baptism or wedding out of **friendship** for the people involved, for **respectability** or because of **family duty**. Or even to get their kids into a certain **school**.

2) **Davie (1994)** argued people may **not attend church** because of their **lifestyle** even though they believe in God. Church attendance **doesn't** tell you about **belief**. Some evidence seems to back up Davie's point, for example, the 2011 census found **59.3%** of people in England and Wales still identified themselves as Christians. However, this isn't a very **reliable** measure of secularisation — people may **identify as Christian** but not be **religious**.

3) In addition, to make comparisons with the past you have to use **old statistics**, which may not be reliable.

Pluralism Gives People Choice

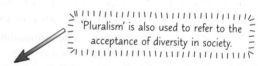

> 'Pluralism' is also used to refer to the acceptance of diversity in society.

Pluralism is the idea that **society** is very **diverse**, with a huge range of **opinions**. **Religious pluralism** has both created and been influenced by **diversity** in types of religious organisations and beliefs in society. As a result, the **established, national church loses its influence** in integrating people into **shared values**. **Multicultural** societies are more likely to have **religious pluralism**. Sociologists **disagree** over whether religious pluralism can **explain secularisation**.

> **Some sociologists see pluralism as evidence against secularisation**
>
> 1) The increase in New Age movements since the 1980s can be seen as proof that the **sacred** is becoming **important** again — this is called **resacralisation**.
>
> 2) It can be argued that pluralism is evidence of religion being **transformed**. It shows a trend towards **individuation** — people being free to search for their **own religious meanings** (to become '**spiritual shoppers**').

> **Other sociologists see pluralism as supporting evidence for secularisation**
>
> 1) Pluralism gives people **choice**. People might feel freer to choose to **reject religion altogether**.
>
> 2) Although some people in modern society have joined **new religious movements**, they are still a **small proportion** of the population. Some sociologists claim the **growth** in NRMs has been **overestimated**.

Postmodernists like **Lyotard (1984)** argue that people have lost faith in the old **metanarratives** of organised religion and politics (see p.5). Postmodernists argue that organised religion has become **less influential** in postmodern society. **Zygmunt Bauman (1992)** suggested that a **religious vacuum** has been left behind — a "**crisis of meaning**". He argued that this vacuum is being filled by **new and diverse types of religiosity** such as New Age movements.

Religiosity in the Contemporary World

Desacralisation is Where Supernatural Belief is Less of a Force in Society

1) **Weber** predicted **desacralisation** (see glossary) in his idea of **disenchantment**. He thought that magic and myth were less important in modern society. Similarly, **Bruce (1995)** sees **science** and rational explanations as **undermining religion**.

2) Instead of turning to the supernatural or religion to **explain our problems**, we might turn to **science**. We demand pills if we are ill and we explain natural disasters using science. This change in **belief** is another **possible explanation** for secularisation.

3) However, the **death** of a loved one, **injustice**, **natural disasters** and **terrorist atrocities** still sometimes lead people to prayer and faith in the supernatural. Modern science **can't explain everything** to everyone's satisfaction.

The Church May have Lost Some Functions and Become Disengaged

1) **Differentiation** is where **society becomes more specialised** so each **institution** in society has **fewer functions** than in the past. For example, the **church** used to have an important **educational** function. But since the 19th century, separate institutions have taken over this role and state involvement has increased. **Bruce (1995)** argues that religion becomes less important in society as some of its previous functions are taken over.

2) **Disengagement** is when the church becomes **separated from the state**. As a result, it has **less influence**.

3) **Parsons (1974)** claims that although the church may have lost its functions and become disengaged from the state and politics, religion can still be **significant in everyday life** and encourage **shared values** in society.

4) Religion is still closely linked to **politics** in places like the **Middle East** and **Northern Ireland**.

> **Some religious institutions have become 'secularised'**
>
> 1) **Secularisation** of **religious institutions** is when the church becomes less religious in its beliefs to **fit in** with the rest of **society**. For example, many churches will now allow divorced people to marry.
>
> 2) American sociologist **Herberg (1956)** thinks church attendance shows **commitment to community** and not religion — people go to church to **meet up with friends** and to feel like **part of something**.
>
> 3) Remember that **not all religious institutions** have become more **secular**. The **New Christian Right** don't compromise their beliefs to fit in with society — they're against divorce, homosexuality and premarital sex. The more extreme end of the religious right are also against women working outside the home.

Secularisation is Very Difficult to Measure

> ⟅ There's more about sociological research methods in Section One. ⟆

1) There are lots of different **measures of secularisation**. Some are more valid and reliable than others. **Surveys** show **high levels of religiosity**, but **quantitative measurements** of **church attendance** are **low**. **Different religious groups** measure membership in **different ways**, anyhow.

2) The term **secularisation** is a general term that's sometimes applied just to Christianity. It's important to know **what's being measured** — the decline of **religion in general** or the decline in **Christianity** in particular.

3) It's difficult to measure the significance of religion and make comparisons because sociologists use **different definitions of religion**. Some sociologists use **substantive definitions** which say **what religion is** — e.g. "religion is belief in the sacred". Some sociologists use **functional definitions** saying **what religion is for** — e.g. "religion is for creating value consensus".

4) To measure whether society has become **more secular** you have to compare it to **the past**. Some sociologists argue that we see the past as a **golden age** of religion where **everyone** believed and **no one** was sceptical. This is **far too simplified**.

5) Research into secularisation can also be rather **ethnocentric** — e.g. focusing on **Christianity** and what the **predominantly white British mainstream** does. Islam, Hinduism and Sikhism are also changing and developing in different ways.

Practice Questions

Q1 How does religious pluralism provide supporting evidence for secularisation?

Q2 What is meant by desacralisation?

Q3 Define the term disengagement, with reference to religion.

Exam Question

Q1 Analyse two explanations for why religion has lost some of its significance in today's society. [10 marks]

Bruce (1995) sees surnames as completely unnecessary...

There's some clear evidence both for and against the secularisation theory — which you need to learn. Oh, and don't get confused like I did — the Bryan Wilson with the theory on secularisation isn't the Brian Wilson who was in the Beach Boys.

Religiosity in the Contemporary World

Many recent changes in religion are because of globalisation (how the world is becoming more and more connected).

Globalisation affects religion in Different Ways

Peter Beyer (1994) claimed that **globalisation** has had three very different impacts on religion:

1) **Marginalisation** — religion has been **pushed out** of politics and public life and into the **private sphere**. In the UK, there is a **debate** over how much **influence** (if any) religion should have over **politics**.

2) **Particularism** — religion has been used by groups who feel **threatened** by globalisation. They use it to express a sense of identity through a mix of **fundamentalism** (see next page) and **nationalism**.

3) **Universalism** — globalisation can result in the emergence of an understanding of **common values** between religions. Beyer gives the example of **religious environmentalism**, in which many faiths come together in **common concern** for protecting a 'God-created' world.

Religion is no longer linked to National Boundaries

1) In the past, most countries had strong links with a **state religion**, so they would be known as 'a **Christian** country', 'a **Muslim** country' and so on. **England** even developed a **state denomination** — its own version of Christianity called the **Church of England**. **Wars** between countries were often fought over **differences** in **religious beliefs**.

2) However, due to **globalisation**, **national boundaries** are being **broken down** — which means that **national identity** and **religious identity** are now less closely **linked** than they once were.

3) At the same time, in the **West**, **secularisation** and **multiculturalism** have helped break down the **importance** of **religion** as a part of **national identity**. For most people in the UK, **Christianity** is no longer closely connected to ideas of 'Britishness'. In contrast, **Nanda (2008)** argues that **worshipping Hindu gods** is now closely linked to **nationalism** in **India**. A **2007** survey also found that **religious belief** is **growing** among Indians, despite globalisation.

4) However, religion continues to be **important**, both in the **UK** and **worldwide**. Some countries still identify strongly with their **state religion** (e.g. Islam in Egypt). Also, the **proportion** of people with a religion is actually **growing worldwide**.

5) It can be argued that **religious identity** is becoming more **globalised**. People are exposed to a **variety** of religions, and **technology** allows believers to be part of **international religious communities**.

Some Global Movements may be a Reaction to Poverty and Exclusion

1) **Pentecostalism** (a form of **Christianity**) has grown very quickly around the world, especially in **poorer** parts of **Latin America**, **Africa** and **Asia**. **David Martin (1997)** contrasted Pentecostalism with **Catholicism**, a more **traditional** version of Christianity, to try to explain this.

2) Martin argues that Pentecostalism succeeds mainly because it is designed to make its members feel **empowered** and **important**. By contrast, traditional religions like Catholicism make them feel **powerless** and **insignificant**.

Pentecostalism

1) Pentecostalism is **chosen** by its members, so they have a stronger sense of **commitment** and **religious identity**.

2) It benefits from the **positive** aspects of globalisation, and so is associated with **change** and **growth**.

3) It's also a **reaction** against the **negative** aspects of globalisation, such as **capitalism's** emphasis on **material wealth** and **consumer goods**. Instead it values **piety** (strict following of religious belief), **self-discipline** and **loyalty** to the **nuclear family**, which can all be achieved **without economic capital**. This makes this Christian denomination attractive to the **poor** and **powerless**.

4) It's not tied to any particular **country** — Pentecostalism is **international**.

5) It's **non-hierarchical**, so all members have **equal status**, and it can **change** and **adapt** to **local communities**.

Catholicism

1) Catholicism is usually **inherited** — it's a Christian denomination you are **born into**, which makes it less likely to lead to strong feelings of **commitment**.

2) It's an **old** denomination. It was **slower** than Pentecostalism to take advantage of **new technologies**, and is associated with **tradition**.

3) The Catholic Church is enormously **wealthy**.

4) Catholicism is the **state religion** in many countries and is strongly associated with **political power**.

5) It is extremely **hierarchical** and has **rigid structures** that are the same all over the world.

See p.146 for more on denominations.

Religiosity in the Contemporary World

Peter Berger says we need to Rethink Secularisation Theory

1) It's clear that **Europe** is **highly secularised**, but religious belief is **growing** in much of the **rest of the world**. This suggests that secularisation theory (see p.150) is too **Eurocentric** — it focuses too much on Europe.

2) The **USA** is **highly religious**. This suggests that the **basic idea** of secularisation theory (which states that **modernisation** leads to **secularisation**) must be **wrong**.

3) Berger argues that what we have seen is not secularisation but **extreme pluralisation** (where there are many **competing beliefs** in world society).

Globalisation has Changed the way religions work

1) Religious groups often make use of **global communication networks** (such as the internet) to **recruit** more members. This can sometimes be **contradictory**, as their **values** might **clash** with those of the modern globalised world, but they still use **modern technology** to help spread their message.

2) Postmodernist **David Lyon (2000)** says religion has relocated to the **sphere of consumption**. He argues that religion has become a **consumer product** — people can now '**pick and mix**' their religious experiences and are no longer tied to the **traditional structures** of the church.

3) One benefit of the **globally-connected society** has been to increase opportunities to **reduce conflict** through **interfaith dialogue** (different religions talking to each other).

Globalisation has also led to an Increase in Fundamentalism

Giddens (1991) argues that globalisation creates **insecurity** and **doubt**, due to its often **conflicting** and **confusing messages**. In contrast, **fundamentalist teachings** offer a **simple**, **reliable** world view. Fundamentalism involves the **fundamental**, **literal interpretation** of religious texts and gives a set of **strict rules** to live by. Fundamentalist groups **fervently** follow their beliefs — they want to create a more **conservative** society and return to '**traditional values**'.

In both of the following examples, **fundamentalism** provides **certainty** and **meaning** in periods of **uncertainty**.

1) Islamic Fundamentalism in Iran

Iran was a **traditional** society that **quickly modernised** under the **Shah** in the **early 20th century**. **Women** wore **Western clothes, alcohol** was freely available and there was **secular education**. There was also **inequality** in society — the upper class were **very rich**, and working-class areas were **neglected**.

Traditional Muslims were **unhappy** about the direction that Iranian society had taken, and saw the Shah as **corrupt**. They started to oppose the Shah, led by a **fundamentalist** religious leader called **Ayatollah Khomeini**. There was a revolution in 1979 and the Ayatollah came to power. He established a society based on **Islamic Sharia law** — alcohol was banned, there were harsh punishments for crime, and women were required to cover their bodies in public.

2) Christian Fundamentalism in the USA

The **New Christian Right** in **America** argues that American society is in **decline** and in a state of **moral crisis**. They think this is caused by **liberal reforms** — e.g. easy **divorce**, legalised **abortion, gay rights** and **secular education**. The New Christian Right **oppose** the teaching of **evolution** in schools, because it disagrees with their fundamentalist interpretation of the Bible. They started some **universities** that offer not only degrees, but also a strict **Christian education**. They promote their views through **mass communication**, e.g. TV and Christian publishing.

Practice Questions

Q1 Describe three differences between Pentecostalism and Catholicism.

Q2 Explain why Peter Berger thinks that secularisation theory is wrong.

Q3 Define the term 'fundamentalism'.

Exam Question

Q1 Evaluate the idea that globalisation has had a major effect on religions across the world. [20 marks]

Ooo I do like pick 'n' mix...

Islamic fundamentalism has become a major focus in today's society (especially in the media), but there are fundamentalist versions of all world religions. I guess the thing to remember is that these groups are always a minority within their religion.

Theories of Development

There are different ways of defining and measuring development and underdevelopment, and tons of theories to explain why some countries are more developed than others.

The Exact Words used to Describe Development are Important

1) The term '**development**' is used to mean economic growth, industrialisation, and high living standards, e.g. high life expectancy and universal education. Countries which have achieved this are called **MEDCs** (More Economically Developed Countries). Countries which haven't are called **LEDCs** (Less Economically Developed Countries).

2) Richer countries are also referred to as **developed**, poorer countries as **developing**. **Underdeveloped** countries are less developed than other countries with the same resources.

Ethnocentric means looking at everything from a certain viewpoint and assuming certain values are superior.

3) All these terms are **ethnocentric**. They define development in terms of 'Western' ideals.

4) '**First World**' and '**Third World**' are **out-of-date** expressions. The First World was **wealthy** countries like the USA and Japan. 'Third World' was used to describe the **poorest countries**.

5) '**Northern**' and '**Southern**' are also used to describe **differences** between countries — **developed** countries are often in the **northern** hemisphere and **developing** countries are often in the **southern** hemisphere. These terms are more **neutral**, but not always accurate, e.g. Australia is a **developed** country in the **southern hemisphere**.

Development is Measured in Different Ways

1) Capitalists argue that **economic indicators** such as **Gross Domestic Product** (**GDP**) are the only effective ways of defining a country's potential for developing (along capitalist lines).

GDP = the total economic value of goods and services produced by a country over a year.

2) However, GDP doesn't tell you how wealth is **distributed**. In a country with a high average GDP per capita (per person) there may be a **minority** living in **deprivation**.

3) Some claim **development** and **underdevelopment** are better measured by **social factors**. They measure development using **lists** of **basic human needs** — e.g. the **Human Development Index** (HDI), **Human Poverty Index** (HPI) and **Physical Quality of Life Index** (PQLI). These can show that there is **deprivation** even in 'developed' countries.

4) It can also be useful to look at **global inequality** (i.e. comparing things like income between different countries). For example, in 2002, the **poorest** people in **America** were still **richer** than all but the very **richest** people in **India**.

Marxist Theory says Capitalism Exploits Underdeveloped Countries

1) **Marx** said that **capitalism** and **industrialisation** were about obtaining the **maximum** amount of **profit**.

2) Many modern Marxists say that there's now a **global capitalist system**. They argue that the capitalists in developed countries **exploit** underdeveloped countries to get **raw materials** and a wide **market** for their goods. This is known as **dependency theory** (see next page).

Modernisation Theory says countries Progress towards Liberal Capitalism

Modernisation theory says that **all countries** move **towards liberal capitalism**. **Undeveloped** countries are seen as **inferior** to **developed** countries that have achieved a higher rate of **production**, **consumption** and **wealth**.

Rostow (1971) suggested that all countries go through a five-stage process of development:

1) Basic, **agricultural** society.

2) **Transition**, or preparing for 'take-off' — farmers produce a surplus and make money from selling cash crops. Small towns develop, and there's some industry on a very small scale.

3) **Industrialisation** or 'take-off' — rapid growth of manufacturing. People move from rural to urban areas.

4) **Drive to Maturity** — lots of investment, and the right social conditions for growth. Large cities develop.

5) **Mass consumption**, or 'developed economy' — wealth spreads, people buy more and the service sector grows.

The explanation for **poverty** and **underdevelopment** is **insufficient agricultural surplus** to fund investment, **insufficient investment in technology**, and **not enough hard-working business people** to create opportunities.

Kerr (1962) focused on **cultural factors** — he believed that countries need **Western-style politics** and **social values** in order to develop, and they should replace **traditional culture** with **Western values**. This is a very **ethnocentric** view.

Theories of Development

Neo-liberalism *believes in using* Free Trade *to help countries* Develop

1) **Neo-liberalism** says that government intervention **distorts** the natural economic processes of the **free market**. Neo-liberals like **Friedman (1962)** believe **free market trade** can be used to help countries develop.

2) Organisations like the **International Monetary Fund** and **World Bank** favour neo-liberalism. They point to **Newly Industrialised Countries** (NICs) such as the **'tiger economies'** to prove that removing **tariffs** (charges for importing and exporting) and encouraging **free trade** can lead to development. 'Tiger economies' are **South-East Asian** countries (**Singapore**, **Hong Kong**, **South Korea** and **Taiwan**) that experienced a period of rapid growth from the 1960s to the '90s.

3) However, both **neo-liberalism** and **modernisation theory** are criticised for being **ethnocentric** (see p.154), and critics say this leads them to distort the **true history** of Western involvement in developing countries.

4) Neo-liberals and modernisation theorists also argue that Western methods of development are **easily imitated** and likely to **succeed** — which isn't necessarily true. In fact, the tiger economies got into **serious economic trouble** in **1997** after attempting to **extend too far** and **too fast**.

Dependency Theory *says* Developed *countries* Exploit Underdeveloped *ones*

1) **Dependency theory** was a reaction **against modernisation theory**. The key dependency theorist is **Frank (1967)**.

2) The theory says that developed countries **exploited** underdeveloped nations during colonial times (especially in the 1800s) when they controlled them as part of an **empire** (see p.158), and prevented them from industrialising.

3) When the underdeveloped nations got **political independence**, they were often still **economically dependent** upon their **former imperial rulers**. The poor nation's **main trading partner** is often its former colonial ruler. The theory says richer developed nations organise **trading relationships** in their favour. They set the price for goods.

4) **Dependency theory** is Marxist — it argues that **workers** in the poorest nations are **exploited** by the **ruling class**. They're paid very **low wages**, so the **profits** from the goods they make and grow go to the **ruling class**. Developed nations pay a **low market price** for the goods, and the goods are sold in the developed nation for a **profit**.

The theory doesn't fully **define** what development is or give **realistic suggestions** for how the situation can be resolved. It also doesn't explain why **socialism** also **exploited** and **created dependency** — e.g. the Eastern European satellite states depended on Russia. Dependency theory is criticised for being **deterministic** — it assumes that **everyone** in **LEDCs** will be **exploited**, and it doesn't accept that some LEDCs might **choose** capitalism, instead of being pushed into it.

Other ideas include Environmentalism *and* Post-Development Theory

1) **Environmentalist** perspectives focus on how **development** harms the **ecosystem**. There are concerns that development might not be **sustainable** — **pollutants** from **industry** and **chemicals** from **modern farming methods** (e.g. pesticides) **damage** the planet. Environmentalists are worried that **environmental issues** will always lose out to **capitalism**, and that rapid development in **LEDCs** is leading the world to an **ecological crisis**.

2) **Post-development theory** criticises **development itself**, claiming that the terms **'developed'** and **'underdeveloped'** are **Western constructions** that **undermine** different countries and cultures. **Arturo Escobar (1995)** believed that Western countries helping other countries to develop was another form of **colonialism** (p.158-159) in disguise. He argues that this sort of development is **materialistic** and **unachievable**, and that we should let other societies evolve in their **own way**.

Practice Questions

Q1 What are the five stages of development, according to Rostow?
Q2 What is the central idea of dependency theory?

Exam Question

Q1 Outline two ways that developed countries can exploit underdeveloped countries. Explain each one. [10 marks]

Singapore and Hong Kong have stripy economies that go 'RAAAR'...

Important reminder — don't use the terms 'first world' and 'third world'. They're out of date now, so it's better to talk about MEDCs and LEDCs instead. Make sure you're happy with what 'ethnocentric' means — it comes up quite a lot in this section.

Theories of Globalisation

This fine pair of pages is about international trade and globalisation. Globalisation has economic, political and cultural aspects. No, don't switch off, this really isn't that boring. Honestly. Look, there's a photo of a burger and everything.

World Systems Theory *says there's* One Worldwide Economic System

1) **Wallerstein (1974)** suggested **World Systems theory**, which treats the entire world as **one economy**, rather than looking at economies country by country. World Systems theory divides the world into **core** (developed countries), **semi-periphery** (e.g. South Africa, Mexico) and **periphery** (e.g. Ethiopia).

2) According to the theory, **core** countries make **full use** of the worldwide economy, and can affect any other country — in other words, they have a global '**reach**'. Core countries are the ones which get the most out of capitalism.

3) World Systems theory says the **semi-periphery** countries are **exploited** by the core countries, but they also **exploit** the **periphery** countries. In the theory, because they are exploiters as well as the exploited, they aren't fully 'on the same side' as the periphery countries — **no unity** amongst the exploited means **no united action** to change the system.

This theory is criticised for being too **deterministic**. It doesn't allow for **individual countries' characteristics**.

Globalisation *has resulted in a* Global Economy

Giddens (1990) notes that **technological change** has transformed the way people live — global **communication** and **travel** are now easy. Goods can be **transported** across the world, and **information** can be transferred across the world **instantaneously**.

1) **Globalists** (sociologists who believe that society is becoming **globalised**) argue that **international trade** and investment have caused national economies to blend together into a **global economy**.

2) **Transnational Corporations** (**TNCs**) operate across national boundaries. They tend to have their headquarters in MEDCs and set up production in countries where there's **cheaper labour**, in order to maximise their profits.

3) **Fröbel et al (1980)** first referred to the '**new international division of labour**' — manufacturing tends to be done in developing countries, and knowledge-intensive work is done in MEDCs. **International division of labour** also means that **different stages of production** can be done in **different countries** — the car industry is a good example.

4) **TNCs** have a **positive** effect — they bring **jobs** and **investment** to developing countries, which can help with their national strategy for development. There's also a benefit for **international consumers** — cheap consumer goods.

5) However, some argue that this is a new form of **exploitation**. **Neo-Marxist** critics of globalisation say that the people of the developing world are turned into '**wage slaves**' for the capitalist system.

6) TNCs aim to create **global markets** for the goods they manufacture. They affect cultures throughout the world.

7) **TNCs** also have an effect on the **business culture** of host nations. TNCs can be categorised as three types — **ethnocentric** (headquarters in country of origin runs everything and sets corporate culture), **polycentric** (managed locally, according to guidelines set by headquarters) or **geocentric** (management is integrated across all countries).

Weberian sociologist Ritzer (1993) writes about global standardisation and 'rationalisation'.

1) He refers to a '**McDonaldisation**' of production across the world. He says products are made with the same values as a **fast food** outlet: the product is made in **assembly line** conditions, it must be **inexpensive** to make and must be **standardised** at all times, across all the countries where it's made and sold. A Big Mac® is the same everywhere.

2) Ritzer picks out five themes within this McDonaldisation — **efficiency**, **calculability** (emphasis is on quantity and speed rather than quality), **predictability**, increased **control**, and the replacement of **human** workers by **machines**.

Sweet, juicy global standardisation.

There's also Globalisation *in* Politics

1) Politics is increasingly carried out on an **international** level, rather than a national level.
2) The United Nations is responsible for enforcing international law, and peacekeeping etc.
3) There's increased **international political cooperation** — e.g. the **European Union**.
4) **International** non-governmental organisations (**NGOs**) coordinate **aid** and **campaigning**.

Theories of Globalisation

Increased Communication spreads Cultural Goods across the world

1) The increase in **international media** communication in the last few decades has meant that cultures that were once **local** have become **international** and **global**. This is called **cultural globalisation**. British and American pop music is everywhere. American and Indian films are seen internationally.

2) Postmodernists argue that this allows people to consume a **plurality** of cultures. They think that cultural globalisation leads to **cultural hybridisation** (a **mixture** of cultures) rather than one culture being **imposed** over another.

3) They also say that **cultural globalisation** is a **two-way process**. Western culture is transmitted to **new societies**, and other identities and cultures get passed on to societies in **MEDCs**. An example of this would be the increase in screenings of **Bollywood films** in Western mainstream cinemas.

4) Critics point to the concentration of the **production** of cultural goods in the hands of a few large **TNCs** which have a lot of power in developing countries. They fear that TNCs will replace **traditional culture** with **Western culture** to try and **create new markets** for **Western cultural goods**. These critics say globalisation leads to **cultural imperialism**.

> cultural goods = films, clothes, food, music, books etc.

Global Organisations are seen by some as More Powerful than Governments

1) TNCs operate in many countries — they have a global reach. Many are as powerful as nation states in economic terms, and some critics point to their perceived lack of respect for local cultures as a key feature of globalisation.

2) National governments often find it hard to control TNCs and are reluctant to act against the interests of the TNC. The host nation risks losing large numbers of jobs if the TNC decides to pack up and move to another country.

3) International political agencies, such as the United Nations and the European Union (EU), have taken some power and decision-making away from national governments.

4) Critics claim that this means nation states lose the ability to determine their own future, as they must constantly negotiate with other governments and agencies to try and get the best policy for the nation.

Leslie Sklair (2000) sees globalisation as a form of **transnational capitalism** (capitalism which crosses national boundaries). He thinks it isn't worth analysing nation states — power is held by TNCs, bureaucrats and global media.

There's Evidence to say that the Nation is still as Important as ever

1) **Realists** point out that **national interest** still determines **most policies** within a nation and in international negotiations. For example, the US refused to agree to the terms of the **Kyoto Protocol** (an international environmental strategy) partly because of the potential effects on US **employment**.

2) **Hall (1995)** argues that in a globalised world, **national identity** becomes very **important** to people as a way of **maintaining differences** between the countries of the world. As a result, the nation state can be strengthened.

3) Increasing fears over the loss of power from national government to the EU has meant that many people in the UK are even more determined to protect the **sovereignty** of the nation.

4) There's a trend towards **devolution** — i.e. giving power to local bodies, as has happened with the Scottish Parliament and Welsh Assembly. Nations **within** the UK have reasserted their identity and control over key issues and policies.

Practice Questions

Q1 Explain why some theorists say we now have a global economy.

Q2 What is the 'new international division of labour'?

Q3 Why do critics of cultural globalisation refer to it as cultural imperialism?

Exam Question

Q1 Evaluate the idea that transnational corporations benefit the countries they operate in.   [20 marks]

So the world is turning into McDonald's? I reckon Ritzer was just hungry...

Hallucinations and bizarre fantasies are pretty common during extreme hunger. But seriously, globalisation is a big thing in sociology. It's a many-armed beast, with cultural, political and economic aspects that you need to know about for the exam.

Debt, Aid and Development

There are different sociological perspectives on how to help countries to develop. And unfortunately, you have to know them all.

The **History** of **Colonialism** has shaped **International Trade Relations**

1) A colony is a territory that's **controlled** by a **foreign power**. Back in the 16th and 17th centuries, **European** countries began to **colonise Asian**, **African** and **American** territories. The height of colonialism was in the **19th century**.

2) European nations colonised foreign territories for three main reasons:

- Colonies were **economically important**. **Raw materials and food** were sourced in the colonies, and taken back to Western Europe to fuel **industrial-capitalist development**.
- Having **colonies** and building up an **empire** added to a nation's **power** and **influence** — the colonising country could put **military bases** and **trading ports** in the colony.
- Europeans also saw colonialism as a way of 'civilising' native people. They saw traditional Asian, African and American cultures as **inferior**, and tried to **replace** them with Western values, including Christianity.

3) Colonialism strongly shaped **economic development** in the colonies. The colonisers set up plantations to grow **cash crops** such as coffee and cotton. They used **slaves** and **low-paid labour** and sold the crops for **high prices** in Europe.

4) Former colonies are often **under-industrialised**, because they were used only for primary sector industries such as agriculture and mining. Former colonies didn't get the chance to develop **manufacturing** industry.

5) Former colonies which rely on **agricultural exports** are hit hard by **global recession** — when the **market price** of cash crops drops, their **national income drops**.

Many **LEDCs** face a **Debt Crisis** — they spend more on **Debt** than **Investment**

1) Throughout the 20th century, **LEDCs** have had to **borrow money** from **richer nations** and **international lending organisations**, both for survival and for development projects.

2) A **loan** from your **bank** comes with conditions — you have to pay **interest**, and you have to pay a certain amount **back** each month. If you don't pay enough, the **interest** starts to **pile on**, and you can find yourself in **financial trouble**.

3) It's exactly the same with **nations**. Many poor countries spend **more** repaying **debts** and the interest that's built up on their debts than they spend on their own **infrastructures**. As **Hayter** points out, that's **not good** for **development**.

Dependency theory puts the crisis down to colonialism, corruption and greed

1) Dependency theorists argue that many countries are poor because **colonialism** restricted their economic development. Countries that gained **independence** were forced to **borrow money** to fund development.

2) Dependency theorists also argue that **aid** doesn't go to the right place — much of the money that's donated disappears, either because **governments embezzle** it (i.e. steal it for themselves) or invest in products that **don't help** a country to develop (e.g. **weapons**). This leaves an **investment gap** that has to be filled with **loans**.

3) In the 1980s and early 1990s, the **richest nations** and the **international lending organisations** significantly raised levels of **interest** paid on loans. Countries had to **borrow more** to meet **interest payments**. Dependency theorists think this rather suited the West, as they saw an **increase** in the **debt owed** to them.

There's an ongoing **campaign** to **reduce debt**, or **scrap** debts entirely. Many countries have had their **total debt** reduced, but this hasn't yet made a **significant impact** on the **absolute poverty** experienced by people within the poorest nations.

International Trade and **TNCs** can help **Development**

1) A recent view, influenced by the **New Right** (see p.159), is that **trade** is more productive for development than **aid**.

2) Not all trade-based strategies come from New Right theorists — e.g. in the **fair trade movement**, businesses pay farmers a fixed 'fair' price for their crops, whatever the **global market price** is. However, **neo-liberals** claim that fair trade is just **aid under another name**, and say that **subsidies** don't encourage producers to be efficient and enterprising.

3) The **World Trade Organisation** (WTO) sets rules for **international trade** to ensure that all countries are treated **fairly**.

1) **TNCs provide investment** to developing countries, which can help with their national strategy for development. They also provide **jobs**, which increases the host nation's **wealth** and the **spending power** of the workers.

2) But TNCs can cause **rapid economic growth** which can be **too fast** for a host nation's **infrastructure** to cope with.

3) Those who define development in **quality of life** terms are concerned about **working conditions** in TNC factories.

Debt, Aid and Development

Aid can be given in *Three Different Ways*

The United Nations recommends rich countries should give 0.7% of their national income in aid. In 2015, the UK made a law that requires the country to meet this target each year.

1) **Bilateral Aid** is where a **government** gives **direct financial support** to another **government** that needs help (e.g. Malawi).

2) **Multilateral Aid** is **grants** or **loans** from **international organisations** such as the World Health Organisation, the International Monetary Fund (IMF) and the World Bank (see p.160).

3) **Non-Governmental Organisations** (NGOs) give **logistical support** and **direct financial donations**. They get their money from the **public**. Examples of NGOs are Oxfam and Christian Aid (see p.160).

Different Theories have *Different Views* of *Aid*

Modernisation theory says aid helps LEDCs 'Westernise'

1) **Modernisation theorists** believe that developed countries should give **aid** to countries that are prepared to accept Western styles of development, i.e. **industrial capitalism**.

2) Modernisation theory sees aid as having a **'trickle-down effect'**. The argument is that aid goes to the elites of LEDCs, and the elites create wealth and prosperity. Associated factors such as **employment** and **increased standards of living** should **filter down** to **local economies** and **local people**.

3) Modernisation theorists were largely justified in the mid-20th century, as many poor countries received aid and experienced **growth**. However, growth **stalled** later, and in some countries the poverty gap actually **increased**.

Neo-Marxist dependency theorists see aid as a tool to serve capitalism

1) Aid is often given with **conditions** attached. A common condition is that local markets should be opened up to **free trade**, allowing foreign companies (including TNCs) to import and export goods without trade or customs levies. Neo-Marxists view this very **negatively**, believing that LEDCs are often exploited economically by TNCs.

2) **Bilateral aid** (where one country gives aid to another) is often **tied** — the aid has to be **spent** in the country that **donated** it. This might mean that the **recipient** nation has to **buy goods** from the **donor** nation, or employ **technical experts** from the donor nation. These requirements help the **donor** nation.

3) Critics of Western aid such as **Hayter (1971, 1981, 1989)** see it as a tool for the richest countries to **politically influence** LEDCs. **Western** countries tended to give aid to countries with **right-wing** governments rather than to countries with **socialist** or **communist** governments. This happened a lot during the Cold War.

4) To get a loan from the World Bank or IMF, LEDCs have often had to agree to make **political** and **economic changes** called 'Structural Adjustment Programmes' (see p.160). These are often **industrial-capitalist** in nature. Evidence shows that some of these programmes **haven't succeeded** in developing poor nations.

New Right theory says that aid creates dependency

1) **New Right theorists** argue that aid teaches LEDCs to be **dependent** on MEDCs, rather than standing on their own two feet. They say that LEDCs start to see aid as a **right**, rather than a **last resort**.

2) **Neo-liberals** believe that aid messes about with the proper operation of the **free market** — they think that the free market is the best way of encouraging development, through **enterprise** and **investment**.

Practice Questions

Q1 What are the causes of debt, according to dependency theorists?

Q2 What are the three categories of aid that are given to less developed countries?

Q3 Explain how the 'trickle-down effect' works, according to modernisation theory.

Exam Question

Q1 Evaluate the idea that aid is merely a tool for spreading capitalism to less developed countries. [20 marks]

Lend us 20 million euros, would you...

As with most of sociology, nothing is ever straightforward. You'd think aid would be simple — helping countries that need it — but it's much more complicated than that. Make sure you know the different types of aid, and the different views on them.

NGOs and International Bodies

These pages look at the impact that international organisations have on the developing world — and it's a bit of a mixed bag.

NGOs and Charities used to provide mainly Emergency Aid

NGOs (non-governmental organisations) are private organisations, some of which carry out campaigning, aid and development work. They are economically and politically **independent** from **government**.

1) **NGOs** and **charities** such as Oxfam, Save the Children® and the Red Cross/Red Crescent mainly respond to **emergencies** — e.g. the 1984 **famine** in Ethiopia, the 2004 **tsunami** in South-East Asia and the **refugee crisis** in **Syria**.

2) **Disaster and emergency relief** is obviously a **short-term** thing. It's different from **long-term development strategies**. That being said, economic and social development **can't take place** where large numbers of people are starving or homeless. It's essential to **fix** the **immediate damage** before going on to **plan strategies** for the long term.

3) NGOs also participate in **development**. They develop **local communities** through education and village clinics, and work with **governments** and **businesses** to coordinate national development.

Four stages of NGO and charity involvement

1) Relief and aid	**Food** programmes, **urgent** medical care
2) Community development	Community **health centres**, community **education**
3) Systems development	Working with **government** and **private businesses**
4) People's movements	Encouraging **locally managed development**

4) The **number** of NGOs has **grown massively** in the past **50 years**, as has the range of their different **aims** and **structures**. **Robbins (2005)** suggests a number of reasons for this:

1) **Better communications** — for example, the **internet** has made it easier for NGOs to organise, publicise and plan.

2) **Raised public awareness** — from extensive **mass media coverage** of global development issues and crises.

3) **Increased funding** — some national governments have increased funding to NGOs as an alternative to taking action themselves. This is because of a **neo-liberal** belief in **private** over state action (see p.155). The increase in funding has also been driven by the belief that NGOs are more likely to **deliver results**...

NGOs can be More Effective than Governments

In some cases, the work of NGOs can actually **advance** the **development** of a country more than its own government can.

1) **NGOs** don't have to consider **political motivations** as much as governments do, so they're less likely to be **corrupt**.

2) Many have **developed networks** and **expertise** — they work with **local people** and understand their **needs**.

3) This means they can **respond** to local issues **effectively** and they often have a reputation for getting assistance where it is needed **quickly**. They are also more **flexible**, because they can **choose** to work with **various** local organisations.

International Lending Organisations try to help countries Develop

1) The **IMF** (International Monetary Fund) is an organisation made up of 188 countries which provides **loans** to states going through **financial difficulties**. It also provides **advice** to the governments of LEDCs on handling their economies.

2) The **World Bank** provides **grants and loans** to help developing countries build **infrastructure** (e.g. roads, electricity networks, telephone networks) and alleviate **debt problems**. It also advises LEDCs on how to grow their **economies**.

To get Loans countries have to accept certain Conditions

Structural Adjustment Programmes (SAPs) were originally introduced by the World Bank and the IMF in the early 1980s. SAPs combine **aid** and **debt assistance** with **conditions** based on **free-market economics**. These conditions include:

1) The **deregulation** of private-sector business and industry to remove limits on foreign investment and competition.

2) The **privatisation** of state-owned industries.

3) **Currency devaluation** to encourage foreign investment.

4) Tight **restrictions on government spending** on education and health.

5) Gearing the economy for the **export market** rather than the domestic market.

SAPs are designed to help countries to develop more long-term economic stability, but they also take economic control away from governments.

From 1999, SAPs have been partially replaced by **Poverty Reduction Strategy Papers (PRSPs)**. These are documents, agreed with the **IMF** and **World Bank**, which outline the country's **social** and **economic strategy**. PRSPs put more emphasis on the country's sense of **ownership** of, and **involvement** in, the policies adopted.

NGOs and International Bodies

SAPs *have been criticised as an* **Ideologically Driven** *development programme*

Hong (2000) has argued that the impact of SAPs has been negative on LEDCs. She argues it's led to:

1) **Increased poverty** — the result of **low pay** and **regressive taxation** (tax that hits the poor harder than the rich).
2) **Poor social conditions** — caused by **low funding of state health** and **social care provision**. Also caused by low pay and poor working conditions due to **lack of regulation**.
3) **Corruption** — **reduced regulation** has provided an **open door for corrupt practices**.
4) **Environmental damage** — production for the **export market** rather than the domestic market has resulted in damaging practices such as **monoculture** (growing one crop exclusively), **deforestation** to make way for plantations of **'cash crops'**, and increased **carbon emissions**.
5) **Social unrest** — Hong cites the example of **Sierra Leone** where the combination of **grinding poverty** and the lack of **services** and **welfare** led to serious upheaval in the 1990s.

Not all the activities of **International Organisations** *are so* **Controversial**

1) In 2005 the **G8** (an organisation made up of eight of the richest countries in the world) **wrote off the debts** of 18 of the poorest developing countries.
2) **Dalmiya and Schultink (2003)** argue that the work of the **World Health Organisation** — the section of the UN that deals with public health matters — has significantly **reduced disease** and **improved nutrition** in the developing world.

Transnational Corporations *are huge businesses operating across borders*

Some **transnational corporations** (**TNCs**) are richer than many nation states. The **impact** of such corporations on LEDCs can therefore be **immense**. TNCs have been **criticised** for their activities in LEDCs. Harmful practices include:

- **Driving down prices** paid to producers in LEDCs followed by **profiteering** when these lower costs are not passed on to consumers in the developed world.
- **Exploiting their workforce** in LEDCs, by using unregulated markets to pay very low wages for very long hours.
- Having a **negative impact** on the environment.

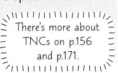
There's more about TNCs on p.156 and p.171.

Isabella wasn't colouring outside the lines — she was 'operating across borders'.

There are **Potential Benefits** *to TNC activity*

Contreras (1987) suggests that TNC activity in the developing world can lead to **significant benefits**. For example:

1) It leads to increases in **tax income**, which governments can spend on **health and education**.
2) The **advanced technology** that TNCs bring with them can provide a **catalyst** to further economic growth.
3) TNCs increase **employment opportunities** and therefore income.
4) TNCs need **skilled workers**, which provides an incentive for improvements in education and training.

Practice Questions

Q1 What are NGOs?

Q2 Give four conditions a country might have to meet to qualify for a loan from the IMF.

Q3 List the potentially negative effects of Structural Adjustment Programmes, according to Hong (2000).

Exam Question

Q1 Outline two ways that NGOs can help countries to develop. Explain each one. [10 marks]

You're gonna have to learn this stuff — you can bank on it...

The SAPs are a big ol' bone of contention with a lot of people — while the IMF and World Bank would claim they're just trying to help, some see them as part of a big conspiracy to spread Western values throughout the globe. For me they're another crazy acronym to learn. It's worth getting to grips with both sides of the argument — no matter what your opinion.

Urbanisation and Industrialisation

Some sociologists say that cities are a focal point for economic development. Others say that cities don't help the poor, and damage the environment. The rest just live in them and leave it at that. Those last ones are my favourite type of sociologist.

Urbanisation goes along with Industrialisation

- **Industrialisation** means the change from **agriculture** and small-scale cottage industry to large-scale **manufacturing** in factories. Factories are **centralised workplaces** — they require people to move to where the work is.
- **Urbanisation** means the increase in **urban populations**, compared to **rural populations**. During periods of industrialisation, people have **migrated** from rural areas to urban areas in search of **work**.

> In Western Europe, industrialisation and urbanisation mainly happened in the 19th century. In countries like Mexico, they happened in the 20th century.

Modernisation theory argues that Urbanisation is key to Development

1) In **modernisation theory**, the growth of **cities** symbolises the triumph of **Western models of development** and **Western ideals**. The city is seen as a place that rejects **traditional goals** and aspirations and replaces them with notions of **meritocracy**, **activism** and **individualism**.

2) **Hoselitz (1964)** argues that the **cities** encourage people to **work**, and contribute to the economy, because **urban society** is focused on **achieved status** (success based on achievement rather than social position) and **meritocracy** (see p.105).

3) Critics argue that this theory is **ethnocentric**, as it's based on Western **cities**, Western **capitalism** and Western **ideals**.

4) Additionally, it's seen as rather **unclear** in places — it doesn't say **how** power, wealth and development move from urban areas into rural areas. It just **assumes** that they do.

Some see Development as the move from Rural Lifestyles to Urban ones

1) Some sociologists, especially **modernisation theorists**, see development as the shift from **rural** life to **urban** life.

2) Taking this view means that it's **easy** to measure development — it's just a calculation of how **urbanised** society has become. This can be measured by counting the number of **people living**, **working** and **socialising** within **cities**, and comparing it to the number of people who live, work and socialise in the **countryside**.

Dual Economy theory says that Rural and Urban economies are Separate

1) **Dual economy** theorists argue that urbanisation leads to two very **different** types of society within one country — **rural** society and **urban** society. They function as **two separate economies** with little connection between them.

2) The **rural** economy is **localised** and focused on **subsistence**. The **urban** economy is **national** and **international** and focused on **economic growth** and development.

3) The theory is based on the idea that **colonialism** (p.158) pushed progression in **urban** areas at a cost to **rural** areas.

4) It's a useful theory to explain that the needs and problems of **urban** areas are very **different** from those of **rural** areas.

5) However, **critics** point to the fact that dual economy theory assumes that rural economies are 'backward'.

Dependency Theory — Poverty in LEDC cities is caused by Colonialism

1) **Dependency theorists** believe the cities described by modernisation theorists **don't exist**. They say cities in **LEDCs** aren't **success stories** of meritocracy and achieved status, where hard work always brings big rewards. They're actually polarised between the '**haves**' and the '**have nots**'. They blame **colonialism** for this.

2) Dependency theory says that urbanisation doesn't bring solutions to the developing world, just more **problems**, e.g. **inequality**, **urban poverty**, **bad public health**. The developing world doesn't have the **infrastructure** to deal with them — there's **poor health care**, limited access to **education**, and little **social security** (if any at all).

3) According to the theory, only the parts of the city where **capitalist elites** live and work are anything like the modernisation theory model of a city. Those parts were **designed** under colonialism to house the **colonial elite**.

4) The theory says LEDC cities **depend** on trade with **rich nations**, and **serve** rich nations rather than their own people.

5) However, dependency theory **ignores** countries where urbanisation **has** brought **economic benefits** for the people.

Urbanisation and Industrialisation

The Two Main Approaches to Industrialisation are ISI and EOI

1) **ISI** is short for **Import Substituting Industrialisation**. The developing nation works to substitute **home-grown alternatives** for goods it used to import. **Trade tariffs** and **taxes** are used to **protect** local manufacturers from **foreign competition**. A state applying ISI has to be **interventionist** — protecting markets, patrolling borders and overseeing the industrialisation process.

2) **EOI** stands for **Export Orientated Industrialisation**. The developing country focuses on producing **consumer goods** for **export**. There is **high demand** for the goods in MEDCs, which have **moved away** from labour-intensive manufacturing. LEDCs have **cheaper labour costs** and can sell their products at attractive prices.

ISI has Advantages and Disadvantages

On the plus side, **ISI** helps LEDCs become **less dependent** on the developed world. They can **target** and **plan** their own economies and **invest the profits** they make in further development. But on the down side...

1) With **no foreign competition** local industries have less incentive to be competitive. Businesses can become **inefficient** and **corrupt** or even fail.

2) **Protectionist policies** (e.g. refusing to buy goods from abroad) can **aggravate potential customers**, who may **refuse to buy** the developing country's goods.

3) With **no real incentive to expand** their business, some firms **cut wages** as an easy way of boosting profits. This can drag down **wage levels** in the country as a whole.

EOI has Positive and Negative Effects too

EOI has worked very well for countries like **South Korea**, **Hong Kong**, **Taiwan** and **Singapore** (sometimes referred to as the '**tiger economies**'), which became Newly Industrialised Countries (NICs) in the 1970s and 80s. People living there now enjoy a much **improved standard of living** and **health**.

But the focus on export markets can mean the manufactured goods are **too expensive** for the domestic population to buy. **Fierce competition** in international markets can lead to **wage cuts**.

EOI had worked well for Gustav.

Industrialisation can bring Too Many People to the Cities

1) **Rapid industrialisation** can lead to **massive social problems** as workers move from the countryside to the city. Newcomers often can't afford ordinary city housing and build temporary homes in **shanty towns** — these don't get any of the usual city **services** like a proper **water** supply, **health care** or **policing**. Standards of living are **extremely low**.

2) **Webster (1984)** described this as **over-urbanisation**. Over-urbanisation is caused by **push** and **pull factors**.

Push factors	Poverty, loss of land, natural disasters, war/civil war.	Result: people leave the countryside
Pull factors	More chance of employment in new factories, better access to education, escape from familial, religious or cultural constraints.	**Result: people move to the city**

Practice Questions

Q1 What is industrialisation?

Q2 What is the dual economy theory?

Q3 Give examples of two 'push' and two 'pull' factors which can contribute to over-urbanisation.

Exam Question

Q1 Analyse two explanations for how urbanisation can cause problems for a developing country.   [10 marks]

And the city streets are paved with gold and diamonds — honest...

When you look at interpretations of urbanisation, remember that modernisation theory and dependency theory are pretty much opposite. So, given that modernisation theory says that cities are wonderful and promote development, dependency theory must say they're awful. If modernisation theory says something is black, dependency theory says it's white. And so on.

The Environment

There's a major downside to LEDCs attempting to become more economically developed — the negative impact it has on the environment. Sociologists mostly agree that it's hard to balance building a good economy and being environmentally friendly.

Industrialisation is a major cause of Environmental Damage

1) **Development** is often in the form of **industrialisation**, which creates **environmental problems**, such as:

Water pollution	Deforestation	Desertification
Kingsbury (2004) suggests that clean water is scarce in some areas due to **industrial pollution**.	**Rainforests** are logged for **hardwoods** or to make way for **agriculture**.	Poor farmers may be forced to over-cultivate and over-graze their land. Eventually the land is exhausted and turns to desert (desertification).

2) As a country develops, it can suffer from **over-urbanisation** (p.163).

3) Urban areas are **polluted** by **industry** and by **motor traffic**, which is bad for **public health** and the **environment**.

4) The new **international division of labour** (p.156) means that polluting heavy industry is concentrated in **LEDCs**.

5) LEDCs don't have **equal access** to 'clean' technology — e.g. equipment to reduce air pollution from power plants. Also, they often aren't able to **afford** cleaner methods of production, so their development can **harm** the environment.

There are different Theoretical views on how to Manage the Environment

The Neo-Liberal View

According to **neo-liberal** theories, countries need to calculate the **costs** and **benefits** of any development strategy. If a country works out that the **environmental cost** of a development strategy is **too high**, then neo-liberals expect that they'll decide not to pursue that strategy. But this may make them **less competitive** in the **global market**.

The Structuralist View

Structuralist theories argue that the developing world would do more about environmental issues if it was **debt-free**. As long as the developing world is struggling to **catch up economically**, the **economy** will always **take priority** over the environment.

> *Structuralist theories are the ones that say the structure of society is responsible for social problems. Marxism is a structuralist theory.*

Some sociologists argue that Sustainable Development is the solution

1) **Sustainable development** is development that aims to **protect** the environment for **future generations**.

2) The term 'sustainable development' came from the **Brundtland Commission (1983-87)**. This was an organisation set up to research **environmental problems** caused by **development**. It described the **three pillars** of sustainable development: **economic**, **environmental** and **social**:

Protection of the environment — this pillar focuses on the 'sustainable' part, e.g. using **renewable energy** in industry, instead of using **fossil fuels**.	**Economic growth** — this pillar focuses most on 'development'. It tries to deal with the fact that we are using **too much** of the **Earth's resources**.

Social equality — this pillar states that sustainable development should have **ethical benefits** too. It should provide **equal opportunities**, access to **education** and **equal rights**.

> *This pillar addresses the claim that the same industries that damage the environment often exploit and mistreat their workers as well.*

3) When economic development uses **natural resources sustainably** and **minimises pollution**, it is known as **green growth**, or **ecological modernisation**.

4) Marxists criticise sustainable development for being too focused on the interests of **wealthier countries**, at the expense of poorer ones. **Redclift (1987)**, a Neo-Marxist, also says that some environmentalists don't give enough priority to relieving **poverty**, because they focus too much on the **environmental** aspects.

5) The **short-term needs** of economic development are often **prioritised** over **long-term environmental issues**, e.g. the UK still expands its **road network**, despite the **pollution** it causes. **Radical environmentalists** argue that the only solution is **de-industrialisation**.

Controlling the green growth of his hedges was Fred's favourite hobby.

War and Conflict

If you're worried that pollution and global warming might destroy the planet in the next hundred years or so, don't panic — there's a good chance we won't have to wait that long. A good, old-fashioned war could destroy the planet in no time at all.

Ethnic Division, Poverty and Political Instability can lead to War

Wars are more likely to take place in **LEDCs** — there are many different causes and explanations for this.

1) Many wars in developing countries are **ethnic conflicts** — struggles between different **ethnic groups** (such as the **Hutus** and **Tutsis** in the **Rwandan Civil War**). Some sociologists argue that ethnic conflicts, especially those in **Africa**, arise from **colonialism**. The colonialists created new national **boundaries**, without considering **ethnic differences**. For example, new national boundaries might **split up** existing ethnic groups, or put **warring** groups in the **same nation**.

2) However, **Frances Stewart (2002)** says that while many conflicts may have an ethnic, cultural or religious dimension, the underlying causes of most are **economic**. Economic causes of war could include **political**, **economic** or **social inequalities**, **poor government services** and **high unemployment**.

3) **Paul Collier (2000)** produced a **conflict risk analysis**, which considers a number of factors that can **lead to war**. These factors include **poverty**, the **resource curse** (where precious **natural resources**, e.g. oil or gold, lead to **conflict** rather than **stability**), **ethnic divides** (as above) and **political instability**.

4) In today's **globalised** world, **developed countries** often get involved in wars in **LEDCs**. They might stage a **military intervention** (sending armed forces to help one side in a war) or **supply weapons** to a developing country.

> **Mary Kaldor (1999, 2007, 2012)** introduced the idea of **'new wars'** — usually **civil** or **ethnic conflicts**. Instead of fighting **enemy soldiers** on the battlefield, these wars target **civilians** with **violence** and **human rights abuses**. Kaldor believes that the **breakdown** of the **nation state** due to **globalisation** is a major cause of new wars — they can **cross national borders** due to the **global arms trade**, **terrorism** and **online** promotion of **extremist views**.

War has an effect on a country's Development

1) If governments are spending their money on **war** and **weapons**, they have less money to spend on **development**.

2) **Kaldor (2007)** identified a link between conflict and **long-term problems**, such as the outbreak of **diseases** (especially in **refugee camps**, where they spread rapidly) and an increase in **poverty**. War can also make **famines** worse, as **food** and **aid** are harder to distribute in a war zone. All of these problems will **hold back** development.

3) **Infrastructure** (e.g. **transport** and **communication networks**) is often **damaged** in conflicts, which harms development.

4) **Schools** are often affected by war — either the school itself is too **damaged** to be used, or it becomes too **dangerous** for children to go to school. **Education** and **literacy rates** fall, which hinders future development. This usually affects **girls** more than boys — especially in countries like **Afghanistan**, where there has been conflict since 2001.

Practice Questions

Q1 Name three types of environmental damage caused by industrialisation.

Q2 What are the three pillars of sustainable development, according to the Brundtland Commission?

Q3 What are ethnic conflicts?

Q4 What are 'new wars'?

Exam Question

Q1 By applying material from Item A, analyse two explanations for why war and conflict can hinder a country's development.

[10 marks]

> **Item A**
> Countries that are engaged in wars often spend large amounts of money on weapons. It can also be harder to ensure that the population are fed during a war. Conflicts can also cause physical damage to schools, or make them too dangerous to attend.

Make tea not war...

Interesting sociology fact: Mary Kaldor and Frances Stewart are sisters. I know, right? Totally blew my mind. Anyway, when sociologists look at war and conflict they're interested in a) what causes the violence, and b) the effects conflict has on future development. There's an easy short answer to b) — not good (but you might want to give a bit more detail in your exam).

Aspects of Development: Demography

Demography is the study of population change. It's been a big thing in sociology since, well, forever.

Population is growing Fast in the Developing World

1) This chart shows **world population growth** since 1750, and predicts what could happen between now and 2050.

2) Population is growing much **more quickly** in the **developing world** than in the industrialised nations.

3) However, it should be noted that the actual **rate** of population growth is now **slowing down** (even though the population is still increasing).

4) The population of the world is also **ageing** — the proportion of **older people** is **increasing** in societies across the world. This is partly due to better **health care**, so it affected **MEDCs** first, but with wider access to health care, the populations of most **LEDCs** are now ageing too.

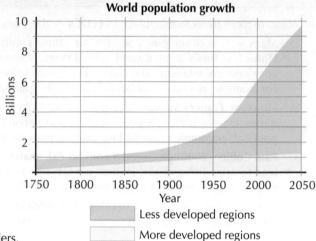

World population growth

Less developed regions
More developed regions

5) Worldwide, there is a roughly **even** balance between genders. However, in some countries, there is a significant **gender imbalance**. For example, **China** has a very **unbalanced** society — there are more men than women. This could be a result of a combination of its **one-child policy** and the perception that male children are **more valuable** than female children. This may have resulted in some parents choosing to illegally **abort female foetuses** so that they could have a **boy**.

Malthusians and Modernisation Theorists Worry about Population Growth

Malthus (1798) thought that population growth could cause **problems** — a population could grow faster than its capacity to **feed itself**. He pointed out that **limited resources** would cause **death**, which would **balance** the birth/death equation.

Neo-Malthusian **Ehrlich (1968)** believed that the '**population explosion**' was putting too much **stress** on the resources of the world, leading the developing world in particular to experience problems such as **famine** and **malnutrition**. He believed **over-population** was damaging **development** and the **environment**.

Artie just didn't feel that over-population was his fault.

1) The work of Malthus and Ehrlich has been used by **modernisation theorists** who argue that over-population in the developing world is one of the **biggest obstacles** to **development**. Any **economic surplus** has to be spent on **feeding** the population and building an **infrastructure** to cope with increased population, instead of on **industry**.

2) Modernisation theorists argue that the solution is to persuade governments to **promote birth control**, and for **Western governments** and **international organisations** to **fund birth control** programmes.

3) Modernisation theorists also suggest that money should be spent on **educating women**, because educated women tend to have fewer babies.

4) Ehrlich has even suggested that men in the developing world who have had 3 children or more should be **sterilised**.

5) Some organisations such as **USAID** (United States Agency for International Development) and **UNFPA** (United Nations Population Fund) spend **hundreds of millions** of dollars each year on worldwide **family planning programmes**.

6) Countries like **China** and **Singapore** have used **legal restrictions** and **economic incentives** to encourage their citizens to have fewer children.

Ehrlich's Theory of over-population has been Criticised

1) **Carnell (2000)** showed that Ehrlich's predictions about population growth were **wrong**. The population is growing more **slowly** than Ehrlich thought.

2) **Harrison (1990)** points out that the **birth rate** isn't the cause of population growth. Population growth is actually caused by a **decline** in the **death rate**, especially the **infant mortality rate**. People are having the **same number** of babies, but **fewer** are **dying**. Harrison does agree with Ehrlich that population growth threatens the **environment**.

Aspects of Development: Demography

Most attempts to **Lower Birth Rates** have **Failed**

1) Some religions, including **Islam** and **Roman Catholicism**, discourage or do not approve of using **contraception**.

2) **Harrison (1990)** notes that the fastest rates of population growth in the developing world are found in **Muslim** countries where traditional ideas about **women** and the **family** predominate.

3) **Feminists** have suggested **significant progress** won't be made on population control until developing countries become **less patriarchal** and the position of **women** in society improves so they are able to **take control** over their own bodies.

4) Much of the evidence does suggest that making **contraception** and **contraception advice** available is **not enough**. It needs to go hand in hand with **changing the position of women in society**.

Marxists say population growth is **Not** the **Problem**

1) Modernisation theorists say over-population is the fault of the **governments** of the developing world, **religious organisations** and the **people** themselves. **Marxists** blame the **global capitalist system** (p.154).

2) Modernisation theorists believe over-population is a **problem** because they assume Malthus was right when he said **growing populations** can outstrip **food supplies**. Marxists believe the real cause of **starvation** and **famine** is not over-population but **unfair distribution of world resources**. There is enough food for everyone, but **capitalist market forces** mean food goes where the **money** is and not where it is **needed** most.

Other theorists also **Support Redistributing Resources**

1) There's not a lot of evidence that **food resources** aren't coping. **Food production** has **increased**, and the world could produce **more** food than it does now, although it might be difficult to do this **sustainably**. **Boserup (1965)** said that **population increase** determines **agricultural change**, so agricultural production always keeps up with the population.

2) **Dependency theorists** argue that the West continues to take the very **best resources** a developing nation has, leaving the inhabitants with little land of any quality. They argue that **land reform** and **redistribution** to the poor would be a better solution than population control.

3) **Adamson (1986)** says focusing on population growth distracts us from the **real causes** of poverty, e.g. **unfair distribution of resources**. We should study the developed world's contribution to this issue — **over-consumption**, **environmental damage**, and **economic exploitation** of the developing world. ← Adamson points out that, in 1986, an American used on average 300 times more energy than a Bangladeshi.

4) **Adamson** also suggests that **poverty** causes high population. Poverty forces parents to see children as **economic assets** who will bring money into the household and support them in **old age**. Where there are **high levels** of **infant mortality**, parents have more children to increase the **chances** of at least one **surviving** into adulthood.

Some believe **Population Growth** can **Encourage Development**

1) Some theorists see population growth not as a problem but as a **cause of development**. As population growth creates pressure on resources it encourages people to **innovate** and find ways to be more **productive**.

2) One example is 19th century **Britain**, where many historians see population growth as a major **cause of industrialisation**.

Practice Questions

Q1 Why do modernisation theorists believe over-population is an obstacle to development?

Q2 Why have policies aimed at reducing population in the developing world had limited impact?

Q3 What positive effects does an increasing population have according to some theorists?

Exam Question

Q1 Evaluate the idea that rapid population growth is a significant obstacle to development. [20 marks]

Malthus thought we had problems in 1798...

... imagine if he could see us now. The world's population was only about 1 billion then — it's over 7 times that now. Sociologists disagree about what's to blame for over-population — too many babies, too few deaths, capitalism... the list goes on.

Aspects of Development: Education

You might not believe this, but good education has been proven to improve living standards and make for a harder-working, happier populace. So it's maybe not surprising that developing countries have increased spending on education in recent years.

Good Education improves the Living Standards of people in LEDCs

In **Rostow's** model of development (see p.154), an **educated workforce** is necessary for **industrial take-off**. Many other sociologists, in particular **functionalists** and **modernisation theorists**, also think education is very important for development.

1) **Economic development** requires **expert, technical knowledge** on a **local level**. Not all expertise can be brought in from other countries. International organisations and MEDCs are generally keen to see LEDCs **train** their own people in the **specialist skills** required for the long-term development of a country.

2) Education also gives people the **values** and **attitudes** required in the process of development. **Literate, numerate** people can fully understand what action is required for development and **participate** in deciding what action to take in their **communities** and their **country**.

3) Education can act as a **unifying force**. It can give people a common set of **values** and ideas about their country, which helps to overcome **class, ethnic** and **religious differences** in a country.

4) Many people in the developing world are keen to participate in education because they want to obtain **achieved status** — a qualification, improved employment opportunities, etc. Education acts as an **empowering** tool for groups in society that have traditionally been **excluded** from **social mobility**, e.g. **women** and the **poor**.

Universal Education is still Unavailable for many in the Developing World

1) **External aid** and **increased investment** in the developing world have led many countries to introduce **universal education** — but provision can be **patchy**. Some countries have universal education for **primary school** age (up to about 11 years old), some have it up to 14 or 16 years old, and some still haven't introduced universal education.

2) Even in countries that have **universal education** as a policy, not every child **actually goes to school**. This is because of other **family commitments** and needs — e.g. children may be required to **work** on the **family farm**.

3) In many countries, parents still have to **pay school fees** to get their child into school. Also, **school supplies** aren't provided by the state like they are in the UK. Families have to **buy** books and other resources.

4) The **growth** in education doesn't necessarily mean **quality** education, either.

   - Much of the **increase** in education has had to be supplied by education **systems** that were designed to meet the **basic needs** of a **few**. Basic education systems have been put under **strain**.
   - Lessons aren't always of **high quality**. Some education doesn't provide enough **useful knowledge**.

The Growth in Education has raised problems with Employment

1) While young people are in schools and colleges being educated, they're not contributing to the **economy**.

2) Because more people are studying and fewer people are working, governments get **less revenue** from income tax. Governments have less money coming in but have to **pay out more** to **provide education**.

3) Bright, educated people from **rural** areas tend to **migrate** to the **cities** to look for jobs. This contributes to **over-urbanisation** and urban **overcrowding** (see p.162-163).

4) The more educated citizens **sometimes struggle** to find **employment** in their own country, or they can simply earn a lot more by moving away to countries that have **better job prospects** — leading to what is called the '**brain drain**'. The end result is that the country **fails to develop** because the educated have **left**, to use their education elsewhere.

Marxist Dependency Theorists see Education as Cultural Imperialism

Dependency theorists really frown on the idea that education **trains** people for **development**. They **strongly disapprove** of education that gives people the **values** and **attitudes** that are needed for 'imperial-capitalist' (i.e. Western) development — this is **cultural imperialism** (see p.157).

Dependency theory sees **education** as a potential **tool** for keeping people **culturally** and **economically dependent** on the developed world — it trains them to get the kind of **jobs** that **benefit TNCs** and the **developed world**.

Aspects of Development: Health

In the early 21st century, health in the developing world is still poor compared to the developed world.
Good health care provision is essential for the protection of people and for a developing country's future prospects.

Physical Quality of Life Index (PQLI) Measures Health and Education

1) **David Morris** developed the PQLI in **1979**. It measures **infant mortality**, **literacy** and **life expectancy**.
   It's useful for sociologists concerned with **development** as a **social issue** rather than an economic issue.

2) The PQLI also allows you to compare **trends** across countries. However, there are problems in collecting **reliable** data.

Education, Poverty and the role of MEDCs all impact on Health in LEDCs

1) **Poverty** forces people to suffer a **bad diet** and **poor public health**, and also prevents them from
   gaining a good quality of **health care**. Universal free health care is **rare** in the developing world —
   people usually have to **pay** to see a doctor. There are also **not enough doctors** and **nurses** to go around.

2) The lack of good **health education** in the developing world means many people (particularly those in
   traditional, **rural areas**) do not know how to **prevent disease** and are not aware of **basic treatments**.

3) Some drugs companies sell drugs in the developing world that are **banned** in the **West** for **safety** reasons.
   Or they may set the **price** of life-saving drugs so **high** that many people in LEDCs can't afford them.

4) **Western products** may be used **inappropriately**. For example, **baby formula milk** is heavily advertised in LEDCs.
   But some mothers don't have access to **clean water** to make the milk with, so many babies die from **infections**.

5) Also, **TNCs** that have set up in developing countries often pay little attention to the **environment**, or **health and
   safety**. For example, the **Bhopal poison gas leak** of 1984 happened because safety procedures were **inadequate**.

> **Example: HIV/AIDS in South Africa**
> - **Insufficient health education** in poor areas meant people **didn't know** how HIV was transmitted.
> - Clinics could be a **day's walk** away.
> - **Transnational drugs companies** refused to allow local drugs companies to make **cheap**
>   versions of anti-HIV drugs. This practice was banned by the courts in 2001. *They doubted that HIV caused AIDS.*
> - In the 1990s, the **South African government** was **reluctant** to **distribute** anti-HIV drugs.

There are different Theoretical Views about Health Inequalities

Modernisation theorists and **functionalists** believe **Western** medicine is **superior**, and that Western medicine and **health
education** can **solve** the problems of **high infant mortality** and **low life expectancy**. Rostow (1971) said **high-tech medicine**
used in the developed world should be **transferred** to developing nations so that **quality health care** can be provided.

Marxist **Navarro (1976)** believed that high-tech Western health care is not the immediate priority for the developing
world. Poor nations need to focus on **basic health procedures** to **save lives** and **improve quality of life**. **Doctors** from
these nations need to be encouraged to **stay** and **work** in their own countries, not to migrate to MEDCs for **better pay**.

Dependency theory blames **colonialism** and **exploitation**. Colonialism introduced **European diseases** to
Africa, America and Asia. Colonialism also replaced **food crops** with **cash crops**, resulting in **malnutrition**.

Practice Questions

Q1 Give two examples of how education can cause employment problems in developing countries.

Q2 What do modernisation theorists suggest could improve health care in the developing world?

Exam Questions

Q1 Outline two ways that education can be used as a tool for development in LEDCs. Explain each one. [10 marks]

Q2 Evaluate the idea that Western standards of health care should not be applied to LEDCs. [20 marks]

This subject is certainly draining my brain...

*It's those dreaded words 'cultural imperialism' again. This topic can often feel like 'them and us' thinking — either assuming
that the West knows best, or assuming that the West is all bad and that poor countries should be left to get on with it.*

Aspects of Development: Gender

Recently, sociologists (particularly feminists) have pointed out that women and men experience development in different ways.

There's **Gender Inequality** in the **Developing World**

Evidence from studies into gender in LEDCs shows that in many cases women get a worse deal than men:

- Women have lower life expectancy than men in some countries (usually women live longer than men).
- Women are paid less than men and get less education than men.
- Women's health is poorer than men's health, and women have less access to health care than men do.
- There's even a greater chance of abortion if a foetus is female (see p.166).
- Women have very poor reproductive rights. They don't get to choose whether to have children, or how many to have, because local religious attitudes are against contraception and abortion.

The Gender Empowerment Measure (GEM) is an indicator of the progress made by women in a society

1) The GEM focuses on social indicators of gender equality — female and male participation in decision making, economic participation and economic power.

2) In other words, it monitors whether women have the right to vote, how many women there are in parliament, how many women have top management jobs and the GDP per capita of the female population.

3) This measure has continually shown that women haven't reached social equality with men.

The Gender-related Development Index (GDI) measures several development-related factors

1) The GDI measures life expectancy, literacy, years in school, number of women in work and women's income.

2) Men still tend to have better income and literacy, but women have improved in most of the categories measured.

3) Women's literacy and numeracy has improved, and the chance of death during or after childbirth has fallen.

Technology can change **Women's Employment Patterns**

1) **Swasti Mitter (1995)** writes about the impact of ICT on female employment in LEDCs. She says that computer technology can be a real advantage to women — it allows them to work from home and work flexible hours.

2) Many ICT jobs which have been outsourced to NICs from MEDCs go to women — e.g. call-centre jobs.

3) Mitter points out that many women in LEDCs like India, Malaysia and Brazil now work in ICT, but they're concentrated towards the bottom end of the work ladder.

Radical, Socialist and Marxist Feminists have **Different Views**

1) Some radical feminists see development as a tool to make women more dependent upon men.

2) Radical feminists say TNCs actively seek to employ women as they are cheaper, more efficient and more docile.

3) If women do experience improvement in their position in society, e.g. greater life expectancy through better health care or increased income, it's because the patriarchy of the developed world allow it for productivity reasons.

Radical feminism can be criticised for failing to see the exploitation experienced by men.

1) Socialist feminists argue that socialism can bring about a society that isn't gendered — i.e. that treats men and women equally. They push for a socialist revolution that totally changes the way people see 'men's jobs' and 'women's jobs', as well as moving ownership of the means of production from employers to workers.

2) Socialist feminist Mies (1986) argues that traditional Marxism and capitalism both undervalue the work women do.

1) According to Marxist feminists, women may feel the negative side effects of development more than men. Women experience a dual burden of paid work and domestic responsibilities.

2) When a country industrialises, men go from one form of work (agriculture) to another form of work (manufacturing industry), but women go from one form of work (housework and childcare) to two forms of work (housework and childcare plus a paid job outside the home).

This is quite simplified, and it's a broad generalisation anyway.

Aspects of Development: Employment

Big international companies often move their factories, call centres, or whatever it is they need, to developing countries because wages are cheaper there. That means jobs for local workers, but many people would say the workers aren't treated fairly.

Developing Countries Encourage TNCs to Relocate

1) **Labour costs** are much much lower in **LEDCs** than in the developed world. As a result, many **TNCs** (transnational corporations) prefer to set up factories in LEDCs, or pay companies in LEDCs to make goods on their behalf.
2) Many LEDCs have actively encouraged TNCs to do this by setting up **Export Processing Zones** (EPZs) — these are a type of **Free Trade Zone** (FTZ).
3) In the EPZs, companies may be offered **tax breaks**, **training grants**, **low regulation** and **low wage costs**. **Trade unions** are often banned.
4) There are now **more than 100** countries in the developing world that have these zones.

Not to be confused with Evenly Patterned Zebras.

Conditions Favour the TNCs, not the Workers

Typical EPZ industries include **garment-making** and assembling **electronic goods**. Workers are not usually **directly employed** by the TNCs. They work for **local manufacturers** who have to **compete** to win contracts from the TNCs. The manufacturers' main concern is to **keep costs down**. This can lead to very **poor working conditions**.

1) Often **hours are long** and **pay is low**. In the garment industry, workers in **Sri Lanka** received the lowest wages in 2013 — **$68** per month on average. Workers in **Thailand** were better paid, earning **$237** per month. In Europe, workers in **Turkey** doing similar work earned around **$494** per month in 2014.
2) **Health and safety** issues, and basic comforts like breaks or washrooms, may be **ignored**.
3) Many firms use **flexible** or **casual labour**, which means that workers have almost **no job security**. They are employed on **short-term contracts** — often on a **weekly** or even **daily** basis.
4) **Highly paid jobs** like **marketing** and **design** are usually done at the TNC's sites in MEDCs. Workers in the LEDC factories tend to have **basic unskilled jobs**. There's very little **training** or chance of **progression**.
5) In EPZs, **women** usually make up the majority of employees. In garment-making it can be up to **90%**. Because women usually earn less than men in LEDCs, it can be argued that the TNCs are **profiting** from women's **lower status**. Some companies in EPZs also use **child labour**.
6) When **trade unions** are **banned** or restricted, it's hard for workers to campaign for **better pay** or **conditions**.
7) There are still so many people **willing** to work that employers have **no incentive** to offer a better wage.

There are Arguments For and Against the special Zones

1) Marxists like **Fröbel (1980)** are highly critical of EPZs. They see them as a new version of **exploitative colonialism**.
2) **Globalists** say that EPZs benefit world consumers as a whole by **keeping prices down**.
3) **Wages** in EPZs look low compared to what people are paid for the same work in industrialised nations. However, they're often **relatively good** when compared to average wages in the developing world.

Practice Questions

Q1 What do the GEM and the GDI suggest about gender inequality? Why do they differ?
Q2 Why do TNCs locate manufacturing in LEDCs?

Exam Question

Q1 Evaluate the idea that women are disadvantaged in the developing world. [20 marks]

Relocation, relocation, relocation...

Employment, health, education, gender issues, the environment, demography... There can't be many issues that global development doesn't touch on. The most important thing to get straight about this section is the difference between Marxist, modernist and dependency theories. Once that's clear you can pretty much predict what they'll say on a particular issue.

SECTION TEN — GLOBAL DEVELOPMENT

Ownership and Control of Media

The media is one of the most powerful influences in modern society because it's part of all our lives.
The study of the media has had to change just to keep up with new developments.

Media is All About Communication

You use **media** to **convey ideas** and **information** to **other people**. Society also talks about '**the media**':

1) '**The media**' includes all the different **forms of communication** that society uses to give information to the **public** — like newspapers, websites, radio, cinema, advertising and TV.

2) **Organisations** who **own** these methods of communication are part of the media too.

3) One of the main **functions** of the media is to **deliver news** to society.
   It's also used to **educate** and **inform** the public, and to provide **entertainment**.

'The media' doesn't exist as a physical, united organisation — it refers to all of these separate forms of communication.

Sociologists Disagree over what Counts as 'Media'

1) There's some **debate** about what counts as media — for example, some theorists would include **all mobile phone technology**, but others would only include it when it's used to communicate to a **large audience**. So, texting a friend wouldn't count, but **subscribing** to a **service** that sends you football scores by text **would** count, and so would visiting a football **website** on your phone.

2) Since the 1980s there have been **huge changes** in the media. There are now a lot more **specialist** media outlets communicating with smaller, **niche groups** rather than to the whole 'mass' of the public — e.g. subscription TV channels for fans of particular football teams, special interest magazines, podcasts about special interest topics.

3) Also, **new media** (p.175-176) allow audiences to **interact** with media providers. Communication isn't **one-way** any more. Some media are more of a **multi-way network**, e.g. the internet.

4) Some theorists include a lot more things when they talk about 'media'. **Marshall McLuhan (1964)** included **any** kind of technology that helped people communicate — even cars and clocks.

Well, OK, I suppose a car lets you drive from A to B to have a meeting, and a clock lets you be on time.

Sociologists Analyse and Research the Media and its Effects

Content Analysis — measuring how often a word, phrase or theme is used in a piece of media

1) In the social sciences, content analysis means **formal**, **quantitative** measuring. For example, you could **count** how many times a news report used the words 'economic crisis'. It's most suited to **written texts**, or to **transcripts**.

2) Content analysis can also be used to investigate the **relationship** between two phrases or themes (e.g. by looking at how often they appear together).

3) The main **downside** of content analysis is that it **takes a long time**. It also doesn't take **context** into account.

Semiotics — studying the signs and codes of media

1) A sign is **anything** that can be used to **mean something else** — e.g. a word or an image. Semiotic analysis looks at the **meanings** of the signs in a piece of media.

2) **Advertisements** are particularly open to semiotic analysis. Ads use **signs** to associate their product with **positive ideas**, e.g. attractiveness, happiness and success. They don't **directly** say, 'buy this product and you will be happy'.

3) Semiotic analysis is open to **subjectivity** and **bias**. The **values** of the researcher may influence how they **interpret** a sign, or the **relative importance** they place on different signs in a piece of media.

A sign can have a very simple meaning, e.g. the written word 'cows' means, well, the idea of cows (the technical term for this kind of meaning is denotation). A sign can also suggest meaning, e.g. a photo of a couple holding hands on the beach at sunset means the idea of romance (this kind of meaning is connotation).

Experiments — studying how an actual audience responds to media

1) One example would be to monitor people's **behaviour** after viewing a violent film.

2) Short experiments like this don't tell you about **long-term media effects**.
   People also tend to **behave differently** when they know they're in an **experiment**.

3) **Audience research** means things like showing media to a **sample audience**, then **interviewing** them or giving them a questionnaire. You have to **formulate good interview questions** to get useful and **meaningful** results and **avoid bias**.

Ownership and Control of Media

The Media is *Owned* by *A Few Powerful Companies* and *Individuals*

The media is **produced** and **transmitted** by **media outlets**, e.g. film studios, TV channels and radio stations. The **same companies** often own **different forms of media** — this is called **cross-media ownership**. It's often not publicised.

1) Media companies **diversify** — they buy other companies that make **different kinds of media**, and they also buy companies in **other business sectors**.

- Rupert Murdoch's **News Corp** owns TV stations, newspapers, book and magazine publishers, and websites.
- In Italy, **Silvio Berlusconi** owns three national TV channels, an advertising agency and a magazine publisher. He part owns a banking company and a cinema firm. (He also owns football club **AC Milan**.)

2) Some media companies **own media** in **several different countries**. News Corp owns newspapers in Australia, Britain and the USA. It owns TV networks in Australia, Europe, Asia, North and South America.

3) Over the last 30 years, media ownership has become concentrated into fewer and fewer hands. Research by **Bagdikian (2004)** found that the American media was now mostly owned by just **five huge corporations** — TimeWarner, Disney, News Corp, Bertelsmann and Viacom®.

4) More recently, **Comcast** and **CBS** have replaced Bertelsmann and joined the four remaining companies identified by Bagdikian — together they are known as the '**Big Six**' and they own **90% of the media in the US**.

The individuals who own and control those companies have **huge power and influence** in society. They can **control** the **information** we receive **if they want to**. A **great example** is **Italy**, where **Silvio Berlusconi** was voted in as prime minister for the third time in 2008 — he stayed in power until 2011. **He owns a lot of media outlets** and some people claim he used them to **control the reporting** of his political party and the opposition.

Some Messages get *Removed* from the *Media*

1) The process of **controlling** the content of the media is called **censorship**.

2) Media messages which are considered **harmful** or **offensive** to society can be **removed** before the audience receives them.

3) Censorship can be done for **moral**, **political** or **security** reasons.

Anita was traumatised after watching a nature documentary on polar bears.

Marxists *say Media Ownership Controls Media Content*

Traditional Marxism — media owners control what we see in the media

The idea is that the owners of the media **exploit their power position** to **manipulate** the content of the media. Capitalist media owners **tell news editors** what **stories** to cover and what **views** to put across. **Miliband (1969)** said that these messages **encourage** the **proletariat** to be **subordinate** and happy to serve the **bourgeoisie**.

Neo-Marxism — media reflect the ideas of the ruling class (including media owners)

Neo-Marxist theory is **more complicated** — it says that control over the media is **indirect**. Neo-Marxism says the **world view of the elite class** is **broadcast** and **reinforced** by the media. The **values** and **ideas** of the **ruling class** are presented as the **natural, common-sense** views to have. This is called '**cultural hegemony**' — one set of ideas **dominating** over other ideas.

> In the 1970s, a study by the Glasgow University Media Group (GUMG) discovered that the majority of people working in the media were white, middle-class men.

1) Some neo-Marxists believe that people who work in the media are **trained** to present a **certain view of the world**. This view becomes **natural** and '**obvious**' to them and the audience. The media workers and the audience are **unaware** that the media is pushing a certain view.

2) Neo-Marxists don't say that **alternative** views are **suppressed** — they say they're **allowed**. This gives the **impression** that **all** views get a **fair** shout — which makes it seem perfectly **fair** for the **dominant view** to stay on top.

3) Marxist sociologists say the control of ideas **doesn't just happen in news** or factual programmes. For example, family entertainment programmes are presented as light-hearted fun, but they present a specific **idea of British family life**.

4) The **Frankfurt School** (who were neo-Marxists) argued that **advertising** in the media makes people **feel** that they **need** the goods produced in the **capitalist economy**. They call these '**false needs**' (p.38).

Ownership and Control of Media

Pluralism says the Media Reflects the Values and Beliefs of Society

1) **Pluralists** argue that society is made up of lots of **different** and **interacting** parts, each producing their own **opinions**.
2) **Postmodernists** say that **consumption** is hugely important in today's society — the **cultural products** and **media** that you **buy** and **consume** form your **identity**.
3) So **postmodernist pluralists** say that because people can **choose** to **consume** any of these **different opinions** media outlets **produce content** that they think people **want** to read and buy.

The audience chooses what media to consume...

1) **Pluralists** argue that no one group or person can push their views on society because there's always another voice that provides an **alternative view**.
2) Pluralists say that this gives normal people **consumer power** over media outlets — if you **don't like** what you are reading or hearing, then you can choose a **different media source**, which causes the old one to **lose money**.
3) **Owners** of the media organisations want to **stay in business**, so they mostly stick to publishing **stories** that **won't offend** their readers — views that are seen as **extreme** often **don't** get published.

Journalists can choose what to write about...

1) **Journalists** and **editors** decide what media content they are going to publish — postmodernist pluralists argue that this **limits** the **power** of owners and **creates** more **media diversity**.

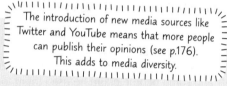
The introduction of new media sources like Twitter and YouTube means that more people can publish their opinions (see p.176). This adds to media diversity.

2) Journalists often have to follow **professional codes** that make sure that they are reporting in an objective, **unbiased** and **honest** way — this is called **journalistic integrity**. This makes it **harder** for owners to **interfere**.
3) **Neo-pluralists** admit it can be **hard** for journalists to be **impartial** and stick to these codes.

The State restricts the power of media owners...

1) In the UK, there are lots of groups and organisations who **regulate** the media — these groups make sure that **media owners** don't have **too much power** and that **journalists** are acting in a **responsible** way.
2) Public Service Broadcasters are also regulated — the **BBC** is publicly funded and the media it produces has to represent as many views as possible **by law**.

Some Sociologists have Criticised the Postmodernist Pluralist view...

1) **Curran (2003)** disagrees with the pluralists — he thinks that **owners still interfere** in the production of media for lots of **different reasons**. Curran also argues that the UK media has been controlled by a small number of individuals for a **long time** — in 1937, **four men** owned **nearly 50% of all UK newspapers**.
2) **Miliband (1973)** thought that owners, who **favour capitalism**, have ultimate control. He argued that issues that show capitalism in a **bad light** are rarely mentioned in the media — things like the existence of inequality and poverty.

Practice Questions

Q1 Give one drawback of semiotic analysis.
Q2 What does 'censorship' mean?
Q3 Describe the traditional Marxist view of media ownership and control.

Exam Question

Q1 Evaluate the idea that media owners have little control over media output.   [20 marks]

CGP — subconsciously spreading Cumbrian values since 1995...

The big difference between Marxist and postmodernist pluralist views is whether the media controls the audience or whether the audience controls the media. It's a good question. You've got traditional Marxists, who think the media's all about making profits for capitalism, and you've got neo-Marxists who say it passes on ruling-class values without even meaning to.

New Media

These pages explain how the fairly recent development of digital technology and the internet has led to a growth in new media. These developments have changed the way everybody communicates and spreads their ideas and opinions.

The **New Media** have **Distinctive Characteristics**

In recent decades, the 'digitalisation' of media has contributed to **changes** in the way we access and experience media.

New media have different **characteristics** to **older**, **printed** forms of media (e.g. newspapers and books):

1) New media are **accessible** — the growth of new methods of **digital communication**, especially the **internet**, means that digital media can be **shared** quickly, easily, and often for **free**.

2) You can use **one digital device** (like a smartphone) to access lots of **different** new media content — this is known as **convergence**. You can play music, visit news sites and read an e-book using the **same** device.

3) **User control** has increased — there is more **power** in the hands of the **audience**. **Streaming** and **catch-up** services now give viewers **control** over the programmes they watch and **when** they want to watch them.

4) There is more **interactivity** — the audience is **directly engaged** with the media. For example, you can **contact** a **live** radio show using Twitter, email or Facebook®. You can also use the **red button** to **vote** on reality TV shows.

Sociologists **Disagree** about Whether New Media are **Revolutionary**

1) Some sociologists argue that **cultures**, **economies**, even **individual personalities** are all **transformed** by new media. For example, attitudes to **privacy** have been completely changed by **social media**. It's now common to **share personal details** on the internet — this puts people at **risk** of **losing control** over who has **access** to their **identity**.

2) **Cornford and Robins (1999)** disagreed with this idea that new media are **revolutionary**. They argued that they were **evolutionary** because they evolved from technology that **already existed**, e.g. most people **still** have to use a phone line to access the internet.

3) They also argued that **interactivity isn't exclusive** to new media — **letter columns** in **newspapers** have allowed people to **share** their views for years. They believe that the only **characteristic** of new media that's **entirely new** is its **speed** of **communication**.

Boyle, Haynes, Cornford and Robins were writing before more revolutionary inventions like wireless internet, smartphones and social media were developed. New media are always changing, which may mean studies become outdated quite quickly.

Some sociologists have studied the **evolutionary impact** of new media on **existing media**:

- **Boyle and Haynes (2004)** looked at media coverage of sport after the development of **mobile phones** and 3G internet. **Phone manufacturers** claimed there would be dramatic, **revolutionary changes** in football broadcasting and marketing.
- They found that **integration** (joining together) of mobile technology and football media was actually an **evolutionary** process. Mobile technology offered **extra** options for viewing football, instead of **replacing** traditional options (like TV broadcasting).

Use of New Media **Varies** According to **Age**, **Location** and **Consumer Power**

1) **Young people** are the **biggest** users of new media. A **2015** survey found that about **5900** UK citizens had **never** used the internet. Only **31** of them were **aged 16-24**.

2) **Older people's** use of new media is **increasing**, though. Another **2015 survey** found that the percentage of **over 65s** who reported using a **smartphone** to access the internet **doubled** between 2012 and 2015.

People who **Can't Access** New Media are part of a **Digital Underclass**

Things like **getting a passport** and **registering to vote** are now mainly carried out **online**. Lack of internet access can be a **major barrier** to accessing these kinds of services.

- People who are in **poverty** are often **excluded** from new media — they can't **afford** to pay for **broadband** or new media **devices**. They form a **digital underclass** — they can't **fully** take part in society because they **lack access** to digital services.
- Some people in **rural communities** also have **limited internet access** — wires capable of transmitting **modern broadband** might not be installed in remote areas. Many rural areas also have **poor coverage** for 3G and 4G internet connections.

Alan became a local hero after discovering the only spot with 3G signal for miles around.

New Media

Curran and Seaton *Divided* Attitudes *to New Media into* Two Types

People **disagree** over whether the development of new media is **good** or **bad** for society. **Curran and Seaton (2003)** divided people into **two groups** — **cultural pessimists** and **neophiliacs** — according to their **attitude** towards new media.

Cultural Pessimists see the rise of new media in a negative way

1) They point out that new media are mainly **controlled** by powerful **multinational corporations** like Microsoft® and News Corp. Increasing **globalisation** means that they have **far-reaching influence** over consumers (p.173).

2) New media are also **controlled** by the **state** (p.173). This **reduces** everyone's **privacy**. For example, in 2013, the **whistleblower** Edward Snowden revealed that American state security were **secretly hacking** thousands of people's emails.

A whistleblower is a person who has knowledge of corruption or scandal and decides to share what they know with the public to stop further wrongdoing.

3) The **consumer benefits** of new media (e.g. **online shopping, next-day delivery**) come at a **social cost** — some online retailers have been criticised for **avoiding taxes** and **exploiting** their workers so that they can offer these services without **losing profits**.

4) **Freedom of information** on the internet means that **offensive** views can be spread — **misogynistic** (based on a dislike of women), **racist** and **terrorist** material can be easily **shared online**.

Neophiliacs see new media as a positive force

1) They say the development of **technology** leads to increased **consumer choice** — the growth of online shopping means you can shop around for the **best deal**. Companies use **global** websites like Facebook® to **advertise** their products, so consumers can buy products from **multiple countries**.

2) You can also **share more information** — this makes society more **democratic** because people are exposed to lots of different views.

3) Inventions like **satellite TV** mean that **viewers** can access TV content from **many countries** — some shows become **global phenomena** (e.g. *Game of Thrones* and *Doctor Who*). This creates a sense of **shared culture**.

There is a Debate *about whether* New Media *are* Democratic

1) Some sociologists argue that **new media** can be used to break down **cultural hegemony** (where a certain set of views is **dominant** over others — see p.173).

2) **Online media platforms** make communication **less regulated** — websites like **YouTube**, **Tumblr** and other **blogging websites** give you the opportunity to **create your own media** and present your **ideas** to a **global audience**. This means media are **more representative of society as a whole** because **anyone** can write or say what they think.

However, cultural pessimist **Andrew Keen (2007)** argued that the **democratic** nature of the **internet** can harm the **quality** of media content. Keen says that media like **Wikipedia®** that are **crowd-produced** (anyone can create and edit them) may be more **democratic** than other media, but they are filled with **badly written, uninformed** and **unchecked** content. These sources are **free** and **easy** to access, so they often **replace** traditional, **professional material**.

Practice Questions

Q1 Describe two characteristics of new media.

Q2 Briefly explain the difference between revolutionary and evolutionary views of new media.

Q3 Who are the 'digital underclass'?

Q4 Give two arguments made by neophiliacs in favour of new media.

Exam Question

Q1 Evaluate the idea that new media have brought about a social and cultural revolution. [20 marks]

New media — providing quality procrastination solutions since 1998...

Before new media, if you wanted to watch cats being ridiculous, you actually had to leave the house and find a cat. It was awful. Anyway, as usual in sociology, no one agrees on anything. Neophiliacs are big fans of new media and their revolutionary effect on society. Cultural pessimists say new media give too much power to businesses, the state and people with extreme views.

Selecting and Presenting the News

Sociologists have studied the news, which reaches many people in society, as an example of how the media works. The news is a social product full of ideas and values — it's not an objective reality 'out there', waiting to be discovered by journalists.

News is **Influenced** by **Practical Constraints** — *time, space and money*

The news is **presented** to us as the most **factual**, **objective** form of media — the reporting of what's happened that day. In reality, newspapers, radio and television run to tight **deadlines** and **constraints**, which **influence** what appears as the news.

1) **Time constraints** mean the most **easily available stories** make it onto the TV/radio news or into the newspaper. Editors and journalists have **contacts** they use **again and again** for convenience, meaning a **limited number of viewpoints** are used. Also, all news organisations have a 'news diary' of regular events. This means they can plan coverage of regular events in advance.

2) **Technical constraints** influence the news. Some places are **easier** to get **cameras**, **microphones** and **journalists** into and these are the places **top stories** will tend to come from. A story will rise and fall in significance **partly** on **how easy it is to report**.

This can lead to, for example, disasters in far-flung places being ignored or under-reported.

3) News organisations all run to a **budget**. Stories and reports from places where they **already have reporters** or **established contacts** are **cheaper to produce**. Many newspapers **can't afford** to have **many reporters** of their own so they **buy stories from news agencies**. These agencies then have a **huge influence** over what becomes news.

4) **Competition** affects the **selection** of the news. Newspaper editors are more likely to publish stories that they believe will make their newspaper the most **popular** that day. It's very important for newspaper editors that their paper **sells more** than their rivals. News stories that can be **sensationalised**, or **celebrity gossip** are often popular.

It's common these days for celebrities, politicians and groups in society to issue **press releases**. Press releases give the story **straight to the newsroom**, which makes it much more likely to be used because it **saves time and money**.

Also remember that stories have to shrink or expand to **fit the space available**. The same story could be on page 2 one day and page 17 the next.

Key studies are **Cohen and Young (1981)** and **Grossberg et al (1998)**. Both refer to the above as common practices in the media.

My editor had to take drastic action when we ran out of space.

News is **Influenced** by the **Values** and **Practices** of **Journalists**

Journalists who report the news learn to follow **certain rules** and **ideas**, which tend to be based on what they believe the general public want to hear about. **Galtung and Ruge (1965)** referred to these as '**news values**'. There are different types of news values which influence the news the media chooses to report.

Bureaucratic news values:
News should be **current**.
News should be **simple**.
News should be **brief**.
Big news is better than **small** news.

Cultural news values:
News should be **unexpected**.
News should focus on **important people**.
News should be **relevant to the audience**.
Bad news is preferred to **good news**.

The relative importance of the different news values to an individual journalist will depend partly on the type of publication or programme they work for.

Two key practices used by journalists which you must know are **agenda-setting** and **gate-keeping**.

Agenda-setting

Journalists and **editors** 'control the news agenda'. News **only becomes news** when **journalists** and **editors** **select it** as news. When a story is selected, journalists choose what **angle** to take when reporting it. This has a **direct effect** on how the audience will **perceive** the story. Agenda-setting may not be **conscious**. It comes from **learnt practices** of journalism — usually based on what **catches the audience's attention**.

Gate-keeping

This comes from work by **Gans (1979)** which describes how the editor decides **which stories are featured** and **how much space** is given to each story. Gans says it's like a gate — the editor opens it for some stories and closes it for others. **Dutton (1986)** says that editors **filter** the news by choosing which stories to print.

Selecting and Presenting the News

The *Selection* and *Presentation* of *News* can be *Biased*

The Glasgow University Media Group (GUMG) studied television news

The GUMG studied **television news** over a long time period (1970s and 1980s) to look for evidence of **bias**. They focused on coverage of workplace **strikes**. They used **detailed content analysis** (p.172) of **TV news bulletins**.

Finding	Examples
The **selection of news** was biased in favour of dominant class values.	**Picket line violence** was **reported more** than police violence.
The **voice-overs** were biased in favour of dominant class values.	**Leading terms** such as **'trouble-makers'** and **'pointless strike'** were used.
Management were given **more access** to the media than strike leaders.	Television interviews with management were **more frequent** and longer than those with strike leaders.
The **filming** and **editing** was biased in favour of the police.	Cameras were often placed **behind police lines**, showing the police viewpoint.

GUMG have a neo-Marxist perspective (p.173).

The work of the GUMG is used to demonstrate **bias in the news** and in the **values and assumptions** of the people who **produce** and **construct** the news. Their work is **highly respected** because they've studied **a lot of news** in **great detail**. Remember though, this study was done in the 1970s and 1980s, so think before you start blithely applying it to the news today.

The **image** of the news as **objective** reporting of fact makes this bias more **important** and more **powerful**. When people **think the news is unbiased**, they're **more likely to believe it**.

This is linked to postmodernist ideas about reality (see p.189).

News is *Influenced* by *Society* — *it's Socially Constructed*

1) All media sociologists agree the **news is socially constructed**, but they disagree over **whose values** are behind the social construction of news — those of the **dominant class** or those of the **majority** of society.

2) From a **pluralist** perspective, **practical constraints** are more significant in influencing the content of the news than ideological bias. The values of journalists are the **common values in society**.

3) From a **Marxist** perspective, the **ideological influences** are most important, and practical constraints can't be separated from ideology. Journalistic values are part of the **dominant ruling-class ideology**.

New Media have had an *Impact* on the *Selection* and *Presentation* of *News*

1) People don't sit down and spend a whole coffee break reading an **online** newspaper — they tend to click on what look like the most **intriguing, juicy headlines**. Editors tend to **select interesting**, **scandalous** or **wacky** stories and present them with a headline that makes them appear **even more** interesting, scandalous or wacky.

2) Audiences can **'have their say'** on news stories via online commenting, text and email. This **interactivity** seems popular with news editors. They may **select** stories that will **stir up** a big response, and **invite audience response** when **presenting** them.

3) There are **hundreds** of **news websites** — you can **compare and contrast** how they present a story. Some stories are **exactly the same** on lots of websites, where news providers have used the **same press release** or **news agency feed**.

These headlines and stories are sometimes called 'clickbait'. They are designed to entice people to follow links to pages that have advertising on them.

The widespread use of **smartphones** (with **cameras** and **internet access**) and **social media** means that **anyone** can **film** and **publicise** something that they select as **newsworthy**. This is sometimes known as **'citizen journalism'**.

1) **Bowman and Willis (2003)** described **citizen journalism** as the public actively taking part in reporting the news. Often, it's the **audience** who tell the **first part** of a story — initial images and reports spread quickly on **social media**.

2) The rise of websites like **Twitter** makes **citizen journalism** easier. **Hashtags draw together** all the content on **one subject**. **One news story** is formed out of everyone's **photos** and **comments**, including the content from individuals who are **directly involved** in developing events.

3) As a result, citizen journalism is at the **centre** of events **as they are happening**. However, it can also be **unreliable**, as individuals can present **rumours** as fact, or **misinterpret events**.

Selecting and Presenting the News

Media Professionals make Assumptions about their Audience

1) **Yvonne Jewkes (2004)** argues that **news content** is **influenced** by the way that **news professionals** construct stories — journalists use **news values** (see p.177) to decide how much '**public appeal**' a story will have.

2) Journalists make **assumptions** about what their **audience** wants to read, watch or hear. They **frame** stories so that they will appeal to them — they adopt a certain **tone**, use **strong images** and **focus** on certain parts of the story.

3) Journalists **judge** whether a story is in the **public interest**. **Politicians** and **businessmen** often influence this process — Jewkes points out that '**public interest**' is often more about what is good for the **government**.

Advertisers and the Government Can Influence News Content

1) **Herman and Chomsky (1988)** argued that media outlets are always **profit-seeking**. They often **rely** on the **government** and **big corporations** for stories. These bodies can **influence** media outlets by threatening to **damage** their profits.

2) **Edwards and Cromwell (2006)** pointed out that **some advertisers** didn't want to appear next to **images** of the **Iraq War** (2003-2011). These kinds of images were suppressed in favour of **less serious content**, so papers could continue to **advertise** and **make money**.

3) Edwards and Cromwell also argued that the **media** often **omits** (leaves out) **criticism** of UK government actions. For example, they pointed out that the media **blamed** the **negative impact** of the Iraq war on those in power in Iraq.

Some Argue that News Content Should be Regulated by the Government

Media professionals have their own organisation, the **Press Complaints Commission (PCC)**, to **monitor standards** and deal with **audience complaints**. This means the **content** of the press is **self-regulated**. **Social media bloggers** aren't regulated, so they have more **freedom**. However, they still have to **obey the law** — contempt of court laws are designed to stop them from publishing anything that might **damage** a **court case**, and **libel** laws are designed to stop them from publishing **lies**.

1) In **2011**, it was widely reported that **journalists** writing for the now disbanded British newspaper *The News of the World* had been **hacking** into the **mobile phones** of people connected to **major news stories**.

2) This triggered the **Leveson Inquiry (2011-12)**. It looked at whether **the press** should be **allowed** to carry on **self-regulating** through bodies like the **PCC** or be regulated by the **government** instead.

3) In the end, the Leveson Inquiry recommended that the **PCC** should be **replaced** by a body with **legal backing**, to make press **self-regulation** more **effective**. It did **not** recommend **government regulation** of the press, though.

- The debate over the **freedom of the press** is pretty important. Some believe it's the **duty** of the press to hold **powerful people** to **account**. Allowing the **government** to **regulate** the press would **limit** its ability to do this.

- On the other hand, sociologist **Paul Hodkinson** argued in 2012 that the idea that the press **represent** 'the people' against those in **power** is actually **false**. He points out that the **Leveson Inquiry** revealed that the press have sometimes **worked with** the **government** and **police** in a way that's **not** in the **public's best interest**.

Practice Questions

Q1 Describe what is meant by 'news values'.
Q2 Explain how the process of gate-keeping takes place in news production.
Q3 Give two examples of ways that new media have influenced the presentation of the news.
Q4 What was the Leveson Inquiry and what did it recommend?

Exam Question

Q1 Analyse two explanations for why journalists can be said to create rather than discover the news.   [10 marks]

I always thought it was funny how the day's events exactly fill the newspaper...

You think you know what news is, and then you read these pages. Suddenly, you know a lot more, but everything isn't so clear-cut any more. News is as much of a social construct as anything else. People choose what to put in the papers and on the telly, and people aren't unbiased and neutral — they're affected by all sorts of social factors, and all sorts of ideas.

Media Representations

The media often stereotypes ethnic minorities, gay people, old people, young people and disabled people. That's a lot of people.

Media Messages about Gender are Stereotyped

Most **editors** are **men**. **Croteau and Hoynes (2000)** found that in the mid 1990s in the US only 6% of top newspaper management and only 20% of top TV management were women. Also, women **don't appear in the media as often as men**. **Cumberbatch (1990)** found 90% of all advertising voice-overs were male and 66% of all people in adverts were male.

There are male and female stereotypes in the media

1) Women in the media are often presented as **ideals** for other women to aspire to. **Naomi Wolf (1990)** and **Susan Orbach (1991)** both reckon that the rise in eating disorders in women is a direct result of this.
2) The media tends to portray women in a **limited range** of roles. **Tuchman (1978)** argued there were only two female roles portrayed in the media: **domestic** and **sexual**. He said that the **achievements** of women are presented as less important than their **sex appeal** — this is a form of **'symbolic annihilation'**.
3) Women are often represented as **victims** (e.g. of sexual or domestic violence) by the media.
4) **Ferguson (1983)** researched **women's magazines**, and found they gave **advice and training** on being (stereotypically) **feminine** — i.e. **sexual**, **domestic** and **romantic**.
5) Some adverts portray **men** as **incompetent** at stereotypically female **domestic tasks**.
6) Action films portray **men** as **violent**, and show male violence in a **positive** way.

'Symbolic annihilation' happens when a social group is represented negatively or falsely, or is completely ignored.

Media stereotypes of gender are often influenced by binary opposition

1) **Binary opposition** means looking at the world in terms of **pairs of opposites**. **Levi-Strauss (1963)** said that one half of a binary opposite pair is **culturally marked** as being **more positive** than the other. For example, in the binary opposition of **male/female**, male is culturally determined as positive.
2) The **media** often **uses** these binary oppositions in **stereotypical** representations of gender — e.g. by portraying women as housewives and men as breadwinners.
3) **Binary opposition** includes the idea of **'the other'**. The **dominant** half of the binary pair (men) is seen as the **normal**, standard, regular version. The half of the binary pair perceived less positively (women) is the **'other'**.

Some Sociologists argue that Gender Representation in the Media is Changing

1) **Westwood (1999)** argues that there are lots of **female characters** on **TV** and in **film** who **do not conform** to gender roles. These characters are seen as **'transgressive'**, because they **go beyond** stereotypical representations of women.
2) **Gauntlett (2002)** identified **changes** in media portrayal of **masculinity**. He found that some **men's magazines** mirrored the format of **women's magazines**, with advice on health, looking good and attracting the opposite sex. They often promoted the **'metrosexual male'**, who cares about **how he looks**, **respects women** and displays traditionally **feminine traits**. However, Gauntlett also says that many men's magazines still **sexualise** women.
3) Gauntlett says that **diverse** representation of gender creates a **wider range** of gendered images to **choose** from.
4) Postmodernists like **Hermes (1995)** think people can **reject media messages** about gender.

Representations of Sexuality in the media are Stereotyped

'LGBT' means lesbian, gay, bisexual and transgender.

The media often presents **inaccurate stereotypes** of **LGBT** groups, or **ignores** them altogether. As a result, media representation of people with LGBT identities can be **negative** or even **non-existent**. This is another form of **'symbolic annihilation'**.

- **Batchelor (2004)** said media representations of homosexuality often suggest that being gay is an embarrassing problem. She also argued that lesbianism was completely ignored by media aimed at young people.
- **Craig (1992)** argues that gay men are often stereotyped as either 'camp', 'macho' or 'deviant'. Many TV shows use 'camp' gay characters as comic relief. Being gay is often characterised as a problem — lots of gay characters are presented as struggling with their sexuality.

See p.53 for more on representation of homosexual relationships in the media.

Gauntlett (2008) argues that things are improving — people are now more **accepting** of a wide range of sexual identities. **Positive representation** of sexuality in the media is **increasing**. Gauntlett argues that this will lead to more **acceptance**.

Media Representations

Disabled People are Under-represented in the Media

1) There's **very little representation of disabled people** in the media. **Cumberbatch et al (2014)** studied a selection of the **most popular** British factual, drama and entertainment **TV programmes**. UK government statistics show that about **19%** of the population has some form of disability, but their study found that people with disabilities had a far lower proportion of **speaking roles** in these programmes.

2) **Fictional representations** of disability (both **supporting characters** and **lead characters** who were important to the plot or narrative) were slightly **more common**.

> **Roles for disabled people can be quite limited.**
>
> Research by **Cumberbatch and Negrine (1992)** looking at British TV over six weeks found the roles for disabled people were based on **pity** or **comedy**. They found that **disabled actors** never appeared **just as actors** playing a person who **just happened to have a disability**, only in **roles particularly about disability**.
>
> However, there are **some positive portrayals** of disabled people in films and on TV — e.g. of Stephen Hawking's experience of **motor neurone disease** in *The Theory of Everything*. **Cumberbatch et al (2014)** also discovered that roles for disabled people on **popular TV** are now **more likely** to be **serious** than comedic.

3) Disabled people are **poorly represented** in **powerful positions** in the media. Those who do hold powerful positions have often **specialised** in disabled issues. For example, the **radio journalist** Peter White (who was **born blind**) hosted **radio shows** about disability before becoming a **disability correspondent** and reporting on the **2008 Beijing Olympic games**.

> **Sociologists have looked at the link between media representation and stereotypes of disability.**
>
> 1) **Barnes (1992)** argued that disabled people are often presented as being **reliant** on the **charity** of others — shows like *Children in Need* may **reinforce** this **stereotype** without meaning to. He also noted that people with disability tend to be presented as being unable to **contribute** to their **local community**.
>
> 2) **Audience response** depends on people's **actual experience** of disability. **Cumberbatch and Negrine** found that people with limited or **no real-life experience** of disability **accepted** the media stereotypes with **little concern**. People **with experience** of disability were **critical** of the media and **rejected** stereotyped images.

Some Sociologists say there are Class Stereotypes in the Media

1) Media **editors** and **executives** are almost all **middle class**. **Middle-class** people also **appear on TV** more often than working-class people, both in **dramas** and on **news** programmes.

2) **Drama roles** for working-class characters are mostly limited to **soap operas**. **Upper-class** characters are often seen in **historical costume dramas** — which tend to give a **romantic** picture of life and class.

3) **News** often represents **working-class** people as a **source of trouble** — 'anti-social behaviour', riots, strikes, crime, etc. The neo-Marxist **Glasgow University Media Group (1982)** suggest that the media is spreading the view that the working class are trouble to ensure the dominance of capitalist ideology (see p.178 for more on this).

Emotional costume dramas could be too much for Marvin.

> ### <u>Glennon and Butsch (1982) looked at 40 years of families on TV in the USA</u>
>
> They found that only **4% of sitcoms** featured a family where the head of household was a **manual worker**. In real life, **36%** of American families were like this. Nearly **half** the **TV families** had a **professional** as head of household — in real life, only **25%** were like this. Most of the TV families were wealthy and glamorous.
>
> Glennon and Butsch thought that most **working-class dads** were portrayed as **stupid** and **comical**, for the audience to laugh at.

4) **Newman (2006)** argues that the media gives **positive attention** to things that only the **wealthy** can afford. For example, **newspapers** devote lots of **space** to reporting on **stocks** and **shares**, but most of the UK population don't own any. According to Newman, the media **blames** the working class for **poverty** and **unemployment** and when **poverty** is discussed, the media talks about **statistics**, instead of **human suffering**.

This is their opinion, not necessarily what the TV audience thought.

Media Representations

Media Stereotypes can Influence Class Identity

Research from **Medhurst (1999)** showed that when middle-class students were shown the programme *The Royle Family*, which featured **deliberately exaggerated** and **stereotypical** working-class characters, they thought it was an **accurate** portrayal of **working-class life**.

Roger overdid things a little when he tried to fit in with his upper-class friends.

Stuart Hall (1982, 1992, 1996) thinks that the media has always portrayed the **middle classes** in a **positive** light and the **working class** in a **negative** light. He says that the media has **reinforced** people's class identities — which keeps the **divide** between the classes going strong.

Media Representations of Ethnicity are often Stereotyped

Cumberbatch et al (2014) looked at representations of ethnicity in TV programmes

When **Cumberbatch et al (2014)** studied the **60 most popular** British factual, entertainment and drama **TV programmes**, they found that the **percentage** of people from ethnic minorities who held a **speaking role** in these shows was **quite representative** of the overall **proportion** of ethnic minorities in the UK population.

However, some ethnic minority groups were **over-represented** (e.g. Black African Caribbean groups) and some were **under-represented** (e.g. South Asian groups).

The study found that people from ethnic minorities are **most likely** to appear in **entertainment shows**. They're also fairly well represented in **factual** shows as '**key contributors**' (e.g. interviewees). However, representation in more major roles is limited — ethnic minorities are **less likely** to be **presenters** or have **lead roles** in drama.

1) **New technology** means there are now more specialist satellite and digital TV and radio channels. These often **cater for specific ethnic minorities** and they're controlled by people from those ethnic minorities (e.g. Bangla TV, BBC Asian Network). However, there aren't many people from ethnic minorities in positions of **power** in **mainstream media**.

2) Tabloid newspapers sometimes stereotype some ethnic minority groups as being a **problem** or a **threat**. **Van Dijk (1991)** made a detailed content analysis of **headlines** in five British national newspapers. He argued that there was often an **association** in the headlines between **ethnic minorities** and **violent** and **negative language**.

3) Some media representations of **multiculturalism** have been **criticised**:

Media portrayal of **ethnic minorities** can also be part of a media representation of **multiculturalism** (e.g. TV and newspaper coverage of the Notting Hill carnival). Some representations of multiculturalism are **utopian** (they suggest that everything's perfect) and some admit there are **problems**, e.g. the film *Bend It Like Beckham*.

Cottle (2000) points out that media portrayals of ethnic minorities **reinforce** views of **non-whites** as the '**other**' (see p.180). He also criticises media portrayals of **multiculturalism**. He says that they **gloss over problems** such as **power imbalances** between different ethnic groups, and the historical effects of **colonialism** and **racism**.

Audiences May React to Ethnic Stereotypes in Different Ways

Hartmann and Husband (1974) analysed **children's responses** to media. They **compared** the responses of children in **two** parts of Britain.

- In an area with **low ethnic mix**, children **believed** negative media content and thought of 'race relations' in terms of **conflict**. In the area with a **high ethnic mix**, children **rejected** media stereotypes in favour of their **own experience**.

- Therefore, **audience response** to ethnic minority stereotypes varies depending on the **real-life experience** of the **audience**. People don't always accept media stereotypes if they **know** better themselves.

Media Representations

Images of Young and Old are Stereotyped in the media

1) There's often a sexist **double standard** in the way older people are represented in the media. The **older** a **woman** gets, the **less likely** she is to get a leading film role or a TV presenting job. It's a different story for men. Older male actors like Sean Connery and Harrison Ford are 'allowed' to be romantically paired with young women. There are lots more **older men presenting TV programmes** than there are older women.

2) **Biggs (1993)** found lots of representation of **older people** in entertainment shows. However, they were often in **stereotyped roles** like 'forceful', 'vague' and 'difficult'.

3) In America, **Signorelli (1989)** studied prime-time TV characters and found that both young and old were under-represented — TV representation was biased towards **middle-aged** people.

4) **Featherstone and Hepworth (1995)** found that magazines for older people tended to push ← an image of 'youthful' older people — enjoying holidays, wearing 'young-looking' clothes, etc.

The media is starting to appeal to older people — advertisers have recognised that they can make money from an ageing population.

5) **Newman (2006)** found that **class** influences representation of age. Older **upper-class** and **middle-class** people are often cast in TV dramas as characters with **high social status** and **advanced careers**.

6) There are also **stereotypes** relating to **young people**. **Children** are often represented as **innocent**. Slightly older '**youth**' are often seen as a **social problem** — prone to drug abuse, binge drinking, petty crime and unplanned pregnancy.

Wayne et al (2008) looked at the representation of young people in the **news**.

1) They found that young people are often presented as a **threat** to the rest of **society**. Also, they have **few opportunities** to express their **views**, which means they can't **influence** the way they are presented in the media.

2) As a result, the serious **problems** that young people may face (e.g. unemployment, money issues and poor mental health) are often **devalued** or **ignored**. **Lack of sympathy** for young people can make these problems **worse**, because the **government** and the rest of **society** don't think they're **important** enough to address.

Changes in Media Representation of Young Girls are Linked to Consumer Culture

McRobbie (2008) argued that, in the last few decades, media representations of **young girls** have **changed**.

1) In the **1970s**, **young girls** were often presented in **magazines** as being '**passive**' and **led** by a desire to **impress boys**. By the **1990s**, TV shows and magazines aimed at **young girls** moved away from this representation. They used the language of '**Girl Power**' to suggest that girls were **free** to be what they wanted to be.

2) This presented girls as **active consumers** who could **choose** how to express themselves. McRobbie argued that the media wanted to create a **consumer market** for products aimed at **young girls** and **women**. The media even encourages **young girls** to **desire products** aimed at **teenagers**, so that they will become consumers too.

Practice Questions

Q1 Briefly explain the findings of Cumberbatch and Negrine (1992) about disabled people and the media.

Q2 Give an example of newspaper bias in relation to ethnic minorities in Britain.

Q3 How does real-life experience affect how people respond to stereotypes in the media?

Exam Question

Q1 Apply your own knowledge and material from Item A to evaluate the idea that media representations of age are based on stereotypes.

[20 marks]

> **Item A**
> News reports involving young people often suggest that they pose a threat to society. Fictional representations of teenagers also focus on the idea that young people are wayward and have lots of problems. Representation of older people on TV is often quite negative, and can suggest they are difficult or forceful.

I've got lots of stereo-types — my MP3, my CD player...

The stuff on these pages makes you think a bit. Loads of studies show how ethnicity, gender, class, disability, age or sexuality (phew... I think that's all of them) have been stereotyped in the media — and some identities aren't represented in the media at all. Things have changed for the better in some cases, but the media has a long way to go before it treats everyone equally.

Media and its Audience

The media constructs and sends out messages to the public — but the impact of the messages depends on how the audience responds. People can accept media messages, or dismiss them as complete rubbish.

The **Hypodermic Syringe** Model — Media **Directly Influence Audience**

Way back in the **1920s**, when **radio** and **newspapers** were just starting to get **important** in society, sociologists developed theories about how the media affected people.

1) The **hypodermic syringe model** says the media **injects** its message into the mind of the audience in the same way as drugs are **directly injected** into the body. The idea is that the media is **so powerful**, its message **directly influences** the individual and they're **powerless** to **resist** the message or **reject** it.

2) This theory says that **all individuals** in the audience are **affected** in the **same way**.

> In **1938**, Orson Welles recorded a radio production of H G Wells' story *The War of the Worlds* in which Martians invade Earth. The broadcast included **fictional news bulletins** reporting the Martian invasion. Some radio listeners **believed** the fake bulletins were true, and **panicked**.
>
> This was used as **evidence** of the **dangerous** and **direct power of the media**, and it created concern in society. For the people who believed in the hypodermic syringe model it was proof enough.

3) Some sociologists decided that the hypodermic syringe model was **too simplistic** to explain how adults view media content. Critics of the hypodermic syringe model think it treats people as **passive** and very easily led.

4) Critics also point out that **not all audience members react in the same way** to the same piece of media (see next page). Studies showed this as far back as the 1920s. It did stay popular as a theory of how the **media** can **influence children**, though (see p.186).

> **The growth of new media means that audiences can directly influence the media too**
>
> During the **refugee crisis** in **2015**, photographs of the body of 3-year-old **Aylan Kurdi**, a **Syrian refugee** who drowned off the coast of Turkey, were **shared** on social media. Lots of people used the images to **criticise European governments** for their approach to the crisis. After this, **mainstream media messages** about refugees became **more sympathetic** — they fell in line with the attitudes their **audience** had shown on social media.

The Media Message is **Interpreted** and **Passed On** by **Key Individuals**

The **two-step flow model** was developed in the 1950s. It says that the media does influence people, but **not everyone is influenced directly**.

1) The **first step** is the **media message** reaching an audience member. All simple so far.

2) The important **second step** is how their **understanding** of the message is **shaped** by **social interaction** with other audience members. For example, if workers in an office chat about a soap opera during their coffee break then these discussions affect individuals' opinions of the storyline and characters.

3) **Katz and Lazarsfeld (1955)** said that there were **key individuals** in each community whose reaction **directly influenced others**. These 'opinion leaders' openly expressed their reaction and opinions, and others **followed** their lead.

4) Katz and Lazarsfeld studied **media influence on American voters**. They concluded that most people followed the opinion leader's views on who they should vote for, but the opinion leaders themselves often got their **ideas straight from the media** messages.

5) It doesn't have to be just two steps — a message can go through several stages of interpretation. **Hobson (1990)** studied an office environment and found that a few **key individuals** influenced what the others watched on television and their **reactions** to the programmes. These opinions were **passed on** to another bunch of colleagues. A **social norm** of what to watch **spread** through the **whole office**. **New recruits** had to **conform** to fit in.

"Did you see X Factor last night, George?"

> It's easy to imagine this happening: "Did you see The Great British Bake Off?" "Wasn't that cake a disaster?" If you don't watch the show, you're left out of the conversation. If you don't agree with the opinion leader, you're made to feel like an outsider.

Media and its Audience

Social and Cultural Context affect how an Audience Responds to the Media

1) **Cultural effects theory** introduced the idea that **social context** is important when looking at the effects of the media. In short, this theory claims that **different people** interpret the media in **different ways**.

2) The idea is that an audience **interprets the media** in the **context** of the **culture** they already belong to. This means that the **effect** of the media is quite **complex** — it's not the same for everyone.

3) 'Culture' refers to the **small, subcultural groups** an individual belongs to and also to the **wider, general culture of society**. For example, in England an individual's response to Arsenal winning the Premiership will **depend** on whether the **individual** supports Arsenal. But audience response to media reports of **England winning the World Cup** would be broadly **similar** for most of the population because there's a **cultural norm** of supporting your country's sports teams.

> Here's a **second look** at the audience response to the *War of the Worlds* broadcast — this time from a **cultural effects viewpoint (Cantril, 1940)**.
>
> 1) The response was **caused** by the **cultural context** in which it was heard. If it was on the radio **today** it wouldn't create the same response.
>
> 2) At the time of the broadcast there was **insecurity** in American society because of a **financial crisis** and the move towards **war in Europe**. Radio programmes were **frequently interrupted** for news reports, and there was a general expectation of bad news.
>
> 3) People **wouldn't have been surprised** to hear a **real report** of bad news interrupting a drama programme on the radio. This made it **more likely** that some members of the audience would **believe** the story.

A key criticism of the cultural effects approach is that it's hard to quantify 'causes' and 'effects', e.g. it's hard to measure the intensity of effects like 'fear' or 'panic'.

We interrupt this A-level sociology book...

4) Neo-Marxist **Stuart Hall (1980)** argued that the media has **dominant ideological** messages 'encoded' into it, but that people of different backgrounds can '**decode**' these messages differently — with varying degrees of **agreement** or **opposition** to the ideology expressed.

Media Reporting of Deviance can Cause Moral Panic

> **Stan Cohen (1973)** described how **media reporting** of expected 'trouble' could **create a moral panic**.
>
> 1) Cohen used the example of the **Mods and Rockers** in the 1960s. The media reported that there would be **fights** between two youth subcultures — the Mods and the Rockers.
>
> 2) Lots of people turned up to fight or watch, partly because of the **media publicity**. The public then **panicked** over reports of how many people turned up to fight.
>
> *Moral panic — public demands that something is done about it*
>
> Small group behaves in a deviant way → Media report the story → Media report similar stories again → Original group labelled as threat to social order → More people join in with deviant behaviour

The Effects of Media Messages Build Up Over Time

1) Media effects can build up over time to **create** or **reinforce** cultural **norms**.

2) For example, **images of women** in the media create **stereotypical images** and place **expectations** on girls and women. There's been a long-running campaign by some feminists to remove pictures of **topless women** ('Page Three Girls') from national newspapers, because they argue that these images **reinforce** the dominant view that it's OK to **objectify women** as sex objects. *The Sun* newspaper **ended** its 'page three' feature in **January 2015**.

3) Some theorists think it's not just the **content** of the media that has a long-term effect on society — the **technology** of the media has an impact too. For example, internet technology has transformed the way people communicate, shop, apply for jobs etc.

The big catchphrase to remember from McLuhan is 'The medium is the message.'

> **Marshall McLuhan (1964)** claimed that media technology actually had a **greater effect** on society than media content — it's the **type** of media we consume that matters. He said **different forms** of media can be described as 'hot' or 'cool'. '**Hot' media**, like films, don't require much **effort** to be understood, but '**cool' media**, like comics, need to be **interpreted** by the reader. Different forms of media require different levels of **engagement**.

4) It's **difficult** to **objectively measure** long-term media effects, so the discussion of long-term effects is mostly **theoretical**.

Media and its Audience

Sociologists have looked at the **Effects** of **Violent Media** on **Audiences**

Lots of research has focused on the **effects** of **violent media** on the **behaviour** of **audiences**. Sociologists have focused on **young children** in particular, as they are often seen as **impressionable** (they might **repeat** behaviour that they see).

1) **Newson (1994)** says that you can become 'desensitised' to violence if you see enough of it on **TV** and in **films** and **games** — this means you get **used** to seeing violence in the media, so you don't see it as **shocking** any more.

2) The most famous example of **violent media effects research** is **Bandura et al (1963)**. They argued that **children** who are **exposed** to violent media go on to **imitate** violent behaviour that they've seen.

- **Bandura et al (1963)** played children a **film of a man hitting a doll**. They then left the children to play with the **same doll** which they'd seen on the film.
- The children who'd seen the violence on film hit the doll, while those who hadn't seen the film played with the doll in a non-violent way.
- Bandura et al said this showed that **violent media could cause violent behaviour**.

The **hypodermic syringe model** (p.184) has been used to link **fictional media violence** with **shootings**.

1) In 2012, a gunman killed 12 people at a screening of the Batman film *The Dark Knight Rises* in Aurora, Colorado. He was dressed as the villain from the film, the Joker, who commits various acts of violence throughout the film.

2) This caused the media to link the attack to the film itself — they suggested that the gunman was directly influenced by this violence. Other mass shootings in America are often blamed on violent films and computer games, even when there is no evidence that an attacker has consumed, or been influenced by, violent media.

The **Glasgow University Media Group** has Researched **Media Effects**

The **Glasgow University Media Group** (GUMG) has looked at **media effects** since **1974**.

1) The GUMG has done a lot of research into the **effects** of **news** and **current affairs** reporting. They **analyse** media content by looking at its **messages** and **values**.

2) They have also **surveyed** and **interviewed audiences** to find out how much **influence** the media has on them.

> **The GUMG argue that the media strongly affect audiences' attitudes and beliefs**

They studied **reactions** to reports of **violence** during the **miners' strike of 1984-5**. **54%** of their **audience sample**, who had seen **media coverage** of the strike, **believed** that the **picket lines** were mostly **violent**. **Police** and people who were on the picket line said that there wasn't as much **violence** as the media suggested. The audience based their **beliefs** on what the media **told** them was happening.

Some have **Criticised** the Idea that **Violent Media** have **Negative Effects**

Others have **criticised** the idea that violent media **normalise violence**.

Cumberbatch (2004) says there is still **no clear evidence** that **violent media** influence the **behaviour** of children or adults. He reviewed over **3500 research studies** about the effects of violent media. According to him, **none** of these studies **prove** for certain that a link exists.

'Sensitisation' is the opposite of 'desensitisation' (when you get used to violence and respond to it less).

Young (1981) argues that violent media may actually have a **positive effect** on **attitudes** towards violence. He says that viewing violent media may result in 'sensitisation' to violent crime, because it **increases awareness** of the **consequences** of violent acts. Individuals can **learn** from **fictionalised examples** of violence (and their **aftermath**) — as a result, they may **avoid** committing violent crimes.

Fesbach and Sanger (1971) argued that violent media give people an **opportunity** to let out all of their **aggression** in a **positive way**. For example, shouting at a computer game is a **safe** way to **release anger** and **relieve** negative emotion, because nobody gets hurt. This process is known as '**catharsis**'.

Media and its Audience

David Gauntlett *thinks* Effects Research *has been Pretty* Ineffective

Gauntlett (2008) criticises some of the methods used in effects research. He's positive about the effects research done by the GUMG, but he criticises most other media effects research.

1) For example, he attacks the experimental method used by Bandura et al in their doll experiment (see p.186). This experiment was carried out in a laboratory environment. Gauntlett thinks this makes the results of the experiment artificial, because the experiment doesn't reflect the way children behave in the real world. Away from the lab, children are influenced by their parents and other children, and might behave differently.

2) He also says that lots of effects research is based on a myth that children are powerless puppets of the media. Other research suggests that children can recognise from an early age that it's not acceptable to imitate fictional violence.

3) Gauntlett prefers to use what he calls imaginative methods. For example, he asked a group of schoolchildren in Leeds to make their own videos about the environment, and then he observed the results. He studied the children in their natural setting, instead of in a lab — this is called an ethnographic study (see p.18).

Bess liked to do 'the YMCA' whenever her owners weren't looking.

There are Other Criticisms of Media Effects Models

1) Some argue that media effects studies don't always make it clear what they mean by 'violence' — often, they only look at fictional violence. They often don't consider how audiences will react to different kinds of violence.

2) This is a problem for research that uses the hypodermic syringe model (p.184). This method doesn't take account of how different people in an audience react. Age is a factor, but so is maturity — for example, some ten-year-olds are more mature than others, so they will have different reactions to the media.

3) Morrison (1999) thinks that context is key — some studies ignore the fact that violent media are presented in different contexts, which can affect the way the audience interprets the violence. For example, viewing violence that is meant to be funny or that appears in a comic context may have a different effect to seeing images of brutal violence in a real-life warzone.

Practice Questions

Q1 Briefly explain the hypodermic syringe model of media influence.

Q2 Define the two steps in the two-step flow model of media influence.

Q3 Explain what's meant by the term 'opinion leader'.

Q4 Briefly explain cultural effects theory.

Q5 Give two reasons why media effects research methods can be criticised, according to Gauntlett.

Exam Questions

Q1 Outline two arguments which support the view that violent media can affect audiences. Explain each one. [10 marks]

Q2 By applying material from Item A, analyse two arguments that support the idea that audiences are directly affected by media messages. [10 marks]

> **Item A**
> Audiences can be affected by images and messages that are transmitted through the media. People often discuss what they've seen in the media with other people and share their opinions. Sociologists have developed different models to study and explain how media might affect audiences.

The hypodermic syringe model — it gets right under your skin...

This theory lark can be a bit tricky. You read one theory and think, "ah, that explains it", then you read the next theory and think, "ah, that explains it" — and they're two totally contradictory theories. I suppose they can both be right some of the time, or they can give you different parts of the picture. The most important thing is that you can write about them in the exam.

Interpreting the Media

Here's more about how people interpret what they see and hear from the media. Some sociologists think people can be quite active in deciding what media messages they want to see and hear.

Audiences *Actively Use* and *Interpret* the Media to *Suit Their Own Needs*

Some theories argue that the audience responds **actively** to media content and messages. Instead of 'what the **media** does **to** people', they look at 'what **people** do **with** the media'.

Uses and Gratifications Theory

1) This theory was developed by theorists such as **Blumer and Katz (1974)** and says that people **use** the media to **meet their needs**. The audience **actively chooses** what media to experience, using such cutting-edge tools as free will and the remote control. Everyone chooses for themselves, so each person's media diet is **unique**.

2) A good example is the study of **soap opera audiences** by McQuail (1972). He looked at how audiences used **Coronation Street** to fulfil a need for **social companionship**. Many audiences felt part of the characters' lives and felt interest and concern for what would happen next in a storyline.

3) **Lull (1990)** listed the social uses of television in the UK — and found men, women, young and old all used the media to meet different needs.

4) Uses and gratification theory is **functionalist** — it says that the media exists to serve the **needs** of the public.

Ben chose to use his computer to fulfil his need for games, homework and plotting world domination.

In media language, 'to engage with' a piece of media means to find it interesting and pay attention to it — to be 'into' it.

Selective Filter Model

1) This theory says the audience **choose** which media to **experience** and also **control** which parts of the media message to pay attention to and **engage with**. The audience pick out the parts of a message which **fit in with their view of the world** and **ignore the rest**.

2) **Fiske (1988)** says individuals become very **experienced readers of the media**. He says that individuals can understand one '**media text**' in several **different ways** on several **different levels** — and in relation to **other** '**media texts**' on the same subject.

'Media text' means a piece of media — e.g. a TV programme, a newspaper article or an advert.

3) **Klapper (1960)** argued that to get its message across, the media has to go through **three selective filters**:

- **Selective exposure** — people only consume the media they want and are able to get.
- **Selective perception** — people ignore messages they don't want to hear.
- **Selective retention** — people tend to remember only what they agree with.

Klapper said this makes it easier for the media to **reinforce** what people think than to **change** people's minds.

4) This model emphasises the **power of the individual** to control his/her experience of the media and says that people use media in a **sophisticated** way. It's a little **postmodern** in that way.

5) The selective filter model has been criticised for **overestimating** the control of the individual over very **powerful media messages**.

Structured Interpretation Model

1) This theory says there's a **dominant interpretation** of media messages which audiences go along with. Like the other two theories, individuals actively **pick** which media they **engage with**, but this theory says the process takes place in a **social context**. The social context creates a '**preferred reading**' of the media message (by 'reading' they mean 'interpretation'). For example, a film is written, presented and promoted with a **preferred reading** in mind — the makers of a film like *Spectre* want you to find the story **intriguing** and **convincing**, not stilted and boring.

2) **Different social groups** have **different dominant interpretations** of the same text. So, this theory isn't the same as earlier theories which saw the audience as a mass who all respond in the same way.

3) **Morley (1980)** studied how the television audience responded to one **news programme** — *Nationwide*. He showed the same programme to several **different social groups** and found that their responses to the programme **varied** hugely, **but within each group** most individuals responded in the **same way**. Trade unionists saw it as biased towards management, and management trainees saw it as pro-union.

Interpreting the Media

Postmodern Theory says the audience gets Lots of Meanings

- Postmodernists say that there are many, many meanings to any social or cultural aspect of life. They say there isn't any aspect of life where there's one single, objective truth or reality that absolutely everyone experiences.
- The postmodern audience picks and chooses between a range of images, messages, ideas and meanings.

Postmodern Theory also says the Media Takes the Place of Reality

1) The development of the media and technology have meant everyday life is **chock-full of images** and messages competing and **conflicting** with each other. The media presents so many different images and stories **woven into everyday life** that the boundary between **reality and the media** is **blurred** — the **media becomes reality**.

- The explosion of **reality TV** and the **obsessive interest** people have with **soap stars** are good examples of this. With **reality TV, real** people get put in an **unreal situation** which is presented as **real**, and the audience follows it like a **soap**. With a soap, **pretend** characters get treated by the press and by audiences **as if they're real**.
- There's an example with **news media** — when something's on the news, it seems like that '**proves**' it's real and true. Images on the news can be taken out of context, though. And news is **influenced** by all kinds of factors (see pages 177-179). The news isn't **objective truth**. But the news is presented as reality, and **becomes reality**.

2) This idea is related to the **postmodernist** idea of a **simulacrum** (p.110). A simulacrum is something that **looks real**, but **isn't**. It's like a copy but **without any kind of connection** to the **original**. Postmodernist theorists say that these simulacra actually **replace** reality. 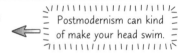 Postmodernism can kind of make your head swim.

3) French postmodernist **Jean Baudrillard (1981, 1994)** suggested that **everything** had been replaced by simulacra. He called this replacement of reality **hyper-reality** — he said that hyper-real images seemed **more real than real**, and that meant they took over from reality. He suggested that **obviously made-up images** were used to give people the impression that they could **tell reality from a simulacrum** when in fact they **couldn't**.

4) In *The Gulf War Did Not Take Place*, **Baudrillard (1995)** argued that the 1991 Gulf War existed more as images on TV screens than as actual fighting. The Gulf War as media **spectacle** or video game type **simulation** became reality.

5) In the media, a piece of information or an image can be **distorted** intentionally in order to **make it appear correct** to viewers. So it's actually **made less true** in order to **appear more true**.

Critics say Postmodernism is too Theoretical and too Obscure

1) **Critics of Baudrillard** say his writing is **deliberately obscure**, and that it **dismisses** the reality of **suffering** and **inequality**.

2) **Postmodernism** has also been **criticised** for being **too theoretical**. It's really **hard to find** (or even think of) any kind of **evidence** which would **prove** postmodernism **right** or **wrong**.

3) I mean, if you're starting out from the premise that no idea has a **straightforward meaning** and individuals create their **own reality** so that there's no one definition of what's '**real**' or '**true**' and that reality has been **replaced** with something that just looks a lot like it — *where on earth do you go from there...*

Practice Questions

Q1 Give an example of a criticism of the selective filter model of audience response.

Q2 Explain the term 'preferred reading' in relation to the media.

Q3 What are simulacra?

Exam Question

Q1 Outline two ways that media audiences actively select and filter the content and messages they receive. Explain each one. [10 marks]

Whenever I fancy feeling like I've shoved my head in a blender...

... I read a little bit of postmodernism. There is kind of a point behind it, though. If you narrow it down to 'people treat media images as if they're real when they're not' and 'it's hard to tell images from reality', then it's not so bad. Having said that, I dare you to read some of Baudrillard's actual work — I only made it through a few pages before I started to question my entire existence.

Globalisation and Popular Culture

The global nature of the media has an effect on society. This all links back to the Culture and Identity topic. If you didn't study that, don't worry — just take a look at p.36-37 and p.56-57 to help you get to grips with these pages.

Media Culture is Popular Culture — some say the Media is 'Dumbed Down'

Culture can be divided into **high** and **low** culture, with high culture being seen as 'good' for society. The division of culture is often considered an elitist **binary opposition** (see p.180).

1) Other theorists refer to **mass culture**, which is passed on by the **media**. **Popular culture** is another way of looking at the culture of the **'masses'**. Some theorists prefer it as it's a more **positive** term than low culture.

2) The idea of **popular culture** is based on an **active audience** who can shape their culture, unlike the concept of **mass culture** which relies on a **passive, media-controlled audience**.

1) There's a debate about 'dumbing down' in the media — simplifying content and avoiding intellectually challenging the audience. For example, the news contains more sensationalism and celebrity gossip than it used to.

2) Popular classical artists such as Katherine Jenkins, Il Divo, etc. can be seen as popularising high culture and bringing it into mainstream popular culture — or as replacing high culture with a dumbed down mass culture substitute.

3) The dumbing down argument isn't new. Back in 1869, the poet and social commentator Matthew Arnold feared that high culture was under threat.

4) Pluralists argue that audiences get the media they want. So dumbing down can't be the fault of the media.

5) Frank Furedi (2004) claims that intentionally simplifying cultural content is itself an elitist activity — it's not done by the 'masses' but done for them, and it assumes that they are too stupid to understand complex content.

The Media is a Global Industry and creates a Global Culture

In recent decades, there has been **concentration of media ownership** — a few media corporations dominate the global market (see p.173). This has caused **media globalisation**.

1) **Devereux (2003)** points out that most of the large media corporations are based in the West, so images from **Western** societies **dominate** the global media market.

2) Commercial **satellite** and **cable TV** services mean that media content can be broadcast across the world.

3) **Global advertising** has contributed to the growth of **global capitalism**. **Strinati (1995)**, a postmodernist, said that media promotes the **consumption** of logos and brands, which fuels this **global economy** and **global culture**.

4) Some sociologists argue that **governments** in Europe and the US have **deregulated** the media. These governments allow **capitalist media corporations** to set up **global media networks**, which **allows** the corporations to influence **culture** on a **global scale**.

Global Media has created a 'global village'

1) The idea of the **global village** comes from **McLuhan (1962)**. He suggests that new technologies bring people closer together — our neighbours aren't just next door, they're on the **other side of the world**.

2) We hear **news and gossip** about people all over the world, and we can **talk to people** all over the world. At the time McLuhan was actually writing, this was only on the **phone**, but **new media** technologies like email and blogs are a great example of his ideas.

The internet has changed the relationship between the media and the state — there are no national boundaries on the internet.

The Internet has had an Impact on Global Culture

Globalisation of media exposes us all to **cultural** and **social commentaries** and **news** from lots of countries. This helps us to **understand** how our culture is **similar** to other cultures — we develop a sense of **shared global culture**.

1) **Matos (2012)** argues that, before the development of **new media** in the **1990s**, most of the world's media focused on **national issues**. Now, media have a much more **global outlook** — the **internet** allows newspapers to report on **global events** that affect us all.

2) The **internet** has made global communication **cheap** and **easy**. People can create their **own media content** and share their **cultural experiences** and **values** with others, without direct **government** or **media outlet** involvement.

3) Some think that **new media** will lead to **divisions** in the 'global village' imagined by McLuhan. People who have access to the **internet** and **IT education** will have an **advantage** over people who don't (the **digital underclass** — see p.175).

4) Countries with **better communications** networks will have a **stronger cultural influence** than countries with poorer internet connectivity.

Some sociologists argue that Western culture is becoming the dominant culture around the world. There's more on this on the next page.

Globalisation and Popular Culture

Some Argue that *Globalisation* of the *Media* has led to *Cultural Imperialism*

There is a debate over whether **globalisation** of culture is **harmful** to **national cultures**. Some argue that **Western culture** is **taking over** across the globe — they call this '**cultural imperialism**'. Others say that we're actually experiencing a **blending** of **national** and **global cultures** into lots of **hybrid cultures** — they call this '**cultural hybridisation**'.

Cultural Imperialism

1) **McBride (1980)** suggests that there is **cultural imperialism** — Western media products flow into less developed parts of the world and **change local cultures**. This makes a **ready market** for Western consumer goods.

2) People in many parts of the world share the **same consumption patterns** as a result of **global advertising** from companies such as Disney, SONY, Coca-Cola® and Virgin. The **internet** has allowed **national boundaries** to be **broken down**. Google™ has **revolutionised** the way companies **advertise** to **global audiences**.

3) **Klein (2000)** says that this leads to increasing **cultural homogenisation** — everyone's culture is becoming the **same**.

4) It has been argued that **technological advancement** has made national culture **less important**. The spread of the internet and satellite TV means that **all** countries are '**victims**' of **global cultural homogenisation**.

5) Some theorists claim that globalisation is specifically **Americanisation** — it's American culture that gets copied.

6) There are **four** main **global news agencies** that **media outlets** across the world use as a **source** for news. These agencies have been accused of spreading **Western cultural prejudices** through their reporting.

Cultural Hybridisation

1) Since the **1990s**, some sociologists have suggested that globalisation of culture is actually resulting in **cultural hybridisation** — **local**, **national** and **global** cultures are all **mixing together** to create a series of **hybrid cultures** across the world.

2) **Sreberny-Mohammadi (1996)** suggests that many local cultures have **resisted cultural imperialism**. She points out the strong and **growing media industry** in Asia and South America, which actually **exports media products** back to the West — e.g. **Bollywood** films influence Western culture, and Brazilian soap operas are sold to TV stations all over North America, South America and Europe.

3) This is often referred to as culture moving in '**multidirectional flows**' — culture flows in **lots of directions**, not just from **America** into other countries. This creates **cultural diversity** — **not** cultural homogenisation.

Curran (2000) has Criticised the Theory of Cultural Hybridisation

1) **Curran** argues that some studies that talk about **cultural hybridity** ignore the role of **economic factors**. He argues that **media corporations** use their power to **control** the culture an **audience** is exposed to. This creates certain '**cultural preferences**' among audiences that companies can then capitalise on to **make money**.

2) For example, **Matos (2012)** says that the idea of '**exotic**' **cultural difference** is used by big media companies to make money. They can **advertise** and **sell** 'exotic' products to consumers across the world who have been exposed to lots of **multicultural influences** through the **internet** and **satellite TV**.

For sale: exotic birds. **Reason for selling**: they won't shut up about cultural hybridisation.

Practice Questions

Q1 Why do some theorists prefer the term 'popular culture' to 'low culture'?

Q2 What did McLuhan (1962) mean by a 'global village'?

Q3 Briefly explain two ways that the internet has contributed to globalisation.

Q4 What does 'cultural imperialism' mean?

Exam Question

Q1 Outline two arguments which support the view that media globalisation is damaging national and local cultures. Explain each one. [10 marks]

There'll be no dumbing down around here...

I'm not sure I like all this stuff about dumbing down high culture. Who's to say we shouldn't watch Britain's Got Talent instead of The Royal Ballet? Anyway, make sure you know the difference between cultural imperialism and cultural hybridisation.

Stratification

There are a scary lot of syllables in the title of this section. I'll get some definitions straightened out for you first, don't worry.

Societies are Stratified — divided into Layers

Differentiation means the way a society is **divided up** into different **groups**, e.g. by age, sex, class or religion.

Stratification means the way societies are divided into **layers**. The **most powerful** are at the **top** and the **most powerless** are at the **bottom**. In between are lots of **strata** (layers, like the layers in rock) organised in a **hierarchy**.

A society can be **stratified** by things like **status**, **social class**, **ethnicity**, **gender** and **age**.

Social class is the main stratification system in **modern, Western capitalist societies** like the **UK**. Social class is partly based on **economic** factors — **jobs**, **income** and **wealth**. Social class also has elements of **power** and **prestige**.

Other stratification systems include the **caste system** used in India, and the **feudal system** used in medieval Britain.

Sociologists often talk about Four Social Classes in the UK

It can be **difficult** to **define** social class, but **sociologists** often try to fit people into one of **four** categories:

1) The **upper class** are **wealthy** and **powerful**. Wealth is **passed on from generation to generation**. People who have **become** wealthy (e.g. from business or the entertainment industry) are also sometimes thought of as upper class.

2) The **middle class** earn their money from **non-manual work**. Teachers, doctors, managers and pretty much anyone who **earns their living sitting in an office** are middle class. The middle class is **getting bigger** these days.

3) The **working class** make their money from **manual work**. Farm labourers and factory workers are working class. The working class have **poorer life chances** than the middle class.

4) The **underclass** get their money from **state benefits**. They include the long-term unemployed and the homeless. The underclass have **the poorest life chances**.

> Sociologists have most often focused on the division between the middle class and the working class.

Relating Class to Occupation poses Problems

1) Occupation **does** bring **status** and **prestige** with it. People **judge** each other by the jobs they do.

2) Two individuals in the **same occupational class** can have very different **income** and **prestige** status — e.g. a highly paid consultant neurologist compared to a low paid junior doctor.

3) Basing class entirely on occupation misses out most of the **upper class** — a lot of them **don't have jobs** as such, but live off **rental income** from property, and income from **share ownership**.

4) Using occupation as a measure of social class also **misses out younger generations** who are **not yet working**. Using **education level** as a measure (e.g. whether or not they have a degree) allows sociologists to study social mobility **patterns** for **younger people**.

> **Research** into the prestige of different jobs often only asks about the 20 or so **most common** occupations. The prestige of all the other jobs in society has to be based on **inferences** from these **small-scale** studies.

The Government used to use a scale of Five Classes called the RG scale

1) This scale is called the **Registrar General's Scale** (RG scale), and was used in Britain until 2000.

2) The **never employed** weren't included, and **unemployed** people were classified according to their **last job**.

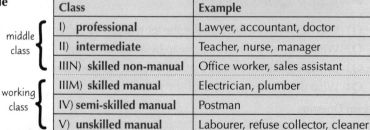

Class	Example
I) professional	Lawyer, accountant, doctor
II) intermediate	Teacher, nurse, manager
IIIN) skilled non-manual	Office worker, sales assistant
IIIM) skilled manual	Electrician, plumber
IV) semi-skilled manual	Postman
V) unskilled manual	Labourer, refuse collector, cleaner

middle class { I), II), IIIN) }
working class { IIIM), IV), V) }

3) The RG scale was based on the **head of household's** occupation (usually the man).

4) **Married women** were classified according to their **husband's job** — this was **sexist**.

5) Also, because the RG scale only considered the head of household's job, it didn't matter what kind of job **other people in the home** had. For example, it **wouldn't distinguish** between a household made up of **two lawyers** and a household made up of a **lawyer** and a **cleaner**.

6) There can be **huge variations** in **income** and **life chances** between different occupations within a class.

> 'Head of household' meant highest male earner, or if no male, highest female earner.

Stratification

The *Government* now uses a scale of *Eight Classes* called the *NS-SEC*

Since 2000, the **government** has used a new scale — the **National Statistics Socio-Economic Classification** (**NS-SEC**). The NS-SEC has **eight classes** based on **type** of employment, rather than **skill level**:

1) **higher managerial** and **professional**	Lawyer, doctor, company director
2) **lower managerial** and **professional**	Nurse, social worker, police officer
3) **intermediate**	Secretary, personal assistant, paramedic
4) **small employers** and **self-employed**	Owner of a restaurant, self-employed plumber
5) **lower supervisory** and **technical**	Builder's foreman, sales floor supervisor in a shop
6) **semi-routine**	Postman, receptionist, sales assistant in a shop
7) **routine**	Waitress, van driver, farm labourer, cleaner
8) **never worked** and **long-term unemployed**	Last worked more than a year ago

Class 1 can be divided into a) large employers and managers, and b) higher professional.

Looking at market situation is a Weberian approach — see p.197.

1) The NS-SEC is based on three areas:
   - **Employment relations** — whether someone is an **employer**, **self-employed** or **employed**, whether they're **salaried** or paid a **weekly wage**, and how large an organisation they work in.
   - **Labour market situation** — income, benefits, job security and promotion prospects.
   - **Work situation** — where the person is in the **workplace hierarchy**, and how much **control** they have at work.

2) The RG scale was replaced by the NS-SEC because of the recent changes in **employment patterns**. There were fewer **manual** workers and far more workers in **service industries**, so **skill level** was no longer a good way to classify workers.

3) The NS-SEC takes into account **changes** in **social position** of some occupations (e.g. shop assistants).

4) Each **individual worker** is classified, rather than classifying a whole **household** by one person's job.

5) The NS-SEC still doesn't account for the 'idle rich' — wealthy **upper class** people who don't need jobs.

Class can be defined both *Objectively* and *Subjectively*

1) An **objective** definition of social class is based on something **definite** which can be **measured** or **classified**, e.g. income or occupation — the NS-SEC is an **objective** way of defining social class.

2) A **subjective** definition relies on factors which **can't be measured** — e.g. what an individual feels their social class position is. For instance, a **self-made millionaire** may be **middle class** by all **objective** standards of wealth and income, but may still **perceive** themselves to be **working class**, have working-class friends and share a working-class culture.

Traditional Class Analysis tended to Ignore Women

The old RG scale classified the social class of all members of a family by reference to the occupation of the **head of household** (usually the **man**). **Michelle Stanworth (1984)** suggested that by using this sociologists miss some important issues, saying that often the social class experience of women within a household is very different to that of the men.

Stanworth's ideas have been backed up by research into social mobility by **Abbott and Payne (1990)**. They concluded that women were far **less likely** to be **upwardly mobile** than their husbands and partners and that those very few women who were upwardly mobile didn't get much further than social class 3. There's more about women and social mobility on p.210.

Practice Questions

Q1 Identify two groups that were not included in the Registrar General's scale.
Q2 Give an example of a semi-routine occupation from the NS-SEC scheme.
Q3 What's the difference between subjective and objective definitions of social class?

Exam Question

Q1 Analyse two explanations for why objective definitions of social class can be problematic. [10 marks]

Oh how I wish this was a classless society — there'd be less to learn...

What a lot of class schemes. For the bare basics, learn the NS-SEC, the RG scale, and the differences between them. Oh, and remember that these are both objective ways of defining social class — some sociologists would prefer a subjective definition.

Class Inequality and Stratification

So, there's no dispute that power, status and economic assets aren't equally distributed within society. There is an awful lot of debate about why, though. A sociologist's answer depends on their fundamental beliefs about the nature of society.

The **Higher** an individual's **Social Class**, the **Better** their **Life Chances**

This is almost **common knowledge** — but in sociology you have to give **evidence** to go along with it.

1) Class affects an individual's life chances **from birth**. The chances of a child **dying** before their first birthday are much higher if they're born into a **lower social class** (and the **gap** has actually got **bigger** in recent decades).

Infant Mortality Rates in the UK (per 1000 live births)	1991	2001
Professional class	5.1	3.6
Unskilled manual class	8.2	7.2
Overall rate	5.3	4.6

Social Trends 33 (2003)

2) In **education**, a child's chances of achieving **good results** are better if they're in a higher social class (see p.24-25).

3) **Goldthorpe and Payne (1986)** found that people are more likely to become **unemployed** if they're from a working-class background. This could be because unskilled, manual jobs tend to have **less job security**. However, some people argue that today's **professional workers** are also suffering from job insecurity, because of the rise in **temporary** jobs.

A person's life chances are their opportunities to achieve the things that their society values (e.g. status, money, comfort).

4) An individual is more likely to suffer **ill health** and **poor medical resources** if they're **working class**. The **Black Report (1980)** documented this in detail, and found that the difference was **increasing** (see p.96).

> Some sociologists argue that **cultural deprivation** is to blame for this difference in **health chances** — that working-class culture is often based on **poor diet** and **bad habits**, like smoking. Other sociologists argue that **material deprivation** means working-class people **can't afford** healthy lifestyles. Alternatively, some argue that the health care system is **biased** against the working class, e.g. **middle-class doctors** may be **intimidating** to them, and they suffer from **long waiting periods** for operations because they can't afford private health care.

The **underclass** have the **worst** health chances. The longer someone is **unemployed**, the greater their risk of **illness**.

5) Finally, social class affects **how long** a person **lives**. On average, **men** from the **higher managerial and professional** class live nearly **six years longer** than men from the **routine** class. For women, the difference is nearer **four years**, but it has **increased** since the early 1980s.

Functionalists say the **Class System** helps society to **Run Smoothly**

1) Fundamental to **functionalism** (try saying that quickly...) is the **strong belief** that the class system enables each individual to find their **right place** and **role** in society. The **most important** positions in society must be filled by the brightest and most able people.

2) Functionalism says that society is a **meritocracy** — people in the **top** strata of society are there because of their **talents** and **efforts**, not because of the class of their **parents**.

Functionalists believe that the education system is a key institution that promotes meritocracy.

3) The high **status**, **power** and **income** in these top strata are **rewards** for conforming to society's values.

4) According to functionalists, most people **don't object** to people in powerful positions getting **extra status** and **rewards**, and this shows that they **support** the values which underpin the system.

Talcott Parsons argued that stratification is fair and functional

1) **Parsons (1953)** established the functionalist position that stratification is **inevitable** and **useful** in all societies.

2) He argued that stratification systems **evaluate** individuals in terms of **common social values** — high status is a reward for **conforming** to society's values.

3) In Parsons' view, stratification **reinforces** the **collective goals** of society and establishes **order**.

Jenny was confident that she'd found exactly the right place in society for her.

Davis and Moore (1945) argue that without a stratification system, society would break down

According to Davis and Moore, stratification has the function of **role allocation**. It makes sure the most **able** and **talented** do the most **important** jobs.

Inequality in reward (pay) and **status** are essential to **motivate** the best individuals to take on the most important roles and jobs. These roles usually require long periods of **training**. High rewards **compensate** people for spending a long time in education and training.

This argument may sound familiar — it's often used to justify high rewards given to company directors and even famous sports stars.

Class Inequality and Stratification

The New Right argue that the Social Stratification system is Unequal but Fair

New Right thinking became popular in the 1980s. New Right thinkers see the **free market** as the **best** way of sorting out everything in society, from boredom to backache. New Right theory says **governments shouldn't intervene in the market** or promote equality as this takes away motivation for people to **pull themselves up by their own bootstraps**.

New Right thinking is sometimes known as **neo-functionalism** (or **political functionalism**) because it pursues similar themes.

1) **Peter Saunders (1990)** is a key British New Right sociologist. Saunders argues that societies with stratification systems based on economic differences **aren't inevitable** (as Parsons thought), but they are a **good idea**.

2) Saunders says **stratification** is a good idea because **unequal rewards motivate** people to **work hard**. He says that in a society with equal rewards, some people wouldn't **pull their weight**. He sees physical force as the only alternative to unequal rewards — and obviously prefers unequal rewards.

3) Saunders says that **inequality** promotes **economic growth**. Individuals are motivated to **start businesses** so that they can make money, which **benefits society** by creating **jobs** and **wealth**. He points to the rise in small businesses and entrepreneurs in modern society to demonstrate how anyone can do well if they work hard enough.

4) New Right thinkers like Saunders believe in legal equality and **equality of opportunity**, rather than **equality of outcome**. Saunders says that it's more important for society to be a **meritocracy** than for society to be **equal**.

5) In a **free market**, market forces control who earns what, according to the **supply of talent** and **demand for talent**. People whose skills are highly **demanded**, but in short **supply**, can earn a lot of money. A system based on the free market is **unequal** (some people earn a lot more than others), but it's **fair** according to New Right thinkers.

> 1) **Saunders (1996)** sees Britain as pretty **close** to being a **meritocracy**. He thinks that **economic rewards** match up with **merit** and **ability**.
>
> 2) He argues that what **looks** like **inequality of opportunity** between middle class and working class is actually caused by **inequality of ability** and **effort**. In other words, he thinks that middle-class children **deserve** better jobs because they're more able, and they work harder.

Unsurprisingly, this view is highly controversial...

Critics of Functionalism and New Right theory claim it Isn't Fair At All

1) **Tumin (1953)** criticised functionalism, and claimed that there's actually **inequality of opportunity** in society.

2) He also criticised Davis and Moore's ideas that some jobs are more **functionally important** than others. In any case, the usefulness and importance of a job doesn't seem to match up to the rate of **pay**. Tumin pointed out that **pay inequality** between groups may be to do with differences in **bargaining power**, rather than differences in usefulness.

3) Tumin argued that instead of **motivating** people, stratification could actually be a **barrier to motivation**.

4) Critics of functionalism also point out that the functionalist view of stratification **ignores the negatives**. Stratification is a system of haves and have-nots, and people in the bottom strata can feel **excluded** from society.

5) **Gordon Marshall** and **Adam Swift (1993)** say that capitalist societies are not as **meritocratic** as the New Right claim. They argue the **free market** does not guarantee a **fair chance** for all. Opportunities vary according to which class you are born into — for example, inherited wealth makes it easier to start a business. **Luck** can play a part in success, too.

6) Evidence shows that people from **working-class** backgrounds are **less likely** than middle-class people to get top jobs — even when they have the **same educational qualifications**. **Class** plays a part even when people have **equal ability**.

Practice Questions

Q1 In what way did Parsons say that stratification was useful for society?

Q2 Explain what Davis and Moore mean by role allocation.

Q3 Why does Saunders say stratification is a good idea?

Q4 Give one criticism of New Right thinking on stratification.

Exam Question

Q1 Evaluate the idea that social inequality is an inevitable product of a successful society. [20 marks]

New Wrong thinking had even more critics than usual...

There's a pattern to sociology teaching at A-level: you study the main theories about each topic and then evaluate and compare them... It's a good approach because it teaches you to look at topics from different points of view. It can get a bit repetitive though. The same theories come up over and over again. What about Zoroastrian views? Huh? Rastafarian?

Class Inequality and Stratification

Surprise — some more theories of stratification! Sorry, I should have warned you on the last page. That was a cruel trick.

Marxists *see stratification as a* Deliberately Divisive *tool for* Exploiting *workers*

1) For Marx, **class** was the key to understanding **absolutely everything** in society. And I mean e-v-e-r-y-t-h-i-n-g.

2) Marx argued there are **only two classes** (strata) in society — the **proletariat** and the **bourgeoisie**. For Marx, a class is a **social group** who share the same **relationship to the means of production**.

Producers	Proletariat or subject class	Majority	Only own their labour	Poor
Non-producers	Bourgeoisie or ruling class	Minority	Own the means of production	Wealthy

The subject class are the producers

1) They only own their labour power, so they have **very little control** in society. They're **completely dependent** on the **ruling class** for wages to live on.

2) Marx said that people are **fulfilled** when they see the **product** of their **labour**. The subject class have their products **taken** from them, so they become **alienated** — distanced from themselves and others.

The ruling class own the means of production

1) Those who own the means of production can control both the **price** at which they **sell** the goods produced, and the **wages** they pay those who produce the goods.

2) It's only by paying the workers **less** than they **sell** the goods for that they can make a **profit**. It is this profit which gives them the **wealth** and **power** to **control** the rest of society in their own interests.

3) Marx argued that all other forms of power come from **economic** power.

4) Marxism says the **education** system, **legal** system, **police** and **media** are all instruments of ruling-class power. This is because those with **economic power** also have the power to **shape** and **control** the institutions in society. According to Marxism, all these institutions serve to keep the **subject class** in its place — **powerless**.

5) Neo-Marxists focus on how the ruling class also use **institutions** to **communicate** their **ideology** (ideas and beliefs about society) to everyone. This means that the ruling class's ideology becomes **dominant**. For example, the idea that society is meritocratic is **spread** by institutions like the **education system**, so everyone accepts that society is **fair**. Marxists claim that spreading these 'false truths' **suits** the ruling class because it prevents workers from rising up against them. 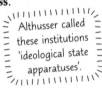 Althusser called these institutions 'ideological state apparatuses'.

Marx thought that Workers *should* Revolt *and bring in* Communism

Marx thought society could be **equal** if the **means of production** were owned by **everyone**. He was certain that workers would eventually develop a '**class consciousness**' — they would **realise** they were being **oppressed** by **capitalism**, see their own power and overthrow the ruling class in a **revolution**, creating a new equal society which Marx called **communism**.

The 20th century saw the **start** and **end** of some large-scale communist societies such as the USSR. The **failure** of these communist societies, and the high levels of both **corruption** and **inequality in communist societies**, have caused many sociologists to say that Marx was wrong and **egalitarian societies aren't possible**. However, modern Marxists have argued that the USSR **wasn't true communism**.

Neo-Marxist *theories of stratification try to explain the* Middle Class

Traditional Marxism didn't predict the **growth** of a **large middle class** such as the **UK** experienced in the **twentieth century**. **Neo-Marxists** have grappled with different ways of **explaining** this.

1) **Erik Olin Wright (1978, 1989)** developed a Marxist analysis of class which explained the middle class of salaried professionals which grew in the late 20th century. This group have some control over the **means of production**, and may own bits of it, but they don't control large sections of labour power. This group is called the **petty bourgeoisie**.

2) Wright says these individuals may experience '**contradictory class locations**' — they have **things in common** with **both** classes at **different** times. For example, they may own shares (part-ownership of modern means of production) but may also lose their livelihood at the will of the ruling class (e.g. if they lose their job, or the share price falls).

3) Wright concludes that **class conflict** and **exploitation** are more **complicated** in the late 20th (and now 21st) century than Marx predicted, but **class** is **still** the basis of **power** and **wealth** in society.

4) **Edgell (1993)** accuses Wright of leaving Marx behind and having more in common with **Weber**.

The **key message** from neo-Marxists is: **don't dismiss Marx completely** just because he didn't focus on the middle class.

Class Inequality and Stratification

Weber argued Class is 'Unequal Access to Material Resources'

Weber considered many of the same issues as Marx. Like Marx, he argued class and stratification have an **economic** basis. Unlike Marx, he didn't go into any detailed predictions about the future, or analysis of the past. He thought about different types of **social status**, and said that there are **three distinct dimensions** or forms of **stratification** in modern society:

Class power	Economic power to access material goods and resources in society.
Social power	Status and prestige, and being respected by others.
Party power	Political power and ability to influence decision-making.

These tend to be **interlinked** in real life — a person with **social power** is also likely to have **political** and **economic** power.

1) **Weber** argued that an individual's **class power** and **class position** derives from their **market position** — i.e. their **economic chances**, and their ability to **control** their **wages** and **working conditions**.

2) An individual's **market position** varies partly depending on how **in demand** their skills and talents are — i.e. how much someone will pay for their services. Market position also covers **ownership** of **property** and **assets** (e.g. shares).

> Weber developed the concept of life chances (see p.194). He believed that good life chances are dependent on a good market position. This means that an individual's life chances can change throughout their life, depending on how in demand their skills are at different times. People from the same class will have similar life chances.

3) For Weber, stratification isn't a case of **two classes** opposed to each other (Marx) or a **meritocracy** (functionalism and New Right) but a hierarchy of **four layers**, each with their own **unique combination** of class, social and party power:
   - The upper class have lots of property, providing a very high market position, and lots of social and party power.
   - White collar professionals have a good market position from owning shares. They have some social and party power.
   - The petty bourgeoisie may own some property (e.g. a small shop), but have lower social and party power.
   - The working class lack property and share ownership, and also lack social and party power.

4) White collar professionals and the petty bourgeoisie can be seen as the **upper** and **lower** parts of today's **middle class**.

Postmodern theory argues that Class isn't as Important as it used to be

1) Postmodernists claim that **other differences** such as gender, age and ethnicity are **at least** as important.

2) **Pakulski and Waters (1996)** say that **cultural differences** (values, lifestyles and beliefs) are what classify individuals into particular groups or strata in current society — not economic position.

3) Crucially, postmodernists say that stratification can be **subjective**. Individuals can **define themselves** as belonging to social groups or social strata and **freely move** from one to another by choosing their **lifestyle** and **identity**.

4) An important part of the way in which individuals define their own social status is through '**symbolic consumption**'. This is the way that the things people **buy** (as well as the things they **think about** and **talk about**) define their **identity** (see p.56). Postmodernists see **consumerism** as a form of differentiation.

Postmodernism allowed Simon to define himself as the croc he always knew he was.

Practice Questions

Q1 What are the two classes described by Marx?

Q2 What three types of power does Weber acknowledge in his theory on stratification?

Q3 What do postmodernists say about class?

Exam Question

Q1 Outline two ways that stratification by social class can cause inequality. Explain each one.　　　　　[10 marks]

'Petty bourgeoisie' is a great one for practising your French accent...

Marx ignores the middle class (there wasn't really one back then). Neo-Marxists admit that today's society is more complex. Weberians base everything on labour market position. And postmodernists say that class doesn't exist anyway. I need a brew.

Changes in the UK's Class Structure

The British stratification system underwent considerable change in the 20th century — alongside changes in society.

There have been Changes in Work Patterns and Wealth Distribution

1) There are **fewer** people in **manual** jobs and **more** people in **non-manual** jobs compared to the early 20th century.

2) Service industries such as **leisure** have grown, and primary and manufacturing industries have decreased.

3) More **women** now work — this has risen from 53% of working-age women in 1971 to nearer 70% now.

4) Between 1945 and 1980 income and wealth became more **evenly distributed**. However, from 1980 onwards, the wealth/income gap has actually started to **widen** again.

5) Many state-controlled industries were **privatised** in the 1980s and 1990s. 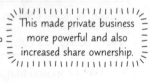 *This made private business more powerful and also increased share ownership.*

6) One thing hasn't changed massively — most **wealth** is still owned by a small **minority**.

The Ruling Class has Changed — opinions differ on just How Much

The **New Right** say that the **ruling class** has **disintegrated**. **Saunders (1990)** argues that because more people **own shares** in the UK, power is spread more widely. The small minority in power has been replaced with a **nation of stakeholders**.

Marxists insist the **ruling class** is **alive and kicking**.

1) **John Scott (1982, 1991)** agrees with Saunders that **more and more people own shares** in the UK but argues this hasn't led to a break-up of the ruling class. Most individuals own a **few** shares but hold **very little** real **power**.

2) Scott, and **Westergaard and Resler (1976)** say there's still a **power elite** who control business and the economy.

The Middle Class has Grown, but may be Breaking Up into Several Classes

1) Functionalists and Weberians cite the rise of **professions** (e.g. lawyers) as evidence of an expanding middle class.

2) **Embourgeoisement** means working-class people **becoming middle class** in lifestyle and values as their **incomes increase**. It was a popular idea with sociologists in the 1950s and 1960s.

3) **Goldthorpe et al (1968)** tested the **embourgeoisement thesis** by interviewing **car workers** in **Luton**. They concluded that affluence had **not** made the workers middle class, and **clear differences** remained between them and the non-manual middle-class workers — e.g. their **attitudes** to work and their possibility of future **promotion**.

Some say the middle class is fragmenting into several middle classes with different life-chances and experiences.

1) **Goldthorpe** says there's an **Intermediate Class** of low-grade non-manual workers who have **little in common** with middle-class professionals. In terms of wages, perks, and relationship with employers, these groups are **distinct**.

2) Marxist **Harry Braverman (1974)** says many non-manual workers have been **deskilled** by technology, so that they now have more in common with the working class in terms of job security and wealth. This is **proletarianisation**.

3) **Roberts et al (1977)** interviewed 'middle class' workers about their view of their **own class position** and found **wide variations** in how groups saw themselves. They decided the middle class is **fragmenting** into **smaller strata**.

4) **Giddens (1973)** disagrees — he says there's a **distinct middle class**. The middle class is distinct from the working class because its members can sell their 'brain power' as well as, or instead of, their labour power.

Postmodernists Pakulski and Waters (1996) say that Class is Dead

Pakulski and Waters give the following evidence to suggest that **class** and therefore **class analysis** in social science is **dead**:

1) **Wealth** became more **equally distributed** during the 20th century. This means not only that economic class differences are less pronounced, but that more people have more **spare cash** to buy consumer goods (see p.197).

2) **Educational status** has become **more important** in deciding life chances, and class background less important.

3) There's a **new postmodern politics** based on non-economic issues such as ethnicity, identity, and the environment.

4) People are **less likely** to **vote along class lines** — e.g. manual workers don't always vote for left-wing parties.

Pakulski and Waters argue that society changed from an **economic class society** in the 19th century, to a **hierarchical class society** in the first half of the 20th century, to a **status society** in the late 20th century.

However, Marxist sociologist **John Westergaard (1995)** suggests that because gaps between rich and poor are widening and big business is more powerful, class is **more** significant in the late 20th and early 21st century — not less significant.

Changes in the UK's Class Structure

The 20th Century Weakened and Divided the British Working Class

The decline in the **traditional working class** sectors of **manufacturing** and **heavy industry** in the 20th century **reduced** the **size** of the British **working class**.

1) **Ralph Dahrendorf (1959)** argues that instead of uniting, the working class has disintegrated. He said that the working class has been divided into groups of **skilled**, **semi-skilled** and **unskilled** workers, and that this is because of changes in **technology**.

2) Dahrendorf is criticised by **Penn (1983)**, whose research into cotton mills in Rochdale suggests that the working class has been **divided** into **skilled**, **semi-skilled** and **unskilled** since at least the **1850s**.

3) **Crewe (1983)** argues that the working class is **splitting into groups** with different **concerns** and **interests**, so it can no longer be considered a 'real' class. He says that there's a 'new working class' who live mainly in the **South**, work in the **private sector** and own their **own homes**. They have **very different life experiences** to the 'old working class' who live mainly in the North in council houses, and work in the public sector.

The idea that the working class is on its way out has been criticised, particularly by Marxist sociologists.

1) **Marxist** sociologists say that the working class can **change its occupation** and **still be working class**.

2) **Beynon (1992)** points out that the old working-class jobs have been replaced by **new occupations** which are **equally badly paid** with poor conditions and rights — e.g. call centres, fast-food outlets and hotels. Beynon says that **cooking burgers** is **manual**, **repetitive labour**, just like working on an assembly line in a factory.

3) Marxists argue what hasn't changed is the **status**, **rights** and **power** that go with the employment — the lack of these things is what makes it working class.

Remember the connection to **globalisation** — part of the reason that working-class manufacturing jobs have vanished in the UK is because they've **moved abroad** to cheaper labour markets (see p.171).

Some Sociologists say there is a growing Underclass below the working class

The idea that the most **disadvantaged** groups in society are a **separate group** from the working class **isn't new**. Marx referred to the 'lumpenproletariat' (beggars, pickpockets) and the 'relative surplus' (people who aren't part of the regular labour market, but who do casual labour when needed). The idea of an **underclass** gained support in the late 20th century.

1) The **New Right** see the **underclass** as **dangerous** to society. American sociologist **Charles Murray (1989)** defines the underclass by **behaviour** — **uneducated**, **delinquent** and **work-shy**.

2) **Runciman (1990)** defines the underclass as people who are **permanently dependent** on **welfare benefits**.

3) **Giddens (1973)** defines the underclass as the **most disadvantaged** in the job market, e.g. illegal immigrants. He says there's a **secondary job market** of **low-paid** jobs with **low job security**, which are the best the underclass can get.

4) **Dahrendorf (1987)** argued that the underclass is **growing rapidly**. This may be because of **globalisation** — as manual work now goes overseas, there is less demand for manual workers. **Automation** (using machines instead of people to perform tasks) also decreases the need for manual workers. In addition, as the labour market becomes more **flexible**, there's much more **insecure**, **temporary** or **casual** low-paid work.

Practice Questions

Q1 Explain Saunders' argument that the ruling class is no longer relevant in modern Britain.

Q2 Explain what sociologists mean by the terms 'embourgeoisement' and 'proletarianisation'.

Q3 Give two reasons why working-class manufacturing jobs have declined in modern Britain.

Exam Questions

Q1 Outline two reasons for changes in the British class structure in the 20th century. Explain each one. [10 marks]

Q2 Evaluate the idea that the working class became so divided in the 20th century that it can no longer be considered a 'real' class. [20 marks]

Breaking up is so very hard to do...

There are a ridiculous number of sociologists on these pages. I know it's a sociology book, but still. I mean, for heaven's sake. It starts off OK until we reach Peter Saunders, and then they just start closing in on you. Scott starts agreeing and Goldthorpe starts testing and then Giddens disagrees and Penn criticises Dahrendorf... please, sociologists, just give it a rest. Seriously.

Globalisation and Class Structure

Many sociologists believe that globalisation has created new forms of class inequality, not just between individuals, but between countries too. Remember that globalisation is about the ways in which the world is becoming more connected.

Analysis of Social Class is not always about Individual Nations

1) In the past, sociological research into class structure has focused on **one nation**, e.g. the working class in the UK.

2) Today, **production**, **producers** (workers) and **capital** (the things that most theories of stratification are based on) all **move between nations**. This has led some sociologists to argue that stratification is also a **global phenomenon**.

3) **Political power**, another important part of stratification, has arguably become globalised. **International organisations**, like the EU and the UN, mean it's now harder to define how much political power someone has without considering their **international influence** too.

Nations can be Stratified in terms of their Development

1) How '**developed**' a country is refers to things like its **economic growth** and the **living standards** of its population. In sociology, **richer** countries are often called '**developed**' countries, and **poorer** countries are '**developing**'.

2) Some sociologists argue that **globalisation** has **increased inequalities** between countries. **Luke Martell (2010)** says that there are now three levels of **global stratification**:

   - The previously **developed world** (e.g. the UK and the United States) has **got richer**.
   - Some parts of the developing world have experienced **fast economic growth**.
   - Other parts of the developing world have **remained poor**.

Martell argues that globalisation ultimately favours the developed world.

There are still problems in fast-developing nations

Since the 1970s, some countries (e.g. South Korea and China) have focused on **manufacturing** goods for **global export**, such as textiles, electronics and cars. **Lower labour costs** mean that these countries can sell their products **cheaply**. This has generated a lot of **capital** and there's been **rapid economic growth**.

This has led to an **improved standard of living** for many people, but these **fast-developing** nations still suffer from high levels of **absolute poverty** (p.80). **Wages** are **low**, and manufactured goods are often **too expensive** for the **workers** themselves to buy. Working **conditions** can be **poor**, with **long hours** and poor standards of **health** and **safety**.

Some Marxists have written about the Transnational Capitalist Class

1) Martell says that **individual nations** can be sorted into **different strata**, depending on their development. Other sociologists have looked at how **global classes** can **operate across multiple nations**.

2) Neo-Marxist **Leslie Sklair (2001)** argues that the world is now dominated by big **transnational corporations** (TNCs). These corporations are often very **rich** and have a lot of **political influence**. Sklair and others refer to the people involved in these companies as the **transnational capitalist class** — they're like a **global ruling class**.

3) **Sklair** says that there are **four fractions** within the transnational capitalist class. They all contribute to the **power** of the TNCs in different ways.

The Corporate Fraction	**Owners** and **top executives** who **control** the TNCs and often have **power** in **other** organisations, e.g. charities and universities.
The State Fraction	**Bureaucrats** and **politicians** who use their **political influence** to promote the interests of the TNCs.
The Technical Fraction	**Professionals** who work in key roles for TNCs. They use their skills to **develop** the corporations' **products** and **services**.
The Consumerist Fraction	**Merchants** and the **media** have control over the organisations that **deliver** these **products** and **services** to the public.

The mathematical fraction was loving its new power.

4) Some sociologists also argue that there's a **global working class** alongside this global ruling class. **Fröbel et al (1980)** claim that there's a **new international division of labour** — TNCs are **managed** in **developed** countries, whilst the labour-intensive, manufacturing work takes place in **developing** countries. Often, the people doing the manufacturing work have **few rights** and **low pay**.

Globalisation and Class Structure

The Food Industry shows the Power of the Transnational Capitalist Class

1) Sklair and others argue that the transnational capitalist class use their **money** and **political influence** to **exploit** the **global working class**, affecting their **health** and well-being.
2) For example, **food activists** argue that **junk food** and **soft drinks companies** (the corporate fraction) have deliberately **targeted** the **poorest** people in **Mexican** society.
3) TNC professionals (the technical fraction) persuaded the Mexican government (the state fraction) to support **junk food imports**.
4) Then the **media** and **marketing** companies (the consumerist fraction) helped to make these products **very popular**.
5) The result was an **epidemic** of **obesity** and **diabetes** amongst the **Mexican poor**.

The idea of a Transnational Capitalist Class can be Criticised

1) This idea depends on the belief that **global stratification** is replacing **national stratification**. This might not be true. For example, you could argue that the **existing class structure** hasn't really **changed** in Mexico — the TNCs simply **took advantage** of it.
2) The state fraction doesn't **always** support the TNCs, e.g. the Mexican government has recently introduced a '**soda tax**' to reduce the levels of soft-drink consumption in their country.

Capital isn't the Only Thing that Moves Around the World — People do too

1) There are **over 200 million migrants worldwide**. Most movement is from **developing** countries to **developed** ones.
2) Some of this migration is **economically** motivated — people seeking **work** or **higher pay** in other countries. Other migrants are seeking **asylum** — they're moving away from **war zones** or **oppression**, looking for a **safe place** to live.

There isn't really one agreed definition of a 'migrant'. Broadly speaking, though, a migrant is someone who moves to live in a different country.

Immigration can impact a country's class structure

- Lots of immigrants are prepared to fill **low-skill** or **unskilled** jobs. This **grows** the **working class**. Studies suggest that these immigrants tend to **remain** as members of the working class, even in **future generations**.
- **Modood et al (1997)** found that some **skilled immigrants** moved **down** the class scale when they arrived in the UK. However, the **children** of these immigrants, especially those of **Indian** or **Chinese** origin, tended to have skilled, **middle-class** jobs.
- In **developed** countries, one consequence of **mass illegal immigration** has been the formation of a new **sub-class** of exploited workers. These people may have been **trafficked** into the country against their will in the first place. They may also be exploited by **employers** who threaten to hand them over to the **authorities** if they object to their **low pay**, **long hours** and **poor working conditions**.

Practice Questions

Q1 What are the four fractions of the transnational capitalist class, according to Sklair?
Q2 Give one example of the transnational capitalist class exploiting the global working class.
Q3 Give two reasons why people migrate from one country to another.

Exam Question

Q1 By applying material from Item A, analyse two arguments that support the idea that traditional models of social class are now less relevant because of globalisation. [10 marks]

> **Item A**
> Some sociologists claim that the existence of international social classes has made national models of social class less significant. They point to the political influence of a global capitalist class, which crosses national boundaries.

I've just migrated to Budapest — I was Hungary...

The basic thing to grasp is that there are two elements to global stratification: 1) you can compare countries against one another, placing them in strata according to how developed they are, and 2) you can look at how social classes stretch across countries, forming a global ruling class and a global working class and so on. So many exciting possibilities. Lucky you, eh?

Inequality and Gender

Feminist sociologists identify gender stratification as an important area of sociology that should be studied in its own right.

Sociologists say that *Sex* and *Gender* are *Different Things*

1) Sex refers to the **physical** and **biological** differences used to **differentiate** men from women.
2) Gender refers to the **socially constructed roles** of what's considered '**masculine**' and what's considered '**feminine**'.
3) Sociologists don't see gender roles as fixed. Because they're **created by society** and don't depend purely on a person's sex, gender roles can therefore **change over time** and can be very **different** in different **cultures**.

Women experience *Inequalities* in the *Stratification System*

1) In the UK, women's **work chances** are worse than men's. The labour market is **vertically segregated** in terms of gender — men on one level, and women on another. Women **earn less** than men and are **less likely** to be in the **top jobs**. Even in professional sectors, women can face a '**glass ceiling**' — a barrier to top managerial positions.

> **Barron and Norris (1976)** say that companies often base **promotions** on **continuous service**, which **favours men** (since women often take time out to give birth).

2) The labour market is also **horizontally segregated** in terms of gender (men on one side and women on another, within the same level of the class hierarchy). There are **more women** than men in **clerical** jobs, in **retail**, and in **catering**. Primary school teaching is almost exclusively female. Some of these 'feminine' jobs may be **lower paid** than **equivalent** 'masculine' jobs.

> In contrast, **girls** are now **outperforming boys** in **education** — this used to be the other way around (p.28-29). Girls achieve better results in nearly every **GCSE** subject, and more women than men go to **university**. However, there's still an imbalance in the **professional** side of higher education — in the 2013/14 academic year, only about **1 in 5 professors** were **female**.

"In my day, the only glass ceiling was the one in the conservatory..."

Liberal Feminists blame inequality on *Discrimination* and *Socialisation*

1) Liberal feminists believe in changing **attitudes**, and overcoming **prejudice** about the roles of men and women.
2) To promote **equal opportunity**, liberal feminists believe in campaigning to **change laws** — from votes for women in the 1920s to the more modern **anti-discrimination** legislation such as the Sex Discrimination Act (1975).
3) According to **liberal** feminists, **inequality** in male and female **life chances** begins with **socialisation**. They argue that **girls are encouraged to take on an **expressive** (emotional) role in society, whilst **boys** are encouraged to **lead**. They also say that **gender roles** encourage girls to prioritise **marriage** and **children** over building their own **career**.
4) When **Sue Sharpe (1976)** studied teenage girls' attitudes in the **1970s**, her findings supported this idea. However, when she repeated the research in the **1990s**, she found that teenage girls **did** now have **career ambitions**.

There have been *Some Changes* to the *Law*, but there's still a *Gender Pay Gap*

1) The **2010 Equality Act** replaced existing laws against **discrimination** in the **workplace** for **gender**, ethnicity and disability, **strengthening** them under a single law. This included the **1975 Sex Discrimination Act**, which made it illegal to advertise a job for specifically a man or specifically a woman.
2) The **gender pay gap** refers to the **difference** in the **hourly earnings** of all working men compared to all working women. The **1970 Equal Pay Act** and its **1984 "equal pay for equal work"** amendment helped to **narrow** the pay gap. However, it's now widened again — in 2015 a woman earned about **80p** for every **£1** a man earned per hour.
3) There are several reasons for this. The 1984 amendment said that a woman should be paid the same as a man in a job of **equal worth** — but it can be difficult to decide which jobs are equivalent to each other. Women are also more likely to take **career breaks** to have and care for children, and do more **unpaid work** per week **caring** for other adults (e.g. older relatives) and doing **housework**. There's also evidence of ongoing **discrimination** in the workplace.

There are also *Health Inequalities* between women and men

- On average **women** in the UK **live** four years **longer** than men, but they spend a greater proportion of their life with a **disability**, and visit a **doctor** more frequently.
- Women are more likely to be **diagnosed** with mental health problems. Some sociologists say this is because of more **stressful** lives, while others say it's to do with **sexism**, e.g. **doctors** seeing women as more **unstable**.

> There are several reasons for men's lower life expectancy, e.g. men smoke and drink more than women. They also do more physical and dangerous jobs, and take more risks.

Inequality and Gender

Radical Feminists *say there is* Conflict *between* All Men *and* All Women

1) **Patriarchy theory** is favoured by radical feminists. Radical feminists suggest that society is run in the interests of patriarchy — male power. According to this view, men take most of society's rewards and privileges for themselves. Men are the **ruling class**, and **all women** are oppressed by **all men**.

2) Radical feminists argue that men also use their control of culture to create the belief that **gender inequality** and **patriarchy** are 'natural'.

3) **Sexual oppression** is seen as the most fundamental form of inequality, with all others such as class and ethnicity being seen as **secondary**.

4) **Female biology** and the way it's treated by society are seen by radical feminists as a cause of gender inequality.

It had a lovely big moat to keep out all the men.

> Shulamith Firestone (1970) asserts that gender inequalities are the direct result of biology. She says pregnancy and childbirth lead to physical, psychological and social disadvantages. She claims that gender inequality can only be put right when women take control of the reproduction process. She advocates abortion and contraception and ultimately calls for a future where human reproduction takes place in artificial wombs.

Marxist *feminists blame gender inequality on* Capitalism *as well as* Patriarchy

1) Marxist feminism says that gender inequality can only be understood in a **social and economic** context.

2) From this perspective, it **suits capitalism** that women are exploited by men on many levels. Engels even suggested that the emergence of capitalism had resulted in 'the world historical defeat of the female sex'.

3) Marxist feminists say that **capitalism exploits women's work** in specific ways:

   - Women are treated as a **'reserve army of labour'** to be hired and fired as needed.
   - Male workers try to **exclude females** from their **trades** and **crafts**.
   - Husbands **exploit** their wives' **unpaid housework**.

4) Marxist feminists see the **bourgeois family** in capitalist society as **patriarchal** and **unequal**. They say that this is because it is set up by men in order to pass **property** on from fathers to sons. Women are seen as working for the benefit of this system, rather than for their own benefit. The logic of this argument suggests that **without private property** there would be no need to do this.

5) For Marxist feminists the solution to gender inequalities is therefore the **end of capitalism** through socialist revolution.

Black Feminism *and* Triple-Systems *theory say* Ethnicity *is also important*

In *Ain't I a Woman?* **(1981) bell hooks** (yes, she does spell her name without capital letters) argues that because they **benefit indirectly** from living in a **racist society**, white feminists are not enthusiastic about tackling racism. She says that mainstream white feminism makes the **false claim** that black and white women face **exactly** the **same problems**.

Sylvia Walby (1990) said women are oppressed in three systems: **gender** (through patriarchy), **social class** (through capitalism) and **ethnicity** (through racism). This is known as a **'triple-systems theory'** of patriarchy.

Practice Questions

Q1 What is the difference between sex and gender, according to sociologists?

Q2 Give three pieces of evidence to support the view that there is gender inequality in society today.

Q3 Briefly outline the similarities and differences between liberal, Marxist and radical feminism.

Exam Question

Q1 Evaluate the idea that socialisation is the most significant contributing factor to gender inequality in the UK. [20 marks]

Ah, more sociological disagreement — always fun...

If you were just flicking through this book, and not really bothering to revise, you probably wouldn't realise that there are so many different strands of feminism. So make sure you learn this lot properly. Remember that you can apply these feminist ideas to many other topics that you've studied — e.g. education, representations of women in culture, female crime rates.

Inequality and Ethnicity

Lots of evidence suggests that different ethnic groups have different life chances.

Sociologists make a distinction between **Ethnicity** and **Race**

1) '**Race**' as a word is usually used to refer to groups sharing a particular physical or biological set of characteristics (usually skin colour). Sociologists, however, **reject** the concept of 'race' for two very important reasons:

   - There's **no scientific basis** to ideas of race — the genetic differences between groups of humans are **tiny**.
   - Ideas of race were largely **discredited** in the early to mid-20th century with pseudo-scientific ideas such as Social Darwinism being used to **justify** horrendous persecution in places such as Nazi Germany.

2) Instead, sociologists prefer to differentiate by **ethnicity**, which places emphasis on **culture** (shared norms and values). **Ethnicity** is therefore something which is **socially constructed**.

3) There are still **difficulties** in using the concept of ethnicity, though. Many ethnic groups are **huge** and subdivided into very different subgroups, e.g. 'Asian' covers an enormous range of different cultural experiences.

Ethnic Minorities are more likely to experience **Inequality** and **Discrimination**

1) The three groups with the **highest proportion** of **unemployed men** are people of '**Other Black**', **Black Caribbean** and **White and Black Caribbean** origin. For women, it's those of **Black African**, **White and Black Caribbean** and '**Other Black**' origin. ('Other Black' is an ethnic group that refers to Black people who aren't African or Caribbean.)

2) Amongst **employed** people, **Pakistani**, **Black African** and **Bangladeshi** men are the most likely to have **low-skilled jobs**. For women, the three groups are **Gypsy or Irish Traveller**, **Bangladeshi** and **White and Black Caribbean**.

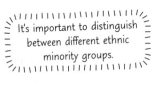
It's important to distinguish between different ethnic minority groups.

3) **Black** households are more likely to be living in housing in the **social rented sector** (rented from the council and housing associations) than **white** households. People from minority ethnic groups make up **almost half** of **overcrowded households** in the UK.

You can use **Examples** of ethnic inequality from **Other Units** you have studied

Education

According to research by Modood et al (1997), Black Caribbean boys are the lowest achievers, and Chinese and Indian pupils the highest achievers. Some sociologists argue that this is because of discrimination within the education system, e.g. teachers labelling black pupils as troublemakers, and an ethnocentric curriculum. Others argue that it's because of cultural and material deprivation outside school (p.26-27).

Health

Bangladeshi people report some of the highest levels of ill health. This may be because there are high proportions of Bangladeshi people in lower social classes (who tend to have poorer health). Some sociologists argue that some ethnic minority groups are less able to access health care, either because of prejudice from medical professionals or the cultural values of the NHS (p.99).

There is evidence of **institutional racism** in the police force:

1) The **Gifford Report (1989)** found evidence of **widespread racism** in the police force. Ten years later, the **Macpherson Report (1999)** found that the **Metropolitan police** was **institutionally racist**.

2) More recently, the Metropolitan Black Police Association has claimed that **ethnic minority officers** struggle to **progress** within the police force, and face a disproportionate amount of **disciplinary action**.

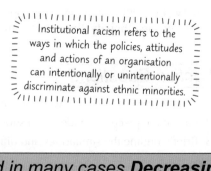
Institutional racism refers to the ways in which the policies, attitudes and actions of an organisation can intentionally or unintentionally discriminate against ethnic minorities.

Patterns of ethnic disadvantage are **Changing** and in many cases **Decreasing**

Andrew Pilkington (1999) gives the following as evidence:

1) Large numbers of people from ethnic minorities have **high status jobs** in non-manual/professional occupations.

2) The **labour market position** of all ethnic minority groups has improved at a **faster rate** than for whites.

3) The **continuing disadvantage** of some ethnic groups (e.g. Bangladeshis) has a lot to do with **cultural** factors — e.g. attitudes to women working outside the home, and linguistic deprivation (not having fluent English) in new immigrants.

Inequality and Ethnicity

Functionalists believe Ethnic Inequality is only Temporary

Functionalist **Sheila Patterson (1965)** suggests that disadvantages will gradually melt away as the immigrant communities and the host communities **adjust to each other** and the meritocratic principles of society start to take effect. Patterson says racism and disadvantage are therefore only **temporary** — eventually and inevitably the immigrants take on the **values** of the host culture and **assimilate** into the host society, and the hosts **accept** the immigrants.

Functionalists cite as evidence the successful assimilation of minority groups in the UK and USA. They have been **criticised** for assuming that assimilation is somehow inevitable and **ignoring** the obstacles of **racism** and **class conflict**.

Marxists suggest that Capitalism Benefits from Ethnic Inequalities

1) **Castles and Kosack (1973)** say that capitalism benefits from a working class **divided** by ethnic inequality.

2) They argue that ethnic differences are used to **distract** the working class from the real cause of their problems. For instance, ethnic minorities get the blame for problems such as **unemployment** and **housing shortages**. The power of the working class is diminished so long as some ethnic groups see themselves as **superior** to others. Instead of uniting to start a revolution, the working class **fights amongst itself**.

3) Castles and Kosack say that ethnic division also creates a **reserve army** of **relatively cheap ethnic minority labour**. Capitalism therefore encourages ethnic division and disadvantage.

Weberians see Ethnic Inequalities in terms of Labour Market Position

1) Weberians like **Rex and Tomlinson (1979)** use the term **'underclass'** to mean people who have the lowest social class and lowest social status. They say the underclass are **beneath** the rest of the working class, and are **cut off** from the rest of the working class. They feel this describes Britain's **ethnic minorities**.

2) **Barron and Norris (1976)** state that there are **two types of job** and **two types of worker**. In the **primary labour market**, workers have secure jobs, good wages, opportunities for training and high status. In the **secondary labour market**, jobs are less secure, wages are low, there are few opportunities for training, and workers are not valued by employers. Their evidence shows a disproportionate number of people from **ethnic minorities** are in the **secondary** labour market.

New Right sociologists use Cultural Explanations of ethnic disadvantage

1) New Right theorists like **Charles Murray (1984)** and **Peter Saunders (1996)** agree that the **underclass** is disproportionately made up of people from **ethnic minorities**. Because they believe society is a **meritocracy**, they blame ethnic minority groups rather than society, or racism.

2) Murray suggests that the distinct **subculture** of some ethnic minorities causes their disadvantage. He believes that this subculture contains an **unwillingness to work**, a tendency to value criminal activity and a tendency for **lone-parent families**. He says this leads to dependency on State welfare benefits and ultimately leads to poverty.

3) New Right ideas have been challenged by sociologists who argue that in 'blaming the victim' they **ignore** both the damaging influence of **racism** and the **structural causes** of poverty. **Giddens (1973)** says that **poor access to education** means people from ethnic minorities are often **underskilled** and **underqualified**.

Practice Questions

Q1 Why do sociologists use the term 'ethnicity' and not 'race'?

Q2 Give three pieces of evidence that suggest there are differences in life chances between different ethnic groups.

Q3 Briefly outline the Marxist explanation for ethnic inequality.

Exam Question

Q1 Outline two ways that ethnic minorities can suffer from discrimination. Explain each one. [10 marks]

Sociologists blame the usual suspects...

In other words, it's the fault of the labour market, capitalism or the victim. Remember that not all ethnic minorities are poor, or trapped in low-paid work, so you need to be able to write about different ethnic minority groups. If you get a question in the exam about the life chances of ethnic minorities, try to think about education and health too — it's not all about work, y'know.

Inequality and Age

People are also treated differently based on how old they are. Sometimes this is very sensible — three-year-olds on mopeds would probably cause carnage. On other occasions, people can be unfairly discriminated against because of their age.

Age Categories are Socially Constructed

Views about age **aren't fixed** or **universal** — they can change with **time**, and vary between different **societies** and cultures.

1) **Age** is part of social **identity**. People are **socialised** to accept the **norms** and **values** of the **society** they live in. So the way a society **views** certain age groups affects **people's behaviour** and **treatment of each other**.

2) Assumptions about at what age someone becomes an '**adult**' or at what age someone is '**old**' can **vary** between different societies and cultures.

3) The **law** affects how different age groups are **treated**. For example, people **under 18** can't buy **alcohol**.

> Bradley (1997) argues that age **isn't as important** as other means of differentiation, such as social class, gender and ethnicity, because age is **temporary**. For example, people under 18 know that they won't be that age **forever**.

There is Stratification by Age — Older People face Inequality...

1) **Retirement** is frequently accompanied by a **loss of status**, self-respect and influence. Older people may become **socially isolated**, because of the decline of the **extended family**.

2) Older people can have unequal access to **health care**. When surveyed, **over half** of older people said their symptoms were **dismissed** by doctors because of their age. Older people may also be dismissive **themselves**, and decide not to go to a doctor about their symptoms.

3) Historically, older people have faced inequality in the workplace — being **forced to retire** before they want to, or being passed over for promotion or training opportunities due to **stereotyped** views of their **capability**. The **Equality Act (2010)** makes it **illegal** to discriminate on the grounds of age.

4) It's also harder for older people to access **education**. Education **policies** often focus on the **under 25s**, meaning that people older than this can struggle to learn **new skills**. Continued learning is important for **work chances**, but it's also important for individual **mental health**.

Betty showed her boss exactly what she thought of age discrimination.

Until about **fifteen years ago**, pensioners were more likely than non-pensioners to live in poverty. Now, they're **less likely** to be in **poverty**. This could be because more generous **benefits** for pensioners have been introduced, such as winter fuel allowances.

However, older people are still **vulnerable** to money problems — particularly those who rely on the **state pension**. The state pension age is actually **rising**, meaning that people will have to wait **longer and longer** to claim this support.

...and so do Children and Young People

1) In work, young people are **paid less** than older workers — this is partly to be expected, as they lack job **experience**. The **minimum wage** is **lower** for workers under 22 than workers over 22, and lower still for workers under 18.

2) Young people in work often experience **low pay**, low responsibility, and **low status work**. In 2001, around a quarter of a million young people were being paid no more than the **minimum wage**. A new **national living wage** (which is based on the minimum amount needed to live) is now being introduced, but this will only apply to people **over 25**. Also, **Income Support** is paid at a **lower rate** to **under 25s**.

3) In **further education**, the Education Maintenance Allowance (which helped with the cost of going to sixth form or college) has been **removed** in England. In **higher education**, students face large **debts** after they graduate — university **tuition fees** rose from a maximum of £1000 per year in 1998 to a maximum of £9000 per year in 2012.

4) Children and young people experience **discrimination** in society. They are often **stereotyped** (especially by the **media**) as **irresponsible** and lacking the knowledge and experience to make judgements and choices.

There are changes to patterns of stratification by age

1) Young people today stay **dependent** for far longer than in earlier generations. Before 1944, people could leave school and start a full-time job at the age of **14**. Recently there's been a big increase in the number of people going on to **further or higher education** rather than full-time work.

2) With **rising house prices**, and a **reduction in housing benefit**, fewer young people are able to **move out** of home.

Inequality and Age

There are **Different Sociological Explanations** of Age Inequality

Functionalists see age inequality as useful to society

1) Functionalists like **Parsons (1977)** say that passing through age groups has the important function of **integrating people** into society. The **role sets** of the different age groups allow a person to develop **full functioning** in society.

2) There's a criticism — functionalism doesn't explain the role of **older people**, who tend to **disengage** from society.

Marxists see age inequality as helping capitalism by providing cheap labour

1) Capitalism benefits from treating young workers differently because they can be **paid less**, and **hired and fired** more easily than more mature workers — and society tends not to object. Paying young people less means more profits can be made. Also the low pay of the young can help to **keep general wages lower**.

2) **Phillipson (1982)** says older people become **stigmatised** as a **burden** on society, especially if they are poor. Rich older people who have been able to plan a relatively **affluent retirement** can maintain status in a capitalist society, but others become **irrelevant** and **marginalised**. Once again, Marxist sociologists see **class inequality** as the inequality that takes precedence over all the others.

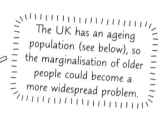
The UK has an ageing population (see below), so the marginalisation of older people could become a more widespread problem.

Weberians explain age inequality by reference to labour market position

1) Both younger and older people have a **poor labour market position** compared to people in middle age.

2) For Weberians, social status and political power are also important in social stratification. Both older and younger people have relatively low **social status**, and may find it difficult to influence **political decision-making**.

Attitudes to **Old Age** have **Changed** because of the UK's **Ageing Population**

1) Between 1971 and 2009, the **percentage** of people aged **over 75** rose from **4.7%** to **7.8%** (Social Trends 41 (2011)).

2) This is partly because **life expectancy** is **increasing**. **Giddens (1986)** argues that **longer life expectancy** also affects **family life** — e.g. people are more likely to have living grandparents or even great-grandparents. But this also means that younger people have to take on the responsibility of **caring** for older relatives for **longer**.

3) **Postmodernists** also claim that **changing attitudes** mean old age is seen as more 'youthful'. **Featherstone and Hepworth (1993)** found that magazines now portray older people **playing sport** and wearing **fashionable** clothes. Cosmetic surgery and advances in health care and beauty products also mean that older people have more ways to **look younger**.

The Lives of **Children** are **Changing Too**

1) **Neil Postman (1994)** argues that today's children **grow up very quickly** — so much so that **childhood** is now **disappearing**. For example, the **internet** has meant that children (and teenagers) can now access **content** that would previously only have been available to **adults**.

2) **Palmer (2007)** argues that this has been **harmful** for children, making their lives more **stressful** and **sexually active**. She claims that a '**toxic childhood**' has developed.

Practice Questions

Q1 Give three ways in which children and young people may face disadvantage in society.

Q2 What is the Marxist view of age inequality?

Exam Question

Q1 Evaluate the idea that older people face disadvantage in modern UK society. [20 marks]

Not to be ageist or anything, but it's the same 'old' story...

Just like with discrimination by gender, ethnicity and disability, age discrimination is actually illegal. It's not as simple as passing a law and *boom* the inequalities instantly vanish, though. You still have to change attitudes, which can be a toughie.

Inequality and Disability

Although it's illegal, people with disabilities are still discriminated against in the UK.

Disability affects Work Chances

1) Disability has a **serious impact** on a person's **work chances**. Disabled people are **more likely to be unemployed** than able-bodied people. This is despite the **Equality Act (2010)**, which **in theory** makes it **illegal to discriminate** against disabled people. Disabled people **in work** are more likely to be in **low-paid** jobs than the general population.

2) Disabled people may be **physically unable** to do certain jobs, or to work at all. They may only be able to have a **part-time job**, or have to take frequent **sick leave**. Some sociologists also argue that **employers** aren't doing enough to **help** disabled people **access work opportunities**.

3) The result is that **large numbers** of disabled people in the UK suffer **poverty** and live on **state benefits**.

People with disabilities have Unequal Education, Leisure and Health chances

1) Traditionally, disabled people went to **special schools** instead of mainstream schools, where opportunities and facilities were sometimes limited. Nowadays, many people with disabilities do attend **mainstream schools**, but in some cases they can't get the **support** they need to get the best out of mainstream education.

2) **Attainment levels** amongst disabled people are considerably **lower** than for non-disabled people, e.g. disabled people, including those with a learning disability, are only **half as likely** to have a **degree** as non-disabled people.

- Despite the Equality Act (2010), disabled people still have **practical difficulties** in accessing cultural and leisure amenities — e.g. lack of wheelchair ramps, signs that aren't clear enough for the visually impaired.
- They may also experience social **stereotyping** and **social exclusion** from clubs and activities — due to able-bodied people's **prejudices** about their abilities.
- Some children and teenagers with disabilities don't have the opportunity to **socialise with other kids** without **adult carers** being present.

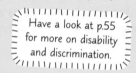
Have a look at p.55 for more on disability and discrimination.

3) Disabled people can also face barriers to **health care**, whether **physically** (e.g. the lack of a ramp into the dentists' surgery) or in terms of **communication difficulties** (e.g. struggling to explain symptoms or book appointments).

4) They can also suffer from '**diagnostic overshadowing**' — where symptoms are **wrongly diagnosed** as part of the person's disability, when they're actually nothing to do with it.

5) People with **learning disabilities** have a lower **life expectancy** than the rest of the population. A **MENCAP (2004)** study found that learning-disabled adults were sometimes **discriminated** against by health care professionals.

Recent Sociology of Disability focuses on Disability as a Social Construct

1) Traditionally, a **biomedical model** of disability (p.94) has shaped society's attitudes towards disabled people. It focuses on the **physical impairment** and tries to 'fix' it.

2) More recently, sociologists such as **Oliver (1990)** and **Shakespeare (1994)** have suggested that disability discrimination has less to do with **actual impairments** and is more to do with disabling **social** and **environmental factors** — e.g. attitudes, **stereotypes**, lack of access, and lack of rights. They suggest disability is a **social construct**, and that it's **society** that needs to be fixed, not people with disabilities. This is a **social model** of disability (p.95).

3) It has prompted changes in **social policy**. The most important is the **Disability Discrimination Act (1995)**, which made **equal access** a legal requirement for employers, shops, schools and train stations etc.

Practice Questions

Q1 When was the Equality Act, and what did it make illegal?

Q2 Explain the difference between the biomedical and social models of disability.

Exam Question

Q1 Analyse two explanations for why disability can impact a person's life chances. [10 marks]

I can think of a huge barrier to leisure — it's called work...

Make sure you revise the views of sociologists like Oliver and Shakespeare, who point out that social policies and attitudes can be as much of a problem for a disabled person as their actual impairment. Shakespeare should be an easy one to remember.

Social Mobility

Social mobility is about how easy it is for people to change class, e.g. if you want to go next door and start A-level history.

Learn these **Definitions** of **Mobility**

Social mobility = the movement from one stratum (class) to another.

Intra-generational mobility = social mobility of the same person within their **lifetime**.

Inter-generational mobility = social mobility **between generations** (i.e. if a person stays in the same class as their parents).

Absolute Mobility = how much social mobility there is in the society as a whole.

Relative Mobility = how much social mobility different social groups have relative to each other.

Ascribed status = status given to a person at birth either through family (e.g. a prince) or through gender or ethnicity.

Achieved status = status resulting from hard work, merit and effort.

Societies which allow for **achieved status** are called **open systems of stratification**.

Societies where social position is **ascribed** are called **closed systems of stratification**.

Open systems have a lot of social mobility, and they're meritocratic.

The **First** major study of **Social Mobility** in Britain was in **1949**

This study was done in 1949, but published in 1954.

Glass (1954) compared the social class of fathers and sons using statistical data

Results:	He found there was a high level of social mobility — two thirds of sons were in a different social class from their father. This mobility was equally split — one third upward and one third downward.
	But, the social mobility was mostly short-range. Most sons moved to the next class up or the next class down. (Glass categorised seven classes.) The study also found that the upper class had fewer people moving in or out of it than the other classes.
Conclusion:	The impact of social mobility is that individuals have unequal chances to reach the top in British society.

The **Oxford Mobility Study** found **Higher** rates of **Social Mobility** in **1972**

This study was conducted by **Goldthorpe et al**. You'll see it referred to as the **Oxford Study**, the Goldthorpe Study or the Nuffield study. Whatever the name, it's the same study.

This study was done in 1972, but not published until 1980.

Goldthorpe et al (1980) also compared the social class of fathers and sons

Results:	There were higher rates of social mobility than in 1949 — half of all sons were in a different social class from their fathers. More of this movement was to a **higher social class** than down to a **lower** one.
Conclusion:	Opportunities for working class individuals had improved in the second half of the 20th century. This has been used by functionalist sociologists to show that Britain has become a more open and meritocratic society.
However:	Closer analysis showed that the chances of getting into the higher classes were much greater for those whose fathers were already there. There was some movement but relatively those born upper class were still better off.

A neat summary of the probabilities of upward mobility and downward mobility is given by **Kellner and Wilby (1980)**. The data revealed a **1:2:4** rule of 'relative hope' — whatever the chance of a **working-class** son being in the **professional class** as an adult, it was **twice** as much for an **intermediate-class** son and four times as much for an **upper-class** son.

So, this study has also been used by sociologists to show Britain is an **unfair society**.

Other Studies have also found that Britain Lacks Social Mobility

1) **Goldthorpe and Payne (1986)** did a follow-up to the Oxford study, looking at mobility rates during the **economic recession** of the 1970s. They concluded that mobility rates had **increased generally** but the chances of reaching **top classes** remained **unequal** in favour of those whose parents were upper class.

2) **Payne's 1987** study found that **region** was a factor in social mobility. For example, working-class people from the **south** of England were more likely to be **upwardly mobile** than those from the **north**.

3) The **Essex study** by **Marshall et al (1988)** looked at 1984 data and found that social mobility was increasing, but it was mainly short-range. Working-class children were less likely to get top jobs. The **Essex study** also showed that working-class people who got upper-class jobs were less likely to retain them than upper-class people.

Social Mobility

Upper-class people tend to be Born Upper Class

1) There's a much greater chance of **higher class** people **staying** in that class than **working-class** people **moving up**.

2) The top classes in the UK remain very **static** — the majority of members come from families who have been in the upper class for **generations**. The elite recruit the sons of those **already** in the elite (**elite self-recruitment**).

3) **Stanworth and Giddens (1974)** found that of the top company positions in over 400 British companies, only **1%** were occupied by individuals with **working-class origins**.

4) Upper-class people have great **life chances** (p.194) — in education, work and health.

There are Difficulties in Measuring Social Mobility

1) All of these studies have mainly focused on the **middle** and **top** of society. The **long-term unemployed** aren't studied.

2) They are mainly **quantitative** rather than **qualitative** studies. They **ignore feelings** about and **experiences** of class.

3) They're based on crude five- or seven-point **scales**, and don't measure changes **within** those groups. Life might be very **different** at the 'bottom' of a range compared to the 'top'.

4) The scales are **employment-based**. Not all jobs **easily fit** into a class 'range'.

5) They compare the **older generation** with the **younger generation** (whose status may still be changing).

6) As **technology** and **work develops**, it is harder to **compare** jobs from one generation to the next.

7) The studies didn't include **women** (see below), so the discovered patterns may not be **significant** for women.

Glass actually criticised his Own Study

1) Glass acknowledged that his study was **crude**, and only intended as a **starting point** in an area that **hadn't been studied before**.

2) He didn't have **enough information** to measure **trends** and **changes over time**.

3) There was **no comparative work** so he couldn't compare the UK with **other countries**.

Upward mobility is fun.

Goldthorpe has been criticised too

1) Goldthorpe's 1972 study found an unexpected **improvement** in **absolute mobility** (see p.211), but he chose to **ignore** it and concentrate on **relative mobility**.

2) **Saunders (1990)** said this was because Goldthorpe was **too focused** on the idea of **class injustice**.

Women's Social Mobility wasn't studied until 1981

1) One of the biggest problems with the **usefulness** of social mobility studies is that almost all major studies failed to take any account whatsoever of the class position of **girls** and **women**.

2) The **first time** women were included in a study was in 1981. **Heath (1981)** went back and looked at the statistics for 1971 and 1975 and compared **fathers'** and **daughters'** social class positions (still no mothers). He found that in classes I and II (see p.192), **daughters** were much more likely to be **downwardly mobile** than sons.

3) **Goldthorpe and Payne (1986)** concluded that women's mobility rates varied according to which class they were in — just the **same as men**. They argued from this that the non-inclusion of women in previous studies didn't affect the overall results. Class **overrode gender**.

4) The **Essex study (1988)** by **Marshall et al** looked at male and female mobility and found that women moved both up and down into the **routine non-manual** group — most routine non-manual work was done by women regardless of their class of origin.

5) **Savage and Egerton (1997)** looked at male and female mobility and found that class affected opportunity less for daughters than it did for sons. This may be because middle-class sons can access an '**old boys' network**', or because of sexism in traditional upper middle-class jobs.

A woman's class used to be defined by the class of the **male** she lived with (see p.192-193). **Feminist sociologists** used to argue that as long as that was the case, social mobility studies **couldn't reveal much** about the impact of gender on social mobility. In **2000**, government statistics switched from a scheme that measured women by the **man's job** to a scheme which measured women by their **own job**, so female social mobility is now being studied in its **own right**.

Social Mobility

Some sociologists say the **Social Mobility Data** shows Britain is **Meritocratic**

There **aren't many** sociologists who interpret the data as evidence of **equality of opportunity**, but there are some.

1) The main man is the New Right thinker **Peter Saunders (1996)**. He uses research like the Essex study to conclude that the **opportunities** are there for social mobility, but the **individual** has to put in the **effort**.

2) Saunders argues the inequality that exists results from differences in the **talent** and **hard work** of the individual — not their class of origin.

3) Saunders has been **criticised** by many sociologists. His **methodology** is criticised — he **doesn't include** the **unemployed** and **part-time employees** in his analysis.

> Look back at the Education section, especially p.24-25.

4) Saunders' views have also been criticised because **class bias** at school could mean that school achievement reflects class background rather than ability. **Labelling** and **stereotypes** at school might discourage **working-class** pupils from applying themselves to their studies.

5) Research published in 2013 by **The Sutton Trust**, an educational equality charity, found that by the age of **15**, **clever boys** from **advantaged** backgrounds in England were **more than two years ahead** of **clever boys** from **disadvantaged** backgrounds in **reading**. In Scotland, they were **almost three years** ahead.

> Savage and Egerton (1997) analysed the same development survey as Saunders, but came to a very different conclusion. They found that those with the same ability didn't all have the same chances of ending up in the higher classes. Factors such as social networks, confidence and cultural advantages helped upper-class children get to the top — e.g. Savage and Egerton say that educational qualifications and tests are based on middle- and upper-class culture and values.

There's a **Continuing Trend** in **Absolute Social Mobility**

1) **Goldthorpe's 1972** study found that opportunities to become a **professional** had **improved** for **working-class** people. However, Goldthorpe argued that this **didn't** necessarily mean that Britain was becoming more **meritocratic**.

2) The introduction of the **Welfare State** after the Second World War had created lots of new jobs in areas such as health care and education. The **financial sector** was also expanding, whilst **manufacturing** decreased.

3) This all means that there was a large increase in the **number** of **service-sector jobs** available. **Absolute mobility** was **improving** (society as a whole was moving towards the service sector) but relative mobility wasn't (people from advantaged backgrounds were still more likely to get these service-sector jobs).

4) This trend in **increased absolute mobility** has **continued** into the 21st century:

- the **service**, **business** and **professional** sectors have **grown**
- **skilled trade** jobs (e.g. metalworking) have **declined**
- **admin** and **secretarial** roles have **declined**

> These types of jobs traditionally provide working-class people with opportunities for skills development and career progression.

5) Some sociologists are **worried** that the labour market is going to **polarise** — there'll be plenty of **professional** jobs at the top, requiring **high-level qualifications**, and lots of **low-skilled** jobs at the bottom, requiring few or no qualifications, but a **big gap** in the **middle**. This could be a problem for **relative mobility** — people from working-class backgrounds, who struggle to access the top jobs, won't have many other **opportunities** to progress.

Practice Questions

Q1 What's the difference between ascribed status and achieved status?

Q2 What did the Oxford mobility study find out about social mobility?

Q3 What's meant by saying that the upper class is 'static'?

Exam Question

Q1 Outline two ways that measuring social mobility can be problematic. Explain each one. [10 marks]

I'm upper class — I have to go up three flights of stairs...

This may not be your favourite topic. You may be pining for the heady days of 'Section Eight — Crime and Deviance'. Thing is, you've got an exam coming up, and this could be a good opportunity to get some marks squared away. Learn the studies — the Oxford study, Goldthorpe and Payne's follow-up, and the Essex Study are three good ones to learn and remember.

Do Well in Your Exam

These pages are about how to use all of that lovely sociology knowledge you've just learnt to do well in your exam.
For your A-Level, you'll do three papers — make sure you know what to expect in each of them, and how to get the marks.

Each Paper *lasts* 2 Hours *and is Worth a* Third *of the A-Level*

Each paper is worth **80 marks**.

Paper 1 *is on* Education *and* Theory and Methods

This is made up of **three sections**:

- The first section is on **Education** — it's worth a whopping **50 marks**.
- The second is on '**Methods in Context**' (the context is **Education**). It contains just one **20-mark** question.
- The final section is on '**Theory and Methods**'. This contains a **10-mark** question about **what sociology is** (e.g. is it a science?) or how sociological **research** should be done.

Paper 2 *is on* Topics in Sociology

This paper tests the **optional topics** you've studied — it's made up of **two sections**:

- In the first section you pick one of these four topics and answer **all** the questions on it: '**Culture and Identity**', '**Families and Households**', '**Work, Poverty and Welfare**' or '**Health**'.
- You choose one of **four** different topics in the second section of the paper: '**Beliefs in Society**', '**Global Development**', '**The Media**' or '**Stratification and Differentiation**'.

Each section is worth a tasty **40 marks**.

Paper 3 *is on* Crime and Deviance *and* Theory and Methods

This is made up of **two sections**:

- The first is on '**Crime and Deviance**' — it's worth **50 marks**.
- The second is on '**Theory and Methods**' again and is worth **30 marks**.

Sadly, my teacher's attempt at reverse psychology didn't produce the results he was hoping for.

You Get Marks For...

AO just means 'Assessment Objective'.

AO1 — Showing what you know about sociology
You need to show that you **know** your sociological **theories**, **concepts**, **evidence** and **research methods**. Make sure you **define** any sociological terms fully, and **spell** the names of any **sociologists** correctly.

AO2 — Applying what you know about sociology to a situation
To get these marks, you have to **relate** what you know to the topic **in the question**, e.g. you often have to give **reasons** for a pattern in society (such as **why** one social group is **more likely** to do something than another).

AO3 — Evaluating sociological ideas, and weighing up competing ideas to draw conclusions
This involves discussing **different perspectives** and **debating** which side is the **strongest**. At the end of **some** answers, you'll be expected to draw everything together to form a **conclusion**.

Short-answer questions don't require an essay — they're worth 4 or 6 marks. They test **AO1 and AO2 skills**.

Essay questions (worth between 10 and 30 marks) test **all three** AOs.

For these questions you might **lose marks** if you don't:

- use **continuous prose** — so no bullet points.
- **organise information** clearly — it's worth **thinking through** your answer before you start writing.
- use **specialist vocabulary** where appropriate — so learn that **sociology jargon**.
- use appropriate **examples** to illustrate your points.

Don't forget about the basics:

- Write as **neatly** as you can.
- Use good **grammar** and **punctuation**.
- Check your **spelling** — especially of sociological terms.
- Make sure you **answer the question**.

Do Well in Your Exam

Here are some Hints for Short-Answer Questions

1) If you're asked for **two** things, give **two** things. **Not one**. Not three. Or four. Five is **right out**.
2) If you're asked for multiple things, spend **equal time and effort** on **each**. You **won't** get full marks for a **lopsided** answer.
3) Use the **number of marks** as a **guide** for **how long you should spend on each question**. The more marks a question is worth, the longer you should spend answering it.

Here are some Example Exam Questions and Answers

4-Mark Questions Usually Ask for Two Things...

There's a 4-mark question in the 'Education' section of Paper 1 and in the 'Crime and Deviance' section of Paper 3.

01 How might schools influence differences in educational achievement by ethnic group? Outline two ways. [4 marks]

The school curriculum may be ethnocentric [1 mark], suggesting that it may not accommodate some ethnic minority students [1 mark].

Teachers may have different expectations of different ethnic groups [1 mark]. This can lead to self-fulfilling prophecies of success or failure [1 mark].

Don't waste time writing about more than two problems.

02 How might inequality cause crime? Outline two ways. [4 marks]

An individual may feel deprived in relation to someone else in society [1 mark]. They may turn to crime in order to acquire the resources to remove this feeling of deprivation [1 mark].

Inequality may deny some individuals the opportunity to succeed in mainstream society, leading to status frustration [1 mark]. They may then turn to illegitimate means of achieving status, e.g. through joining criminal gangs [1 mark].

Clearly outline each problem, e.g. don't just say, 'People may have status frustration'.

...and 6-Mark Questions Usually Ask for Three Things

6-mark questions also pop up in the 'Education' section of Paper 1 and the 'Crime and Deviance' section of Paper 3.

03 Why do girls outperform boys at most stages of education? Suggest three reasons. [6 marks]

Traditionally 'male' employment sectors such as heavy industry and factory work have declined [1 mark]. It can be argued that this has left boys with greater uncertainty over what they can aim for in life — some are disillusioned and feel no incentive to work hard at school [1 mark].

The number of female teachers has increased [1 mark]. This means that boys have fewer role models at school than before, which arguably means they are less likely to try to push themselves to achieve [1 mark].

The trend is also likely to be partly self-perpetuating. Boys are considered to be underachievers, so some teachers negatively label them [1 mark]. That negative labelling can become a self-fulfilling prophecy, causing boys to continue to underachieve [1 mark].

A new paragraph for each new point makes it clear that you've suggested three things.

04 Why are some ethnic groups more likely to be convicted of crime than others? Suggest three reasons. [6 marks]

The police and court system may be institutionally racist [1 mark], meaning that they are more likely to suspect and convict people from some ethnic groups [1 mark].

People from some ethnic groups are much more likely to be unemployed than others [1 mark]. This can cause them to reject mainstream society and turn to crime [1 mark].

Young black males are often labelled as criminals [1 mark]. This can create a self-fulfilling prophecy, where black males live up to their label and engage in criminal activity [1 mark].

Explain each point by stating the reason, and then explaining why it causes more convictions.

Here are some Hints for Longer Essay Questions

1) This is where the **essays** start, so remember to write in **continuous prose**.
2) Come up with a **structure** before you start writing, and use **paragraphs** to show that you've **organised** your ideas. Start a **new paragraph** whenever you start a **new point**.
3) These questions will have marks for **AO1, AO2 and AO3**. So you have to show that you **know** all the theories and concepts AND that you can **apply** them to the issue AND that you can **evaluate** the arguments. In 20- and 30-mark questions, you also need to draw a **conclusion**.

Alan paid the price for his careless approach to structure.

Do Well in Your Exam

Some *10-Mark* Questions have an *Item* to Read

Refer to the content of the **item** at least once, but **don't** just copy a bit of it — you need to **analyse** it by discussing an argument for or against it. You **don't** need to draw a **conclusion** for 10-mark questions.

---

01 **By applying material from Item A, analyse two explanations for why pupils from working-class backgrounds do not achieve as highly in education as children from middle-class backgrounds.** **[10 marks]**

Item A

Pupils from middle-class backgrounds generally leave school with much better GCSE results than pupils from working-class backgrounds. For example, middle-class students are more likely to go on to study A-levels. In the UK, class is the strongest determinant of educational achievement. There is a huge gap between the achievement of children from professional backgrounds and those from working-class backgrounds.

Read the item carefully. It'll give you ideas for what to write about.

One explanation for why pupils from working-class backgrounds do not achieve as highly in education as children from middle-class backgrounds is that they may be labelled differently by teachers. Teachers may not expect children from working-class backgrounds to achieve highly, so may place them in lower streams or sets, where they do not have access to high levels of knowledge. This limits their opportunity to achieve in education. Pupils may also become frustrated with their low set or stream and respond by forming anti-school subcultures where education is viewed as unimportant. This attitude will be a barrier to learning and doing well in exams. In contrast, teachers may have higher expectations of children from middle-class backgrounds, so may place them in higher streams and teach them more advanced content, resulting in them getting better GCSE results. However, it could also be argued that this approach is too deterministic and that negatively labelled pupils are not always destined to fail. For example, the way individual pupils react to being labelled may influence how much their educational achievement is affected.

Use sociological terms correctly.

Use the content of the Item.

A second explanation is cultural deprivation outside of school. Sugarman (1970) and Hyman (1967) argue that class-based cultural attitudes to education are linked to educational achievement. They argue that children from middle-class backgrounds have higher aspirations than working-class pupils, and they value education more highly. This leads to higher educational achievement. Also, Bourdieu (1971, 1974) argued that middle-class children have more cultural capital than working-class children — books, internet access and visits to museums, galleries and theatres all improve their cultural knowledge. Bourdieu argued that this improves their educational ability. In addition to this, Douglas (1964) found that parental attitudes towards education were the most important factor in educational achievement, and middle-class parents are more likely to show interest in education by attending open evenings, for example. A problem with the cultural deprivation argument is that it treats working-class and middle-class pupils as homogenous groups and doesn't take into account variation in aspiration across all social classes. Many working-class families do place a high value on education, for example.

Start a new paragraph for each explanation.

Apply your own knowledge and illustrate with examples.

Analyse the explanations by thinking about their flaws.

Here's a *10-Mark* Question on *Theory and Methods*

---

02 **Outline two advantages of a sociologist using unstructured interviews. Explain each one.** **[10 marks]**

One advantage of unstructured interviews is that they provide detailed, qualitative data. Because they use open-ended questions and don't have a rigid structure, interesting and in-depth information can result from them. The interviewer can encourage the interviewee to elaborate on the points they make and can ask for clarification if any answers are unclear. This would not be possible with a questionnaire or a more structured interview. From an interpretivist perspective, collecting such explorative, individualised data is very beneficial. Positivists, who prefer a more scientific approach to research, would criticise unstructured interviews for being unreliable, since the data is harder to analyse and repeat. However, even if this is the case, the insights provided by unstructured interviews could act as a valuable springboard for conducting other, more quantitative research.

Show that you understand what the research method is.

Apply knowledge of sociological perspectives.

Another advantage of unstructured interviews is that they provide the interviewer with the chance to gain the interviewee's trust. This means they're good for researching sensitive issues such as domestic violence. Unstructured interviews may also be highly suited to interviewing children, who might be intimidated by a more formal interview and who may need support to articulate their views. This does mean that interviewer effects can make the data from unstructured interviews less value-free than data from closed questionnaires. For example, the interviewee might give the answers they think the interviewer wants to hear, making the data invalid. They may have answered an anonymous questionnaire more honestly. However, it could be noted that Becker (1970) found that an aggressive interviewer style produced more useful answers, so perhaps the interviewer's influence on the interviewee can be a strength of the method, if it's approached thoughtfully.

Analyse explanations by weaving their strengths and weaknesses into your answer.

Comment on the reliability and validity of the method.

Illustrate with examples or studies where appropriate.

Do Well in Your Exam

Here's an Example 20-Mark Question about Methods

1) Here's an example of a **longer exam question** based on an **item**. It's the kind of question you get in the **Methods in Context** part of **Paper 1** — you have to apply a **sociological method** to an **educational issue**.

2) In this example, you'll notice that the **sociological method** is the **same** as the one on page 214. This is to show how **different** your answer needs to be when **applied** to a topic.

---

03 Apply your own knowledge and material from Item A to evaluate the advantages and disadvantages of using unstructured interviews to investigate the link between social class and educational achievement.   **[20 marks]**

Read the item carefully. It'll give you ideas for what to write about.

Item A
Investigating social class and educational achievement

Sociologists have studied the extent to which there is a link between social class and standards of achievement in education. Some sociologists believe that a negative attitude towards schooling (often reinforced by a peer group) can affect educational achievement. Some also note that such attitudes are more common amongst working-class students. This trend may be due to the approaches of teachers. Alternatively, it may be due to factors outside of school affecting attitudes to education.

Sociologists researching the link between social class and educational achievement may use unstructured interviews. Unstructured interviews have the advantage of allowing students to elaborate on their views, but they do take a considerable amount of time, so are usually only used for small-scale research.

Unstructured interviews take the form of an unrestricted, free-flowing conversation between the researcher and the subject, providing qualitative data through a range of open-ended questions.

Give a brief description of the research method you're discussing.

A key advantage of using unstructured interviews for researching social class and educational achievement is that they allow the researcher to build up a rapport with the interviewee. This can be important for encouraging a child to open up and be honest in their answers, resulting in more valid data. Furthermore, unstructured interviews allow the researcher to follow up any ambiguous or unusual responses, to gain greater clarity and detail. This could be very important if a child struggled to articulate themselves clearly. This is why unstructured interviews are most appropriate when taking an interpretivist approach to research, which is focused on empathising with individuals and discovering the motivations and emotions behind their behaviour.

Apply your sociological knowledge to the research method you're discussing.

Unstructured interviews are a good way to research individuals' attitudes, which may be key when researching educational achievement. For example, Willis (1977) used a range of methods, including unstructured interviews, to research the working-class anti-school subculture. The boys in this subculture had very negative attitudes towards education and were disruptive in school. The unstructured interviews allowed him to build a rapport with the boys and gain an insight into their motivations and beliefs. This opportunity for rapport wouldn't have been possible using methods such as official statistics or questionnaires.

Another advantage of using unstructured interviews to research this topic is that it is a sensitive and subtle approach for working with young people. For example, Labov used this method when investigating whether 'linguistic deprivation' might be a factor in working-class children underachieving in education. A different approach, such as formal, structured interviews, may have been intimidating to the children in the study.

Discuss both strengths and weaknesses.

On the other hand, there are some disadvantages of unstructured interviews as a research method. Firstly, the results are not always reliable. For example, if another sociologist repeated Willis's research with a different group of working-class boys, they may get different results. In addition, the research sample tends to be small because it's a time-consuming and therefore expensive method. For example, Willis used a sample of only twelve boys. It's difficult to generalise from the results, because answers tend to be specific to individual subjects. This also makes it difficult to make direct comparisons between one interviewee and another.

Show that you're applying the Item at least once in your answer.

Furthermore, unstructured interviews may not be the best approach for studying how negative labelling by teachers can affect educational achievement. Teachers may be unwilling to admit to having lower expectations of working-class students, as they want to show themselves in the best possible light. In this situation, observation may be a better approach, as it would avoid this bias.

Positivist researchers would also find alternative methods more appropriate. For example, a self-completion questionnaire using a large sample would be more likely to provide reliable, quantitative data that could be used to make generalised conclusions. For example, a possible correlation between factors outside of school, such as economic deprivation, and educational failure might be easier to research using a positivist approach, because quantitative data on household income and exam results could be compared.

You still need to mention sociological perspectives on research methods.

In conclusion, unstructured interviews are a useful research method for the topic of social class and educational achievement, to some extent. They are particularly appropriate for interpretivist sociologists researching individuals' views on this reasonably sensitive issue. However, they would be less useful for large-scale research, such as collecting data from a representative sample of many schools across the UK.

Sum up with a short conclusion.

Do Well in Your Exam

You need to Debate Different Perspectives in 30-Mark Questions

1) You'll get a **30-mark** question on **Education** in Paper 1 and another on **Crime and Deviance** in Paper 3.
2) 30 marks is **loads**, so it's **vital** that you know how to tackle these **mammoth** questions in the exam.

---

04 Apply your own knowledge and material from Item C to evaluate the idea that class differences in conviction rate are mainly the result of the structure of society.   **[30 marks]**

Item C
The working class is the social group most commonly convicted of crime. Traditional Marxist sociologists hold the view that individuals are forced into crime by the structure of capitalist society. In particular, they see crimes such as robbery and property theft as inevitable responses to the wide gap between the rich and poor.

One argument for why the working class are most commonly convicted of crime is that society is structured so that the legal system is biased against them. Crime is a social construction, so the laws that exist to sanction it are determined by society. From a Marxist perspective, since the ruling class has more power than the working class, the law reflects their interests. These interests include protecting the property on which capitalist exploitation is built and controlling the working class so they continue to provide labour. For example, the law is more concerned with property crime, which is more likely to be committed by the working class, than it is with white-collar and corporate crime, such as breaking health and safety laws. Though the ruling class do break laws as often as the working class, this system means they are in a better position to escape convictions. Reasons for this include selective law enforcement, more lenient treatment by the legal system, and being able to afford better legal advice.

Marxists argue that, in capitalist society, varying pay levels within the working class keep individuals competing against each other and prevent them from uniting together to threaten capitalism. This means that although everyone (including the very richest in society) may feel relatively deprived, working-class people are more likely to have this feeling. According to left realists, this is a major factor in the committing of crime. For example, Young (2002) pointed out that the media allows the working class to see what other people can afford, which intensifies their feelings of relative deprivation. This viewpoint is criticised because it doesn't explain why some people experiencing relative deprivation turn to crime while others don't. ◄ *Include criticisms of viewpoints.* Furthermore, capitalist societies don't necessarily have more crime than others. For example, there's crime in socialist societies like Cuba, whilst some capitalist societies, such as Switzerland, have very low crime rates.

A further argument for the structure of society leading to more working-class criminal convictions is provided by the functionalist Robert Merton. He said that most individuals share the goal of success and wealth, known as the 'American Dream'. He said that the main, legitimate means of achieving these goals is through the education system, and that when individuals fail to do so, due to factors beyond their control, it causes strain. Merton's strain theory identifies five adaptations to strain. One of these is 'innovating', which means that they find alternative paths to success and wealth, the most obvious path being crime. Another adaptation is 'retreating' from society, for example by drinking to excess, or taking drugs. These activities can also lead to the individual committing crimes. Children from working-class backgrounds generally have poorer academic achievement, so they are most at risk of not becoming successful by legitimate means. Many middle-class parents can pay for a high quality education for their children, which improves access to employment and wealth. Even if middle-class pupils perform poorly at school, they may well secure a job through their network of contacts. *Refer to key sociologists who support the view or argue against it.*

Even those sociologists who don't see criminals as passive victims of capitalism still see society as contributing to rates of working-class crime. Taylor, Walton and Young's *The New Criminology* (1973) argues that crime is a conscious, meaningful and deliberate choice individuals make to try to fight the structural inequalities of capitalist society. This viewpoint sees working-class crime as a method for redistributing wealth that is unfairly concentrated among the members of the ruling class. Therefore, the unequal structure of society might cause working-class individuals to respond by committing crime. *Use your own knowledge to strengthen your answer.*

On the other hand, New Right sociologists argue that working-class crime comes from cultural values which are different to those of mainstream society. They say that the working class have formed an underclass that accepts criminality as a response to structural inequalities in society. The subcultural theorist Miller (1962) argued that successive working-class generations pass down cultural values that encourage working-class men to break the law. However, Bordua (1962) argued that the basis of this argument is flawed, because there is no evidence that the working class live their lives in cultural isolation. Even if we accept Miller's point, it could be argued that the cultural values that supposedly shape working-class attitudes to crime may have developed as a result of structural inequalities in society in the first place. *Create a balanced argument using different points of view.*

This kind of complexity suggests that the critical criminology proposed by Taylor, Walton and Young may actually be the best way of understanding rates of working-class convictions. Their view of working-class crime as the result of individual decision-making and a host of interplaying structural factors does recognise structural inequality, but within a contextualised approach to deviance. *Sum up with a short conclusion that answers the original question.*

Evaluate the view that revision will get you quite a lot of marks...

The more stuff you learn, the more you'll be able to write. Make sure you keep it relevant — don't waffle on about something else just to show how much extra stuff you know, e.g. if the topic is questionnaires, don't go on about interviews for ages.

Glossary

absolute poverty Not having the essentials needed for life — food, warmth and shelter.

achieved status Status you get by working for it.

agenda-setting A practice in journalism where an editor or journalist selects what to include in the news and chooses a particular angle to take when reporting it, so affecting how the story is perceived by their audience.

alienation Having no control over the products of your work and becoming detached from yourself and society as a result.

anomie Durkheim's term for a state of moral confusion in society, resulting from an absence of the common shared norms and values that bind a society together. He argued that this was bad for both individuals (who are uncertain of how to behave in particular situations) and for society as a whole. Anomie (or 'normlessness') is a state that is typical of societies undergoing sudden change.

ascribed status Status you have from birth.

beanpole family A family structure where a small number of members from each generation all live together in one household, e.g. a retired couple living with their daughter, son-in-law and grandchildren.

binary opposition A view of the world that is based on pairs of opposites, e.g. male/female, good/bad. One half of the pair is seen as more dominant and more 'normal' than the other.

biomedical model A model of health and illness that considers only factors within the body. It ignores social, psychological and environmental factors.

bourgeoisie Marxist term for the capitalist ruling class. They own the means of production (e.g. factories, equipment, raw materials).

capitalism An economic system based on private ownership of the means of production, distribution and exchange of commodities. In the capitalist system, labour becomes a commodity which employers buy for wages. Capitalism is associated with free trade and individual enterprise. It started in Europe and the US and has spread to become the dominant economic philosophy in most countries.

censorship The control of the media (TV, newspapers, film etc.) through banning certain works, scenes, images or language from being broadcast or published.

census A government survey of all people within a defined geographical area. The British census is an obligatory survey of the entire population that is carried out every 10 years.

civil disobedience Protest action that breaks laws.

class A way of stratifying society, on the basis of people's social and economic status. Class is hierarchical — some classes are more privileged than others. The 'class system' is criticised by Marxists.

collective consciousness The shared values and norms that hold society together.

commodity fetishism When capitalist society encourages people to become obsessed by products that are not essential to survival.

communism A system of government which is theoretically based on a classless society and where private ownership has been abolished. It is influenced by the ideas of Marx and Engels.

conformity Adherence to the norms and values of society. The opposite of deviance.

conjugal roles Husband and wife roles — who does the paid work, who does the washing-up etc.

consensus Fundamental agreement within a society, especially about that society's basic values. Functionalist theory suggests that, as a result of socialisation, the people in a society all share the same norms and values and this contributes to consensus.

convergence The ability to access lots of different types of media using one device.

critical criminology A theory of crime and deviance that challenges traditional theories of crime and argues that crime is a result of inequality within society. It says that criminals commit crime deliberately to provoke change.

critical victimology The theory that groups who are oppressed (e.g. women) are more likely to be victims of crime.

cult A religious group with no fixed set of beliefs. Cults often focus on the inner power of individuals and mysticism. They're often short-lived and don't usually have a hierarchy.

cultural capital The skills and cultural know-how that children learn from their parents.

cultural deprivation theory This theory says working-class culture makes people disadvantaged.

cultural effects theory A media effects theory that focuses on the social context of media and its audience.

cultural hybridisation When local, national and global cultures blend together to form a series of hybrid cultures.

Glossary

cultural imperialism The idea that Western culture is replacing local and national cultures in many parts of the world.

culture The 'way of life' of a society or group. Culture is made up of things such as language, customs, knowledge, norms and values. It is passed on by socialisation.

culture of dependency The idea that generous welfare policies create a culture where people are happy to claim benefits instead of looking for work.

cybercrime Crime that is carried out on the internet.

dependency ratio The number of people who are not of working age (e.g. children, pensioners) compared to the number of working-age people.

dependency theory A development theory which blames underdevelopment on colonialism and exploitation.

deregulation When government involvement in an industry is decreased or completely removed.

desacralisation Religious and spiritual beliefs becoming less important in society.

desensitisation When being exposed to something repeatedly or regularly makes you less sensitive to it, e.g. consuming lots of violent media may make you react less strongly to real violence.

deviance Something that goes against society's norms and values. Deviant behaviour is behaviour that society doesn't approve of.

deviance amplification When levels of deviance are exaggerated or overreported by the media, and authorities respond with social control, which provokes further deviance. The authorities respond with more intense social control, and the cycle continues.

deviant career When a person is labelled as deviant and shamed by society, and they resort to more deviant behaviour to escape the feeling that they've been rejected. This reinforces the label, which makes it harder for the person to escape their deviance.

differentiation The division of society into different groups. These groups may be based on a person's abilities, on biological features like their age or sex, or on cultural differences like class or religion.

disability A limited ability to perform certain tasks because society hasn't made provision for an impairment.

emotional work Dealing with the emotions of a family.

ethnic group A group of people with a common culture — language, religion and way of life.

ethnocentric Centred around the values and interests of one particular ethnic group.

ethnography Research which studies the culture and way of life of a community by looking at social relationships, organisations, customs and practices. It is usually done by observation, and may also use interviews and case studies.

extended family A family which includes more than just parents and children, e.g. including grandparents, cousins, uncles and aunts.

false consciousness Marxism says that workers are in a state of false consciousness about their place in society. They have learnt ruling-class values and beliefs through education, the media and religion, which prevent them from realising how unfair capitalist society is.

false needs Things people think they need but which don't really satisfy them. Marxists say these false needs have been created by a capitalist culture which encourages consumerism.

falsification Proving a hypothesis wrong.

feminism A broad movement which believes that social organisations and culture have been dominated by men to the exclusion of women. Feminists claim that this has devalued and disadvantaged women into a marginalised status. Feminist sociologists think that mainstream sociology has ignored the lives of women. There are many varieties of feminism, e.g. liberal feminism, Marxist feminism and radical feminism.

folk devil A scapegoat for things going wrong in society.

Frankfurt School A neo-Marxist group that formed in Germany in the 1930s. They combined Marxist ideas with psychology.

free market An economic system that lets supply and demand control prices, wages etc., rather than the government.

functionalism An important sociological perspective about how society works, founded by Durkheim, which argues that everything in society exists for a reason. Functionalists believe that society is made up of a number of institutions, each of which has a useful function and helps society to run smoothly, e.g. the family, the education system, religion. These institutions work in harmony because of agreed norms and values, and this is essential for society to survive. Functionalists say that individuals internalise these norms and values (socialisation).

Glossary

ndamentalism Living by a strict set of rules developed according to the literal teachings of a religion's authoritative text, e.g. living by the words of the Bible.

nder Sociologists say that gender (femininity and masculinity) is a social construction. Being male or female is the biological sex you're born with, while masculinity and femininity are identities you're socialised into.

obalisation The breaking down of traditional national boundaries as globally people become more interconnected. This happens due to factors such as the growth of multinational companies, improvements in communications and technology, increased migration of people between societies, and the global marketing of cultural products.

awthorne effect When participants are aware they are being observed and this affects their behaviour.

egemony The domination of one group of people over others, or of one set of ideas and values over others.

dden curriculum The social norms and values that are taught at school, but not as part of the regular curriculum. Includes conformity, respect for authority and other cultural values.

erarchy A system which ranks people according to status. Any system where you have a boss in charge of people is a hierarchy.

ousehold A group of people who live together. They needn't be related.

yper-reality A situation, suggested by postmodernists, where people are unable to tell the difference between reality and representations of reality.

ypodermic syringe model The idea that the media injects its message directly into the minds of the audience. It claims that all people in the audience are affected in the same way, and that they're powerless to resist or reject the message.

ypothesis A statement that makes a prediction which can be tested and proven to be true or false. Hypotheses are often used by scientists to predict how different factors are related. They are tested using experiments and research.

trogenesis Health problems caused by the modern medical system.

entity An individual's sense of self. This can be influenced by social factors such as class, gender, religion and ethnicity.

eological state apparatus Institutions like the media, schools, Church and family which can spread the ideology of the state.

ideology A set of ideas and beliefs about the way things should be — often politically motivated.

impairment A potentially limiting physical characteristic or symptom (e.g. deafness) that a person has.

infrastructure Physical features or networks that help a society to run more smoothly, e.g. roads, public transport networks, electricity networks, buildings.

institutional racism When the policies, attitudes and actions of an institution discriminate against ethnic minorities — sometimes unintentionally.

institutions of society Structures that contribute to the running of society, e.g. the family, the Church, the education system and the health care system.

interactionism Also known as 'interpretivism'. A sociological approach which focuses on the actions and thoughts of individuals. Society is viewed as the product of interaction between individuals. Interactionists favour research methods that look at individual people's motives and feelings.

labelling theory This theory says that the labels given to someone affect their behaviour. Labels also affect how other people treat someone, e.g. teachers might treat a child labelled a 'troublemaker' more strictly.

LEDC Less Economically Developed Country.

Left Realism Sociological viewpoint which developed from Marxism. The approach focuses on working within the capitalist framework and aims to direct social policy to help the poor.

life chances The opportunities people have to gain the things that society values and to improve their own quality of life.

longitudinal study A study done over a period of time.

marginalisation When an individual, social group or organisation is isolated from, or pushed to the edges of, mainstream society and made to feel unimportant.

marketisation of education Encouraging competition between schools in order to create a market within education, where parents have more choice.

Marxism A theory and political ideology based on the views of Karl Marx (1818-1883). Marxists are opposed to capitalism, which they believe is based on the exploitation of the working class (proletariat), who do the work, by the ruling class (bourgeoisie), who own the 'means of production'. Most of the profit from the work that the working class do is kept by the bourgeoisie. The bourgeoisie arrange society to keep the workers down. Original Marxist ideas have been developed and adapted by neo-Marxists.

Glossary

master status A label that dominates the way a person is seen, to the extent that all their other qualities are disregarded. For example, a person who is labelled as 'mentally ill' may find that their other qualities are ignored, because the label 'mentally ill' takes on master status.

means-tested benefit A benefit that people only get if they are below a certain level of wealth.

MEDC More Economically Developed Country.

media Ways of communicating with large numbers of people, e.g. newspapers, TV, magazines, radio and the Internet.

media outlets Companies that produce and transmit media content, e.g. TV stations and newspaper publishers.

media text Any piece of media — e.g. a book, a TV programme, an advert.

medicalisation Taking a previously non-medical human condition and treating it as a medical problem that needs to be studied, diagnosed and treated using medical means.

meritocracy A system where the best (most talented and hard-working) people rise to the top.

metanarrative An overarching, all-encompassing story which gives meaning to history and events.

modernisation theory The theory that all countries are moving towards liberal capitalism. Countries that have developed high levels of production, consumption and wealth are seen as superior to less developed countries.

moral panic A fear of a moral crisis in society. Moral panics are often linked to 'folk devils'. The mass media have a big role in starting moral panics in modern society.

multiculturalism The existence of lots of different cultures (e.g. ethnic, religious, national) in one society or community.

neo-Marxism A movement developed in the 20th century by some of Marx's followers who revised and adapted his ideas to make them more relevant to modern society. Neo-Marxists often stress the importance of culture in sustaining capitalism, e.g. through the hegemony of capitalist ideas.

New Religious Movements (NRMs) Modern religious or spiritual movements that may have roots in established religions, but that are often seen as alternatives to more dominant religions.

New Right Movement which gained influence in sociology in the 1980s. New Right theory believes in the 'moral superiority' of the traditional nuclear family, and tends towards the view that sexual tolerance and single mothers are bad for society. Problems like poverty and unemployment are seen to be caused by an over-generous welfare state.

news values Rules or ideas that influence journalists when they are deciding what to report on. News values are often based on what journalists think the audience wants to hear or read. They can be bureaucratic or cultural.

NGOs (non-governmental organisations) Private organisations, many of which provide both short-term and long-term support to developing countries. They often work with local people to promote development.

non-conformity Not going along with society's norms and values.

norm A social rule about what is correct and appropriate behaviour within a particular culture, e.g. queuing in a shop.

nuclear family Parents and their dependent children living together.

operationalisation Defining a concept and deciding how to measure it.

patriarchy A society where men are dominant. Feminists often describe male-dominated societies and institutions as 'patriarchal'.

peer groups People of the same or similar social status and age, e.g. a group of teenagers.

Pentecostalism A form of Christianity that places a lot of importance on directly experiencing the presence of God and the Holy Spirit.

Physical Quality of Life Index (PQLI) A development index that measures infant mortality, literacy and life expectanc

pluralism The belief that society is diverse and reflects the needs and views of everyone via democracy and the free market.

positivism A theoretical point of view which concentrates on social facts, scientific method and quantitative data (facts and figures). The positivist view is that human behaviour is determined by external social factors, and so is outside the control of the individuals in society.

positivist victimology The theory that a person's actions or characteristics may make them more likely to become victims of crime.

Glossary

postmodernism A theory which says there is no one objective truth or reality that everyone experiences.

postmodern society The world after the modern age — with flexible working, individual responsibility and people constructing their own identity.

primary data Completely new data that has been collected first-hand by the researcher.

privatisation When private organisations or companies are allowed to gain ownership of assets or companies that used to be owned by the government on behalf of the public.

proletariat The working class who, according to Marx, form the majority of society and are exploited by the bourgeoisie.

qualitative methods of research Methods like unstructured interviews and participant observation that give results which tell a story about individuals' lives.

quantitative methods of research Methods like surveys and structured interviews that give results you can easily put into a graph or table.

rational choice theory A theory of crime and deviance that argues that criminals won't try to commit a crime where there is a high chance of them being caught, or if the reward isn't worth the risk of being caught.

relative poverty A measure of poverty that decides whether a person is in poverty by comparing their situation (e.g. level of income) to the situations of others in society.

reliability Data is reliable if other sociologists using the same methods on the same group collect the same data. Quantitative data is usually the most reliable.

religiosity How religious a person is or how important religion is within a social group or a society.

repeat victimisation When someone becomes a victim of the same type of crime on more than one occasion.

Right Realism A view of crime and deviance that says that biology, a lack of socialisation, and rational choice can cause crime.

rite of passage A growing-up ceremony that young people do to prove they aren't kids any more.

sanctions Rewards or punishments that strengthen social norms. These can be formal (carried out by an official organisation) or informal (carried out by the public).

secondary data Data gathered using existing sources of information, such as official statistics, newspapers, emails, and diaries.

secularisation When religion loses its influence in society.

self-fulfilling prophecy When people behave in the way that they know others expect them to behave.

semiotic analysis Looking for hidden meanings in the structure of a text, image or object.

social construct An idea or belief that's created in society, and doesn't come from a scientific fact.

social control When people's behaviour is limited by society, often through shared norms and values, punishments, or rewards. It aims to increase social stability.

social democrats People who think the state should redistribute wealth, and that there should be a strong welfare state paid for out of taxes. Social democrats believe in social equality.

social exclusion Where individuals can't participate fully in society, often because of related problems like poverty, unemployment, poor skills, bad health or family breakdown. These people often find it hard to access public services.

social model of health A model that regards health and illness as social constructs that are influenced by factors outside the body, e.g. diet and damp housing.

social order The stability of a society.

social policy Government decisions which affect society, e.g. raising taxes, changing the benefits system, privatisation.

socialisation Passing on cultural values and norms from one generation to the next, so that they become internalised, i.e. part of everyone's way of thinking.

sociology of personal life A sociological approach that values what individuals themselves think is important, instead of focusing on what sociologists think should be important to them.

status frustration When cultural deprivation limits a person's opportunities to take part in mainstream society, causing them to feel unhappy with their social position.

stereotype A generalisation about a social group — often inaccurate and insulting.

strain theory A theory that says that a person becomes deviant because they are unable to meet the cultural goals of society (e.g. wealth) due to factors they can't control.

stratification The way society is divided up into layers, which form a hierarchy.

Glossary

stratified sample A sample with the same proportions of gender, class, age etc. as the population you're studying.

subculture A group who share values and norms which are different from the mainstream culture. A culture within a culture.

subjective poverty A measure of poverty based on how poor an individual person actually feels, rather than on more standard, official measures.

superstructure In Marxist theory, the superstructure is the institutions in a society which aren't economic (such as legal, political, cultural and religious institutions) and the beliefs and values which these institutions propagate. It has a role in maintaining and sustaining the economic infrastructure.

sustainable development Development that is designed to protect the environment for the benefit of future generations.

symbolic annihilation False, negative or very scarce representation of a particular social group in the media, which may cause that group to be unfairly stereotyped.

symbolic consumption Buying products for their symbolic value (e.g. what they stand for) to reflect aspects of your identity.

symmetrical family A family structure where conjugal (husband and wife) roles are equally shared.

target population A whole group of people (e.g. disabled women, black males) that a researcher wants to draw conclusions about using research carried out on a sample of that population.

third-way politics A political viewpoint that combines elements of right-wing self-sufficiency and left-wing social democracy.

transcarceration When a vulnerable person is moved between several different institutions (e.g. prisons, mental institutions, young offender facilities).

transnational corporations (TNCs) Corporations that do business in more than one country. They often have their headquarters in MEDCs and carry out production in LEDCs to capitalise on cheaper labour.

transnational crime Crime committed by criminal organisations across multiple countries, e.g. people trafficking or money laundering.

triangulation Combining different research methods and data to get the best results.

underclass A social group at the bottom of the social hierarchy. New Right sociologists think they're lazy and dependent on welfare. Left-wing sociologists think they're disadvantaged by the welfare system.

underemployment When people who want to be in full-time, permanent work are employed in part-time or temporary jobs. Also, when a highly-skilled worker performs a job that requires less skill.

universal benefit Benefit that everyone gets, whether they're rich or poor.

validity Data is valid if it gives an accurate picture of what's being measured.

value-free research Research that isn't biased, and isn't influenced by the researcher's beliefs.

values General beliefs held by society and by individuals about what is important or what is right and wrong, e.g. acceptance of mainstream religious beliefs is a value of Western society.

victim survey Survey asking if respondents have been victims of crime.

wealth The worth of everything a person owns (e.g. propert possessions, savings) minus any debts that they owe.

Welfare State The British Welfare State was set up in the 1940s with the aim of wiping out the social problems of society (poor health, housing and education, poverty and unemployment). The Welfare State was designed to be free at the point where people actually needed it (e.g. a visit to hospital) and was paid for by people in work contributing to a national insurance scheme.

World Systems theory Development theory which looks at the world as a single economic system where some countries have a lot of power and others don't have power.

Index

Index

Index

Index

Index

Index